Seventh Edition

COMMUNITY AND PROBLEM-ORIENTED POLICING

EFFECTIVELY ADDRESSING CRIME AND DISORDER

Kenneth J. Peak

Professor Emeritus, University of Nevada, Reno

Ronald W. Glensor

Reno, Nevada, Police Department (Ret'd)

 Pearson

330 Hudson Street, NY, NY 10013

Vice President, Portfolio Management: Andrew Gilfillan
Portfolio Manager: Gary Bauer
Editorial Assistant: Lynda Cramer
Senior Vice President, Marketing: David Gesell
Field Marketing Manager: Thomas Hayward
Product Marketing Manager: Kaylee Carlson
Senior Marketing Coordinator: Les Roberts
Director, Digital Studio and Content Production: Brian Hyland
Managing Producer: Cynthia Zonneveld
Content Producer: Nikhil Rakshit
Manager, Rights Management: Johanna Burke
Operations Specialist: Deidra Smith
Creative Digital Lead: Mary Siener
Managing Producer, Digital Studio: Autumn Benson
Content Producer, Digital Studio: Maura Barclay
Full-Service Management and Composition: iEnergizer Aptara®, Ltd.
Full-Service Project Manager: Sadika Rehman
Cover Design: StudioMontage
Cover Art: ventdusud/Shutterstock
Printer/Binder: LSC Communications
Cover Printer: LSC Communications/Kendallville
Text Font: TimesLTPro

Library of Congress Cataloging-in-Publication Data

Names: Peak, Kenneth J., author. | Glensor, Ronald W., author.
Title: Community and Problem-Oriented Policing
    policing/Kenneth J. Peak, Professor Emeritus, University of Nevada,
    Reno, Ronald W. Glensor, Reno, Nevada, Police Department (Ret'd).
Description: Seventh Edition. | Hoboken : Pearson, 2016. | Revised edition of
    the authors' Community Policing and Problem Solving, ©2012. | Includes
    index.
Identifiers: LCCN 2016041386 | ISBN 9780133590104 | ISBN 0133590100
Subjects: LCSH: Community policing. | Crime prevention—United
    States—Citizen participation. | Police administration. | Police-community
    relations. | Community policing—United States. | Police
    administration—United States.
Classification: LCC HV7936.C83 P43 2016 | DDC 363.2/3—dc23 LC record available at
    https://lccn.loc.gov/2016041386

ISBN-10:   0-13-359010-0
ISBN-13: 978-0-13-359010-4

To the several members of my family circle—attorney, sheriff, police commander, assistant sheriff, and federal agent—who uphold the legal maxim "Mind your manners, tell the truth, know the law."

–K.J.P.

To my wonderful and supportive family: my wife Kristy, daughter and son Breanne and Ronnie, son and daughter-in-law Derek and Katie, and grandchildren Addison, Chloe, Claire, and Heidi.

–R.W.G.

BRIEF CONTENTS

CONTENTS

NEW TOPICS IN THIS SEVENTH EDITION

In addition to updated information, case studies, exercises, and exhibits newly added throughout the book, following are other substantively new materials added to this edition:

Chapter 1: Contributions of the federal government/COPS Office to community policing

Chapter 2: A "new professionalism"; "guardians" or "warriors"? addressing fear of crime; effects of economy; civilian review boards—blessing or curse?

Chapter 3: (Formerly Chapter 10) States crack down on sanctuary cities; lessons from history and Ferguson; how to achieve harmony, justice, and policy; transparency with Web sites and databases; calls for police body cameras; guardian mindset; early intervention systems for identifying problem employees

Chapter 4: (New Chapter) Faces of terrorism—homegrown, lone wolf, cyberterrorist; law enforcement strategies; legislative measures; drones; roles of local police, community policing, social media

Chapter 5: "CHEERS" method for problem analysis; problem solving in New Zealand

Chapter 6: Problem-oriented policing, community, crime prevention as symbiotic relationship; community role in preventing crime and restoring anchor points

Chapter 7: IT comes to policing; federal stimulus; rationale for IT; exploiting young officers' flair for IT; choosing which tools to use; smart policing; using civic apps and applying social media; dedicated software for problem solving

Chapter 8: Revisiting the "new professional's" guardian mindset; constitutional policing and legitimacy; angst caused by hot spot policing; use of force in the new culture of policing; responding to mass demonstrations

Chapter 9: Strategic planning example—planning one's future; a forward-thinking perspective; examples of planning and implementation

Chapter 10: Police training for today's society—Seattle's model; technologies such as gamification and use of avatars; E-learning and distance education; resources on the Web

Chapter 11: Knowledge and skills evaluators should possess; quantitative and qualitative measures; validity; the Evidence-Based Policing Matrix; evaluating agencies' and officers' efforts; RAND's benchmark program; Sweden's use of crime prevention committees

Chapter 12: The changing war on drugs (especially with marijuana, prescription drug abuse, and synthetic drugs); problems and responses with neighborhood disorder

Chapter 13: Cybercrime—types, police tactics, and federal efforts for addressing; human trafficking problems and police strategies

Chapter 14: Technology, terrorism, cybercrime of the future, and what community policing and problem solving can do to address them; applying science to policing; need for strong police leadership (in several areas).

PREFACE

This is a most exciting point in time to be studying (or working in) law enforcement, as evidenced by the fact that, since this book's last (sixth) edition appeared, the new strategies (smart policing, intelligence-led policing, predictive policing, and so on), technologies, and methods that have come into being have changed the field to a major degree. Added to the already challenging philosophy and strategies of community- and problem-oriented policing, these even newer strategies challenge the intellect and ability of today's police officers to address crime and disorder in ways that are more stimulating and exhilarating than ever before.

This book, like its six preceding editions, is what works in policing for combating crime and disorder in our neighborhoods and communities. It is about the evolution of the latest era in policing that began in the mid-1970s, one that centers on collaborating with the community and other agencies and organizations that are responsible for community safety. It examines from many perspectives a philosophy and style of policing that requires officers to obtain new knowledge and tools for solving problems, and it is grounded in strategic thinking and planning to enable agencies to keep up with the rapid societal changes in such areas as homeland defense.

This seventh edition is premised on the assumption that the reader is most likely an undergraduate or graduate student studying criminal justice or policing, or instead a police practitioner with a fundamental knowledge of police history and operations who is working in policing or a government agency and is interested in learning about community policing and problem solving. Citizens who are collaborating with police to resolve neighborhood problems in innovative ways can also be well served by reading this book.

We also impart some of the major theories, research, practices (with myriad examples), and processes that are being implemented under community policing and problem solving. Our ongoing primary emphasis is on the practical aspects of problem-oriented policing—putting the philosophy into daily practice. We continue to emphasize that problem-oriented policing is an individualized, long-term process that involves fundamental institutional change, going beyond such simple tactics as foot and bicycle patrols or neighborhood police stations; it redefines the role of the officer on the street from crime fighter to problem solver; it forces a cultural transformation of the entire police agency, involving changes in recruiting, training, awards systems, evaluations, and promotions.

It has been said that problem solving is not new in policing, that police officers have always tried to solve problems in their daily work. True enough; but as is demonstrated throughout this text, problem solving is not the same as solving problems. Problem solving in the context of community policing is very different and considerably more complex, requiring that police officers identify and examine the underlying causes of recurring incidents of crime and disorder. This policing approach thus seeks to make "street criminologists" of the officers, teaching them to expand their focus on offenders to include crime settings and victims.

We also emphasize that this book is not a call to ignore or discard policing's past methods, nor do we espouse an altogether new philosophy of policing in its place. Instead, we recommend that the police borrow from the wisdom of the past and adopt a holistic approach to the way police organizations are learning to address public safety more successfully. This book describes how many agencies should, and are, actively going about the process of revolutionizing their philosophy and operations.

ORGANIZATION AND CONTENTS OF THE BOOK

As indicated above, like its six predecessors, this book is distinguished by its applied approach. In doing so, it showcases dozens of exhibits and additional case studies and examples of problem solving in the field.

Also newly emphasized in this seventh edition are methods of policing a diverse society—particularly disenfranchised minorities in the "post-Ferguson" era and the call for a re-examination of police methods—as well as the fight against terrorism and applications of new information technologies (IT) for problem solving. In addition, chapters will examine major issues and challenging crime problems (e.g., drugs, gangs, youth and crime, neighborhood disorder, domestic violence, and human trafficking), crime prevention, changing agency culture, evaluating problem-solving initiatives, cyberbullying and cybercrime, and special populations (e.g., the mentally ill), and the future. A chapter-by-chapter breakdown follows.

Part I of the book describes what we term the "long road" to community policing and problem solving. Chapter 1, Evolution, begins with a brief discussion of policing's inception in Britain's and the efforts of Sir Robert Peel leading to the Metropolitan Police Act in England. We also review the onset and evolution of policing in the United States, including a look at policing's three eras (focusing on the emergence of community problem-solving and new strategies for this century and the significant assistance of federal resources); also briefly discussed is the development of the community- and problem–oriented policing for today's challenges and the contributions of problem-oriented policing to homeland security. In Chapter 2, community partnerships are examined in this time of tremendous police–citizen discord, opens with an examination of what is meant by "community," and (as noted above) why all such efforts to involve citizens in addressing crime and disorder have led to community policing. Included is a review of the need for a new professionalism, the police role as "guardians," signs of a healthy community, economic challenges facing police and society, the use of civilian review boards, and how communities can connect with their courts and corrections organizations.

Part II includes two chapters that focus on two police priorities: managing diversity and ensuring that our homeland is protected. Chapter 3, looking at diversity, thus examines the challenges posed by people immigrating to the United States, the history (often very combative) of relations between minorities, how problem-oriented policing can enhance police–community relations, and the need for police to become more transparent and address racial profiling and bias-based policing. Chapter 4, Protecting the Homeland, examines the many faces of terrorism (to include cyberterrorism and bioterrorism) and what the local police and community policing—with the assistance of legislation and technologies—are doing to combat it.

Part III centers on problem solving and its approaches, programs, and practices. Chapter 5, Problem Solving, serves as a bulwark of the textbook as it specifically focuses on the development and methods of community- and problem-oriented policing, which are complementary core components. The problem-solving process, known as SARA (for scanning, analysis, response, and assessment), is discussed as the primary tool for understanding crime and disorder. Included are the basic principles of police problem solving, the role of the street officer within it, some difficulties with problem solving, and some ways to tailor strategies to individual neighborhoods. Crime prevention, discussed in Chapter 6, considers two important and contemporary components for preventing crime: crime prevention through environmental design (CPTED) and situational crime prevention; included are discussions of which crime-prevention approaches work, do not appear to be successful, and hold promise for crime prevention. Chapter 7, Tools for Problem Solving, looks at how IT came to policing as well as the tools that are available for crime analysis and other functions. Included are several relatively new tools for analyzing and managing crime: CompStat, intelligence-led and predictive policing, social media, real-time crime centers, and smart policing.

In Part IV, we examine the necessary organizational foundations required for community policing and problem solving to flourish. In Chapter 8, Changing Agency Culture, we discuss what is meant by organizational culture and the need for some police agencies to modify their culture so as to become more constitutional and legitimate in the eyes of the public; how an organization can move from one that is "good" to being "great"; recruiting quality officers; and the roles and responsibilities of chief executives, middle managers, supervisors, and rank-and-file officers. Chapter 9, Planning and Implementation, discusses the key functions of preparing and initiating problem-oriented policing, which must be accomplished by thoughtfully laying the proper foundation; we also explain the strategic planning process, roles of key leaders in this process, addressing resistance to change, and how to measure whether or not planning and implementation were properly accomplished. Chapter 10 addresses the challenge of providing the best means and types of training, particularly in the context of engaging in constitutional, fair and impartial policing; we also consider the value of higher education, what works best for adult- and problem-based learning, and some technological approaches to training and the basics of a curriculum. The last chapter in this part, Chapter 11, confronts the issue of evaluation, including the different tools and methods for doing so. An ongoing challenge for community policing and problem solving is determining whether or not police responses to crime were successful.

Part V focuses on specific methods and challenges for dealing with crime and disorder in our society. In Chapter 12, we describe the application of problem-solving methods to drug abuse, youth gangs, and neighborhood violence. Chapter 13 continues this same theme, examining what works with the mentally ill population, domestic violence, cybercrime (including identity theft), and human trafficking.

Finally, in Part VI, we look at challenges that will likely confront the police in the future. Chapter 14 explores what kinds of factors will shape and drive change, to include the language of policing, the economy and demographics, technologies, terrorism, cybercrime, applying science to policing, and the need for strong leadership in several areas (e.g., militarization, transparency, succession planning, civilianization, and training).

Two appendices conclude the text; the first includes several award-winning case studies of excellent problem solving, and an example of a problem-oriented policing training curriculum.

We believe this book comprehensively lays out for today's student how problem-oriented policing should be, and is being applied in the United States. As noted above, the major strength of this book lies in its many case studies, exhibits, and "learn by doing" segments, which demonstrate how the concept is planned, implemented, operationalized, and evaluated. As Samuel Johnson wrote, "Example is always more efficacious than precept."

We are extremely grateful for the helpful suggestions made by the following reviewers of this edition: Jay Berman, New Jersey City University; Douglas Davis, Mary Baldwin College; Jennifer Estis-Sumerel, Itawamba Community College; and Michael Pittaro, American Military University.

INSTRUCTOR SUPPLEMENTS

Instructor's Manual with Test Bank. Includes content outlines for classroom discussion, teaching suggestions, and answers to selected end-of-chapter questions from the text. This also contains a Word document version of the test bank.

TestGen. This computerized test generation system gives you maximum flexibility in creating and administering tests on paper, electronically, or online. It provides state-of-the-art features for viewing and editing test bank questions, dragging a selected question into a test you are creating, and printing sleek, formatted tests in a variety of layouts. Select test items from test banks included with TestGen for quick test creation, or write your own questions from scratch. TestGen's random generator provides the option to display different text or calculated number values each time questions are used.

PowerPoint Presentations. Our presentations are clear and straightforward. Photos, illustrations, charts, and tables from the book are included in the presentations when applicable.

To access supplementary materials online, instructors need to request an instructor access code. Go to **www.pearsonhighered.com/irc,** where you can register for an instructor access code. Within 48 hours after registering, you will receive a confirming email, including an instructor access code. Once you have received your code, go to the site and log on for full instructions on downloading the materials you wish to use.

ALTERNATE VERSIONS

eBooks This text is also available in multiple eBook formats. These are an exciting new choice for students looking to save money. As an alternative to purchasing the printed textbook, students can purchase an electronic version of the same content. With an eTextbook, students can search the text, make notes online, print out reading assignments that incorporate lecture notes, and bookmark important passages for later review. For more information, visit your favorite online eBook reseller or visit www.mypearsonstore.com.

Ken Peak

Ron Glensor

ABOUT THE AUTHORS

Kenneth J. Peak, Ph.D., is a professor emeritus and former chairman of the criminal justice department at the University of Nevada, Reno, where he was named "Teacher of the Year" by the UNR Honor Society and also served as acting director of public safety. He has authored or coauthored 31 books on policing, justice administration, women in law enforcement, and police supervision and management; two historical books (on bootlegging and temperance); and more than 60 journal articles and additional book chapters on a wide range of justice-related subjects. He has served as chairman of the Police Section, Academy of Criminal Justice Sciences and a past president of the Western Association of Criminal Justice. Prior to coming to UNR, Dr. Peak held positions as a municipal police officer, criminal justice planner; director of a Four-State Technical Assistance Institute; director of university police at Pittsburg State University; and assistant professor at Wichita State University. He received two gubernatorial appointments to statewide criminal justice committees while in Kansas and holds a doctorate from the University of Kansas.

 Ronald W. Glensor, Ph.D., is an assistant chief (retired) of the Reno, Nevada, Police Department (RPD). He has accumulated more than 36 years of police experience and commanded the department's patrol, administration, and detective divisions. In addition to being actively involved in RPD's implementation of community-oriented policing and problem solving since 1987, he has provided such training to thousands of officers, elected officials, and community members representing jurisdictions throughout the United States as well as Canada, Australia, and the United Kingdom. He is also a judge for the Herman Goldstein International Problem Oriented Policing Awards held annually throughout the nation. Dr. Glensor was the 1997 recipient of the prestigious Gary P. Hayes Award, conferred by the Police Executive Research Forum, recognizing his contributions and leadership in the policing field. Internationally, he is a frequent featured speaker on a variety of policing issues. He served a six-month fellowship as problem-oriented policing coordinator with the Police Executive Research Forum in Washington, D.C., and received an Atlantic Fellowship in public policy, studying repeat victimization at the Home Office in London. He is coauthor of *Police Supervision and Management in an Era of Community Policing* (third edition) and was coeditor of *Policing Communities: Understanding Crime and Solving Problems.* Dr. Glensor has also published in several journals and trade magazines, is an adjunct professor at the University of Nevada, Reno, and instructs at area police academies and criminal justice programs. He holds a doctorate in political science and a master's of public administration from the University of Nevada, Reno.

PART I

The Long Road to Community Policing and Problem Solving

This part consists of two chapters, which together will map the movement away from traditional policing methods, the development of community policing and problem solving, and the important role of the community in those processes. Chapter 1 traces the professionalizing of policing in England and its subsequent journey to, and elaboration in, the United States, including its various iterations and strategies; Chapter 2 focuses on the community's role in shaping, guiding, and controlling the police as well as the courts, and corrections subsystems.

Evolution:
The Geneses of Community Policing

LEARNING OBJECTIVES

As a result of reading this chapter, the student will understand:

- The evolution and development of professional policing from its early use of volunteers in England to its modern-day practices in the United States
- The characteristics of each of the three eras—political, professional, and community—of policing in the United States
- The foundations and strategies of both community policing and problem-oriented policing, to include contributions of the federal government
- How empirical studies resulted in major changes in police methods and approaches
- How to distinguish the three generations of community policing and problem solving
- The contributions of community policing and problem solving to homeland security
- How, when viewing the entire history of policing, it may be said to have come full circle in its contemporary emphasis on community

TEST YOUR KNOWLEDGE

1. The "architect" and "crib" of professional policing—the person and agency where most initial practices were developed—was Robert Deal, in the Philadelphia Police Department.
2. Modern-day policing in the United States originated with the onset of volunteer night patrols in New York City in 1866.
3. Policing in the United States has gone through three eras: the political, the professional (or reform), and the community eras.
4. The professional "crime fighter" model of policing has served it well and continues to prevail today.
5. The community era of policing emphasizes that the police cannot solve crimes without citizen input and assistance.
6. Community-oriented policing and problem solving relies heavily on the use of statistics: calls for service, response times, and numbers of arrests by officers.
7. The federal government has had no influence or provided any assistance with the spread of community policing and problem solving.

Answers can be found on page 278.

When we pull back the layers of government services,
the most fundamental and indispensable virtues
are public safety and social order.

—HON. DAVID A. HARDY, WASHOE COUNTY
DISTRICT COURT, RENO, NEVADA

To understand what is, we must know what has been, and
what it tends to become.

—OLIVER WENDELL HOLMES

INTRODUCTION

It is difficult to accurately establish the beginning of community-oriented policing in America. This is possibly because the notion of community policing is not altogether new; parts of it are as old as policing itself, emanating (as will be seen later) from concerns about policing that were indicated in the early nineteenth century.

We also must mention at the outset of this book that community policing and problem solving is not a unitary concept but rather a collection of related ideas. Several prominent individuals, movements, studies, and experiments have brought policing to where it is today. In this chapter, we examine the principal activities involving the police for more than a century and a half—activities that led to the development of community policing and problem solving.

This historical examination of policing begins with a brief discussion of Britain's and Sir Robert Peel's influence and the Metropolitan Police Act in England. Then we review the evolution of policing in America, including the emergence of the political era and attempts at reform through the professional crime fighter model. Next we look at police and change, including how "sacred cow" policing methods have been debunked by research, demonstrated the actual nature of police work, and shown the need for a new approach.

Following is an examination of the community problem-solving era, including what the principles of this new model are, why it emerged, and how it evolved. Included in this chapter are brief discussions of some relatively new police analytical tools—**CompStat**, **smart policing**, **intelligence-led policing**, and **predictive policing** (all of which are discussed in more detail in Chapter 7). Next is a brief discussion of how problem-oriented policing can enhance the nation's defense and homeland security (Chapter 4 is devoted entirely to this subject as well). Then, the chapter concludes with a summary, a listing of the chapter's key terms and concepts, review questions, and several scenarios and activities that provide opportunities for you to "learn by doing" (these are explained in more detail below).

BRITISH CONTRIBUTIONS

The population of England doubled between 1700 and 1800. Parliament, however, took no measures to help solve the problems that arose from the accompanying social change.[1]

London, awash in crime, had whole districts become criminal haunts, and thieves became very bold. In the face of this situation, Henry Fielding began to experiment with possible solutions. Fielding, appointed in 1748 as London's chief magistrate of Bow Street, argued against the severity of the English penal code, which applied the death penalty to a large number of offenses. He felt the country should reform the criminal code in order to deal more with the origins of crime. In 1750, Fielding made the pursuit of criminals more systematic by creating a small group of "thief-takers."[2] When Fielding died in 1754, his half-brother John Fielding succeeded him as Bow Street magistrate. By 1785, his thief-takers had evolved into the Bow Street Runners—some of the most famous policemen in English history.

Later, Robert Peel, a wealthy member of Parliament, felt strongly that London's population and crime problem merited a full-time professional police force, but many English people and other politicians objected to the idea, fearing possible restraint of their liberty. They also feared a strong police organization because the criminal law was already quite harsh (by the early nineteenth century, there were 223 crimes in England for which a person could be hanged). Indeed, Peel's efforts to gain support for full-time paid police officers failed for seven years.[3]

Peel finally succeeded in 1829. His bill to Parliament, titled "An Act for Improving the Police in and Near the Metropolis," succeeded and became known as the **Metropolitan Police Act** of 1829. The *General Instructions* of the new force stressed its preventive nature, saying that "the principal object to be attained is 'the prevention of crime.' The security of persons and property will thus be better effected, than by the detection and punishment of the offender after he has succeeded in committing the crime."[4] It was decided that constables would don a uniform (blue coat, blue pants, and black top hat) and would arm themselves with a short baton (known as a truncheon) and a rattle (for raising an alarm); each constable was to wear his individual number on his collar where it could be easily seen.[5]

Peel proved very farsighted and keenly aware of the needs of a community-oriented police force as well as the need of the public who would be asked to maintain it. Indeed, Peel perceived that the poor quality of policing was a contributing factor to the social disorder. Peel's statement that "The police are the public, and the public are the police" emphasized his belief that the police are first and foremost members of the larger society.[6]

Peel's attempts to appease the public were well grounded; during the first three years of his reform effort, he encountered strong opposition. Peel was denounced as a potential dictator; the *London Times* urged revolt, and *Blackwood's Magazine* referred to the bobbies as "general spies" and "finished tools of corruption." A national secret body was organized to combat the police, who were nicknamed the "Blue Devils" and the "Raw Lobsters." Also during this initial five-year period, Peel endured one of the largest police turnover rates in history. Estimates range widely, but it is probably accurate to accept the figure of 1,341 constables resigning from London's Metropolitan Police from 1829 to 1834.[7]

Peel drafted what have become known as **Peel's Principles** of policing, most (if not all) of which are still apropos to today's police community. They are presented in Box 1–1.

BOX 1–1
Peel's Principles of Policing

1. The basic mission for which the police exist is to prevent crime and disorder as an alternative to the repression of crime and disorder by military force and severity of legal punishment.
2. The ability of the police to perform their duties is dependent upon public approval of police existence, actions, behavior, and the ability of the police to secure and maintain public respect.
3. The police must secure the willing cooperation of the public in voluntary observance of the law to be able to secure and maintain public respect.
4. The degree of cooperation of the public that can be secured diminishes, proportionately, the necessity for the use of physical force and compulsion in achieving police objectives.
5. The police seek and preserve public favor, not by catering to public opinion, but by constantly demonstrating absolutely impartial service to the law, in complete independence of policy, and without regard to the justice or injustice of the substance of individual laws; by ready offering of individual service and friendship to all members of the society without regard to their race or social standing; by ready exercise of courtesy and friendly good humor; and by ready offering of individual sacrifice in protecting and preserving life.
6. The police should use physical force to the extent necessary to secure observance of the law or to restore order only when the exercise of persuasion, advice, and warning is found to be insufficient to achieve police objectives; and police should use only the minimum degree of physical force which is necessary on any particular occasion for achieving a police objective.
7. The police at all times should maintain a relationship with the public that gives reality to the historic tradition that the police are the public and that the public are the police; the police are the only members of the public who are paid to give full-time attention to duties which are incumbent on every citizen in the interest of the community welfare.
8. The police should always direct their actions toward their functions and never appear to usurp the powers of the judiciary by avenging individuals or the state, or authoritatively judging guilt or punishing the guilty.
9. The test of police efficiency is the absence of crime and disorder, not the visible evidence of police action in dealing with them.

Source: W. L. Melville Lee, *A History of Police in England* (London: Methuen, 1901), Chapter 12.

POLICING IN AMERICA: THE POLITICAL ERA

Although the onset of full-time, professional policing in the United States is commonly said to have occurred in New York City in 1844, some police historians believe that the first organized, "modern" form of policing occurred in the South in the form of slave patrols.[8] Indeed, from the time Dutch slave ships began bringing slaves to the U.S. colonies as early as 1670, colonists began attempting to control slaves through informal means. The first such patrol was probably first organized as a special enforcement arm in South Carolina in 1704.[9] These men were well-armed and often visited plantations where they were allowed to flog slaves who were violating the codes.[10] In many colonies and states, anyone could legally apprehend, chastise, and even kill any slave found off of his or her plantation, and runaway slaves could even be killed in some states.[11] The slave patrols eventually became the legal mechanism for social control, particularly in rural areas of the Southern colonies, where they were to maintain the institution of slavery as well as capture runaway slaves and protect the white majority from slave uprisings and crimes.[12]

Early Beginnings

THE NEW YORK MODEL. Americans meanwhile were observing Peel's overall successful experiment with the bobbies on the patrol beat. Industrialization and social upheaval had not reached the proportions that they had in England, however, so there was not the urgency for full-time policing that had been experienced in England. Yet by the 1840s, when industrialization began in earnest in America, U.S. officials were watching the police reform movement in England more closely.

To comprehend the blundering, inefficiency, and confusion that surrounded nineteenth-century police in what would be called the **political era** of policing, we must remember that this was an age when the best forensic techniques could not clearly distinguish the blood of a pig from that of a human and the art of criminal detection was little more than divination. Steamboats blew up, trains regularly mutilated and killed pedestrians, children got run over by wagons, injury very often meant death, and doctors resisted the germ theory of disease. In the midst of all this, the police would be patrolling—the police being men who at best had been trained by reading pathetic little rule books that provided them little or no guidance in the face of human distress and disorder.[13]

New York Police Department officers initially refused to wear uniforms because they did not want to appear as "liveried lackeys." A blue frock coat with brass buttons was adopted in 1853.
Courtesy NYPD Photo Unit.

The movement to initiate policing in America began in New York City. (Philadelphia, with a private bequeath of $33,000, actually began a paid daytime police force in 1833; however, it was disbanded in three years.) In 1844, New York's state legislature passed a law establishing a full-time preventive police force for New York City. This new body was very different from that adopted from Europe, deliberately placed under the control of the city government and city politicians. The mayor chose the recruits from a list of names submitted by the aldermen and tax assessors of each ward; the mayor then submitted his choices to the city council for approval. Politicians were seldom concerned about selecting the best people for the job; instead, the system allowed and even encouraged political patronage and rewards for friends.[14]

The police link to neighborhoods and politicians was so tight that the police of this era have been considered virtual adjuncts to political machines.[15] The relationship was often reciprocal: Political machines recruited and maintained police in office and on the beat while police helped ward leaders maintain their political offices by encouraging citizens to vote for certain candidates. Soon other cities adopted the New York model. New Orleans and Cincinnati adopted plans for a new police in 1852; Boston and Philadelphia followed in 1854, Chicago in 1855, and Baltimore and Newark in 1857.[16] By 1880, virtually every major American city had a police force based on Peel's model, pioneered in New York City.

FROM THE EAST TO THE WILD, WILD WEST.   These new police were born of conflict and violence. An unprecedented wave of civil disorder swept the nation from the 1840s until the 1870s. Few cities escaped serious rioting, caused by ethnic and racial conflicts, economic disorder, and public outrage about such things as brothels and medical school experiments. These occurrences often made for hostile interaction between citizens and the police, who were essentially a reactive force. Riots in many major cities actually led to the creation of the "new police." The use of the baton to quell riots, known as the "baton charge," was not uncommon.[17]

Furthermore, while large cities in the east were struggling to overcome social problems and establish preventive police forces, the western half of America was anything but passive. When people left the wagon trains and their relatively law-abiding ways, they attempted to live together in communities. Many different ethnic groups—Anglo-Americans, Mexicans, Chinese, Indians, freed blacks, Australians, Scandinavians, and others—competed for often-scarce resources and fought one another violently, often with mob attacks. Economic conflicts were frequent between cattlemen and sheep herders, often leading to major range wars. There was constant labor strife in the mines. The bitterness of the slavery issue remained, and many men with firearms skills learned during the Civil War turned to outlawry after leaving the service (Jesse James was one such person).[18]

Despite these difficulties, westerners established peace by relying on a combination of four groups who assumed responsibility for law enforcement: private citizens, U.S. marshals, businessmen, and town police officers.[19] Private citizens usually helped to enforce the law by use of posses or through individual efforts, such as vigilante committees[20] (contemporary examples of such groups would include the so-called Minutemen that patrol the Southwest borders in search of illegal aliens).[21] While it is true that they occasionally hanged outlaws, they also performed valuable work by ridding their communities of dangerous criminals.

Federal marshals were created by congressional legislation in 1789. As they began to appear on the frontier, the vigilantes tended to disappear. U.S. marshals enforced federal laws, so they only had jurisdiction over federal offenses, such as theft of mail, crimes against railroad property, and murder on federal lands. Their primary responsibility was in civil matters arising from federal court decisions. Finally, when a territory became a state, the primary law enforcement functions usually fell to local sheriffs and marshals. Sheriffs quickly became important officials, but they spent more time collecting taxes, inspecting cattle brands, maintaining jails, and serving civil papers than they did actually dealing with outlaws.[22]

Politics and Corruption

During the late nineteenth century, large cities gradually became more orderly. American cities absorbed millions of newcomers after 1900 without the social strains that attended the Irish immigration of the 1830s to 1850s.[23]

Partly because of their closeness to politicians, police during this era provided a wide array of services to citizens. Many police departments were involved in crime prevention and order maintenance as well as a variety of social services. In some cities, they operated soup lines, helped find lost children, and found jobs and temporary lodging for newly arrived immigrants.[24] Police organizations were typically quite decentralized, with cities being divided into precincts and run like small-scale departments—hiring, firing, managing, and assigning personnel as necessary. Officers were often recruited from the same ethnic stock as the dominant groups in the neighborhoods; they lived in the beats they patrolled and were given considerable discretion in handling their individual beats. Decentralization encouraged foot patrol, even after call boxes and automobiles became available. Detectives operated from a caseload of "persons" rather than offenses, relying on their caseload to inform on other criminals.[25]

The strengths of the political era centered on the fact that police were integrated into neighborhoods. This strategy proved useful as it helped contain riots and the police assisted immigrants in establishing themselves in communities and finding jobs. There were weaknesses as well: The intimacy with the community, the closeness to politicians, and a decentralized organizational structure (and its inability to provide supervision of officers) also led to police corruption. The close identification of police with neighborhoods also resulted in discrimination against strangers, especially minority ethnic and racial groups. Police often ruled their beats with the "end of their nightsticks" and practiced "curbside justice."[26] The lack of organizational control over officers also caused some inefficiencies and disorganization; thus, the image of Keystone Cops—bungling police—was widespread.

Emergence of Professionalism

In summary, the nineteenth-century police officer was essentially a political operative rather than a modern-style professional committed to public service. Because the police were essentially a political institution and perceived as such by the citizenry, they did not enjoy widespread

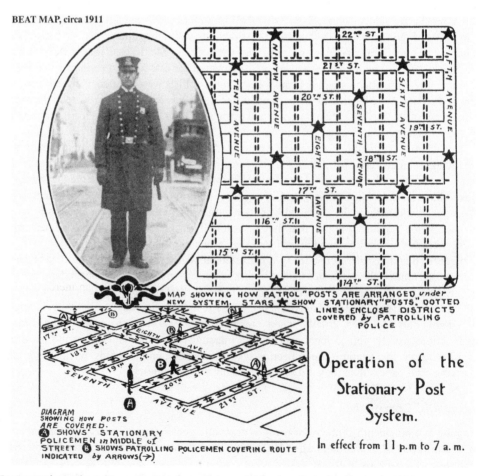

Foot patrol was the primary strategy for policing neighborhoods during the early 1900s.
Courtesy NYPD Photo Unit.

acceptance by the public. As political appointees, officers enjoyed little job security, and salaries were determined by local political factors. Primitive communications technology of the era meant that police chiefs were unable to supervise their captains at the precinct level; thus, policy was greatly influenced by the prevailing political and social mores of the neighborhoods. As a consequence, police behavior was very much influenced by the interaction between individual officers and individual citizens. The nature of that interaction, later termed the problem of **police–community relations**, was perhaps even more complex and ambiguous in the nineteenth century than in the late twentieth century.[27]

THE PROFESSIONAL ERA

Movement Toward Reform

The idea of policing as a profession, however, began to emerge slowly in the latter part of the nineteenth century. Reform ideas first appeared as a reaction to the corrupt and politicized state of the police. Reformers agreed that partisan politics was the heart of the problem. Even reformers in the National Prison Association bemoaned the partisan politics that hindered the improvement of the police. Slowly the idea of policing as a higher calling (i.e., higher than the concerns of local politics), as a profession committed to public service, began to gain ground. Two other ideas about the proper role of the police in society also appeared. One emphasized improvement in the role of police with respect to scientific techniques of crime detection. The other idea was that police could play more of a social work role; by intervening in the lives of individuals, police officers could reform society by preventing crime and keeping people out of the justice system. These reformers were closely tied to the emerging rehabilitative ideal in correctional circles in what is termed the **professional era**.[28]

New Developments and Calls for Reform

There were several important developments in the **reform of policing** during the late 1800s. Policing realized the beginning of a body of literature. Most authors were closely tied to the police and thus painted an inaccurate picture in some respects (e.g., the corruption that existed in many police departments), but their writings were also very illuminating. They provided glimpses into the informal processes that governed police departments and focused on the individual officer, a focus that would be lost in the later professionalization movement with its emphasis on impersonal bureaucratic standards. Furthermore, the late 1800s witnessed improvements in the areas of testing and training. The physical and mental qualifications of police officers concerned new police commissioners, and formal schools of instruction were developed (the best being Cincinnati's, which required a total of 72 hours of instruction). During the late 1800s, there was also the appearance of police conventions, such as the National Police Chiefs Union (later named the International Association of Chiefs of Police [IACP]) and fraternal and benefit societies.[29]

August Vollmer, pioneer of police professionalism from 1905 to 1932, rallied police executives around the idea of reform during the 1920s and 1930s, emerging as the leading national spokesman for police professionalism. What is often overlooked among the abundance of Vollmer's contributions to policing was his articulate advocacy of the idea that the police should function as social workers. The belief that police officers should do more than merely arrest offenders, that they should actively seek to prevent crime by "saving" potential or actual offenders, was an important theme in police reform. It was an essential ingredient in the notion of professionalism. Indeed, in a series of addresses to the IACP, Vollmer advanced his ideas in "The Policeman as a Social Worker" (1918) and "Predelinquency" (1921). He began by arguing that the "old methods of dealing with crime must be changed, and newer ones adopted."[30]

Vollmer's views were very prescient for today, especially given the contemporary movement toward community policing. Vollmer felt that traditional institutions and practices were no longer adequate for a modern and complex industrial society. He believed that the police should intervene and be involved with people before they entered lives of crime, and he suggested that police work closely with existing social welfare agencies and become advocates of additional reform proposals. Vollmer also suggested that police inform voters about overcrowded schools and support the expansion of recreational facilities, community social centers, and antidelinquency agencies. Basically, he was suggesting that the police play an active part in the political

August Vollmer, a national spokesman for and early pioneer of police professionalism, established one of the first fingerprint bureaus and formal police schools while he was chief of police in Berkeley, California. *Courtesy Samuel G. Chapman.*

life of the community, yet the major thrust of police professionalization had been to insulate the police from politics. This contradiction illustrated one of the fundamental ambiguities of the whole notion of professionalism.[31]

Other reformers continued to reject political involvement by police, and civil service systems were created to eliminate patronage and ward influences in hiring and firing police officers. In some cities, officers could not live in the same beat they patrolled, to isolate them as completely as possible from political influences. Police departments, needing to be removed from political influence, became one of the most autonomous agencies in urban government.[32] However, policing also became a matter viewed as best left to the discretion of police executives to address. Police organizations became law enforcement agencies, with the sole goal of controlling crime. Any noncrime activities they were required to do were "social work." The "professional model" of policing was in full bloom.

The scientific theory of administration was adopted, as advocated by Frederick Taylor during the early twentieth century. Taylor had studied the work process, breaking down jobs into their basic steps and emphasizing time and motion studies, all with an eye toward maximizing production. From this emphasis on production and unity of control flowed the notion that police officers were best managed by a hierarchical pyramid of control. Police leaders routinized and standardized police work; officers were to enforce laws and make arrests whenever possible. Discretion was limited to the extent possible. When special problems arose, special units (e.g., vice, juvenile, drugs, tactical) were created rather than assigning problems to patrol officers.

Crime Commissions and Early Police Studies

The early 1900s also became the age of the crime commission, including the **Wickersham Commission** reports in 1931. President Herbert Hoover, concerned with the lax enforcement of prohibition and other forms of police corruption, created the National Commission on Law Observance and Enforcement—popularly known as the Wickersham Commission after its chairman, former U.S. Attorney General George W. Wickersham. This commission completed the first national study of crime and criminal justice, issuing 14 reports and recommending that the corrupting influence of politics be removed from policing, police chief executives be selected on merit, patrol officers be tested and meet minimal physical standards, police salaries and working conditions be decent, and policewomen be used in juvenile and female cases. Many of these recommendations represented what progressive police reformers had been wanting over the previous 40 years; unfortunately, President Hoover and his administration could do little more than report the Wickersham Commission's recommendations before leaving office.

The most important change in policing during this decade was the advent of the automobile and its accompanying radio. Gradually the patrol car replaced foot patrol, expanding geographic beats and further removing people from neighborhoods. There was also Prohibition (which affected the police very little in a long-term way), a bloody wave of racial violence in American cities, and the rise and defeat of police unionism and strikes. The impact of two-way radios was also felt, as supervisors were able to maintain a far closer supervision of patrol officers, and the radio and telephone made it possible for citizens to make heavier demands for police service. The result was not merely a greater burden on the police but also an important qualitative redefinition of the police role.[33]

The 1930s marked an important turning point in the history of police reform. The first genuine empirical studies of police work began to appear, and O. W. Wilson emerged as the leading authority on police administration. The major development of this decade was a redefinition of the police role and the ascendancy of the crime fighter image. Wilson, who took guidance from J. Edgar Hoover's transformation of the Federal Bureau of Investigation (FBI) into an agency of high prestige, became the principal architect of the police reform strategy.[34] Hoover, appointed FBI director in 1924, had raised eligibility and training standards of recruits, giving FBI agents stature as upstanding moral crusaders and developing an incorruptible crime-fighting organization. He also developed impressive public relations programs that presented the bureau in the most favorable light. Municipal police found Hoover's path a compelling one. Following Wilson's writings on police administration, they began to shape an organizational strategy for urban police that was analogous to that pursued by the FBI.

Also by the 1930s, the policewomen's movement, begun in the early 1900s, had begun losing ground. Professionalism came to mean a combination of managerial efficiency, technological sophistication, and an emphasis on crime fighting. The social work aspects of policing—the idea of rehabilitative work, which had been central to the policewomen's movement—were almost totally eclipsed. The result was a severe identity crisis for policewomen: They were caught between a social work orientation and a law enforcement ideology. Later, by the 1960s, women would occupy an extremely marginal place in American policing.[35]

In sum, under the reform era's professional model of policing, officers were to remain in their "rolling fortresses," going from one call to the next with all due haste. As Mark Moore and George Kelling observed, "In professionalizing crime fighting, the 'volunteers,' citizens on whom so much used to depend, [were] removed from the fight. If anything has been learned from the history of American policing, it is that, whatever the benefits of professionalization (e.g., reduced corruption, due process, serious police training), the reforms . . . ignored, even attacked, some features that once made the police powerful institutions in maintaining a sense of community security."[36]

Professional Crime Fighter

EMPHASIS ON EFFICIENCY AND CONTROL. The decade of the 1930s ended the first phase in the history of police professionalization. From the 1940s through the early 1960s, police reform continued along the lines that were already well established. Police professionalism was defined almost exclusively in terms of managerial efficiency, and administrators sought to further strengthen their hand in controlling rank-and-file officers; however, many of the old problems, such as racial unrest and an unclear definition of the police role, persisted. Nonetheless, by the late 1930s and early 1940s, there was a clear sense of mission for the police, a commitment to public service where one had not existed before.[37] Also, policing had begun to develop its own sense of professional autonomy. And, ironically perhaps, the most articulate groups and the most creative thinking were to be found in nonpolice groups: the National Prison Association, the social work profession, and the field of public administration. The efforts by reformers to remove political influence over police, though not entirely successful, were beginning to take hold as police boards and powerful police chiefs met their demise. Police unions reappeared, however, and the emergence of careerism among police officers significantly altered their attitudes toward the job and the public they served.

FBI agents practice shooting from vehicle in the 1930s.
Courtesy FBI.

The professional model demanded an impartial law enforcer who related to citizens in professionally neutral and distant terms, personified by television's Sgt. Friday on "Dragnet": "Just the facts, ma'am." The emphasis on professionalization also shaped the role of citizens in crime control. Like physicians caring for health problems, teachers for educational problems, and social workers for social adjustment problems, the police would be responsible for crime problems. Citizens became relatively passive in crime control, mere recipients of professional crime control services. Citizens' responsibility in crime control was limited to calling police and serving as witnesses when asked to do so. Police were the "thin blue line." The community's need for rapid response to calls for service (CFS) was sold as efficacious in crime control. Foot patrol, when demanded by citizens, was rejected as an outmoded, expensive frill. Professionalism in law enforcement was often identified in terms of firearms expertise, and the popularity of firearms put the police firmly in the anti-gun control camp.[38]

Citizens were no longer encouraged to go to "their" neighborhood police officers or districts. Officers were to drive marked cars randomly through streets, to develop a feeling of police omnipresence. The "person" approach ended and was replaced by the case approach. Officers were judged by the numbers of arrests they made or by the number of miles they drove during a shift. The crime rate became the primary indicator of police effectiveness.

REESTABLISHMENT OF COMMUNICATION: POLICE–COMMUNITY RELATIONS. While much of the country was engaged in "practicing" and "selling" police reform embodied in the professional model of policing, a movement was beginning in Michigan to bring the police and community closer together. Louis Radelet served on the executive staff of the National Conference of Christians and Jews (NCCJ) from 1951 to 1963, when he became a professor in what was then the School of Police Administration and Public Safety at Michigan State University (MSU). In 1955 Radelet, having conducted many NCCJ workshops dedicated to reducing tensions between elements of the community, founded the National Institute on Police and Community Relations (NIPCR) at MSU; he served as institute director from 1955 to 1969 and was also coordinator of the university's National Center on Police and Community Relations, created to conduct a national survey on police–community relations, from 1965 to 1973.[39]

The institute held 5-day conferences each May during its 15-year existence, bringing together teams of police officers and other community leaders to discuss common problems. In peak years, more than 600 participants came from as many as 165 communities and 30 states as well as several foreign countries. As a result of the institute's work, such programs proliferated rapidly across the nation. We believe the stated purposes of the many programs initiated during this period are still applicable today and are listed here[40]:

1. To encourage police–citizen partnership in the cause of crime prevention.
2. To foster and improve communications and mutual understanding between the police and the total community.
3. To promote interprofessional approaches to the solution of community problems and to stress the principle that the administration of justice is a total community responsibility.
4. To enhance cooperation among the police, the prosecution, the courts, and the corrections.
5. To assist the police and other community leaders to achieve an understanding of the nature and causes of complex problems in people-to-people relations and especially to improve police–minority relationships.
6. To strengthen implementation of equal protection under the law for all persons.

The NIPCR was discontinued at the end of 1969. Radelet wrote that its demise was "a commentary on the evolution of issues and social forces pertinent to the field. The purposes, assumptions, and institute design of past years may have been relevant in their time. But it became imperative now to think about police–community relations programs in different terms, with more precise purposes that could be better measured."[41]

Problems with the Professional Model

Several problems with the professional model of policing began to arise during the late 1960s.

Crime began to rise, and research suggested that conventional police methods were not effective. The 1960s was a time of explosion and turbulence. Inner-city residents rioted in several major cities; protestors denounced military involvement in Vietnam; and assassins ended the lives of President John F. Kennedy, Robert F. Kennedy, and civil rights leader Rev. Martin Luther King, Jr. The country was witnessing tremendous upheaval, and such incidents as the so-called police riot at the 1968 Democratic National Convention in Chicago raised many questions about the police and their function and role. Largely as a result of this turmoil, five national studies, each with a different focus, looked into police practices during the 1960s and 1970s: the President's Commission on Law Enforcement and the Administration of Justice (termed the "President's Crime Commission" [1967]), the National Advisory Commission on Civil Disorders (1968), the National Commission on the Causes and Prevention of Violence (1968), the President's Commission on Campus Unrest (1970), and the National Advisory Commission on Criminal Justice Standards and Goals (1973). Of particular note was the aforementioned President's Crime Commission of 1967, charged by President Lyndon Johnson to find solutions to America's internal crime problems. Among the commission's recommendations for the police were hiring more minorities as police officers to improve police–community relations, upgrading the quality of police officers through better-educated officers, and using better applicant screening and intensive preservice training.[42]

The President's Crime Commission brought policing full circle, restating several of the same principles that were laid out by Sir Robert Peel in 1829: that the police should be close to the public, that poor quality of policing contributed to social disorder, and that the police should focus on community relations.

Police administrators became more willing to challenge traditional assumptions and beliefs and to open the door to researchers and their **research findings**. That willingness to allow researchers to examine traditional methods led to the growth and development of two important policing research organizations: the Police Foundation and the Police Executive Research Forum (PERF).

Fear rose. Citizens abandoned parks, public transportation, neighborhood shopping centers, churches, and entire neighborhoods. What puzzled police and researchers was that levels of fear and crime did not always correspond: Crime levels were low in some areas, but fear was high, and vice versa. Researchers found that fear is more closely associated with disorder than with crime. Ironically, order maintenance was one of the functions that police had been downplaying over the years.

Three Selma-to-Montgomery (Alabama) marches in 1965 marked the peak of the American civil rights movement, growing out of the voting rights movement launched by African-Americans. The first march took place on March 7, 1965—"Bloody Sunday"—when 600 civil rights marchers were attacked by state and local police with batons and tear gas.
Courtesy National Park Service.

Many minority citizens did not perceive their treatment as equitable or adequate. They protested not only police mistreatment but also lack of treatment—despite attempts by most police departments to provide impartial policing to all citizens.

The antiwar and civil rights movements challenged police. The legitimacy of the police was questioned: Students resisted police, minorities rioted against them for what they represented, and the public (for the first time at this level) questioned police tactics. Moreover, minorities and women insisted that they be represented in policing if the police were to be legitimate.

Some of the myths on which the reform era was founded—that police officers use little or no discretion and that their primary duty is law enforcement—could no longer be sustained. Over and over, research underscored that the use of discretion was needed at all levels and that law enforcement composed but a small portion of police officers' activities.[43] Other research findings shook the foundations of old assumptions about policing; for example, two-person patrol cars are neither more effective nor safer than one-person cars in reducing crime or catching criminals.[44] Other "sacred cows" of policing that were debunked by research are discussed below.

Although managers had tried to professionalize policing, line officers continued to have low status. Police work continued to be routinized; petty rules governed officer behavior. Meanwhile, line officers received little guidance in the use of discretion and had little opportunity for providing input concerning their work. As a result, many departments witnessed the rise of militant unionism.

The police lost a significant portion of their financial support. Many police departments were reduced in size, demonstrating an erosion of public confidence.

Police began to acquire competition: private security and the community crime control movement. Businesses, industries, and private citizens began to seek alternative means of protecting themselves and their property, further suggesting a declining confidence in the capability of police to provide the level of services that citizens desired. Indeed, today there are more than 1.5 million private police personnel employed in the United States—two to three times more personnel than there are in all federal, state, and municipal police agencies combined.[45] The social upheaval of the 1960s and 1970s obviously changed the face of policing in America. Not to be overlooked is the impact of the courts during this period as well. A number of major landmark Supreme Court decisions curtailed the actions of police and, concurrently, expanded the rights of the accused.

Changing Wisdom: More Recent Studies of Police Work

As a result of the problems mentioned earlier and the civil unrest that occurred during the professional era of policing, research evolved a new "common wisdom" of policing. As will be shown, much of this research shook the foundation of policing and rationalized the changes in methods we offer in later chapters. We discuss what might be termed the two primary clusters of police research that illuminated where policing has been and what officers actually do.

The first cluster of research actually began in the 1950s and would ultimately involve seven empirical studies of the police: the early work of sociologist William Westley concerning the culture of policing,[46] the ambitious studies of the American Bar Foundation,[47] the field observations of Jerome Skolnick,[48] the work of Egon Bittner analyzing the police function on skid row,[49] Raymond Parnas's study of the police response to domestic disturbances,[50] James Q. Wilson's analysis of different policing styles,[51] and the studies of police–citizen contact by Albert Reiss.[52] These studies collectively provided a "new realism" about policing[53]:

- Informal arrangements for handling incidents and behavioral problems were found to be more common than was compliance with formally established procedures.
- Workload, public pressures, and interagency pressures as well as the interests and personal predilections of functionaries in the criminal justice system were found in many instances to have more influence on how the police and the rest of the criminal justice system operated than the Constitution, state statutes, or city ordinances.
- Arrest, commonly viewed as the first step in the criminal process, had come to be used by the police to achieve a whole range of objectives in addition to that of prosecuting wrongdoers (e.g., to investigate, harass, punish, or provide safekeeping).
- A great variety of informal methods outside the criminal justice system had been adopted by the police to fulfill their formal responsibilities and to dispose of the endless array of situations that the public—rightly or wrongly—expected them to handle.
- Individual police officers were found to be routinely exercising a great deal of discretion in deciding how to handle the tremendous variety of circumstances with which they were confronted.

These findings also underscored that the police had, in the past, depended too much on the criminal law in order to get their job done; that they were not autonomous but rather were accountable, through the political process, to the community; and that dealing with fear and enforcing public order are appropriate functions for the police.[54] Other early studies indicated that less than 50 percent of an officer's time was committed to CFS, and of those calls handled, over 80 percent were noncriminal incidents.[55]

The five national studies of policing practices during the riots and the Vietnam War of the 1960s and 1970s (discussed in the previous section) began a quest for new directions. Later, a second cluster of police research occurred that provided further knowledge about police methods. The Kansas City Preventive Patrol Experiment of 1973 questioned the usefulness of random patrol in police vehicles.[56] Other studies showed that officers and detectives are limited in their abilities to successfully investigate crimes[57] and that detectives need not follow up every reported unsolved crime.[58] In short, most serious crimes were unaffected by the standard police actions designed to control them.

Since the 1970s, additional studies have dispelled many assumptions commonly held by police about their efficiency and effectiveness. For example, preventive patrol has been shown to be costly, producing only minimal results in the reduction of crime.[59] Rapid response to calls has been shown to be less effective at catching criminals than educating the public to call the police sooner after a crime is committed.[60] We now know that police response time is largely unrelated to the probability of making an arrest or locating a witness. The time it takes to report a crime is the major determining factor of whether an on-scene arrest takes place and whether witnesses are located.[61] Despite their best efforts, police have had little impact on preventing crime.[62]

Viewing "Sacred Cow" Methods with Caution

What did the studies mentioned previously mean for the police? Was the professional model of policing (discussed earlier) completely off base? No, in fact it can have a positive impact on a police agency's organization, efficiency, and control. However, these studies do show that the police erred in doggedly investing so much of their resources in a limited number of practices that were based on a rather naive and simplistic concept of the police role.[63] Furthermore, as we noted above, the police got caught up in the "means over ends" syndrome, measuring their success by the numbers of arrests, quickness of responses, and so on (the means) while often neglecting the outcome of their work (the ends).

As we have seen, the "We've always done it this way" mentality, still pervading policing to a large extent, may be not only an ineffective means of organizing and administering a police agency but also a costly squandering of valuable human and financial resources. For many police agencies today operating under the traditional incident-driven style of policing, the *beat* (rather than the *neighborhood*) is, to borrow a term from research methodology, the "unit of analysis." Under this timeworn model, officers have been glued to their police radios, flitting like pinballs from one call for service to the next as rapidly as possible. Furthermore, police officers seldom leave their vehicles to address incidents except when answering a CFS. They know very little about the underlying causes of problems in the neighborhoods on their beats.

The results of employing conventional police methods have been inglorious. Problems have persisted or been allowed to go unnoticed and grow while neighborhoods deteriorated. Officers became frustrated after they repeatedly handled similar calls, with no sign of progress. Petty offenses contributed to this decline and drove stable community members away once the message went out to offenders and vandals that no one cares about the neighborhood. Yet many in the police field are unaware of or refuse to accept that the old ways are open to serious challenge.

Time for a New Approach

We believe it is clear from all we've discussed thus far that police agencies must change their daily activities, their management practices, and even their view of their work in order to confront the changes that are occurring. We maintain that given the current levels of violence and the public's fear of it, the disorder found in countless American neighborhoods, the poor police–community relations in many cities, and the rapidly changing landscape of crime and demographics in America, the police need to seriously consider whether a bureaucratic overhaul is needed to meet the demands of the future.

Police research also demonstrated the need for agencies to evaluate the effectiveness of their responses. Both quantitative and qualitative data should be used as a basis for evaluation and change. Departments need to know more about what their officers are doing. Agencies are struggling to find enough resources for performing crime trend analyses; most also do not conduct proper workload analyses to know what uncommitted time is possessed by their officers.

Research has also provided the realization that policing consists of developing the most effective means for dealing with a multitude of troublesome situations. For example, problem solving is a whole new way of thinking about policing and carries the potential to reshape the way in which police services are delivered.[64]

One of several things the police must do to accomplish their mission is to reacquaint themselves with members of the community by involving citizens in the resolution of neighborhood problems. Simply stated, police must view the public as well as other government and social services organizations as "a part of," as opposed to "apart from," their efforts. This change in conventional thinking advocates efficiency with effectiveness and quality over quantity, and it encourages collaborative problem solving and creative resolutions to crime and disorder.

THE COMMUNITY ERA

Team Policing, Foot Patrol, and Shattered Myths

In the early 1970s, it was suggested that the performance of patrol officers would improve more by using job redesign based on "motivators."[65] This suggestion later evolved into a concept known as "team policing," which sought to restructure police departments, improve police–community relations, enhance police officer morale, and facilitate change within the police organization. Its primary element was a decentralized neighborhood focus to the delivery of police services. Officers were to be generalists, trained to investigate crimes and basically attend to all of the problems in their area, with a team of officers being assigned to a particular neighborhood and responsible for all police services in that area.

In the end, however, team policing failed for several reasons. Most of the experiments were poorly planned and hastily implemented, resulting in street officers not understanding what they were supposed to do. Many mid-management personnel felt threatened by team policing; as a result, some sabotaged the experiment. Furthermore, team policing did not represent a completely different view of policing. As Samuel Walker observed, "It was essentially a different *organizational approach* to traditional policing: responding to calls for service, deterring crime through patrol, and apprehending criminals" (emphasis in original).[66]

There were other developments for the police during the late 1970s and early 1980s. Foot patrol became more popular, and many jurisdictions (such as Newark, New Jersey; Boston, Massachusetts; and Flint, Michigan) even demanded it. In Newark, an evaluation found that foot patrol was readily perceived by residents and that it produced a significant increase in the level of satisfaction with police service, led to a significant reduction of perceived crime problems, and resulted in a significant increase in the perceived level of safety of the neighborhood.[67] Flint researchers reported that the crime rate in the target areas declined slightly; CFS in these areas dropped by 43 percent. Furthermore, citizens indicated satisfaction with the program, suggesting that it had improved relations with the police.[68]

These findings and others discussed below shattered several long-held myths about measures of police effectiveness. In addition, research conducted during the 1970s suggested that *information* could help police improve their ability to deal with crime. These studies, along with those of foot patrol and fear reduction, created new opportunities for the police to understand the increasing concerns of citizens' groups about disorder (e.g., gangs, prostitutes) and to work with citizens to do something about it. Police discovered that when they asked citizens about their priorities, citizens appreciated their asking and often provided useful information.

The Community Patrol Officer Program (CPOP), instituted by the New York City Police Department in 1984, was similar in many respects to the Flint foot patrol program. Officers involved in this program were responsible for getting to know the residents, merchants, and service providers in their beat area; identifying the principal crime and order maintenance problems confronting the people within their beat; and devising strategies for dealing with the identified problems.[69]

Early Beginnings of the Problem-Oriented Policing Model

Simultaneously, Herman Goldstein's problem-oriented approach to policing was being tested in Madison, Wisconsin; Baltimore County, Maryland; and Newport News, Virginia. These studies found that police officers enjoy operating with a holistic approach to their work, have the capacity to do problem solving successfully, and can work with citizens and other agencies to solve problems. Also, citizens seemed to appreciate working with police. Moreover, this approach was a rethinking of earlier strategies of handling CFS: Officers were given more autonomy and trained to analyze the underlying causes of problems and to find creative solutions. These findings were similar to those of the foot patrol experiments and fear reduction efforts.

Problem-oriented policing requires not only new police strategies but a new organizational approach as well. There is a renewed emphasis on community collaboration for many police tasks. Crime control remains an important function, but equal emphasis is given to *prevention*. Police officers return to their wide use of discretion under this model and move away from routinization and standardization in addressing their tasks. This discretion pushes operational and tactical decision making to the lower levels of the organization.

Participative management is greatly increased, and fewer levels of authority are required to administer the organization; middle management layers are reduced. Concurrently, many cities have developed what are, in effect, "demarketing" programs, attempting to rescind programs (such as the area of rapid response to CFS and to 911 calls except for dire emergencies) that had been actively sold earlier.

Community problem solving has helped to explain what went wrong with team policing in the 1960s and 1970s. It was a strategy that innovators mistakenly approached as a tactic. Team policing also competed with traditional policing in the same departments, and they were incompatible with

As part of their community policing and problem-solving efforts, many agencies use bicycle patrols to focus on crime prevention and greater interaction with the community.
Kevin Lamarque/Reuters Pictures.

one another. A police department might have a small team policing unit or conduct a team policing experiment, but the traditional professional model of policing was still "business as usual."

The classical theory of police organization that continues to dominate many agencies is likewise alien to the community problem-solving strategy. The new strategy will not accommodate the classical theory of traditional policing; the latter denies too much of the real nature of police work, continues old methods of supervision and administration, and creates too much cynicism in officers attempting to do creative problem solving.

Box 1–2 displays the three key elements of problem-oriented policing: community partnerships (discussed more thoroughly in Chapter 2), problem solving (see Chapter 5), and organizational transformation (Chapter 8)—as we envision its contemporary fundamental structure. This is a very important framework for you to comprehend because, in addition to framing and explaining the construction of problem-oriented policing, it essentially underlies and guides all other chapters that are contained in this book.

BOX 1–2

A Framework for Community Policing: Elements and Principles

Community Partnerships	Problem Solving	Organizational Transformation
Collaborative partnerships between the law enforcement agency and the individuals and organizations they serve, and anyone with a stake in the community.	The process and effect of problem solving should be assessed at each stage of the problem-solving process.	1. Leadership and administration • Policies and procedures • Management approach • Information management • Planning/program evaluation • Resources and finances
1. Agency has multidisciplinary partnerships with community partners, including other government agencies, nonprofit and community groups, businesses, the media, and individuals.	1. General problem-solving approach 2. Problem-solving processes: • Scanning • Analysis • Response • Assessment	2. Human resources • Recruiting, selection, training • Performance evaluation/promotion • Honors and awards • Discipline • Labor relation
2. Existing partnerships bring appropriate resources and level of commitment to community policing activities.	3. General skill in problem solving	3. Field operations • Call prioritization • Alternative reporting • Beat boundaries • Permanent shifts • Reduced specialization
3. Level of interaction between the law enforcement agency and community partners.		4. External relations • Community, media, businesses, local government service providers

Source: Adapted from Gayle Fisher-Stewart, *Community Policing Explained: A Guide for Local Governments* (Washington, D.C.: U.S. Department of Justice, Office of Community Oriented Policing Services, and the International City/County Management Association, July 2007), p. 5, http://www.cops.usdoj.gov/files/ric/Publications/cp_explained.pdf.

Why the Emergence of Problem-Oriented Policing?

Although we will discuss problem-oriented policing in greater detail and from different perspectives in the following chapters, below is a summary of the factors that set the stage for its emergence:

- Narrowing of the police mission to crime fighting.
- Increased cultural diversity in our society and heightened concern with police violation of minority civil rights.
- Detachment of patrol officers in patrol vehicles and of administration from officer and community input.
- Increased violence in our society.
- Downturn in the economy and, subsequently, a "do more with less" philosophy regarding the police.
- Increased dependence on high-technology equipment rather than contact with the public.
- Emphasis on organizational change, including decentralization and greater officer discretion.
- Desire for greater personalization of government services.
- Burgeoning attempts by the police to adequately reach the community through crime prevention, team policing, and police–community relations.

Most of these elements contain a common theme: the isolation of the police from the public. In sum, the police got caught up in the "means over ends" syndrome, wherein they measured their success by the numbers of arrests, quickness of responses, and so on. They often neglected the outcome of their work—the ends. For many decades, this isolation often resulted in an "us versus them" mentality on the part of both the police and the citizenry. The notion of community policing therefore "rose like a phoenix from the ashes of burned cities, embattled campuses, and crime-riddled neighborhoods."[70]

Well Entrenched: Three Generations of Community Policing and Problem Solving

Problem-oriented policing is the established paradigm of contemporary policing, both at home and abroad; it enjoys a large degree of public acceptance[71] and receives widespread attention by academicians who have published a growing number of journal articles and doctoral dissertations on the topic.[72] Furthermore, it has now moved through three generations or eras, according to Willard Oliver: innovation, diffusion, and institutionalization[73]:

1. The first generation of community policing and problem solving, *innovation*, spans from 1979 through 1986, beginning with the seminal work of Herman Goldstein concerning needed improvement of policing,[74] coupled with the "broken windows" theory by James Wilson and George Kelling.[75] Early concepts of community policing during this generation were often called "experiments," "test sites," and "demonstration projects," and were often restricted to larger metropolitan cities. The style of policing that was employed was predominately narrow in focus (e.g., foot patrols, problem-solving methods, and community substations). These small-scale test sites provided a source of innovative ideas for others to consider.

2. The second generation, *diffusion*, spans from 1987 through 1994. The concepts and philosophy of community policing and problem solving spread rapidly among police agencies through a variety of communication means within the policing subculture. Adoption of the strategy was fast becoming a reality during this generation, as evidenced by the fact that in 1985 slightly more than 300 police agencies had adopted some form of community policing,[76] whereas by 1994 it had spread to more than 8,000 agencies.[77] The practice of community policing during this generation was still generally limited to large and medium-size cities, and the style of policing during this generation was much broader than the first, being more involved with neighborhood and quality-of-life issues. The strategies normally targeted drug use and fear of crime issues while improving police–community relationships. Much more emphasis was placed on evaluating outcomes through the use of appropriate research methodologies.

3. The third generation, *institutionalization*, spans from 1995 to the present and has seen widespread implementation of community policing and problem solving across the United States:

> Note that today, according to a 2015 report by the Bureau of Justice Statistics, about 7 in 10 local police departments (including about 9 in 10 departments serving a population of 25,000 or more) have a mission statement that includes a community policing component, and overall, departments with a problem-solving partnership employed 63% of all local police officers.[78] This generation has seen problem-oriented policing become deeply entrenched within the political process and has been featuring federal grant money through the Violent Crime Control and Law Enforcement Act of 1994.

EMERGING STRATEGIES FOR THE TWENTY-FIRST CENTURY

Although we will discuss them more in Chapter 7 as tools for problem solving, here we briefly describe four relatively recently conceived, third-generation police strategies for assisting the problem-oriented policing effort. Certainly there is some overlap in the definitions of the three approaches, but they are today major concepts in the day-to-day practice of policing and are extremely useful for crime analysis in the SARA problem-solving process (discussed in Chapter 5).

CompStat (for "comparative or computer statistics") is a relatively new crime management tool used in the problem-solving process and is designed for the collection and feedback of information on crime and related quality-of-life issues. CompStat requires police managers to generate weekly or monthly crime activity reports, to provide up-to-date information that is then compared at citywide, patrol, and precinct levels.

Smart policing is an emerging paradigm in American policing. It emphasizes the use of data and analytics as well as improved crime analysis, performance measurement, and evaluation research. Smart policing does not prescribe any particular policing model or approach, but stresses the importance of in-depth problem analysis and definition to guide their later efforts; therefore, an impressive array of strategies and tactics have been developed and implemented by local SP sites. For example, while some sites focused primarily on hotspot and place-based policing strategies, others focus primarily on offender-based approaches (e.g., focused deterrence through identification of prolific offenders and strategic application of suppression and social support strategies).

Intelligence-led policing operates on the assumption that a relatively small number of people are responsible for a comparatively large percentage of crimes; it is believed that officers will have the best effect on crime by focusing on the most prevalent offenses occurring in their jurisdiction. Intelligence is simply *information*; furthermore, "information plus analysis equals intelligence," and without analysis, there is no intelligence. Intelligence is what is produced after collected data are evaluated and analyzed by a trained intelligence professional.

Finally, *predictive policing* integrates crime analysis, crime-fighting technology, intelligence-led policing, and more to inform forward thinking crime prevention strategies and tactics. As an example, the police have always known that robberies surge near check-cashing businesses and that crime spikes on hot days and plummets during the rain, but officers' minds can store and remember only so much data. So when the police monitor crime data and query a computer system for historical and real-time patterns, they can predict, more systematically, over a bigger area, and across shifts and time spans, where crimes are likely to occur.

As noted above, these three concepts are discussed in more detail in Chapter 7.

Community policing and problem solving has obviously become the culture of many police organizations, affecting and permeating their hiring processes, recruit academies, in-service training, promotional examinations, and strategic plans. COPPS is also having an impact in the form of community-oriented government and in the criminal justice system.

Having discussed the three primary eras of policing, we show them in Table 1–1.

Next, we discuss the overall effect and contributions of the federal Office of Community Oriented Policing Services (COPS) on problem-oriented policing employment, training, literature, and other resources, as it recently celebrated its twentieth birthday.

TABLE 1-1   The Three Eras of Policing

	Political Era (1840s to 1930s)	Reform Era (1930s to 1980s)	Community Era (1980s to Present)
Authorization	Politics and law	Law and professionalism	Community support (political), law, and professionalism
Function	Broad social services	Crime control	Broad provision of services
Organizational design	Decentralized	Centralized and classical	Decentralized using task forces and matrices
Relationship to community	Intimate	Professional and remote	Intimate
Tactics and technology	Foot patrol	Preventive patrol and rapid response to calls	Foot patrol, problem solving, and public relations
Outcome	Citizen and political satisfaction	Crime control	Quality of life and citizen satisfaction

Source: Adapted from George L. Kelling and Mark H. Moore, *The Evolving Strategies of Policing* (Washington, D.C.: U.S. Department of Justice, National Institute of Justice Perspectives on Policing, November 1988).

CONTRIBUTIONS OF THE FEDERAL COPS OFFICE: AN OVERVIEW

Certainly problem-oriented policing would not have progressed to the position and prominence it occupies in U.S. policing were it not for substantial assistance from the federal government—specifically, from the Department of Justice's Office of Community Oriented Policing Services, or COPS. In September 2014, the COPS Office celebrated 20 years of providing grant funds to assist law enforcement agencies to better keep their communities safe through community policing. Following are some of the highlights of this two-decade effort:

- With an initial objective of putting 100,000 additional officers on the street, COPS took a multifaceted approach and awarded funds under the following primary grant programs:

  - In 1994, the Accelerated Hiring, Education, and Deployment (AHEAD) and Funding Accelerated for Smaller Towns (FAST) programs awarded more than $894 million for hiring more than 12,900 community policing officers.
  - In June 1995, the Universal Hiring Program (UHP) expanded funding efforts to include transit, campus, park, and other police forces serving special jurisdictions. UHP ultimately resulted in awards totaling more than $4 billion for more than 55,000 officer positions between 1995 and 2008. During this time, the Making Officer Redeployment Effective (MORE) program awarded nearly $1.3 billion between 1995 and 2002 to thousands of police departments and sheriffs' agencies for technologies and equipment and to hire civilians for administrative and support duties.

- In sum, during its initial 20 years, the COPS Office had:

  - invested more than $14 billion in hiring, training, and technology funding.
  - distributed more than two million publications concerning training, white papers, and resource materials.
  - funded more than 125,000 officers for more than 13,000 police agencies.
  - trained more than 700,000 officers on community policing and problem solving.[79]

PROBLEM-ORIENTED POLICING AND HOMELAND SECURITY

New Threats and New Measures

Unquestionably, historians of the future will maintain that terrorist acts of the early twenty-first century changed forever the nature of policing efforts in the area of **homeland security** in the United States. Words are almost inadequate to describe how the events of September 11, 2001, forever modified and heightened the fears and concerns of all Americans—and the police—with regard to domestic security and the methods necessary for securing the general public.

Dozens of acts of attacks on American soil have demonstrated this nation's vulnerability. But perhaps none was more shocking than that occurring in September 2001 when hijacked jetliners crashed into the World Trade Center complex in New York City and the Pentagon in Virginia.
Terraxplorer/Getty Images.

Police have several means to address domestic terrorism. First, and perhaps the most fruitful, is military support of law enforcement. The Posse Comitatus Act of 1878 prohibits using the military to generally execute the laws; the military may be called on, however, to provide personnel and equipment for certain special support activities, such as domestic terrorism events involving weapons of mass destruction.[80]

To further combat terrorism, the U.S. Department of Homeland Security (DHS) was formed in 2002.[81]

Role of Problem-Oriented Policing

What can problem-oriented policing contribute to the goal of maintaining our nation's defense? As an overarching answer to that question, 9-11 taught all Americans that we—the police and citizens—must work together to ensure our collective safety; the responsibility of responding to terrorist threats falls directly on the shoulders of state and local law enforcement and their government and community partners. Furthermore, the philosophy underlying police problem solving can be directed toward trying to prevent terrorist activities before they occur. A task force report put it thusly:

> Most of the real frontlines of homeland security are outside of Washington, D.C. Likely terrorists are encountered, and the targets they might attack are protected, by local officials—a cop hearing a complaint from a landlord, an airport official who hears about a plane some pilot trainee left on the runway, an FBI agent puzzled by an odd flight school student, or an emergency room resident trying to treat patients stricken by an unusual illness.[82]

Beat officers are also a vital part of our safety. They know their neighborhoods, provide community policing, track identity theft and fraud, and develop trusted local sources. As one policy analyst put it, "They are in the best position to 'collect' the dots that federal agencies need to 'connect' to forecast the next attack."[83]

Terrorism is obviously a local issue, and homeland security and problem-oriented policing have much in common. Homeland security requires a shift in the culture of law enforcement agencies that involves the creation of external partnerships, citizen involvement, problem solving, and transformation of the organization. Problem-oriented policing serves as a solid framework for the development of an effective prevention strategy for homeland security by local law enforcement agencies.[84]

Certainly crime-mapping systems, data collection and analysis protocols, and other kinds of problem-solving technologies that are discussed in Chapter 7 may be used as platforms for gathering intelligence to assess terrorism vulnerability and to implement preparedness plans. As examples, agencies that use geographic information systems (GIS) to conduct crime mapping and analysis can also use GIS to conduct terrorism target mapping and analysis; agencies that use their Web site to disseminate crime prevention information can use it to disseminate home-land security information. Certainly CompStat, smart policing, intelligence-led policing, and predictive policing, discussed above, can also assist in these endeavors.

We also believe it is important for the police to establish and maintain partnerships and lines of communication with immigrant communities, although there may be cultural, language, and other barriers to overcome. These groups may be in the best position to provide information that could lead to the prevention of a terror attack because they often possess information that is unknown outside of what are often insular communities.

In sum, factors associated with the problem-solving philosophy and the implementation of homeland security strategies are highly correlated. Problem solving also involves intergovern-mental and interagency collaborations with state and federal agencies that are essential for the collection and exchange of intelligence and the sharing of resources in the event of an attack.[85]

A NOTE ON COMING FULL CIRCLE, BACK TO THE COMMUNITY. . .

This chapter overview of the evolution of policing has emphasized its English origins, coming to the United States, and its three eras; included are some of the individuals, events, and national commissions that were instrumental in taking policing through those eras. It has also shown how the history of policing may be said to have come full circle to its roots, wherein it was intended to operate with the consent and assistance of the public. Policing is now attempting to throw off the shackles of tradition and become more community oriented.

This historical overview also reveals that many of today's policing issues and problems (most or all of which are discussed in subsequent chapters) actually began surfacing many centu-ries ago: graft and corruption, negative community relations, police use of force, public unrest and rioting, general police accountability, the struggle to establish the proper roles and functions of the police, the police subculture, and the tendency to withdraw from the public, cling to tradition, and be inbred. As we will see in later chapters, the community era is thriving in today's police world.

Exhibit 1–1	Global Perspective: Legacies of the Past, Struggles of Today in Three African States

Three African states' police forces—all former British colonies—are combatting the legacies of their past and contemporary legislative weaknesses that militate against successful community policing and problem solving. Each nation's police force was created out of a need to stifle dis-sent and maintain colonial rule, and thus was established with single-party governmental author-itarianism that would later impact the independence of police forces and their ability to be accepted by the public.

The Sierra Leone Police (SLP) must cope with high crime rates in urban slums. Corruption is prevalent in the SLP, fostered by poor compensation and working conditions for police offic-ers, which in turn leads to routine bribery. The SLP have no strategic plan for crime prevention, and the small size of the force makes basic police functions lacking. Furthermore, the SLP is highly politicized, with well-connected officers able to act with impunity. Major crimes—terrorism, cybercrime, human trafficking, and the drug trade—serve to reinforce the public's view of the SLP as corrupt and ineffective. Therefore, current police–public relations do not sup-port effective community policing.

The Tanzania Police Force (TPF) is aided by the people's militia, which also has powers of arrest. The latter lacks adequate training, and its members often violate constitutional rights of citizens and engage in corruption. The police, meanwhile, are accountable through parliamentary oversight and national human rights and ethics commissions. The TPF has poor investigation techniques, lacking capability in forensics and evidence handling. Resources are generally inadequate, with the resulting low morale in the force giving rise to corruption, abuse of powers, and fabrication of cases against the innocent. General police training, salaries, and working conditions for police are also inadequate, and the lack of effective crime records and negative public perceptions of the police stifle problem-oriented policing.

The Zambia Police Service (ZPS) likewise has public image problems: more than half of the public is dissatisfied with their performance, while 80 percent rate the police as only "somewhat effective." Much of this perception is due to a shortage of officers and perceived corruption in the ZPS. However, the ZPS has made notable progress in training and sensitizing officers about the needs of lower-class and vulnerable populations. Minimum qualifications for recruits have been increased, and the training curriculum revised to include human rights law. Accountability mechanisms include parliamentary oversight and investigations of corruption, arbitrary arrests, and other unprofessional behavior.

Taken together, these three African states provide a primer on how *not* to implement community policing and problem solving, due to the legacy of the past. In sum, challenges for these three venues include politicization (with abuse of the police to advance personal agendas and oversight bodies being partisan), lack of resources (forces are understaffed and thus the quality of police work suffers), personnel (recruits are not well trained, and training does not address human rights), widespread lack of trust in the police, and corruption (poor pay and conditions lead officers to take bribes, while oversight is inadequate).[86]

Summary

This chapter has shown the evolution of policing in America, up through and including its contemporary community era and its emphasis on homeland defense. Problems with some of the old methods, as well as the willingness of police leaders to rethink their basic role and develop new strategies, led us to community- and problem-oriented policing. It is much more than simply "a return to the basics" but is instead a retooling of the basics, coming full circle.

The incorporation of past wisdom and the use of new tools, methods, and strategies via problem solving offer the most promise for detecting and preventing crime, addressing crime and disorder, and improving relations with the public. These partnerships are essential for addressing the "broken windows" phenomenon[87] (an influential theory asserting that once the process of physical decay begins, its effects multiply until some corrective action is taken). The lesson, Wilson and Kelling argued, was that we should redirect our thinking toward improving police handling of "little" problems. In short, the police need to be thinking like what might be termed "street-level criminologists," examining the underlying causes of crime rather than functioning like bureaucrats. This theme will be echoed at various points throughout the book.

Key Terms and Concepts

CompStat	Peel's Principles	Predictive policing	Reform of policing
Homeland security	Police–community	Problem-oriented	Research findings
Intelligence-led policing	relations	policing	Smart policing
Metropolitan Police Act	Political era	Professional era	Wickersham Commission

Items for Review

1. Describe the British contributions to American policing.
2. Explain when and where modern-day policing first came to America and what its primary challenges were.
3. List and briefly explain the three eras of policing, focusing on their primary differences and foci.

4. Explain what is meant by the new "common wisdom" of policing, and discuss the major research findings of the latter half of the 1900s regarding policing methods.
5. Describe the three generations of community- and problem-oriented solving.

Learn by Doing

As indicated in the Preface, the "Scenarios and Activities: 'Learning by Doing'" section here and at the end of all the other chapters of the book comports with the early 1900s teaching of famed educator John Dewey, who advocated the "learning by doing" approach to education, or problem-based learning. It also comports with the popular learning method espoused by Benjamin Bloom in 1956, known as "Bloom's Taxonomy," in which he called for "higher-order thinking skills"— critical and creative thinking that involves analysis, synthesis, and evaluation.[88] The following scenarios and activities will shift your attention from textbook-centered instruction and move the emphasis to student-centered projects. By being placed in these hypothetical situations, you can thus learn and apply some of the concepts covered in this chapter, develop skills in communication and self-management, at times become a problem solver, and learn about or address current community issues.

1. You have a friend who is a police officer and is instructing a class on problem-oriented policing at the Regional Police Academy. She knows of your academic background and asks that you assist this instruction, focusing on the differences between policing's *political*, *professional* (or reform), and *community* eras. What will be the content of this assignment?

2. Given heightened concerns about terrorism due to the increasing development of nuclear capabilities in the Middle East and elsewhere, your criminal justice honor society plans to conduct a noon forum on campus concerning the role of problem-oriented policing in homeland security. What will be your main points?

3. Your criminal justice professor has assigned a group project in which you are to describe "the benefits of smart policing in the twenty-first century." Set forth what will be your major points, focusing on its philosophy, methods, and tools.

Endnotes

1. David R. Johnson, *American Law Enforcement History* (St. Louis, Mo.: Forum Press, 1981), p. 11.
2. Ibid., p. 13.
3. Ibid., pp. 14–15.
4. Leon Radzinowicz, *A History of English Criminal Law and Its Administration from 1750, Vol. IV: Grappling for Control* (London: Stevens & Sons, 1968), p. 163.
5. Johnson, *American Law Enforcement History*, pp. 19–20.
6. A. C. Germann, Frank D. Day, and Robert R. J. Gallati, *Introduction to Law Enforcement and Criminal Justice* (Springfield, Ill.: Charles C. Thomas, 1962), p. 63.
7. Clive Emsley, *Policing and Its Context, 1750–1870* (New York: Schocken Books, 1983), p. 37.
8. See, for example, Samuel Walker, *A Critical History of Police Reform: The Emergence of Professionalism* (Lexington, Mass.: Lexington Books, 1977); Samuel Walker, *Popular Justice* (New York: Oxford University Press, 1980); also see Phillip Reichel, "Southern Slave Patrols as a Transitional Police Type," *American Journal of Policing* 7 (2) (1988):51–77.
9. Phillip Reichel, "Southern Slave Patrols as a Transitional Police Type," p. 59.
10. Sally Hadden, *Slave Patrols: Law and Violence in Virginia and the Carolinas* (Cambridge, Mass.: Harvard University Press, 2001), pp. 185–187.
11. Reichel, "Southern Slave Patrols as a Transitional Police Type," p. 57.
12. Hadden, *Slave Patrols: Law and Violence in Virginia and the Carolinas*, pp. 185–187.
13. Eric H. Monkkonen, *Police in Urban America, 1860–1920* (Cambridge, UK: Cambridge University Press, 1981), pp. 1–2.
14. Johnson, *American Law Enforcement History*, pp. 26–27.
15. See K. E. Jordan, *Ideology and the Coming of Professionalism: American Urban Police in the 1920s and 1930s* (Dissertation, Rutgers University, 1972); Robert M. Fogelson, *Big-City Police* (Cambridge, Mass.: Harvard University Press, 1977).
16. Johnson, *American Law Enforcement History*, p. 27.
17. James F. Richardson, *Urban Policing in the United States* (New York: Oxford University Press, 1970), p. 51.
18. Johnson, *American Law Enforcement History*, p. 92.
19. Ibid.
20. Ibid.
21. See, for example, Southern Poverty Law Center, "Minuteman Project Leaders Say Their Volunteers Are 'White Martin Luther Kings,' but Their Anti-immigration Campaign Is Marked by Weaponry, Military Maneuvers and Racist Talk" (June 27, 2005), https://www.splcenter.org/fighting-hate/intelligence-report/2005/minutemen-other-anti-immigrant-militia-groups-stake-out-arizona-border.
22. Ibid., pp. 96–98.
23. Ibid.
24. Monkkonen, *Police in Urban America, 1860–1920*, p. 158.
25. John E. Eck, *The Investigation of Burglary and Robbery* (Washington, D.C.: Police Executive Research Forum, 1984).
26. See, George L. Kelling, "Juveniles and Police: The End of the Nightstick," in Francis X. Hartmann (ed.), *From Children to Citizens, Vol. II: The Role of the Juvenile Court* (New York: Springer-Verlag, 1987).
27. Samuel Walker, *A Critical History of Police Reform: The Emergence of Professionalism* (Lexington, Mass.: Lexington Books, 1977), pp. 8–9, 11.
28. Ibid., p. 33.
29. Ibid., pp. 33–34, 42, 47.
30. Ibid., p. 81.
31. Ibid., pp. 80–83.
32. Herman Goldstein, *Policing a Free Society* (Cambridge, Mass.: Ballinger, 1977).
33. Albert Reiss, *The Police and the Public* (New Haven, Conn.: Yale University Press, 1971).
34. See, Orlando Wilson, *Police Administration* (New York: McGraw-Hill, 1950).
35. Walker, *A Critical History of Police Reform*, pp. 93–94.
36. Mark H. Moore and George L. Kelling, "'To Serve and Protect': Learning from Police History," *The Public Interest* 70 (Winter 1983):49–65.
37. Peter K. Manning, "The Police: Mandate, Strategies, and Appearances," in Jack D. Douglas (ed.), *Crime and Justice in American Society* (Indianapolis, Ind.: Bobbs-Merrill, 1971), pp. 149–163.

38. Walker, *A Critical History of Police Reform*, p. 161.

39. Louis Radelet, *The Police and the Community* (4th ed.) (New York: Macmillan, 1986), p. ix.

40. Ibid., p. 17.

41. Ibid., p. 21.

42. William G. Doerner, *Introduction to Law Enforcement: An Insider's View* (Englewood Cliffs, N.J.: Prentice Hall, 1992), pp. 21–23.

43. Mary Ann Wycoff, *The Role of Municipal Police Research as a Prelude to Changing It* (Washington, D.C.: Police Foundation, 1982).

44. Jerome H. Skolnick and David H. Bayley, *The New Blue Line: Police Innovation in Six American Cities* (New York: Free Press, 1986), p. 4.

45. William C. Cunningham, John J. Strauchs, and Clifford W. Van Meter, *The Hallcrest Report II: Private Security Trends, 1970–2000* (McLean, Va.: Hallcrest Systems, 1990).

46. William Westley, *Violence and the Police: A Sociological Study of Law, Custom, and Morality* (Cambridge, Mass.: MIT Press), 1970.

47. American Bar Foundation, *The Urban Police Function*, approved draft (Chicago: Author, 1973).

48. Jerome Skolnick, *Justice Without Trial: Law Enforcement in Democratic Society* (New York: John Wiley & Sons, 1966).

49. Egon Bittner, "The Police on Skid Row: A Study of Peace Keeping," *American Sociological Review* 32 (1967):699–715.

50. Raymond I. Parnas, "The Police Response to the Domestic Disturbance," *Wisconsin Law Review* 4 (1967):914–955.

51. James Q. Wilson, *Varieties of Police Behavior: The Management of Law and Order in Eight Communities* (Cambridge, Mass.: Harvard University Press, 1968).

52. Albert J. Reiss, Jr., *The Police and the Public* (New Haven, Conn.: Yale University Press, 1971).

53. Goldstein, *Policing a Free Society*, pp. 22–24.

54. Ibid., p. 11.

55. Elaine Cumming, Ian Cumming, and Laura Edell, "Policeman as Philosopher, Guide, and Friend," *Social Problems* 12 (1965):285; T. Bercal, "Calls for Police Assistance," *American Behavioral Scientist* 13 (1970):682; Reiss, *The Police and the Public*.

56. George Kelling, Tony Pate, Duane Dieckman, and Charles E. Brown, *The Kansas City Preventive Patrol Experiment: A Summary Report* (Washington, D.C.: Police Foundation, 1974).

57. Peter W. Greenwood, Joan Petersilia, and Jan Chaiken, *The Criminal Investigation Process* (Lexington, Mass.: D.C. Heath, 1977); John E. Eck, *Managing Case Assignments: The Burglary Investigation Decision Model Replication* (Washington, D.C.: Police Executive Research Forum, 1979).

58. Bernard Greenbert, S. Yu Oliver, and Karen Lang, *Enhancement of the Investigative Function, Vol. 1: Analysis and Conclusions, Final Report, Phase 1* (Springfield, Va.: National Technical Information Service, 1973).

59. Kelling, Pate, Dieckman, and Brown, *The Kansas City Preventive Patrol Experiment*:

60. Ibid.

61. Joan Petersilia, "The Influence of Research on Policing," in Roger C. Dunham and Geoffrey P. Alpert (eds.), *Critical Issues in Policing: Contemporary Readings* (Prospect Heights, Ill.: Waveland Press, 1989), pp. 230–247.

62. James Q. Wilson, *Thinking About Crime* (New York: Vintage Books, 1975).

63. Herman Goldstein, *Problem-Oriented Policing* (New York: McGraw-Hill, 1990), p. 13.

64. Ibid., p. 3.

65. Thomas J. Baker, "Designing the Job to Motivate," *FBI Law Enforcement Bulletin* 45 (1976):3–7.

66. Samuel Walker, *The Police in America: An Introduction* (2nd ed.) (New York: McGraw-Hill, 1992), p. 185.

67. Police Foundation, *The Newark Foot Patrol Experiment* (Washington, D.C.: Author, 1981).

68. Robert Trojanowicz, *An Evaluation of the Neighborhood Foot Patrol Program in Flint, Michigan* (East Lansing, Mich.: School of Criminal Justice, Michigan State University, 1982).

69. Michael J. Farrell, "The Development of the Community Patrol Officer Program: Community-Oriented Policing in the New York City Police Department," in Jack R. Greene and Stephen D. Mastrofski (eds.), *Community Policing: Rhetoric or Reality* (New York: Praeger, 1988), pp. 73–88.

70. Robert Trojanowicz and Bonnie Bucqueroux, *Community Policing: A Contemporary Perspective* (Cincinnati, Ohio: Anderson, 1990), p. 67.

71. George Gallup, *Community Policing Survey* (Wilmington, N.Y.: Scholarly Resources, 1996).

72. Willard M. Oliver, "The Third Generation of Community Policing: Moving Through Innovation, Diffusion, and Institutionalization," *Police Quarterly* 3 (December 2000):367–388.

73. Ibid.

74. Herman Goldstein, "Improving Policing: A Problem-Oriented Approach," *Crime and Delinquency* 25 (1979):236–258.

75. James Q. Wilson and George L. Kelling, "Broken Windows: The Police and Neighborhood Safety," *Atlantic Monthly* (March 1982):29–38.

76. Samuel Walker, *The Police in America: An Introduction* (New York: McGraw-Hill, 1985).

77. T. McEwen, *National Assessment Program: 1994 Survey Results* (Washington, D.C.: National Institute of Justice, 1995).

78. U.S. Department of Justice, Bureau of Justice Statistics, *Local Police Departments, 2013: Personnel, Policies, and Practices* (May 2015), p. 8, http://www.bjs.gov/content/pub/pdf/lpd13ppp.pdf.

79. U.S. Department of Justice, Office of Community Oriented Policing Services, *The COPS Office: 20 Years of Community Oriented Policing* (September 2014), p. 3, http://ric-zai-inc.com/Publications/cops-p301-pub.pdf.

80. D. G. Bolgiano, "Military Support of Domestic Law Enforcement Operations: Working Within Posse Comitatus," *FBI Law Enforcement Bulletin* (December 2001):16–24.

81. U.S. Department of Homeland Security, "Creation of the Department of Homeland Security," http://www.dhs.gov/creation-department-homeland-security.

82. U.S. Department of Justice, Office of Community Oriented Policing Services, "Community Partnerships: A Key Ingredient in an Effective Homeland Security Approach," *Community Policing Dispatch* 1(2) (February 2008):2.

83. Michael E. O'Hanlon, "Homeland Security: How Police Can Intervene," *The Washington Times* (August 18, 2004), p. 2, http://www.brookings.edu/view/op-ed/ohanlon/20040818.htm.

84. Jose Docobo, "Community Policing as the Primary Prevention Strategy for Homeland Security at the Local Law Enforcement Level," *Homeland Security Affairs* 1(1) (Summer 2005):1.

85. Ibid., p. 2.

86. Simon Robins, *Addressing the challenges of law enforcement in Africa Policing in Sierra Leone, Tanzania and Zambia*, Institute of Policy Studies (October 2009), http://dspace.africaportal.org/jspui/bitstream/123456789/30885/1/NO16OCT09.pdf?1.

87. Wilson and Kelling, "Broken Windows," pp. 29–38.

88. Benjamin S. Bloom, *Taxonomy of Educational Objectives, Handbook I: The Cognitive Domain* (New York: David McKay, 1956).

Community Partnerships:
Building Accord in a Time of Discord

LEARNING OBJECTIVES

As a result of reading this chapter, the student will understand:

- How and why the police must adopt a "New Professionalism"
- What constitutes a healthy community, and how citizens and police can collaboratively contribute to a sense of social well-being and address fear of crime
- How and why community policing evolved, and what it is and is not
- The purposes and arguments for and against use of civilian review boards for police oversight
- How courts and corrections agencies are practicing community justice

TEST YOUR KNOWLEDGE

1. Studies show that most citizens desire having police officers who are more "warrior" than "guardian."
2. The term social capital is used to denote a community's social networks and relationships, with people bonding and establishing bridges.
3. At minimum, a police department can be said to be actively engaged in community policing by building storefront police substations, adding foot or bicycle patrols, and having a specialized unit of neighborhood police officers.
4. Even before the widely publicized police shootings occurring in the mid-2010s, citizen review boards existed in more than 2,000 communities to evaluate such police actions.
5. Civilian review boards would bring the police and community together, but many police officers believe that citizens are simply unqualified to judge a police officer's actions.
6. Courts and corrections agencies, like the police, have begun initiating formal programs for connecting with the community.

Answers can be found on page 278.

INTRODUCTION

In Chapter 1, we established that policing has evolved through three eras and is currently in its community era. But what defines a "community," and how do the police go about engaging and addressing problems within a changing community having all types of crime? How can the police deal with the fear of crime? And how does the overarching problem of the economy relate to those efforts?

Clearly, working with the community is key—the *sine qua non*—in community policing. This chapter discusses why that is so, beginning with a look at new directions many police agencies and personnel are undertaking in order to focus on being more professional. Next is a discussion of some of the elements that compose a healthy community, to include cohesion, social capital, addressing fear of crime, and volunteerism. Then we look at how the economy has affected policing, and discuss the centerpiece of this chapter: how all of these aforementioned topics relate to the community policing strategy, what it is and is not, and how it differs from traditional policing practices. In this same vein, we look at the use of beat meetings and citizens' police academies for bringing police and communities together, as well as what are felt to be pros and cons of citizen review boards that exist to oversee the police. Finally, we examine community justice, and how courts and corrections agencies are also partnering with citizens and how units of government are reaching out with community service centers and e-government activities. Exhibits 2–1 to 2–8 discuss related activities. The chapter concludes with a summary, a listing of key terms and concepts, some items for review, and several "learn by doing" scenarios and activities that provide opportunities for you to apply your knowledge of this chapter's content.

Note that several weighty police–community issues and problems are discussed in later chapters as well.

Figure 2–1 graphically depicts the kinds of collaborative partnerships between the law enforcement agency and the individuals and organizations they serve that are necessary for developing solutions to problems and increase trust in police.

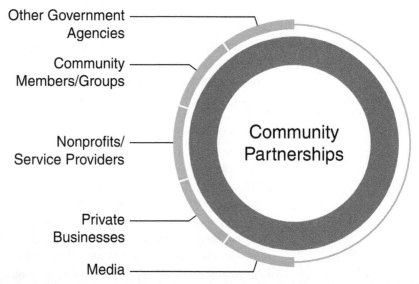

FIGURE 2–1   Collaborative partnerships between the law enforcement agency and the individuals and organizations they serve help to develop solutions to problems and increase trust in police.

FIRST THINGS FIRST: BEING A PROFESSIONAL

A "New Professionalism"

The many drawbacks of policing that existed during the professional era were discussed in Chapter 1. Suffice it to say that citizens had little influence in crime control, and police were reactive, accomplished little in the way of long-term problem solving, and were the "thin blue line." Citizens were no longer encouraged to go to "their" neighborhood police officers or districts, and officers passed by and drove patrol cars randomly through streets while their productivity was judged by the number of arrests they made or the number of miles they drove during a shift. The crime rate became the primary indicator of police effectiveness.

Today, however, police organizations across the United States are striving for what might be termed a New Professionalism,[1] one that includes stricter *accountability* in terms of their effectiveness and conduct, while also increasing their *legitimacy* in the eyes of those they serve, and to encourage continuous *innovation* in police practices. These three goals suggest a fourth element as well: a *national coherence*. Next we discuss these four principles in greater detail.

1. A commitment to *accountability* means having an obligation to account for police actions—not only internally but also to civilian review boards (discussed later in this chapter), city councils and county commissioners, state legislatures, and courts. Also, there is a greater accountability for dealing with crime (in later chapters, we discuss such methods as CompStat, intelligence-led policing, predictive policing, and smart policing). Police agencies might also conduct public surveys in order to learn about crime and disorder and fear of crime. It is also hoped that the New Professionalism will bring reduction in the use of force as police departments become more proficient in analyzing events leading up to use-of-force incidents to determine if the officers were justified in using such tactics.

2. A commitment to *legitimacy* includes a determination to engage in police activities with the consent, cooperation, and support of the community. There must be public support for enforcing the law and a belief that such is being done judiciously and with community approval and engagement. The New Professionalism emphasizes professional integrity and public trust. Traditionally, police often measured their legitimacy in terms of the number of civilian complaints that were lodged against them. This measure is highly problematic, because relatively few people actually make a formal complaint, and those who do complain are often persistent offenders who use the complaint process in an attempt to deter police from stopping them in the future. For these and other reasons, complaints do not serve as a credible measure of public dissatisfaction.

3. A commitment to *innovation* means actively experimenting with new ideas and changing policies and procedures accordingly. Such agencies look for practices that work as they attempt to both prevent crimes and solve problems. Knowledge—its creation, dissemination, and practical application—is essential to genuine professionalism. Police must measure their outcomes, encourage independent evaluations of their policies and tactics, and design experiments that rigorously test new ideas. In sum, police departments need to become learning organizations.

4. *National coherence* means that agencies exemplifying the New Professionalism participate in national conversations about professional policing. They are training their officers, supervisors, and leaders in successful practices and theories. Such organizations as the Police Foundation, the Police Executive Research Forum, the federal Community Oriented Policing Services (COPS) Office, the Office on Violence Against Women, the Office of Justice Programs, the Major Cities Chiefs Association, and other professional associations have helped by nurturing national conversations among practitioners and researchers.[2]

Citizen surveys provide police departments with vital information about their performance and citizens' concerns.
Ronald W. Glensor.

"Guardians" or "Warriors"?

Note that later (in Chapter 3) we discuss policing in a diverse society, the historical and contemporary chasm between police and minorities, and the question of whether or not the police have become too militarized. Here, we merely note that much of that discussion revolves around how the police are now too often being seen as "soldiers" or "**warriors**." Certainly, the recent killings and violence by police involving African-American men such as Laquan McDonald (Chicago), Walter Scott (Charleston, South Carolina), Tamir Rice (Cleveland, Ohio), Eric Garner (New York City), Michael Brown (Ferguson, Missouri), and others have caused many people to ask whether or not there exists within the police culture a "warrior mindset."[3] The "Black Lives Matter" movement was created to campaign against violence toward black people, organize protests in the aftermath of the deaths of black people in killings by law enforcement officers, and address the broader issues of racial profiling, police brutality, and racial inequality.[4] Exhibit 2–1 discusses how policing has changed in the recent climate—with many officers now uncertain about how to do their jobs; the effects and proposed reforms post-Ferguson are discussed in more detail in Chapter 3.

We will discuss the need for a new type of police professionalism, legitimacy, and the **guardian** mindset more in Chapter 8, which concerns how to change agency culture.

Exhibit 2–1	A "Transformational Time" in Policing

Many police officers are now increasingly worried that their next activity on the street might quickly become the next YouTube sensation, depicting yet another highly charged encounter between them and citizens. Many of them observe that, where they once were given respectful nods by the public, now they often receive hostile stares instead and have become strangers in their own neighborhoods. Some city police departments have found themselves "under siege" due to civil unrest, and mayors and police chiefs have lost their jobs. Some police chiefs feel they have also been abandoned by the federal government, which launched more than 20 investigations of police operations from 2009 to 2015. Providence, Rhode Island, Police Chief Hugh Clements maintains that there is a "delicate balance" in this "transformational time" in policing. Chiefs and sheriffs fear that all officers are being judged for the actions of a few, and that the end of police–public discord may not end any time soon.[5]

SIGNS OF A HEALTHY COMMUNITY

Community Cohesion

While there is no agreed-upon definition of **community cohesion**, there is general consensus that it includes the following elements: (1) people in the community share common values, respect each other, and have a common identity; and (2) people in the community share goals and responsibilities and are willing to work with others. Empowerment is the result of community cohesion; it refers to the ability of neighborhood residents to work together to decide what is best for the community, and to transform these decisions into action and desired outcomes.[6] Community cohesion and empowerment are processes rather than outcomes; that is, they entail an ongoing effort by people in the community to work together to achieve shared goals. Fostering a strong **sense of community** is one of the principles of community policing, and it follows that key roles for the police include identifying and addressing issues of neighborhood crime and disorder in order to prevent victimization and fear of crime. This entry discusses how the police and other governmental leaders can empower citizens so that they may have a stake in and provide formal assistance with crime and disorder reduction.[7]

Social Capital

Two of the most fundamental and indispensable qualities of a thriving community are public safety and social order. Police cannot hope to be successful in addressing neighborhood crime and disorder without partnering with the community's members; this is the nexus of "community" and "policing," and it requires high levels of trust and engagement.

Having members of a community who are bonded together, looking out for one another, and willing to engage in collective action when threatened is key to the peaceful coexistence if not the very survival of an orderly society. This is known as **social capital**, and it relates to community policing.

Social capital concerns social networks and relationships, bonding people and establishing bridges between them. It includes fostering goodwill toward each other (social cohesion) and is fundamentally about how people interact with each other. Social capital can concern people who are in close proximity to one another—neighbors—who share rootedness, and involves their social, psychological, and even economic dependence on one another. It also can refer to the institutions, relationships, and norms that help to shape social interactions.

Social capital exists in two contexts or domains: local and public. The local level of social capital is the most basic and concerns individual citizens who have trust and reciprocity with one another. It involves people's informal assumption of responsibility to take care of one another as well as to enforce informal rules of conduct.[8]

Addressing the Fear of Crime

Obviously, a police–community alliance cannot achieve success if citizens are scared away from their streets, parks, and neighborhoods. Gallup surveys have typically indicated over the years that, while there is less crime in America, there is more fear of crime. And while most of the kind of crime that worries people—mugging, vandalism, and robbery—occurs in residential areas, many commercial districts are hurt because some believe that downtowns and neighborhood shopping districts are risky places to walk. Whether it is an older person who feels nervous about walking home, parents who feel anxious about sending their child to the store, or a storeowner who becomes uneasy every time a customer enters their shop, fear of crime can have a devastating effect on our quality of life.[9]

Violent crime rates across the nation sank by more than half in the 1990s. While this is truly a remarkable social phenomenon, Pew Research Center also found that, for the first time in its polling experience, more Americans (52 percent) said that protecting gun rights is more important than controlling gun ownership (46 percent). This is the opposite of most findings of the past 20 years, and reflects that protection is now the top reason gun owners offer for choosing to own a firearm (in the past, it was hunting).[10] It seems, therefore, that we have become a country that remains fearful of crime, is increasingly supportive of "gun rights," and is increasingly persuaded that having a gun in the house provides more safety.[11]

What can the police do about this situation? First, research suggests that when the police partner more generally with the public, levels of citizen fear will decline, and that problem-oriented policing is an effective approach for reducing crime, disorder, and fear. What this

Although juvenile arrests have generally declined since the mid-1990s, concern about youth crime and violence continues.
Monkey Business Images/Shutterstock.

| Exhibit 2–2 | Violent Crimes and House Visits in Reno, Nevada |

In late 2015, after three shootings occurred in a single neighborhood in one month's time, Reno, Nevada, police officers and government leaders immediately undertook outreach measures to address concerns of the affected area. Knocking on nearly 50 homeowners' doors in a single day as part of a formal Neighborhood Contact Team initiative (which is routinely activated when there is a major incident or a crime hot spot), the team gave residents information about community resources that combat poverty and crime, reassured residents that they can feel safe in their homes, and, as one officer put it, helped to "humanize the badge." Several officers high-fived children, hugged residents, and handed out fliers and business cards, while informing residents that they would be returning with food in the near future for needy families. The residents were asked to offer any ideas about ways to combat crime and poverty in the area, informed of an app that could be used for reporting crimes via a Secret Witness program, and given referrals to agencies that would help with mental illness and drug abuse problems. A survey instrument was also disseminated for police to learn how they could better serve the area. One important need that was identified for the area was having more activities for kids, and ways in which parents could become more engaged in their children's lives.

Source: Adapted from Jenny Kane, "Shootings Prompt Friendly House Visits from Police," *Reno Gazette Journal* (January 1, 2016):1A, 6A.

generally means is that, as police increasingly practice community-oriented policing and problem solving attending to crime "hot spots" and using techniques and technologies discussed in later chapters, crime, disorder, and the fear of crime will all be reduced.[12]

Volunteerism

Never in the history of policing—and especially since the aforementioned Great Recession in the United States and budgets were slashed—has there been more of a need to actively involve citizens in police operations. This may be done through a variety of means. For example, volunteers may be widely used. Citizen patrols and crime prevention initiatives are welcomed and encouraged. Area commanders meet often with members of the public to solicit input and feedback. Many internal committees include public participation. Policy decisions typically involve opportunities for input from citizens, and the department has both formal and informal mechanisms for this purpose. Promotional boards include citizens. The department seeks to educate the general public about police work in various ways, including publications, Web sites, public access television, and town hall meetings. The department accepts and even encourages citizen review of its performance.

The International Association of Chiefs of Police maintains a comprehensive Web site that is devoted to describing all types of citizen **volunteerism** programs, at http://www.theiacp.org/VIPSResources. Exhibit 2–3 shows three such examples.

Volunteers provide valuable assistance to police and are used for a variety of tasks, such as traffic control and enforcement, looking for missing persons, code enforcement, and victim services.
Don B. Stevenson/Alamy Stock Photo.

Exhibit 2–3	Volunteering in Police Services (VIPS): Some Examples

Following are three examples of how the police can utilize volunteers:

▶ The Bellevue, Washington, Police Department uses a volunteer program coordinator to outline the volunteers' responsibilities, describe any special skills or abilities the volunteers should have, and set the hours the volunteer will work. The volunteer program coordinator then finds the best available volunteer for the assignment. Volunteers in the program have served as archive managers, case assistants, bicycle registration and recovery specialists, fire lane parking enforcers, community project administrators, quartermasters, and chaplains, to name just a few.

▶ Volunteers assigned to the patrol division in Vacaville, California, issue citations for all nonmoving violations, direct traffic, service police vehicles, relieve school crossing guards, assist with searches for missing persons, report unlicensed businesses, and help enforce municipal codes involving neighborhood blight and reporting violations of all kinds. Volunteers also assist in the records section (releasing crash records, running citations for traffic court, providing customer service at the front counter), the property and evidence section (purging unneeded evidence, updating computer records), the K-9 unit (putting on the protective wear and standing in for the bad guy during training exercises), and the investigations division (coordinating the crime prevention program).

▶ The Hazelwood, Missouri, Police Department's Volunteer Services Unit first requires volunteers to have completed the **citizens' police academy;** they are then eligible to participate in the Citizen Observer Patrol, in which volunteers patrol designated areas of the city, in a marked car or on foot, watching for and reporting suspect activity, looking for disabled automobiles, injured persons, fires, and broken windows and open doors at homes and businesses, watching for teenagers who appear to be involved in mischief, and so on. Volunteers receive quarterly in-service training on such topics as traffic direction, radio procedures, first aid, and CPR.

Source: Adapted from Volunteers in Police Service, "VIPS Focus," pp. 1–3, http://www.policevolunteers.org/pdf/2007%20Award.pdf.

EFFECTS OF THE ECONOMY ON POLICING

Policing has long been an occupation that is considered one of job security, even in times of economic recession. However, such has not been the case since the Great Recession of 2007–2009.

A 2012 study conducted by the Police Executive Forum revealed that 51 percent of police departments had their budgets cut since the recession began.[13] To address budget cuts, many police departments had to lay off officers, make other personnel cuts, or leave various jobs unfilled. Others explored the idea of combining or regionalizing police service. Given that medical costs are the largest service costs for most local government jails, it is unsurprising that cities sought to save money on these expenses. Some counties began treating patients inside of the jails instead of transferring them to external facilities, switching from name-brand medications to generic ones, and privatized the medical services that they provide in their jails in attempting to save money.[14] Some counties that operate jails sought to reduce the use of traditional incarceration by expanding the use of house arrest for pretrial detainees, those who are arrested for committing low-level, nonviolent offenses, serving their sentences at home and monitored by an electronic ankle bracelet.

Finally, many local governments expanded their uses of technologies, particularly in policing, to increase efficiency. Such technologies as traffic cameras, public surveillance systems, GPS systems, and license plate scanners serve to expand the reach of policing. These technologies also assist with (and are required for) identifying specific "hot spot" areas to predict specific times and places where crime is most likely to occur.[15]

There are two schools of thought concerning the long-term effect, if any, that the recent economic recession will have on **community policing** and problem solving (discussed below).

The homeless, inebriates, and panhandlers—many of whom have been sorely affected by the economy—can add to peoples' fear of crime as much as actual crimes do.

Dmytro Zinkevych/Shutterstock.

Some authors believe that the recent economic downturn spells long-term trouble for problem-solving efforts, because they rely so heavily on taking care of the low-level crimes—the underlying notion being that if minor offenses pervade a community, there will come to pass a proliferation of additional and violent crimes, or the so-called "broken windows" theory. They wonder whether the resources that are required to address and process these minor offenses—including the needs and costs of police (some of it overtime pay), prosecutors, jails, social services, and other related entities—can continue in times of economic turmoil and when public safety budgets have been hit hard. Contributing to this argument is the fact that, in order to address budget cuts, many police departments have laid off officers, made other personnel cuts, or left various jobs unfilled.[16]

The importance of community policing in the face of both tough economic conditions and the dynamic global threat environment cannot be overemphasized. While some agencies have perceived a need to shut down community policing programs or eliminate community policing officers, that is not the right approach to take. Community policing has taught us that the building of relationships and the solving of problems are more important, not less, in challenging times such as these.

There are practical reasons for expanding community policing in these challenging economic times. The most important of these is that police must rely on residents and business purveyors to share information about crime and disorder in order to engage in effective problem solving to maintain public order and curtail crime. While some would argue that we can no longer afford the "luxury" of community policing, it is clear that the vast majority of law enforcement executives embrace the realization that we cannot afford to dispense with the ideals and practices of community policing.

WHERE ALL THESE ROADS HAVE LED: COMMUNITY POLICING

An Oft-Misunderstood Concept: What It *Is*

Community policing, recognizing that police rarely can solve public safety problems alone, encourages interactive partnerships with relevant stakeholders. These partnerships can accomplish the two interrelated goals of developing solutions to problems through collaborative problem solving and improving public trust. The public should play a role in prioritizing and addressing public safety problems.

—U.S. Department of Justice,
Office of Community Oriented Policing Services.

As stated by Tom Casady, the Lincoln, Nebraska, Director of Public Safety, community policing is perhaps the most misunderstood and frequently abused theme in police management. While it has become fashionable for police agencies to initiate community policing, there is often confusion about what it actually means.[17] Therefore, it is essential that readers of this book first understand what this term means and what it does not.

First and foremost, community policing is not a temporary program or project. Rather, community policing is a philosophy and practice that permeates the entire police agency, with employees working cooperatively with individuals, groups, and both public and private organizations to identify and resolve issues of crime and disorder. As the federal Office of Community Oriented Services indicated, above, community-based police agencies recognize the fact that the police cannot effectively deal with such issues alone, and must partner with others who share a mutual responsibility for resolving problems. Community policing stresses crime prevention as well as early identification and timely intervention of crime issues before they become unwieldy problems.

Community policing—as opposed to traditional policing, which relied heavily on the use of arrests for addressing crime—has as its foundation a belief that policing is much more than law enforcement and making arrests. Indeed, many studies have shown that actually dealing with crime consumes only 10–20 percent of the police workload; in sum, "chasing bad guys" only has short-term benefit and is only one small part of the job. Community policing officers must understand that resolving a problem with unruly people drinking at a public park, working to reduce truancy at a middle school, marshaling resources to improve lighting in a mobile home park, and removing abandoned vehicles from streets may also represent valid and valuable police work and affect the livability of a neighborhood. Following are some areas in which community policing stands apart from traditional policing in its approach to the job:[18]

- *Geographic responsibility.* Officers identify with their area of assignment, rather than the work shift or functional division. Commanders are assigned to geographical areas and given wide latitude to deploy their personnel and resources within that area. Officers commonly know many of the people who live and work in this area, and are intimately familiar with the area's geography, businesses, schools, and churches. Officers seek out detailed information about police incidents that have occurred in their area of assignment during their off-duty time.
- *Long-term assignment.* Officers can expect to work in the same geographical area for many years. Officers' preferences for areas are considered in making assignments. Rotation of geographical assignments is rare. The organization values the expertise and familiarity that comes with long-term assignment to the same area.
- *Decentralized decision making.* Most operational decisions are decentralized so that field officers are given broad discretion to manage their own uncommitted time. Operational policies serve as general guidelines for professional practice more than detailed rules and regulations. First-line supervisors are heavily involved in decisions that are ordinarily reserved for command ranks in traditional police departments.
- *Participative management.* The department employs numerous methods to involve employees at all levels in decision making. Staff meetings, committees, task forces, quality circles, and similar groups are impaneled so as to obtain input from frontline employees as a part of any policy decision. Supervisors view their role primarily in providing support to field personnel by teaching, coaching, obtaining resources, solving problems, and "running interference."
- *Generalist officers.* Officers are expected to handle a huge variety of police incidents, and to follow through such incidents from beginning to end. Even when specialists are used, their role is to work cooperatively with field officers, rather than assume responsibility for cases or incidents from field officers.
- *Police leadership on community issues.* Police officers and managers are deeply involved in community affairs, often speaking out on issues of community concern. Elected officials consult with police managers and supervisors, and police representation is seen on committees and community organizations.
- *Proactive policing.* The police agency makes blocks of time available for police officers to address identified problems. A range of tactics other than responding to individual incidents are used, such as targeted saturation patrol, bicycle and foot patrol, undercover/plain clothes/decoy/surveillance operations, educational presentations, coordination of efforts with other government or human service agencies, support to volunteer efforts, initiation of legislative proposals, and so forth. Rather than merely responding to calls for service, the department engages in problem-oriented policing (discussed in Chapters 5–7),

identifying emergent problems, gathering data, bringing together stakeholders, and implementing specific strategies targeting the problem.

- **Recognition and professional development.** For the above efforts, officers receive frequent recognition for initiative, innovation, and planning. The department acknowledges and rewards problem-oriented policing projects, and officers receive the respect and admiration of their colleagues as well.

Also per Casady, other means of determining whether or not community policing is being properly embraced by a local agency would include:

1. Observing the daily work of officers (if they are devoting a significant amount of available time getting out of their patrol cars and going into businesses, schools, PTA meetings, recreation centers; being involved in community affairs/cultural events, school events, meetings of service clubs, and so on).
2. Community members knowing a few officers by name, and officers knowing a large number of citizens on their beats and having an intimate knowledge of their area.
3. Officers being relaxed and not robotic when engaged in community discussions, and being involved in tackling significant community issues.
4. The police agency deploying a process for addressing citizen grievances, relating well with the news media, and cultivating positive relationships with elected officials.[19]

What It Is *Not*

Despite the claims of some people, community policing is not soft on crime. Rather, it can significantly improve the ability of the police to discover criminal conduct, clear offenses, and make arrests. Improved communication with citizens and more intimate knowledge of the beat enhances the officers' crime-fighting capability. Moreover, though some of these may be used as specific strategies, community policing is *not* accomplished by merely:

- adding school resource officers, storefront police substations, foot or bicycle patrols;
- writing a grant;
- creating a pilot program in a single area of town;
- adding a specialized unit of neighborhood police officers; and
- launching a citizens' police academy.[20]

When an agency claims to have implemented community policing as of a certain date, that is also a good indication that it has not fully and adequately embraced the practice. Furthermore, the public should not attempt to determine whether or not its local police are engaged in community policing solely on the basis of the agency's press release, organizational chart, or an annual report. Rather, community policing is a process that evolves, develops, takes root, and grows, until it is an integral part of the philosophy and practice of both the agency and the community. It is a change from a style of policing that emphasizes a shift in crime control and "crook catching" to a style of policing that emphasizes citizen interaction and participation in problem solving.[21]

Community policing goes beyond simply doing the above things, redefining the role of the officer on the street, creating a cultural transformation of the entire department (discussed in Chapter 8), decentralizing the organizational structure, and fomenting changes in recruiting, training, awards systems, evaluations, promotions, and so forth (see Table 2–1 and Figure 2–2).

A Definition

It is difficult to find a concise definition of community policing; typically, what one finds as a "definition" is a lengthy listing of its elements and strategies. However, the federal Office of Community Oriented Policing Services offers the following:

Community policing is a philosophy that promotes organizational strategies, which support the systematic use of partnerships and problem solving techniques, to proactively address the immediate conditions that give rise to public safety issues, such as crime, social disorder, and fear of crime.[22]

TABLE 2–1	Traditional Versus Community Policing: Questions and Answers	
Question	**Traditional Policing**	**Community Policing**
Who are the police?	A government agency principally responsible for law enforcement.	Police are the public and the public are the police: The police officers are those who are paid to give full-time attention to the duties of every citizen.
What is the relationship of the police force to other public service departments?	Priorities often conflict.	The police are one department among many responsible for improving the quality of life.
What is the role of the police?	Focusing on solving crimes.	A broad problem-solving approach.
How is police efficiency measured?	By detection and arrest rates.	By the absence of crime and disorder.
What are the highest priorities?	Crimes that are high value (e.g., bank robberies) and those involving violence.	Whatever problems disturb the community most.
With what, specifically, do police deal?	Incidents.	Citizens' problems and concerns.
What determines the effectiveness of police?	Response times.	Public cooperation.
What view do police take of service calls?	Deal with them only if there is no real police work to do.	Vital function and great opportunity.
What is police professionalism?	Swift, effective response to serious crime.	Keeping close to the community.
What kind of intelligence is most important?	Crime intelligence (study of particular crimes or series of crimes).	Criminal intelligence (information about the activities of individuals or groups).
What is the essential nature of police accountability?	Highly centralized; governed by rules, regulations, and policy directives; accountable to the law.	Emphasis on local accountability to community needs.
What is the role of headquarters?	To provide the necessary rules and policy directives.	To preach organizational values.
What is the role of the press liaison department?	To keep the "heat" off operational officers so they can get on with the job.	To coordinate an essential channel of communication with the community.
How do the police regard prosecutions?	As an important goal.	As one tool among many.

Source: Malcolm K. Sparrow, Implementing Community Policing (Washington, D.C.: U.S. Department of Justice, National Institute of Justice: U.S. Government Printing Office, November 1988), pp. 8–9.

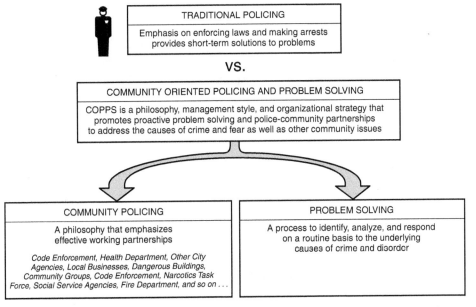

FIGURE 2–2 Traditional Policing Versus Community Oriented Policing, Problem Oriented Policing, and Neighborhood Police Officers.

Two Exceptional Programs: Beat Meetings and Citizens' Police Academies

Two excellent methods of bringing police and citizens together in a constructive manner include beat meetings and citizens' police academies. First, following are descriptions of how three cities are bringing community policing to life through the use of **beat meetings**:

- In Chicago, beat community meetings are held on all 285 police beats in Chicago. Every beat is required to meet at least quarterly, but the majority of beats meet monthly or bimonthly. The primary objective of the beat community meeting is to allow beat residents, other community stakeholders, and police to discuss chronic problems on the beat and to engage in problem solving using the community policing and problem-solving process. These meetings also provide an opportunity for police and community residents to exchange information about conditions in the neighborhood, to identify crime and disorder problems, and to develop strategies to combat those problems. The meeting also provides an opportunity for police and community to get to know one another.[23]
- At the Los Angeles Police Department, Community-Police Advisory Boards (C-PABs) have been meeting since 1993 to provide community members with an opportunity to obtain information and give advice to their respective officers. Each of the 21 geographic areas (community police stations) throughout the city has its own C-PAB. These advisory groups meet monthly to discuss crime and quality-of-life issues. Each C-PAB has two co-chairs, one being the beat commanding officer and the other person a civilian member voted on by the membership. Recently, many C-PABs have formed subcommittees to tackle specific crime and quality-of-life problems with problems involving graffiti, youth, homeless outreach, and traffic.[24]
- In Kansas City, Kansas, community policing is proactive, solution-based, and community-driven. It requires local government, law enforcement agencies, and law-abiding citizens to work together to arrest offenders, prevent crime, solve ongoing problems, and improve the overall quality of community life. Officers regularly attend neighborhood watch meetings and business/merchant association group meetings and meet with citizen activists, church leaders, and other public service agencies and providers. In an effort to improve the overall quality of life in Kansas City, Kansas, the officers network with

Some newer police stations are much more community-friendly, less stark in appearance, and used for citizen gatherings, such as the Los Angeles West Valley "second-generation station house."
John Coletti/Getty images.

other police departments and governmental agencies in an effort to address crime, fear of crime, social and physical disorder, and neighborhood and community decay.[25]

Citizens' police academies are at the core of community policing efforts. Normally lasting 10–12 weeks' duration and meeting once per week, they help police to create more informed citizens, debunk misperceptions about law enforcement, and open lines of communication between the two camps. Normally offered free of charge to civilians 18 and older with no criminal history, class size is typically limited to a few dozen students in order to ensure quality interaction and hands-on experience. Activities typically include giving students a tour of the facility, to include interview rooms, holding cells, and evidence lockers. Ideally, class members will also engage in a number of hands-on activities, such as ride-alongs with officers, touring courts and corrections facilities, and firing weapons at a range. They might also be taught the basics of criminal investigations, defensive tactics, crime scene management, and use of weapons. Instructors and guest speakers are normally chosen for their ability to communicate and engage the class, and enjoy interacting with civilians.[26]

CIVILIAN REVIEW BOARDS: A BLESSING OR A CURSE?

Extent and Rationale

Given the wisdom of community policing's bringing together citizens and police to address crime and disorder and solve problems, it would seem logical that **civilian (or citizen) review boards** should be used in order to involve citizens in investigating and overseeing police activities. This is a commonly discussed approach to police accountability, often arising in the wake of fatal police shootings or corruption scandals. It is commonly argued that the public expects—and that civilian review boards will provide—the kind of independent and transparent oversight of policing that is needed today. There is even a national organization devoted to such boards, the National Association for Civilian Oversight of Law Enforcement, that provides a Web site, programs, training, conferences, and a number of other resources in this regard.[27]

Today there are more than 200 civilian oversight entities around the country, though their powers to investigate and punish officers vary.[28] Some such boards are used to not only investigate disciplinary actions regarding the use of force and in-custody deaths, but also review their police agency's budget and policies, and how police are using body cameras.

Police Distrust

However, there remains a robust debate about whether or not such boards are beneficial, and if so, which model of citizen oversight should be adopted. Tensions run high when this subject is discussed, and fights and scuffles have even broken out at public meetings where citizen oversight is under consideration.[29] The fact that so few jurisdictions use such boards would indicate that police are winning this debate, arguing that the boards are often politicized and unfair to them.

In the words of Jim Pasco, the national executive director of the Fraternal Order of Police, civilians simply are not qualified to judge whether a police officer followed a department's rules governing use of force:

> The fact of the matter is, an officer has to make a split-second decision involving life or death. And the civilian review boards tend to, by definition, be made up of civilians who have no particular experience or insight into what went through that officer's mind . . . what the circumstances were.[30] Some police authorities are also concerned about the boards having a "preconceived agenda," that people appointed to a board by elected officials might feel obligated to pursue specific policies.[31]

Even the establishment and power of such boards can be tricky, especially where they are independently elected officials who are not accountable to county commissioners. In addition, some states' laws protect personnel records of police officers from most public disclosure and block access to investigative records, so experts say it's critical to persuade sheriffs and other law enforcement leaders to cooperate with oversight boards.[32]

Exhibit 2–4	Global Perspective: Eyes on the South African Police

Residents of a middle-class neighborhood in Sandringham, South Africa, felt they had a choice: either work with the police or become vigilantes.

As they became more and more desperate, police offered a police reserve course, which was attended by 150 residents; citizens learned that community policing is what makes a police service different from a police force, and police found it better to solve problems than arrest people.

The group became part of a formal organization known as a Community Policing Forum (CPF), one of 21 that are attached to police stations. CPFs are statutory bodies and possess strong powers under the 1993 interim constitution including the ability to monitor the effectiveness and efficiency of the South African Police Service (SAPS); they also advise police on priorities in the neighborhood and promote the accountability of the SAPS to local communities.

In fact, the preamble to the final Constitution of 1996 notes that the SAPS is accountable to the communities it serves, and that CPFs are to promote communication and cooperation between the SAPS and communities and "to improve transparency and service delivery" in the SAPS. It also refers to "the partnership and joint problem solving between communities and the SAPS."

A crucial CPF task is to notify police of trouble spots, such as dangerous corners where illegal drugs are regularly sold, houses where stolen goods are believed to be stored, or teenage gang hideouts—so that police can move in and stop crimes before they're committed. At the same time, the forums ensure that the police are also doing their job, maintaining transparency and service delivery. They are also vital in crime prevention and crime reduction, mobilize community support in crime detection, improve relationships with the community, and take preventive actions against drugs and child abuse.

A typical CPF consists of 20–30 active members. Some CPFs have subforums, such as special committees to deal with taxis and problems at schools.

Source: Adapted from Barbara Ludman, "How Community Policing Works," City of Johannesburg, South Africa (January 18, 2016), http://joburg.org.za/index.php?option=com_content&task=view&id=88&Itemid=9.

In Sum. . .

It seems that the verdict is apparently still out on whether or not local units of government are helped or hindered by having such citizen input. Because of this ongoing debate, the President's Task Force on 21st Century Policing has recommended that the federal Justice Department fund more research on civilian police oversight models.[33] Note also that in Chapter 3, we discuss the importance of recruiting quality officers for problem solving and policing a diverse society, and also review Early Intervention Systems for identifying problem employees.

Exhibit 2–5	Lessons Learned: Civilian Oversight in Boston

The Boston Police Department (BPD) was selected by the Department of Justice Office of Community Oriented Policing Services (COPS) as one of the four agencies in the United States to receive funding to enhance integrity within the department. The BPD sought to better understand and improve civilian oversight in the complaint review process, while also evaluating the strengths and challenges of the current complaint process in Boston, understand the best practices of complaint and use of force review nationally, and recommend a model of civilian oversight that would meet the specific oversight needs within Boston.

Some of the key principles drawn from the project were:

1. The community has a role in complaint review and oversight, and strong civilian oversight models increase communication with the public.
2. Oversight works best when it is triggered automatically.
3. Oversight should be transparent.
4. There is no one best model—models must fit the local needs, structure, and history.

The BPD has a high rate of sustained complaints in its investigations. However, use of force, including both lethal and nonlethal force, by BPD officers is low compared with other departments of similar sizes and those that serve similar cities. The BPD has a proven track record working with groups outside the department to identify the priorities of the community and work toward meeting common goals.

Source: Office of Community Oriented Policing Services, "Boston Police Department: Enhancing Cultures of Integrity" (April 2010), http://ric-zai-inc.com/Publications/cops-p184-pub.pdf.

CONNECTING WITH COURTS AND CORRECTIONS

In addition to the police–community dyad that exists under community policing, citizen involvement in courts and corrections agencies has come a long way in recent years. Such involvement—known collectively as **community justice**—has inspired innovative programming among court systems, prosecutor and defender offices, and corrections departments.

Closely related to the concept of community justice is **restorative justice**, the elements of which include repairing harm (first taking care of the victim who suffered the harm prior to trying to help the offender become a better citizen), reducing risk (managing the offender in such a way that he or she will not commit another crime), and building community (taking responsibility for the behavior of community members and becoming involved in the resolution process, not just turning crime over to government to be dealt with). Table 2–2 compares the traditional standard of retributive justice with restorative justice, which concerns active involvement of victims and the community.

Next we discuss this sea change in community involvement.[34]

Community Courts

Community courts are neighborhood-focused courts that attempt to harness the power of the justice system to address local problems. They strive to engage outside stakeholders such as residents, merchants, churches, and schools in new ways in an effort to bolster public trust in justice. And they test new approaches to reduce both crime and incarceration. The first community court in the country was the Midtown Community Court, launched in 1993 in New York City. Several dozen community courts, inspired by the Midtown model, are in operation or planning around the country. International interest in community courts includes programs in Canada, Australia, South Africa, and Singapore.[35]

Community prosecution is founded on the idea that prosecutors have a responsibility not only to prosecute cases but also to solve public safety problems, prevent crime, and improve public confidence in the justice system. Around the country, prosecutors are taking on new responsibilities that reflect this shift—working out of neighborhood offices and collaborating with others (including residents, community groups, and other government agencies) in the development of problem-solving initiatives. In many cases, community stakeholders actually help to set the crime-fighting agenda and participate in the solutions. Definitions of success are changing as well. Rather than simply tallying cases won or jail sentences imposed, community prosecutors are measuring the effect of their work on neighborhood quality of life, community

TABLE 2–2 Comparison of Retributive and Restorative Justice	
Old Approach to Justice: Retributive	**New Approach to Justice: Restorative**
Primary objective focuses on punishment for a violation of the law	Primary objective focuses on reparation of harm done to victim or community by offender
Adversarial process with little or no attention to victim	A community based approach to facilitation, dialogue and negotiation to change offender behavior
Traditional treatments of punishment, leniency and prevention	Offender must take ownership of harms committed
Vengeance for wrongs committed outweigh community-based approaches such as mediation and negotiation	Offender must take action to make amends to victim and community
Offender punishment is primary objective	Victim healing is also a primary objective

Source: Adapted from Office of Juvenile Justice and Delinquency Prevention *Balanced and Restorative Justice: Prospects for Juvenile Justice in the 21st Century*, 2004, pp. 467–509, https://www.ncjrs.gov/pdffiles/framwork.pdf.

| **Exhibit 2–6** | Community Prosecution in Seattle, Washington |

Seattle's Law Enforcement Assisted Diversion (LEAD) program is a community-based approach to addressing low-level drug and prostitution crimes. Instead of jail, arrestees are diverted to community based treatment and diversion provided by a variety of support service providers. Officers are provided standardized criteria to guide them in making the proper decision for qualified offenders but they are also allowed some discretion.

The focus of LEAD is improving the community's quality of life. A policy coordinating group - consisting of Seattle elected officials, King County Prosecuting Attorney's Office, Seattle City Attorney's office, King county Sheriff's office, Seattle Police Department and Washington State Department of Correction - oversees the program.

Once enrolled in the LEAD program, a caseworker works with the offender to find an appropriate individually tailored service plan which may include substance abuse treatment, mental health services, housing, and job training and placement.

Source: Adapted from U.S. Department of Justice, Office of Community Policing Services, "Seattle LEAD's on Law Enforcement Diversion," *Community Policing Dispatch* 4 (4), April 2013, http://cops.usdoj.gov/html/dispatch/04-2013/seattle_leads.asp.

---

attitudes, and crime. Working with local prosecutors and national experts such as the Association of Prosecuting Attorneys, the Center for Court Innovation provides technical assistance and training to the field.[36]

Defense attorneys are also engaged in community justice. They know about their clients and the communities from which they come; the staff sees their communities as a series of interconnected family networks. Relatives often call the office out of concern for a person's safety as he or she entered the justice system. The program provides a deeper understanding of clients through continuity of representation and better investigation, better presentation of sentencing options through greater connection to community resources, and greater ability to represent residents' support for a less severe sentence.

A good example of a community court's activities is the aforementioned Midtown Community Court in New York City.[37] This court targets quality-of-life offenses such as prostitution, illegal vending, graffiti, shoplifting, fare beating, and vandalism in midtown Manhattan. Residents, businesses, and social service agencies collaborate with the court by supervising projects and providing onsite services, including drug treatment, health care, and job training. Social services located in the court provide the judge with these services as well as a health education class for prostitutes and "johns," counseling for young offenders and mentally ill persons, and employment training. For offenders with lengthier records, the court offers a diversionary program. Many defendants return to court voluntarily to take advantage of these services, including English as a second language and General Educational Development (GED) classes.

Community Corrections

The size and cost of jails and prisons have grown, as has the awareness of many people that perhaps many nonviolent offenders can do better using alternatives to incarceration in prisons or jails. Citizens are now reconsidering the role of community-based corrections, which encompasses probation, parole, and pretrial supervision. States and counties are moving to shift the burden from institutional to **community corrections**.[38]

In some states, efforts to build capacity, attract new resources, and contribute in significant ways to public safety are at the starting place of educating policymakers and stakeholders on the function and purpose of supervision. States and counties have also begun experimenting with new technologies and practices in their supervision to more efficiently and safely manage offenders in the community. Policymakers and the public must work together to develop a much greater understanding of what is possible for community-based corrections agencies to achieve and the resources it will take to get there.

A new and excellent report by the Vera Institute of Justice's Center on Sentencing and Corrections provides an overview of the state of community corrections, the transformational

Community corrections includes sentencing low-risk offenders to community work projects.
Washoe County Sheriff's Office.

practices emerging in the field, and recommendations to policymakers on realizing the full value of community supervision to taxpayers and communities.[39]

Other partnerships that can involve the courts and citizens include child care during trials for victims and witnesses, law-related education, and job training and referral for offenders and victims. A community-focused court can also practice restorative justice, emphasizing the ways in which disputes and crimes adversely affect relationships among community residents, treating parties to a dispute as real individuals rather than abstract legal entities, and using community resources in the adjudication of disputes.[40]

Exhibit 2–7 demonstrates how one community is partnering with its corrections agencies.

Community Service Centers

Beginning in the mid-1980s, when community policing was becoming more widespread, police storefronts also became more popular. Today, however, cities are going beyond just using a storefront, instead providing a **community service center**, where citizens can do "one-stop shopping"

| Exhibit 2–7 | Corrections Partner with Others in Ohio |

In Richland County, Ohio, a partnership exists between the county adult probation office, sheriff's office, police department (city of Mansfield), and state parole authority, with teams of community policing and community corrections officers conducting major joint operations. They engage in joint inspections of local bars, check for curfew violations, do fugitive surveillance, and perform joint visitations of probationers' and parolees' homes to seek out and question clients for possible violations. Community policing officers handle specific clients, which enhances their familiarity with supervised offenders; likewise, corrections officers supervise offenders in the police department's beat areas, which gives them greater knowledge of the neighborhoods in which their clients reside. Crime statistics reveal a much greater reduction in violent and property crimes in areas where these agencies work together.

Source: David Leitenberger, Pete Semenyna, and Jeffrey B. Spelman, "Community Corrections and Community Policing," *FBI Law Enforcement Bulletin* (November 2003):20–23.

to access government services. In addition to filing police reports or obtaining information, following is a list of some other kinds of services being provided:

- Affordable housing listings
- Alarm permit applications
- Business licenses
- Bus schedules
- City job listings and applications
- Community event information
- Community maps and plans
- Crime prevention information
- City council meeting dockets
- Dog license applications
- Notary services
- Park and recreation class and event schedules
- Passport applications
- Permits
- Social service referrals
- Tax forms
- Water bill payments

E-Government

The Internet is dramatically changing the way government operates—in terms of not only a greater ability of residents or businesses to interact with public agencies but also the manner in which government delivers services: **e-government** at work. Now obtaining information is literally just a click away. The Clearwater Police Department uniquely provides an "Active Calls for Service" Web site whereby citizens can, in near real-time terms, see calls that are being dispatched to police officers. Exhibit 2–8 shows a display of that screen (it may be viewed at http://www.clearwaterpolice.org/cfs/active.asp).

Exhibit 2–8

Summary

This chapter's centerpiece is the partnership between the community and police. In that regard, we defined what police are doing to become more professional, what is meant by "community," several means for bringing the two sides together, and challenges to having a sense of police–community unity (e.g., civilian review boards). Also discussed was how and why community policing evolved and how courts and corrections organizations are also partnering with the public.

These are exciting yet also daunting times for the police and public. Perhaps more than ever, given national outrage toward policing killings and public outcry for greater transparency and accountability, the police must be mindful of their image and the social, political, and psychological impact of their actions. "Business as usual" will not suffice.

Key Terms and Concepts

Beat meetings
Citizens' police academy
Citizen (civilian) review
  board
Community cohesion

Community corrections
Community court
Community justice
Community policing
Community prosecution

Community service
  center
E-government
"Guardians"
  (vs. "warriors")

Restorative justice
Sense of community
Social capital
Volunteerism

Items for Review

1. Describe what some police agencies are doing to gain what is termed "New Professionalism."
2. How do a "guardian" and "warrior" mentality differ with regard to policing?
3. Explain what is meant by "community," including the roles that cohesion, social capital, and volunteerism play in it.
4. How has the recent Great Recession affected policing in general? Community policing in specific?
5. Describe what community policing is and is not, and compare the ways in which community policing differs from traditional policing.
6. How do beat meetings and citizens' police academies function, and serve to foster better police–community relations?
7. How can civilian review boards help policing? What are some arguments against them?
8. How are courts and corrections agencies connecting with citizens?

Learn by Doing

1. Assume that, in the aftermath of several police shootings in your region, your county governing board is hearing public comments concerning the need for police to become more accountable, legitimate, and like community "guardians." As legislative liaison for your county's sheriff's department, you've been asked to prepare a position paper on this topic. What would you identify as being essential in order for the police to accomplish these goals?
2. Your criminal justice honor society is conducting a noon forum for all students in order to briefly explain to new members the

relatively new concepts of community justice, restorative justice, community courts, and community corrections. How will you explain each of these three concepts?
3. Each year your criminal justice faculty sponsors a "Career Day" program. The department chairperson requests that you participate by making a short presentation on potential benefits of, and concerns with, civilian review boards. What will you say?

Endnotes

1. Christopher Stone and Jeremy Travis, *Toward a New Professionalism in Policing* (March 2011), National Institute of Justice and Harvard Kennedy School, pp. 2–19, https://www.ncjrs.gov/pdffiles1/nij/232359.pdf.
2. Ibid.
3. Seth Stoughton, "Police Warriors or Community Guardians?" *Washington Monthly* (April 17, 2015), http://www.washingtonmonthly.com/ten-miles-square/2015/04/police_warriors_or_community_g055130.php.
4. Black Lives Matter, "About the Black Lives Matter Network," http://blacklivesmatter.com/about/.
5. Adapted from Kevin Johnson, "Providence One of Many U.S. Police Forces Feeling Ferguson Aftershocks," *USA Today* (January 1, 2016), http://www.usatoday.com/story/news/nation/2015/12/28/providence-police-force-ferguson-effect-aftershocks/77005198/.
6. Sharon Chamard, "Community Cohesion and Empowerment," in Kenneth J. Peak (ed.), *Encyclopedia of Community Policing and Problem Solving* (Thousand Oaks, Calif.: Sage, 2013), pp. 34–37.

7. Ibid.

8. Kenneth J. Peak, in ibid., pp. 390–391.

9. See Andrew Kohut, "Despite Lower Crime Rates, Support for Gun Rights Increases," Pew Research Center (April 17, 2015), http://pewrsr.ch/1E8OLMu; also see Bill Hart, "Crime, Fear, Guns," Arizona State University, Morrison Institute for Public Policy (April 29, 2015), https://morrisoninstitute.asu.edu/blog/crime-fear-guns.

10. Ibid.

11. Ibid.

12. David Weisburd and John E. Eck, "What Can Police Do to Reduce Crime, Disorder, and Fear?" *Annals of the American Academy of Political and Social Science* (May 2004):46–51, http://cebcp.org/wp-content/publications/WeisburdEck04.pdf.

13. See Police Executive Research Forum, "Survey Indicates Easing of Budget Cuts in Some Local Police Departments, but Most Are Still Being Cut" (April 30, 2012) (Washington, D.C.: Author), p. 1.

14. Ibid.

15. Office of Community Oriented Policing Services, "The Impact of the Economic Downturn on American Police Agencies" (n.d.), http://www.cops.usdoj.gov/Default.asp?Item=2602.

16. Matthew J. Parlow, "The Great Recession and Its Implications for Community Policing," *Georgia State University Law Review*, 28 Ga. St. U. L. Rev. 1193 (Summer 2012), pp. 1210–1211, http://policeforum.org/library/economy/Impactofeconomic crisisonpolicingApril2012final.pdf.

17. Tom Casady, Lincoln, Nebraska, Police Department, http://www.lincoln.ne.gov/city/police/cbp.htm.

18. Adapted from ibid.

19. Ibid.

20. Ibid.

21. Ibid.

22. Office of Community Oriented Policing Services, *Community Policing Dispatch* 1 (1) (January 2008):1, http://cops.usdoj.gov/html/dispatch/january_2008/nugget.html.

23. Chicago PD, "What Are Beat Meetings . . . And Why Are They Important?" https://portal.chicagopolice.org/portal/page/portal/ClearPath/Get%20Involved/How%20CAPS%20works/Beat%20Meetings.

24. See LAPD, "Community-Police Advisory Boards (C-PAB) Meeting Schedule and City-Wide Minutes," http://www.lapdonline.org/mission_community_police_station/content_basic_view/8984.

25. Kansas City, Kansas, Police Department, "Neighborhood Resource Center," https://www.wycokck.org/community-police/.

26. For more comprehensive information, see the Web site of the National Citizens Police Academy Association, at http://www.nationalcpaa.org/.

27. National Association of Civilian Oversight of Law Enforcement, https://nacole.org/.

28. See ibid., for a listing of jurisdictions with citizen review boards.

29. Martin Kaste, "Police Are Learning to Accept Civilian Oversight, but Distrust Lingers," NPR (February 21, 2015), http://www.npr.org/2015/02/21/387770044/police-are-learning-to-accept-civilian-oversight-but-distrust-lingers; also see Ben Brumfield, AnneClaire Stapleton, and Sara Sidner, "In Ferguson's Wake, Police and Citizens Scuffle at St. Louis Meeting," CNN (January 29, 2015), http://www.cnn.com/2015/01/28/us/st-louis-police-citizen-ferguson-outburst/.

30. Quoted in Kaste, "Police Are Learning to Accept Civilian Oversight, but Distrust Lingers," http://www.npr.org/2015/02/21/387770044/police-are-learning-to-accept-civilian-oversight-but-distrust-lingers.

31. Southern California Public Radio, "SoCal Cities Debate the Pros and Cons of Police Oversight Models" (July 30, 2015), http://www.scpr.org/news/2015/07/30/53450/socal-cities-debate-the-pros-and-cons-of-police-ov/.

32. Southern California Public Radio, "SoCal Cities Debate the Pros and Cons of Police Oversight Models."

33. President's Task Force on 21st Century Policing, *Interim Report of the President's Task Force on 21st Century Policing* (March 4, 2015), p. 27 (Washington, DC: Office of Community Oriented Policing Services), http://www.cops.usdoj.gov/pdf/taskforce/interim_tf_report.pdf.

34. For a broader discussion of community justice, see Center for Court Innovation, "Community Justice 2014," http://www.courtinnovation.org/community-justice-2014.

35. Center for Court Innovation, "Community Court," http://www.courtinnovation.org/topic/community-court.

36. Center for Court Innovation, "Community Prosecution," http://www.courtinnovation.org/topic/community-prosecution.

37. See Center for Court Innovation, "Midtown Community Court," http://www.courtinnovation.org/project/midtown-community-court.

38. Vera Institute of Justice, Center on Sentencing and Corrections, "The Potential for Community Corrections to Improve Safety and Reduce Recidivism" (July 2013), http://www.vera.org/sites/default/files/resources/downloads/potential-of-community-corrections.pdf.

39. Ibid.

40. Center for Court Innovation, "Restorative Justice," http://www.courtinnovation.org/topic/restorative-justice.

PART II

Policing's Dual Priorities: Managing Diversity and Homeland Protection

This part's chapters discuss two contemporary issues that pose tremendous challenges for the police: working within a more diverse community and the role of local police in protecting the homeland. Together, these priority issues now—justifiably—consume tremendous amounts of time and resources.

Policing a Diverse Society

LEARNING OBJECTIVES

As a result of reading this chapter, the student will understand:

- The current and projected demographic outlook for the United States, and the inherent challenges diversity poses for the police
- The status of immigration law and policy in the United States and the related problems and challenges involving the police
- The historical background of police–minority relations, as well as how recent events involving police shootings have caused a deeper schism between police and minorities
- The kinds of actions that might be taken to close the police–minority divide, to include transparency (possibly with body worn cameras), adopting a "guardian" mindset, trust building, police recruitment, and addressing biased policing

TEST YOUR KNOWLEDGE

1. Anticipated demographic changes in the United States include an overall younger population, with fewer immigrants and minorities.
2. At present, there is no firm immigration policy in the United States.
3. During the mid-2010s, police–minority relations can be said, overall, to have improved.
4. The issue of police use of body cameras is generally felt to be a "win–win" between police and community, as there are no inherent legal or social problems or issues involved.

Answers can be found on page 278.

I wish I could say that racism and prejudice were only distant memories. We must dissent from the indifference . . . the apathy . . . the fear, the hatred and the mistrust. We must dissent because America can do better, because America has no choice but to do better.

—JUSTICE THURGOOD MARSHALL

INTRODUCTION

As historical and contemporary racial, ethnic, and societal clashes between the police and people they serve would clearly demonstrate, any discussion of community policing must include a discussion of our nation's diverse nature and the problems it has wrought. **Diversity** now means more than embracing variations in race, ethnicity, and gender; it also encompasses variations in age, language skills, culture, religion or belief system, and sexual orientation—all of which can bring the community and police together (or split them apart). As a publicly funded service profession, however, the police are ethically and professionally bound to serve the entire community. Furthermore, a commitment to diversity within the police agency reflects the community it serves and sends a message of inclusiveness and equality. At its root, however, the subject of diversity and its related problems with police involve race and ethnicity; unfortunately, as this nation's population has become more and more diverse, and adding in its wave of immigration, general economic turmoil, war, natural disasters, and a bevy of other social problems, there has also come more of a Great Divide among its citizens. Indeed, in Chapter 2 we discussed some of the challenges in developing police–community relationships in the United States; this chapter is essentially a continuation of that chapter.

We begin this chapter with an overview of the **demographics** of the United States, showing how it is changing in its composition. Then, related to that, we examine the nature and challenges of immigration, a highly polarizing political, social, and economic issue today.

Next—and perhaps constituting the centerpiece of this chapter—we review another longstanding problem: police–minority group relations. After a brief look at what has often been a hostile relationship between police and African-Americans, we examine the recent explosion of problems beginning with the police shooting in Ferguson, Missouri, and other cities; included is a consideration of some possible approaches for the police to bring about harmony and justice in minority communities. Included in this assessment are calls for police body camera, changing the police mindset to one of serving as "guardians," recruiting for diversity, early intervention systems, and racial profiling. Exhibits 3–1 to 3–5 illuminate general issues of policing diversity as well.

The chapter concludes with some items for review and several "Learn by Doing" scenarios, where you are invited to "be the officer" in some delicate situations that police officers might confront.

WHO WE ARE: A DIVERSE—AND CHANGING—NATION

Race, Sex, and Age

According to the U.S. Census Bureau, there are now nearly 319 million people living in America (changes in the size of the population are driven by the projected number of births, deaths, and net international migrants; if immigration levels are maintained at a constant level, the U.S. population will grow to 399 million by 2050).[1] About 23 percent of those persons are under age 18, and about 15 percent are age 65 and over. The proportion of females (50.8 percent) is slightly higher than males. Regarding racial affiliation, persons identifying as white are about 77.4 percent; Hispanic or Latino, 17.4 percent; Black or African-American, 13.2 percent; American Indian and Alaska Native, 1.2 percent; Asian, 5.4 percent; and Native Hawaiian and Other Pacific Islander, 0.2 percent (total exceeds 100 percent; see notes for explanation).[2]

The U.S. population is projected to age over the coming decades, with a higher proportion of the nation's total population in the older ages (65 and over). Overall, the percentage of the total population that is under the age of 18 is projected to decrease.[3]

Following are some of the more salient demographic trends that are expected to occur in the United States between now and 2050:

- As noted above, the nation will grow somewhat older, with the portion of the population that is currently at least 65 years old—13 percent—expected to reach about 20 percent by 2050. This is termed the "graying of America," and is felt by many observers to portend a decline in the nation's eminence, as many other countries are simply not as "gray."

Police must interact with senior citizens to better understand their needs and concerns.
Hill Street Studios/Blend Images/Getty Images.

- As the baby boomers (born between 1946 and 1964) age, the population of working and young people is also expected to keep rising, in contrast to most other advanced nations.
- America's relatively high fertility rate—the number of children a woman is expected to have in her lifetime—was 2.1 in 2006, with 4.3 million total births. Owing largely to recent immigrants, who tend to have more children, and children of the original boomers having children of their own, the nation is expected to see increases in the populations of young and working people and is on the verge of a baby boomlet.[4]

Certainly, the police must prepare for the coming of an older, more diverse nation. Additional demographic information is provided below, in looking at the immigrant population.

IMMIGRANTS TO THE LAND OF OPPORTUNITY

The foreign-born population in the United States consists of about 40.7 million people; this includes 18.6 million naturalized U.S. citizens and 22.1 million noncitizens. Of the noncitizens, approximately 13.3 million are legal permanent residents, 11.3 million are unauthorized migrants, and 1.9 million are on temporary visas.[5]

At the same time, the Pew Research Center reports that there are now an estimated 11.3 million unauthorized immigrants (about half of whom are Mexican) residing in the United States—the lowest number in a decade, and still declining.[6] From 2005 to 2009, an average of 850,000 undocumented immigrants entered the United States annually;[7] since 2009, however, according to the Pew Research Center, an average of about 350,000 new unauthorized immigrants each year.[8] The Great Recession of the mid- and late-2000s resulted in fewer immigrants coming here because jobs were disappearing, and increased patrolling and enforcement had an impact. The federal Immigration and Customs Enforcement (ICE) has stepped up the frequency of its raids on U.S. businesses that employ illegal immigrants.

The immigrant population in the United States has caused a dramatic increase in local, state, and tribal law enforcement encounters with both legally admitted and undocumented immigrants during routine police duties (see Exhibit 3–1 concerning Haitians); accordingly, the need for law enforcement officers to have a working knowledge of **immigration** law and policy has increased concurrently as well. In response to these demands, the federal Office of Community Oriented Policing Services (COPS) funded a web-based Basic Immigration Enforcement Training (BIET) program to train officers in such areas as determining immigrant/nonimmigrant status, identifying false identification, and notifying foreign nationals' embassy or consulate.[9]

Federal Efforts at Law and Policy

At present, there is no definitive federal policy regarding immigration, and the subject remains very polarizing—often placing the police in the middle of the fray. In June 2013, The U.S. Senate passed The Border Security, Economic Opportunity, and Immigration Modernization Act

Exhibit 3–1	A Community Policing Approach with Haitians in Delray Beach, Florida

In the early 1990s, officers of the Delray Beach, Florida, Police Department (DBPD) began hearing people asking more and more often if they understood the Creole language. Eventually, it came to light that the city was in the midst of an immigrant explosion of mostly illegal Haitian immigrants (Creole is one of two official languages of Haiti, the other being French).

Unfortunately, a large element within this population included criminals who fed on the fears of the illegal Haitian immigrants and committed numerous felonies against them. And, because the undocumented Haitians were fearful of the police—and dissuaded by a ruthless system of policing in their home country—they opted to let these crimes go unreported. Only after a few immigrants became legal residents and thus had no fear of being deported, did they come forward and reveal to police the extent of their victimization.

In order to combat the Haitian criminal element, the DBPD realized it would need to engage the Haitian community. The first attempt to do so was the creation of a successful citizens' police academy, conducted in Creole and with 40 individuals attending. Next, a Haitian citizens' patrol was developed, using graduates of the citizens academy to establish more volunteer patrols; members patrolled in specially marked volunteer vehicles and dressed in volunteer uniforms. Volunteers also assisted the DBPD and surrounding agencies with translation, and, during times of crisis, such as an earthquake and hurricane in Haiti, collected five tractor-trailers worth of donated goods to be shipped to Haiti.

The Haitian citizen's academy and volunteers have also helped other police agencies in Florida with growing Haitian communities by providing training for initiating both the citizens academy and volunteer programs. In addition, a youth cadet academy has been launched in a high school so that students can also learn about policing.

Through community policing efforts and creative community partnerships, the DBPD continues to foster trust with the Haitian community, overcome the criminal subculture that took advantage of immigrants, and help Haitian residents take an active role in their community.[10]

Citizens' police academies expose people to police methods and issues.
Elena11/Shutterstock.

of 2013 (Senate Bill 744), an immigration reform bill; this bill would make it possible for many undocumented immigrants to gain legal status and eventually citizenship. It would also make the border more secure by adding up to 40,000 border patrol agents, and provide for points-based immigration system (based on professional skills, family relations, and work history in the United States). Whether the U.S. House of Representatives will even consider the bill is unknown.[11] In the meantime, training and knowledge of the law, together with fundamental community policing principles, will best prepare local police agencies to address the continually growing and changing face of illegal immigration.

Arizona's Law and a U.S. Supreme Court Decision

In April 2010, the Arizona legislature enacted the toughest immigration enforcement law in U.S. history, with passage of a "trespassing" law that criminalized the mere status of being in the country illegally. The law also prescribed jail time for immigrants who fail to carry their federal registration documents and who seek work in Arizona. But the most controversial aspect of the law, and indeed the most critical for community policing, was the requirement that police officers make a "reasonable attempt" to determine the immigration status of a person if the officer has "reasonable suspicion" that such person is an illegal immigrant. Several immigrants' rights groups and other organizations challenged the law, ultimately taking their fight to the U.S. Supreme Court.

The Court issued its 5-3 decision in June of 2012. All of the law's provisions were struck down except the one that most affected police officers, requiring them to act on reasonable suspicion to check a person's immigration status while enforcing other laws.[12] For the police, the Court's decision left more questions than answers. For example, how long must officers wait for federal authorities to respond when they question someone concerning their immigration status? If the police release a person too soon, are they exposing themselves to a lawsuit for failing to enforce the law? How do they avoid being sued for racial profiling? Finally, what justifies reasonable suspicion that someone is in the country illegally?[13]

A National Crackdown on Sanctuary Cities

States around the country are considering laws that would crack down on "sanctuary cities"—cities known to protect undocumented immigrants from being deported. The crackdown was prompted by the July 2015 murder of Kathryn Steinle of San Francisco, who was shot by an undocumented immigrant who had been released from a local jail instead of handed over to federal immigration officials.

Sanctuary cities came into being in recent years in response to a federal program that uses local law enforcement to help identify undocumented immigrants living in the country. People who are arrested on local charges and booked into local jails have their fingerprints sent to the Department of Homeland Security to check for immigration violations. If a violation(s) exists, Immigration and Customs Enforcement (ICE) agents can ask local police to hold the suspect until such time as agents can pick up the person and begin deportation proceedings. Opponents of this practice complained that the program was being abused by ICE to round up people who had been arrested for nonviolent, minor crimes; that, in turn, led to city policies that limit local officials, including police, from assisting ICE in those efforts.

Conversely, ICE has argued that a number of potentially dangerous immigrants were set free. That debate came to a head in July 2015 when, despite a criminal record that included seven felony convictions, Juan Lopez-Sanchez was free and in the country to allegedly shoot Steinle (see Exhibit 3–2).

| **Exhibit 3–2** | *The Case Underlying Challenges to Sanctuary Cities* |

Juan Francisco Lopez-Sanchez, 52, will face murder charges in San Francisco, being accused of fatally shooting 32-year-old Kathryn Steinle in the back while she strolled in the city in July 2015. Lopez-Sanchez, arrested less than an hour later, stated that he had accidentally fired a gun he said he found wrapped in a T-shirt, and that he had taken strong sleeping pills before the incident.

Lopez-Sanchez, who had returned to the United States after being deported to Mexico five times, became the focal point in the debate over immigration law and what are termed sanctuary cities. In March 2015, Lopez-Sanchez completed serving his third federal prison term for felony re-entry into the United States from Mexico. He was transferred to local custody because of a warrant for alleged marijuana possession, but was released after prosecutors decided not to pursue the case.

San Francisco, a sanctuary city, honors immigration holds only if the person has a violent record or if a judge has examined the hold or approved a warrant. Several city politicians have defended the policies as a way to protect immigrants without violent criminal records, and encourage them to report crimes to police.[14]

Federal and state reactions to the shooting were swift. Members of Congress, state legis-latures, and local governments called for changes in the policy, and the U.S. House of Representatives approved a bill (the "Stop Sanctuary Policies and Protect Americans Act") in July cracking down on those cities.[15] The U.S. Senate, however, killed the bill in late October, by a vote of 54-45 (60 votes were required for passage).[16]

At the state level, in October 2015, North Carolina became the first state to enact such a law, its governor saying that "Public safety officials must have the flexibility and tools to inves-tigate crimes and sanctuary city policies deprive law enforcement of those tools."[17]

POLICE AND MINORITIES: A HISTORY OF CONFLICT AND CHALLENGES

A minority group is a group or category of people who can be distinguished by special physical or cultural traits that can be used to single them out for differential and unequal treatment. As will be seen below—and as with the issue of immigration—conflicts between minority groups and governments and their police have a long and sordid history.

Lessons from History and Ferguson

Disraeli said, "No man will treat with indifference the principle of race. It is the key of history." Certainly the riotous events that unfolded in Ferguson, Missouri, in August 2014, following the shooting death of Michael Brown by a white police officer, as well as the in-custody death of Freddie Gray in Baltimore in April 2015 (where six police officers were charged with murder and/or assault) would prove that statement rings true today.[18] Then, police-minority relations took another drastic, negative turn in mid-2016, as tensions between African-Americans and police peaked in the aftermath of policing shootings of Alton Sterling on July 5th in Baton Rouge, Louisiana, and one day later, Philando Castile in Falcon Heights, Minnesota, by white officers. Then, on July 7th, a retaliatory attack occurred against police by an African-American sniper in Dallas, Texas, during a Black Lives Matter protest that killed five officers and wounded several others.

Problems of **police–minority relations** are certainly not a recent phenomenon. Indeed, in March 2015 thousands of people—including President Barack Obama—commemorated the 50th anniversary of "Bloody Sunday" in Selma, Alabama—when state troopers met Dr. Martin Luther King and 25,000 peaceful civil rights marchers at the Edmund Pettus Bridge with batons and tear gas. This peaceful demonstration led to the Voting Rights Act of 1965.[19]

However, not all such protests were as peaceful: during the 1960s major race riots occurred in Harlem, New York; Watts, California; Newark, New Jersey; and Detroit (often fomented by such violent militant groups as the Black Panthers). There were 75 civil disorders involving African-Americans and the police in 1967 alone, with at least 83 people killed. A number of presidential commissions were created to study riots, campus disorder, and minority relations in

A scene from the Walker Report of the 1968 Democratic National Convention in Chicago.

Courtesy of the Walker Report, from the Department of Justice.

A scene from the Walker Report of the 1968 Democratic National Convention in Chicago.
Courtesy of the Walker Report, from the Department of Justice.

general. One such commission, the National Advisory Commission on Civil Disorders (also known as the Kerner Commission), stated in 1968 that "our nation is moving toward two societies, one black, one white—separate and unequal."[20] Then, in the late 1980s and early 1990s, police–community relations appeared to worsen again, with major riots, looting, and burning in Miami, Florida; Los Angeles; Atlanta; Las Vegas; Washington, D.C.; and St. Petersburg, Florida, as well as in other cities. Race riots during the 1960s, such as the one in Watts, California, often pitted police against protesting members of the community.

James Baldwin, the African-American sociologist, was moved to write in 1960 (about Harlem) that:

> None of the Police Commissioner's men, even with the best will in the world, have any way of understanding the lives led by the people they swagger about in twos and threes controlling. Their very presence is an insult, and it would be, even if they spent their entire day feeding gumdrops to children.[21]

Then the new millennium arrived, and **bias-based policing**—also known as **racial profiling** or "driving while black or brown" (DWBB)—became a hot-button issue. A 2007 study released by the Bureau of Justice Statistics (BJS) found that while black, Hispanic, and white drivers were equally likely to be pulled over by the police, black and Hispanic drivers were much more likely to be searched and arrested, and police were much more likely to threaten or use force against such drivers than against white drivers in any encounter. However, the BJS report warned that the findings do not prove that police treat people differently along racial lines and that the differences could be explained by driver conduct or other circumstances.[22] DWBB is discussed more below.

Indeed, for many minorities, the four words that are inscribed over the entrance to the U.S. Supreme Court building in Washington, D.C.—Equal Justice Under Law—ring hollow; for them, justice is neither equal nor blind. The widespread discontent following the April 2015 police shooting of unarmed African-American Walter Scott in North Charleston, South Carolina (see Exhibit 3–3), as well as the shooting of 12-year-old Tamir Rice in Cleveland, the chokehold

---

Exhibit 3–3   *South Carolina's Largest Settlement*

In October 2015, the family of Walter Scott and the city of North Charleston, South Carolina, reached a $6.5 million settlement in Scott's fatal shooting death. Scott was struck in the back by a bullet while running away from officer Michael Slager in April 2015. Slager reportedly pulled Scott over for a broken brake light; he was later charged with murder in the case. A state circuit judge refused to release Slager on bail, saying that doing so "would constitute an unreasonable danger to the community." The settlement represented the largest ever reached in this type of case in South Carolina's history.[24]

A demonstrator protests in Ferguson, Missouri.
Anadolu Agency/Getty Images.

death of Eric Garner in New York City, and the aforementioned death of Freddie Gray, led to thousands of demonstrators marching and staging "die-ins" near the White House and across the country (as well as federal lawsuits against the officers' employing agencies).[23] "Black lives matter" became their rallying cry, and even a new university course of that name was launched at Dartmouth College in Hanover, New Hampshire.[25] Other widely publicized incidents would follow, such as the police shooting death of an unarmed black teenager in the city of Madison, Wisconsin, in March 2015.[26]

The city of Ferguson raged for a week, gas and rubber bullets were used, the National Guard was deployed, and a police officer was shot (two officers were also shot during a protest in March 2014).[27]

Ultimately, five Ferguson officials resigned (including the police chief, city manager, municipal judge, and two police supervisors) and a U.S. Department of Justice issued a scathing report about the widespread racially biased abuses by police, who routinely targeted African-Americans for arrests and ticketing.[28] Much controversy was also raised concerning the use of the state's national guard and military equipment and tactics in Ferguson and across the nation. They point to the millions of pieces of surplus military equipment that have been given to local police departments across the country—including military-grade semiautomatic weapons, armored personnel vehicles, tanks, helicopters, and airplanes. Of course, a competing viewpoint is that the public wants police to utilize whatever tools and resources are required to keep them safe.

How to Achieve Harmony, Justice, and Policy?

What is the solution for such cities as Ferguson, Baltimore, and Baton Rouge and Baltimore—cities that are vastly different in their demographics but quite similar in attitudes and emotions? If someone had the perfect answer to that question, he or she would probably be very wealthy. However, although there are many underlying social problems in such communities that take many years if not decades to build to a boiling point, a priority is to seriously examine their relationship with and understanding of their minority communities. Therefore, in a community such as Ferguson—where 67 percent of the population but only 5 percent of police officers were African-American—and in a nation where many people see discrimination and prejudice when blacks are arrested at nearly three times the rate of people of other races,[29] good starting point is to make every effort to recruit and diversify the agency and thus provide a means for giving people a voice. As one witness told the President's Task Force on 21st Century Policing concerning youth in poor communities:

> By the time you are 17 you have been stopped and frisked a dozen times. That does not make that 17-year-old want to become a police officer. The challenge is to transform the idea of policing in communities among young people into something they see as honorable. They have to see people at local events, as the person who lives across the street, not someone who comes in and knows nothing about my community.[30]

Ray Kelly, former NYPD Police Commissioner, believes that in such cases the state must step in as an outside force, and a new police chief (preferably one of color) must be hired. Others (such as a former Philadelphia mayor and mayors in Baltimore, Maryland, and Gary, Indiana) suggested that city officials and police must reach out to community leaders, meet with civic associations, add African-Americans to the administration, and add an advisory committee on community relations that is composed of people of all colors.[31]

| **Exhibit 3–4** | Global Perspective: Community Policing in Vastly Diverse Papua New Guinea |

Linguistically, Papua New Guinea (PNG) is the world's most diverse country, with more than 700 native tongues. Located approximately 100 miles from the northernmost point of Australia (Cape York), it occupies the eastern half of New Guinea and its offshore islands. It is a nation of immense cultural and biological diversity, known for its beaches, coral reefs, and scuba diving. About 80 percent of the PNG people live in rural areas with few or no facilities of modern life, and the poverty level is high. Many tribes in the isolated mountainous interior have little contact with one another, let alone with the outside world, being dependent on agriculture.[32]

But as scenic and pastoral as PNG might appear, it has high levels of crime and violence, particularly against women. In fact, PNG is one of the most dangerous places in the world to be a woman, with an estimated 70 percent of women experiencing rape or assault in their lifetime. Few perpetrators are brought to justice; lack of access to courts and police, as well as failure by many justice officials to take violence against women seriously, contributes to the extremely low arrest and conviction rates.

There are reports of violent mobs attacking individuals accused of "sorcery," the victims mostly women and girls. Perpetrators of such attacks rarely face justice, and few witnesses will come forward. Additionally, other human rights issues include overall gender inequality, corruption, and excessive use of force by police. Rates of family and sexual violence are among the highest in the world and perpetrators are rarely prosecuted.[33]

Community policing is helping, however. PNG has strong ties with Australia, which has long practiced community policing and sent police officers to support its northern neighbor. Fed up with the immense number of sexual assaults perpetrated against women, police in many communities are working with women's groups to proactively take matters into their own hands by organizing groups to protect and empower them. Also formed is a new women's community policing group, whose members wear their own blue uniforms. Through their work together, these women have begun to shed their fear of men and to initiate many other community projects, including a day care center for children and awareness campaigns on child abuse and HIV/AIDS. The police and women also worked to establish a safe house where women and children can go at any time. When a woman comes to the safe house, a bell is rung. Upon hearing the bell, other women from the community bring whatever food or money they can spare. The underlying theme

Former U.S. Secretary of State Hillary Clinton is greeted by traditional dancers in Papua New Guinea in 2010 as she called for an end to the "culture of violence" against women and announced a new initiative to help reduce the island's staggering levels of violence.

AFP/Getty Images.

is that working together, police and communities can better protect the women and children. Indeed, women's groups are pushing for even more community policing to further benefit women and children.

By combining the efforts of the police, women's groups, other government agencies, and broader communities, PNG is beginning to deal with the issue of forcible rape and domestic violence. They understand, however, that until all members of communities within the nation's hundreds of tribes realize the nature of these crimes and begin to address them, much work remains to be done.[34]

Other reform ideas in the aftermath of Ferguson included that police stop blurring the lines with the military and begin wearing body cameras (discussed below), and even that drugs be legalized (it is asserted that African-Americans distrust the police because so many young black men are sent to prison for nonviolent drug offenses).[35] Also recommended was that the U.S. Department of Justice investigate such shootings to determine whether any civil rights violations occurred, implement training on racial profiling, and create programs to address vestiges of segregation, dehumanization, and stereotyping in our society.[36]

In the Baltimore death of Freddie Gray in April 2015, newly appointed U.S. Attorney General Loretta Lynch announced that the Justice Department's Civil Rights Division and the FBI would investigate the case—which is the normal approach. However, what many people wish to see are not more platitudes (e.g., "What is needed is a national discussion on race relations"), but actual policy changes such as those mentioned above, as well as reviewing accountability standards for officers and (as one African-American minister in Baltimore put it) encouraging warnings rather than a "shoot first" policy when dealing with potential suspects.[38]

Certainly, one form of public policy that might also be examined is the lack of requirement for police officers to possess a college degree; a long line of research—including a 2015 study at Michigan State University—have found that college-educated officers are less likely to use force on citizens; and, as researcher William Terrill stated, "If you use less force on individuals, your police department is going to be viewed as more legitimate and trustworthy and you're not going to have all the protests we're having across the country."[39]

Some Police Responses: Greater Transparency Using Web Sites and Databases

Some police agencies now demonstrate complete openness regarding officer-involved shootings. An example is provided in the "focus on" box, which shows facts and outcomes of such a shooting as provided by the Dallas, Texas, Police Department's Web site.

Also coming to light was the near total lack of national information concerning such shootings. Although one seven-year study ending in 2012 indicated that nearly two times a week in

---

FOCUS ON: Dallas Police Department's Postings of Information Concerning Officer-Involved Shootings[37]

On Monday, December 9, 2013, at approximately 3:11 P.M., plainclothes deployment officers were conducting surveillance on a vehicle at 9524 Military Parkway that had been taken in a robbery offense. The vehicle became occupied by two individuals and a felony traffic stop supported by uniformed officers in marked vehicles was attempted outside the apartment complex. The vehicle did not stop and turned back into the complex. The driver fled on foot and the passenger remained in the vehicle. One officer approached the vehicle, pulled her weapon and fired one time at the B/M/19 suspect striking him. The suspect was injured and transported to Baylor Hospital.

Suspect was unarmed. The officer was terminated for violation of departmental policy and later indicted by a Dallas County Grand Jury for Aggravated Assault. No officer was injured. One officer fired 1 round. Involved Officer: W/F 12 years, 3 months service.

the United States, a white police officer killed a black person (and nearly one in five is black), such information has long been considered flawed and largely incomplete (only about 750 agencies of 17,000 contribute such information, and doing so is voluntary in nature).[40] As a result, in the wake of the police shooting death of Michael Brown in Ferguson, Missouri, measures were put in place to initiate a national database tracking such shootings in the United States. A White House panel—chaired by former Philadelphia Police Chief Charles Ramsey—was appointed to require states to report the deaths of all people in police custody or during arrest to the federal government. The U.S. Senate passed the Death in Custody Reporting Act in December 2014 mandating that all states do so, or risk losing millions of dollars in federal grants.[41]

TRANSPARENCY AND TRUST BUILDING: OPPORTUNITIES AND CHALLENGES

"You don't have to look like the people you police, you just have to care." Thus did Kansas City, Missouri, police officer Octavio "Chato" Villalobos issuing a challenge to the police to build trust between themselves and the community. This section discusses what the police might do in order to accomplish that goal.[42] For preliminary consideration, Table 3–1 shows the mount of confidence people have in the police, by race.

These discussions also indicate that both understanding and transforming the relationship between the police and the community served, particularly minority and disenfranchised communities, are as old as policing. While today's police officers and leaders did not create the contemporary problems of race and policing, to include community mistrust, it is nevertheless their responsibility to try to improve the current state. In fact, the need for law police executives to forge trusting relationships—and their ability to provide effective and respectful policing in a multicultural society—is perhaps their most critical challenge. They must also understand that the inability of police organizations to appropriately handle police misconduct has a direct

---

TABLE 3–1   Confidence People Have in Police, by Race

Good Cop, Bad Cop

How much confidence do you have in police officers in your community...

... to do a good job of enforcing the law?

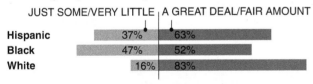

JUST SOME/VERY LITTLE | A GREAT DEAL/FAIR AMOUNT

	JUST SOME/VERY LITTLE	A GREAT DEAL/FAIR AMOUNT
Hispanic	37%	63%
Black	47%	52%
White	16%	83%

... to not use excessive force on suspects?

	JUST SOME/VERY LITTLE	A GREAT DEAL/FAIR AMOUNT
Hispanic	54%	45%
Black	59%	36%
White	24%	74%

... to treat Hispanics and white equally?

	JUST SOME/VERY LITTLE	A GREAT DEAL/FAIR AMOUNT
Hispanic	51%	46%
Black	55%	41%
White	25%	72%

... to treat blacks and whites equally?

	JUST SOME/VERY LITTLE	A GREAT DEAL/FAIR AMOUNT
Hispanic	48%	47%
Black	62%	36%
White	27%	72%

Source: Pew Research Center/USA Today, August 2014.

impact on the organizations' integrity and professionalism—which together are the cornerstones of community trust building.[43]

Next we look at some methods for accomplishing those lofty goals, beginning with the current push for police to wear body cameras, and followed by changing the mindset of the police to one of being a guardian, recruiting for diversity, and what are termed Early Warning Systems toward accomplishing that aim.

Calls for Police Body Cameras

Another outgrowth of the Ferguson, Missouri, Baltimore, and police shootings in other cities is the emphasis on greater police **transparency**—and the cry for officers to wear **body cameras**. With cellphones recording what appear to be a number of questionable if not criminal cases of police use of force—and what also appears for many people to be misrepresentation or cover up of facts by police in the aftermath—many politicians and activists argue that all officers should be compelled to do so. But having such a policy would raise at least two important questions: (1) when, specifically, should the cameras be used; and (2) who should be allowed to view which kinds of footage?

Regarding the first issue, cameras cannot be activated all of the time; officers have a reasonable right to privacy (e.g., during bathroom breaks or in private conversations) just as citizens do; also, many people—such as confidential informants or crime victims or witnesses—would understandably not come forward if they knew they would be recorded. Concerning the second question of who should view the videos, there are similar problems: publicly embarrassing videos of people who are being arrested or are intoxicated raise privacy concerns, while the public would also deem the recording of innocent bystanders, witnesses, victims, children, and people in their homes to be an egregious invasion of privacy.

Finally, as one expert put it, there is an "800-pound gorilla in the room" that needs to be discussed: unless state laws are changed, the ability of and cost for police to dedicate personnel and equipment to store, redact, and provide videos for all open-records requests (to include those by defense attorneys) would be extremely challenging if not impossible.[44] Body cameras can carry tremendous costs—not from the equipment itself (ranging from a few hundred to a few thousand dollars) but from the time required to store and edit the videos, as well as the impact of public disclosure or open records requests under the Freedom of Information Act (FOIA). A related issue is that such FOIA requests are often from individuals or companies wishing to generate income by posting police activity on YouTube and selling advertising space.[45]

The companion box discusses the latter concerns relating to body-camera use.

Some people argue, however, that public officials should not complain that the "sky is falling" in regard to such requests, and that public officials can address such large requests through

A national ramification of the recent rash of controversial police shootings across the United States has been a cry for police body-worn cameras.
Win McNamee/Getty Images.

---

you be the. . . JUDGE:

Police Body Cameras Wanted (or Not?)

Public disclosure requests for all body-cam videos since police begin using them, every 911 dispatch on which Seattle police officers were sent, all videos from patrol-car cameras, all of the reports officers write, and the details of all computer searches by officers for persons' names, addresses, or license plate numbers were expected to financially cripple the city of Seattle, Washington, and result in the demise of a plan to equip Seattle police officers with body cameras.[47]

Within a few weeks of initiating a six-month pilot program to equip officers with body cameras, the city received the above request by an anonymous citizen; Washington state law allows such anonymous requests, and public agencies cannot deny records on the ground a request is overbroad as long as the materials are identifiable.[48]

In one such case, a request for all e-mails received and sent by city employees could have cost the city $110 million in salary and take 1,376 years for one full-time employee to respond. The city of course argues that the administrative costs relating to such requests make honoring them cost-prohibitive.[49]

---

such means as delivering materials in installments and collecting copy fees with each release to make sure the requester is serious. It is also argued that city officials sometimes exaggerate the time and technical requirements required to produce records, and look for horror stories to persuade legislators of the need to change the law.[46]

Although body cameras may appear to be a panacea for police agencies and citizens wanting greater transparency and to resolve civilian complaints efficiently, it is obvious that many issues must be examined before their use becomes the "new normal" in policing. As one author put it,

> Balancing the benefits and drawbacks of this powerful new technology is not an easy task, and the decision to equip police departments with cameras should not be made lightly. Once such a program is deployed, it is increasingly difficult to have second thoughts or to scale back.[50]

Educating the Hearts and Minds of the Guardians

Aristotle said that "Educating the mind without educating the heart is no education at all."[51] His belief can also be said to speak to the challenge of educating the police on the crucial topics of diversity, trust, and police professionalism.

Police agencies must transform themselves so as to ensure that community trust and support will be such that their duties may be performed effectively. As a Denver, Colorado, police executive put it, this transformation can only come about when there is a change in mindset, and a good beginning point for that change is in diversity training, to:

- Focus on seeing all others as people with value and worth and deserving of unconditional respect.
- Contribute to personal development and self-mastery.
- Expand the intellect while touching the hearts of officers—they must learn and "feel" in the educational experience.
- Remember that adults learn best by doing and participating in an experience.
- Provide tools and skills that can be practiced and applied to daily work.

Make educational sessions one part of a continuing process of learning that reinforces a philosophy ultimately leading to a culture shift.[52]

In the same vein, as mentioned briefly in Chapter 2, a member of the President's Task Force on 21st Century Policing 2015 asked the question:

> Why are we training police officers like soldiers? Although police officers wear uniforms and carry weapons, the similarity ends there. The missions and rules of

engagement are completely different. The soldier's mission is that of a warrior: to conquer. The police officer's mission is that of a guardian: to protect. Soldiers must follow orders. Police officers must make independent decisions. Soldiers come into communities as an outside, occupying force. Guardians are members of the community, protecting from within.[53]

More and more articles are being written about the need for police to embrace the "guardian mindset," rather than seeing themselves as soldiers. As a law professor and former police officer put it, "Officers . . . must realize that the public—even a group of noncompliant teenagers—are not an enemy to be vanquished, but civilians to be protected."[54]

Recruiting for Diversity: A Toolkit

The importance of recruiting for diversity in today's community-policing world cannot be overstated. As former Gaithersburg, Maryland, police chief Mary Ann Viverette put it:

> Every day, our officers come into contact with individuals from different cultural backgrounds, socioeconomic classes, religions, sexual orientations, and physical and mental abilities. Each of these groups brings a different perspective to police–community relations and, as a result, our officers must be prepared to respond to each group in the appropriate fashion. Failure to recognize and adjust to community diversity can foster confusion and resentment among citizens and quickly lead to a breakdown in the critical bond of trust between a law enforcement agency and its community.[55]

Policing is a publicly funded service, and is thus ethically bound to serve and represent the entire community. That is easier said than done, however, and the recruitment and retention of a large pool of qualified applicants to help in changing the culture of the agency—as discussed in general in Chapter 8—can be a daunting task. The task of recruiting and retaining women and minorities as police officer is doubly daunting. There are some means of doing so, however, and that is the subject of a major publication by the Office of Community Oriented Policing Services in its 2009 **Law Enforcement Recruitment Toolkit**; those recommendations include the following methods and approaches:

a. Examine the department's diversity and determine which groups are underrepresented. Does the department reflect the community's diversity? What community does the agency want to reflect?

b. Tap into internal knowledge. Assess the experiences of current minority and female members of the department, including the recruitment and selection process.

c. Assess the potential recruiting pool. This assessment includes a basic understanding of the community's racial and ethnic composition to indicate appropriate marketing strategies and to provide a quantitative picture of where agency is falling short of ideal representation.

d. Engage the community. As an example, Sacramento, California, uses a community recruiter program wherein community members are involved in the process of screening acceptable candidates. These recruiters also serve on entry-level and promotional oral panels, providing a valuable opportunity for the department to understand cultural differences, particularly as they relate to interviewing and testing.

e. Use officers as recruiters. The most successful recruitment programs involve every member of the police department in the recruitment of new officers. Studies have shown that officers' demeanor and professionalism during contact with someone powerfully shapes that person's impressions of the police department and policing as a career.

f. Reach out to where prospects live, work, worship, and pray. Recruiters can get their information into the hands of potential recruits by engaging them on their terms and in their neighborhoods. Women- and minority-owned businesses, grocery stores, health clubs, neighborhood council meetings, YWCAs, schools, and universities—especially criminal justice programs, career fairs, and sporting events—are all excellent venues in which to engage potential recruits.[56]

Early Intervention Systems: Identifying Problem Employees

An **Early Intervention System** (EIS) is a computer database police management tool designed to identify officers whose behavior is problematic, as indicated by preselected performance indicator fields determined by the agency. The focus is on helping employees by providing intervention in a voluntary and nondisciplinary format. The program is "early" in the sense that an agency acts on the basis of performance indicators that suggest an officer may be having problems on the job but do not necessarily warrant formal disciplinary action as the initial organizational response. The identification, coupled with a menu of remedial actions, increases agency accountability and offers employees a better opportunity to succeed in their organizations. Evaluations enable supervisors to meet with an employee, discuss his or her performance, and formally record strengths, weaknesses, and expectations. Evaluations also provide supervisors with an opportunity to coach, mentor, and praise desired behavior and to notify employees when unacceptable behavior has been reported.

Most EIS use computer systems or databases to track employee records and are housed as a separate entity from the disciplinary system, usually within Internal Affairs units. The EIS records are intended to track employee behaviors and interventions by supervisors, should that become necessary. As data-driven mechanisms of accountability, these programs rely on a broad array of performance indicators, including use-of-force incidents, citizen complaints, department and community commendations and awards, court appearances, and arrest reports. Supervisors must be adequately prepared to review the data and, as with traditional performance evaluations, conduct appropriate interventions and follow-up with the employee.[57] Through an EIS, many behavior problems could be reduced significantly, resulting in a decrease in the caseload of the Internal Affairs unit.

A good example of an EIS is one that is being closely watched in the San Diego, California, Police Department (SDPD), which chose to implement what it termed the Early Identification and Intervention System (EIIS) (see Exhibit 3–5).

Exhibit 3–5   Investigating and Intervening: San Diego's EIIS

The San Diego Police Department, a leader in the development and practice of community policing and problem solving, has had no dearth of high-profile criminal conduct by a few of its police officers, including sexual assaults of women by on-duty officers (one officer was charged with 21 felony charges related to the sexual assault and victimization of eight women while he was on duty over a four-year period). In early 2011, 10 SDPD officers were investigated for criminal misconduct on charges including rape, domestic violence, driving under the influence, and sexual battery. And in 2014, another officer pled guilty to two counts of felony false imprisonment and three counts of misdemeanor sexual battery involving four victims. In response, the chief sought outside assistance to review the SDPD's systems for detecting and preventing misconduct, evaluate how the department had handled the misconduct cases, and recommend reform measures.[58]

San Diego's Early Investigation and Intervention System (EIIS) is a computer database that is designed to automatically collect data daily in several key areas—citizen complaints, police equipment accidents, use-of-force incidents, officer-involved shootings, internal affairs investigation, shooting range results, and discretionary arrests (of persons who are mentally ill or under the influence of drugs or alcohol). Also watched closely by EIIS is each officer's exposure to high-risk incidents (homicides, shootings, child deaths, traffic fatalities, sexual assaults); some officers are simply exposed to a greater-than-average number of calls for service that involve pain, fear for their safety, and tragedy. Officers who may be hurting but afraid to admit it may be identified by EIIS and given help as needed.

A major feature of the program lies in its ability to identify potentially problematic behaviors early, so that a manager can initiate a private, nondisciplinary, coaching conversation and, if necessary, make referrals to nearly 60 available groups or agencies. Results thus far indicate that only a small number of officers (4–5 percent) appear in EIIS with indicators that would suggest the command staff must take action. Of those employees, the goal is to provide resources to them before they harm their careers, their community, the department, or even themselves.[59]

Many minorities and youths believe they are unfairly detained, interviewed, and arrested, as seen in this New York City candlelight vigil.
Scott Olson/Getty Images.

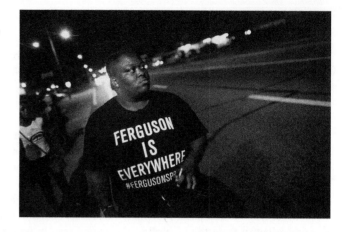

Racial Profiling and Bias-Based Policing

Biased treatment of minorities has been and continues to be one of the most sensitive charges against the criminal justice system as well as a despised police practice in the new millennium. (Actually, the more inclusive and proper term is "bias-based profiling," which includes unequal treatment of any persons on the basis of race, ethnicity, religion, gender, sexual orientation, or socioeconomic status.) Although the exact number is unknown, many states have adopted legislation related to racial profiling; most of these laws include data collection requirements.[60]

The best defense for the police may be summarized in two words: collect data. Collecting traffic stop data helps chiefs and commanders determine whether officers are stopping or searching a disproportionate number of minorities and enables them to act on this information in a timely fashion. Technology—including mobile data computers and wireless handheld devices—is available to the police for this purpose.

The International Association of Chiefs of Police (IACP) has issued a comprehensive policy statement on bias-based policing and data collection. The association "believes that any form of police action that is based solely on the race, gender, ethnicity, age, or socioeconomic level of an individual is both unethical and illegal" but that data collection programs "must ensure that data is being collected and analyzed in an impartial and methodologically sound fashion."[61]

Summary

This chapter focused on the often-fractured relations that have historically come between the police and immigrants as well as the minority communities they serve. Ours is not a perfect world. The Constitution notwithstanding, people are not created equal, at least with respect to legal, social, political, and economic opportunities. This disparity creates confrontations, mistrust, and enmity between many citizens and the police. Certainly those problems have been exacerbated by the recent spate of police killings of unarmed citizens.

As more indictments and news articles go viral about such killings, the police must work even harder to heal the wounds of the past and to eliminate any vestiges of bias-based policing and vigorously pursue those who would commit hate crimes. Policing also needs more women and minorities who are willing to assist as citizens or as police officers to join the cause as well as more culturally informed police training.

For these reasons, many would argue that community policing offers the best hope for improvement, because this strategy fosters a partnership that is based on trust, communication, and understanding.

Key Terms and Concepts

Bias-based policing	Diversity	Police–minority	Law Enforcement
Body cameras	Early Intervention System	relations	Recruitment Toolkit
Demographics (U.S.)	Immigration; extent and law of	Racial profiling	Transparency

Items for Review

1. Describe what sort of nation we are in terms of demographics, and some of the ways in which we are a changing population; include what is meant in contemporary terms by "diversity."
2. Explain how immigration has become a political and social battle for our society and police.
3. Delineate the historical background of police–minority relations, and the events that occurred in Ferguson, Missouri, and other such venues that have caused a schism between police and minorities.

4. Review the kinds of actions that might be taken to close the police–minority divide.
5. Explain how police body cameras, changing the police mindset, recruitment, EI systems, and addressing bias-based policing (racial profiling) have their respective roles to play in police–minority relations.

Learn by Doing

1. You are president of your criminal justice department's national honor society, and have decided to conduct a symposium dealing with the problems police now face with minorities and immigrants. How will you develop this forum? Who might be invited as guest speakers? What kinds of topics would you include?
2. You are a Public Information Officer in your police agency and have been invited to speak at a local civic group meeting. You are asked to describe the kinds of activities that can bring the police and community (particularly minorities) together, particularly

your views of police wearing body cameras. What is your response?
3. Your county sheriff assigns you, as the agency's liaison with the human resources office, to work toward recruiting many more women and minority deputies into your agency. The county manager has also made agency diversity a top priority, so a substantial budget has been appropriated for this purpose. Using the "toolkit" ideas presented in this chapter, what will you recommend to be done in order to reach these individuals in markets that are not normally recruited?

Endnotes

1. U.S. Census Bureau, "Population Projections" (n.d.), https://www.census.gov/population/projections/files/analytical-document09.pdf.
2. U.S. Census Bureau, "Quick Facts," https://www.census.gov/quickfacts/table/PST045215/00. Persons identifying as being of two or more races constitute 2.5 percent; furthermore, Hispanics may be of any race and are included in applicable categories.
3. Sandra L. Colby and Jennifer M. Ortman, *Projections of the Size and Composition of the U.S. Population: 2014 to 2060* (Washington, D.C.: U.S. Census Bureau, 2014), pp. 2, 4.
4. Joel Kotkin, "The Changing Demographics of America," *Smithsonian Magazine* (August 2010), http://www.smithsonianmag.com/40th-anniversary/the-changing-demographics-of-america-538284/?no-ist.
5. Center for American Progress, "The Facts on Immigration Today," October 23, 2014, https://www.americanprogress.org/issues/immigration/report/2014/10/23/59040/the-facts-on-immigration-today-3/#policy.
6. Pew Research Center, "5 Facts About Illegal Immigration in the U.S.," July 24, 2015, http://www.pewresearch.org/fact-tank/2015/07/24/5-facts-about-illegal-immigration-in-the-u-s/.
7. Tara Bahrampour, "Number of Illegal Immigrants in U.S. Drops, Report Says," *The Washington Post* (September 1, 2010), http://www.washingtonpost.com/wp-dyn/content/article/2010/09/01/AR2010090106940.html.
8. Pew Research Center, "Unauthorized Immigrant Population Stable for Half a Decade," July 22, 2015, http://www.pewresearch.org/fact-tank/2015/07/22/unauthorized-immigrant-population-stable-for-half-a-decade/.

9. Office of Community Oriented Policing Services, "Basic Immigration Enforcement Training" (n.d.), http://www.cops.usdoj.gov/default.asp?Item=2044.
10. Anthony Strianese, "Community Policing in the Delray Beach, Florida, Haitian Community," *The Police Chief* 78 (March 2011), pp. 32–33, http://www.policechiefmagazine.org/magazine/index.cfm?fuseaction=display_arch&article_id=2333&issue_id=32011.
11. For a comprehensive examination of federal immigration policy, attempted legislative enactments, and the police role within such policy, see: American Immigration Council, "A Guide to S.744: Understanding the 2013 Senate Immigration Bill," http://www.policeforum.org/assets/docs/Free_Online_Documents/Immigration/voices%20from%20across%20the%20country%20-%20local%20law%20enforcement%20officials%20discuss%20the%20challenges%20of%20immigration%20enforcement%202012.pdf; Anita Khashu, *The Role of Local Police: Striking a Balance Between Immigration Enforcement and Civil Liberties* (April 2009), http://www.policefoundation.org/wp-content/uploads/2015/06/The-Role-of-Local-Police-Narrative.pdf. http://www.immigrationpolicy.org/special-reports/guides744-understanding-2013-senate-immigration-bill; and Police Executive Research Forum, *Voices from Across the Country: Local Law Enforcement Officials Discuss the Challenges of Immigration Enforcement* (2012).
12. K. Johnson and J. Biskupic, "Arizona Immigration Crackdown Raises Flags," *USA Today* (April 30, 2010), http://www.usatoday.com/news/nation/2010-04-29-arizona-immigration_N.htm.

13. National Conference of State Legislators, "Arizona's Immigration Enforcement Laws," July 28, 2011, http://www.ncsl.org/research/immigration/analysis-of-arizonas-immigration-law.aspx.

14. Christine Mai-Duc, "Deportee Accused of Killing Kathryn Steinle to Stand Trial on Murder Charge," *Los Angeles Times* (September 4, 2015), http://www.latimes.com/local/lanow/la-me-ln-kathryn-steinle-sf-shooting-murder-trial-20150904-story.html.

15. Alan Gomez, "States Are Cracking Down on 'Sanctuary Cities,'" *USA Today* (October 15, 2015), http://www.usatoday.com/story/news/2015/10/15/sanctuary-cities-san-francisco-shooting-reaction/73931824/.

16. Kelsey Harkness, "See How Your Senators Voted on Sanctuary Cities," *Daily Signal* (October 20, 2015), http://dailysignal.com/2015/10/20/sanctuary-cities-bill-blocked-in-senate/.

17. Elise Foley, "North Carolina Governor Signs Bill Targeting 'Sanctuary Cities,' Undocumented Immigrants," *Huffington Post* (October 28, 2015), http://www.huffingtonpost.com/entry/north-carolina-immigration-law_56311d41e4b06317991094e7.

18. Michael Pearson, Steve Almasy, and Ben Brumfield, "Freddie Gray Death Ruled Homicide; Officers Charged," *CNN* (May 1, 2015), http://www.cnn.com/2015/05/01/us/freddie-gray-baltimore-death/.

19. See Rick Harmon, "Timeline: The Selma-to-Montgomery Marches," *USA Today* (March 6, 2015), http://www.usatoday.com/story/news/nation/2015/03/05/black-history-bloody-sunday-timeline/24463923/.

20. National Advisory Commission on Civil Disorders, *Report of the National Advisory Commission on Civil Disorders: Report Summary* (New York: Bantam Books, 1968), pp. 1–2, http://www.eisenhowerfoundation.org/docs/kerner.pdf.

21. James Baldwin, *Nobody Knows My Name: More Notes of a Native Son* (New York: Dial Press, 1962), p. 98.

22. Office of Justice Programs, Department of Justice, "Police Stop White, Black, and Hispanic Drivers at Similar Rates According to Department of Justice Report," www.ojp.usdoj.gov/newsroom/pressreleases/2007/BJS07020.htm.

23. CBS News, "Families of Michael Brown, Eric Garner, Tamir Rice to March to Capitol," December 13, 2014, http://www.cbsnews.com/news/families-of-michael-brown-eric-garner-tamir-rice-to-march-to-capitol/.

24. Greg Botelho and Sonia Moghe, "North Charleston Reaches $6.5 Million Settlement with Family of Walter Scott," *CNN* (October 9, 2015), http://www.cnn.com/2015/10/08/us/walter-scott-north-charleston-settlement/index.html.

25. Jamie Gumbrecht, "Dartmouth Launches #BlackLivesMatter Course," http://www.cnn.com/2015/02/04/living/feat-dartmouth-black-lives-matter/.

26. John Bacon, "Peacefully, Madison Processes Police Shooting," *USA Today* (March 9, 2015), http://www.usatoday.com/story/news/nation/2015/03/08/madison-police-shooting-robinson/24612157/.

27. Alan Scher Zagier, "Uneasy Calm in Ferguson After Shooting of Police Officers," Associated Press, March 13, 2015, http://www.msn.com/en-us/news/us/calm-prevails-in-ferguson-after-shooting-of-police-officers/ar-AA9G992.

28. See, for example, Tierney Sneed, "Ferguson Report Prompts Resignations, Court Takeover," *U.S. News* (March 11, 2015), http://www.usnews.com/news/articles/2015/03/11/doj-ferguson-report-prompts-resignations-court-takeover.

29. Brad Heath, "Racial Gap in U.S. Arrest Rates: 'Staggering Disparity,'" *USA Today* (November 19, 2014), http://www.usatoday.com/story/news/nation/2014/11/18/ferguson-black-arrest-rates/19043207/.

30. President's Task Force on 21st Century Policing, 2015, *Interim Report of the President's Task Force on 21st Century Policing*, Office of Community Oriented Policing Services (March 4, 2015), p. 9, http://www.cops.usdoj.gov/pdf/taskforce/Interim_TF_Report.pdf.

31. Rick Hampson, Marisol Bello, and Kevin Johnson, "Nine Solutions to Fix Ferguson," *USA Today* (March 13, 2015), http://www.usatoday.com/story/news/2015/03/12/ferguson-how-to-fix-problems/70230164/.

32. BBC News, "Papua New Guinea Profile—Overview," October 7, 2015, http://www.bbc.com/news/world-asia-15592917.

33. Human Rights Watch, "World Report 2015: Papua New Guinea," https://www.hrw.org/world-report/2015/country-chapters/papua-new-guinea.

34. Shantha Bloemen, "Uniting Communities Against Domestic Violence," January 20, 2006, http://www.unicef.org/png/reallives_4136.html.

35. The Leadership Conference, *Lessons from Ferguson, Missouri—The Need for Sensible Law Enforcement Reform* (n.d.), http://www.civilrights.org/publications/reports/civil-rights-act-report-december-2014/lessons-from-ferguson.html.

36. Ibid.

37. See Dallas Police Department, http://dallaspolice.net/ois/docs/narrative/2013/OIS_2013_311475A.pdf.

38. Amanda Yeager, "As Baltimore Grapples with Police-Community Relations, Columbia Pastor Returns to Ferguson," *Baltimore Sun* (May 5, 2015), http://www.baltimoresun.com/news/maryland/howard/columbia/ph-ho-cf-david-anderson-0507-20150504-story.html#page=1.

39. Quoted in "Do Cops Need College?" *Michigan State University Today* (February 15, 2015), http://msutoday.msu.edu/news/2015/do-cops-need-college/.

40. Kevin Johnson, Meghan Hoyer, and Brad Heath, "Local Police Involved in 400 Killings per Year," *USA Today* (August 15, 2014), http://www.usatoday.com/story/news/nation/2014/08/14/police-killings-data/14060357/.

41. Kevin Johnson, "Panel to Consider Tracking of Civilians Killed by Police," *USA Today* (December 12, 2014), http://www.usatoday.com/story/news/nation/2014/12/11/tracking-cop-deaths/20104193/.

42. Tracie Keesee, "Fairness and Neutrality: Addressing the Issue of Race in Policing," *The Police Chief* (March 2011), http://www.policechiefmagazine.org/magazine/index.cfm?fuseaction=display_arch&article_id=2334&issue_id=32011.

43. Ibid.

44. Richard N. Holden, "The Technology Cycle and Contemporary Policing," paper presented at the *Annual Meeting of the Academy of Criminal Justice Sciences*, March 5, 2015, Orlando, Fla.

45. Ibid.

46. Steve Miletich and Jennifer Sullivan, "Costly Public-Records Requests May Threaten SPD Plan for Body Cameras," *Seattle Times* (November 20, 2014), http://www.seattletimes.com/seattle-news/costly-public-records-requests-may-threaten-spd-plan-for-body-cameras/.

47. Ibid.

48. Ibid.

49. Ibid.

50. ''Considering Police Body Cameras: Developments in the Law,'' 128 Harv. L. Rev. 1794, April 10, 2015, http://harvardlawreview.org/2015/04/considering-police-body-cameras/.

51. Allexperts, Greek/Aristotle Quote, http://en.allexperts.com/q/Greek-2004/2011/5/Aristotle-quote-1.htm.

52. Tracie Keesee, "Fairness and Neutrality: Addressing the Issue of Race in Policing."

53. Office of Community Oriented Policing Service, *Interim Report of the President's Task Force on 21st Century Policing* (March 2015), p. 10, http://www.cops.usdoj.gov/pdf/taskforce/Interim_TF_Report.pdf.

54. Seth Stoughton, quoted in Tim Suttle, "Wise Words from an Ex-Cop: The Police Guardian v. The Police Warrior," *Paperback Theology* (June 9, 2015), http://www.patheos.com/blogs/paperbacktheology/2015/06/wise-words-from-an-ex-cop-the-police-guardian-v-the-police-warrior.html; see also Val Van Brocklin, "Warriors vs. Guardians: A seismic shift in policing or just semantics?" *PoliceOne* (July 1, 2015), http://www.policeone.com/leadership/articles/8633970-Warriors-vs-Guardians-A-seismic-shift-in-policing-or-just-semantics/.

55. Mary Ann Viverette, "President's Message: Diversity on the Force," *The Police Chief* (December 2005), http://www.policechiefmagazine.org/magazine/index.cfm?fuseaction=display_arch&article_id=755&issue_id=122005.

56. U.S. Department of Justice, Office of Community Oriented Policing Services, *Community Policing Dispatch*, "Preparing for Crime in a Bad Economy," http://www.cops.usdoj.gov/html/dispatch/January_2009/crime_economy.htm.

57. For a comprehensive overview of early intervention systems, see Samuel Walker, *Early Intervention Systems for Law Enforcement Agencies: A Planning and Management Guide* (Washington, D.C.: Office of Community Oriented Policing Services, 2003), http://www.cops.usdoj.gov/html/cd_rom/inaction1/pubs/EarlyInterventionSystemsLawEnforcement.pdf.

58. Police Executive Research Forum, *Critical Response Technical Assessment Review: Police Accountability—Findings and National Implications of an Assessment of the San Diego Police Department* (Washington, D.C.: Office of Community Oriented Policing Services, 2015), p. ix, http://www.sandiego.gov/police/pdf/perfrpt.pdf.

59. Carolyn Kendrick and Steve Albrecht, "A Way to Identify and Help Troubled Cops," *The San Diego Union-Tribune* (May 14, 2011), http://www.sandiegouniontribune.com/news/2011/may/14/a-way-to-find-and-help-troubled-cops/; see also San Diego Police Department, *Enhancing Cultures of Integrity* (Washington, D.C.: Office of Community Oriented Policing Services, 2011), http://ric-zai-inc.com/Publications/cops-p184-pub.pdf. http://ric-zai-inc.com/Publications/cops-p052-pub.pdf.

60. Lorie A. Fridell, *Racially Biased Policing: Guidance for Analyzing Race Data from Vehicle Stops—Executive Summary* (Washington, D.C.: Police Executive Research Forum and Office of Community Oriented Policing Services, 2005), p. 1.

61. G. Voegtlin, "Bias-Based Policing and Data Collection," *The Police Chief* (October 2001):8.

Protecting the Homeland:
An International Problem for Local Police

LEARNING OBJECTIVES

As a result of reading this chapter, the student will understand:

- The many "faces" of terrorism, to include definitions and types, the threat posed by lone wolf terrorists in the United States, and the weapons of cyberterrorism and bioterrorism
- How law enforcement has had to adapt and evolve for combating terrorists
- The legislative measures that have been enacted in the war against terrorism
- Whether or not the use of unmanned aerial vehicles (drones) is legal and beneficial
- The role of local police in providing homeland security
- The general role of community policing in providing homeland security

TEST YOUR KNOWLEDGE

1. Currently, all terrorist attacks in the United States and abroad involve well-organized groups.
2. To be considered an act of terrorism, a weapon of mass destruction must have been employed.
3. Homegrown and "lone wolf" terrorists are as yet not a concern for federal authorities, as they have thus far been confined to international venues.
4. Many experts believe it is only a matter of time before chemical/biological weapons are used.
5. The FBI lists terrorism as its highest priority and is the nation's lead federal law enforcement agency for investigating and preventing acts of domestic and international terrorism.
6. Fusion centers conduct analysis and facilitate information sharing for preventing, protecting against, and responding to crime and terrorism.
7. Unquestionably, the U.S. Constitution supports our government's use of drones to strike its citizens, both here and abroad, who fit the profile of a terrorist.
8. Because of the strong and necessary federal involvement for combating terrorism, community policing has but a small role to play in homeland security.

Answers can be found on page 278.

*You will notice that the plane will stop, then will start to fly
again. This is the hour in which you will meet God.*
—FROM THE INSTRUCTION MANUAL FOR THE SUICIDE ATTACKS ON THE WORLD
TRADE CENTER, FOUND IN MUHAMMAD ATTA'S BRIEFCASE

*There is no doubt that our nation's security and defeating
terrorism trump all other priorities.*
—ARLEN SPECTER, FORMER UNITED STATES SENATOR

INTRODUCTION

Osama bin Laden is dead (killed by a team of U.S. Navy SEALs at a compound in Abbottabad, Pakistan, in April 2011), but the fight against terrorism continues. Since September 11, 2001, there has been no cessation of attempts by would-be terrorists to attack people, significant buildings, and military objects in the United States, as happened when al-Qaeda terrorists flew hijacked jets into the twin towers of the World Trade Center complex in New York City and the Pentagon in Virginia, thus bringing international terrorism to the American homeland.

This is also the age of the serious and determined terrorist, and the future of terrorism involves much more than planting a relatively harmless virus in a computer system or hacking into a major corporation's voicemail system.

Protecting our homeland requires the development of new investigative techniques, specialized training for police investigators, and employment of individuals with specialized, highly technological backgrounds. If the police are not prepared, these crimes could become the Achilles' heel of our society.

Still, we remain vulnerable. Even with all of the surveillance and countless personnel and enormous budgets now (and since 9/11) devoted to protecting our homeland, in April 2013 two homegrown, al-Qaeda-influenced brothers with online radical Islamic material and

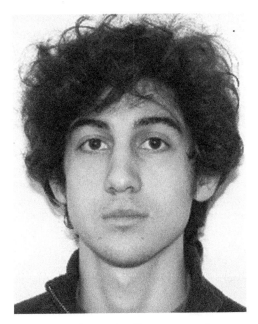

Dzhokhar and Tamerlan Tsarnaev were homegrown, al–Qaeda-influenced brothers who detonated two bombs at the Boston Marathon in April 2013, killing 3 people and injuring 264.
Lowell Sun and FBI/AP images.

bomb-making instructions detonated two bombs at the Boston Marathon (killing 3 people and injuring 264).

A December 2, 2016, holiday party at the Inland Regional Center in San Bernardino erupted in gunfire leaving 14 dead and 22 injured. According to police, U.S.-born radicalized Muslim Syed Farook, 28, and Pakistani wife Tashfeen Malik, 27, used high-powered weapons purchased by his friend and neighbor Enrique Marquez. It is alleged that Farook and Marquez abandoned a plot to attack Riverside City College in 2012. Farook and Malik were killed in a shootout with police soon after the incident. A search of the home by the FBI discovered 12 pipe bombs, 4,500 rounds, and tools for explosives. Reports also suggest that the planned attack was eerily similar to the Tsarnaev brothers' bombing in Boston.[1]

What can be done (if anything) to prevent such attacks? How has law enforcement at all levels—to include the overarching concept of community policing—evolved to cope with such determined people bent on radicalized religious fanaticism? This chapter attempts to answer those questions.

First, we consider the "many faces" of terrorism, to include definitions and types, both in the United States and abroad. Included are brief discussions of **cyberterrorism** and **bioterrorism**. Then we examine how law enforcement has had to adapt and evolve for combating terrorists, looking at what federal agencies are doing and formal programs extant for that purpose. Next is a review of **legislative measures** that have been enacted in the war against terrorism, and also whether or not the use of unmanned aerial vehicles (drones) is legal and beneficial.

The role of local police is then covered, including the need for their ongoing vigilance and having plans in place so as to respond efficiently to terrorist attacks, and finally we discuss the general role of community policing in this war against terrorists.

THE MANY FACES OF TERRORISM

Definitions and Types

The Federal Bureau of Investigation (FBI) succinctly defines terrorism as the "unlawful use of force against persons or property to intimidate or coerce a government, the civilian population, or any segment thereof, in furtherance of political or social objectives."[2] More broadly, terrorism can be both *domestic* and *international* in nature; definitions for both are provided in the United States Code.[3]

As has been demonstrated in the United States, terrorist acts can take many forms and do not always involve bombs and guns; as examples, environmental and animal activists seek to further their agendas by burning greenhouses, tree farms, logging sites, ski resorts, and mink farms. Terrorist acts are also perpetrated by hate-filled white supremacists, and anti-government **extremists** and radical separatist groups.

Homegrown Violent Extremists

Also of particular concern today are **homegrown violent extremists** (HVEs, such as the Boston bombers mentioned above), who encourage, endorse, condone, justify, or support the commission of a violent criminal act in order to achieve a political, ideological, religious, social, or economic goal. Homegrown violent extremists can include U.S.-born citizens, naturalized citizens, green card holders or other long-term residents, foreign students, or illegal immigrants wishing to commit terrorist acts inside Western countries or against Western interests abroad. Some might have been inspired by calls by the Islamic State of Iraq and the Levant (ISIL) for individual jihadists in the West to retaliate for U.S.-led airstrikes on ISIL.[4]

According to Michael Morell, twice an acting director of the Central Intelligence Agency, there is now a compelling threat from the Islamic State (ISIS) on U.S. soil: 3,500 to 5,000 "jihadist wannabes" have traveled from the United States, Western Europe, Canada, and other countries to Syria and Iraq to gain battlefield experience and have easy access to the U.S. homeland (part of at least 20,000 foreign nationals from about 90 countries who have joined ISIS). Morell states that while an attack in the United States from such fighters at the direction of ISIS has not yet occurred, "... it will." Indeed, in November 2014 an individual with sympathies for ISIS attacked two New York City police officers with a hatchet.[5]

Aliases:
Abu Muhammad, Abu Fatima, Muhammad Ibrahim, Abu Abdallah, Abu al-Mu'iz, The Doctor, The Teacher, Nur, Ustaz, Abu Mohammed, Abu Mohammed Nur al-Deen, Abdel Muaz, Dr. Ayman al Zawahiri

DESCRIPTION

Date(s) of Birth Used:	June 19, 1951
Place of Birth:	Egypt
Height:	Unknown
Weight:	Unknown
Build:	Unknown
Hair:	Brown/Black
Eyes:	Dark
Complexion:	Olive
Sex:	Male
Citizenship:	Egyptian
Languages:	Arabic; French

An example of a "Most Wanted Terrorists" poster on the FBI Web site.
AFP/Stringer/Getty images.

The Lone Wolf and Homegrown Terrorists

In December 2015, a husband and wife wearing military-style clothing and black masks entered a Christmas party for employees of the San Bernardino, California, county health department and opened fire with two assault-style weapons, killing 14 people in what was the most deadly terrorist attack in the United States since 9/11. The man and woman were parents and college graduates, solidly middle class and *sans* criminal record, and typical homegrown jihadists. And, like all other such jihadists in the United States, they were not formally affiliated with a foreign terrorist group. Such jihadists—predominantly male (93 percent) and averaging 29 years of age—killed 45 Americans from 2010 through 2015.[6]

Of particularly serious concern at present is the self-radicalized, homegrown, and lone offender—individuals who appear ordinary but are driven to hateful attacks based on a particular set of beliefs without a larger group's knowledge or support. Recent attacks (such as that described above in San Bernardino as well as in Paris, France, in November 2015) and attempted attacks internationally and in the homeland warrant increased security, as well as increased public vigilance and awareness.

As Secretary of the Department of Homeland Security Jeh Johnson stated:

> We worry about the potential domestic-based, home-grown terrorist threat that may be lurking in our own society – the independent actor or 'lone wolf' – those who did not train at a terrorist camp or join the ranks of a terrorist organization overseas, but who are inspired at home by a group's social media, literature or extremist ideology.[7]

Community members are encouraged to recognize and report signs of potential radicalization to violence,[8] which might include individuals prominently displaying a radical Islamic jihadist (a war fought by Muslims to spread or defend their beliefs) ideology on their social media; espousing attacks on prominent symbols of the West, Christians, soldiers, and police officers; or in some other manner indicating they buy into a terrorist agenda and support radical Islamic jihad (see Exhibit 4–1).[9]

An International Problem

Meanwhile, terrorism is on the rise around the world as international terrorist groups become more adept at recruiting "foot soldiers" through the Internet and other means—and these attacks have become increasingly focused on civilian targets, with terrorists using more traditional methods of violence such as guns and hostage-taking rather than large-scale bombings.

Exhibit 4–1	How Does One Become Radicalized? The Case of Zachary Chesser

Zachary Chesser was an average high school student in northern Virginia. He participated in his high school's Gifted and Talented program, joined his high school break-dancing team, was an avid soccer player with aspirations of getting a scholarship to play in college, and worked part-time at a video rental store.

In the summer of 2008, the 18-year-old Chesser converted to Islam and quickly became radicalized, solely on the Internet. He began posting views that supported Islamist terrorist groups, watching sermons by Anwar al-Awlaki, and he exchanged e-mails with the cleric about joining Al-Shabaab. Within weeks, he had quit his job because he "objected to working at a place that rented videos featuring naked women" and became increasingly hostile to his parents.

Soon Chesser had committed himself solely to using his computer and graphics skills to contribute to and promote violent extremist messages. He also attempted to travel to Somalia with his wife to join Al-Shabaab, but was unsuccessful when his mother-in-law hid his wife's passport. Next, he uploaded a video to YouTube in which he threatened the creators of the television show South Park after an episode depicted the Prophet Muhammad dressed in a bear costume. He then attempted to join Al-Shabaab once again, but was held for questioning at the airport. A few days after being questioned, Chesser was arrested for attempting to provide material support to a terrorist organization. He pled guilty to three federal felony charges—communicating threats, soliciting violent jihadists to desensitize law enforcement, and attempting to provide material support to a designated foreign terrorist organization—and was sentenced to 25 years in federal prison.[10]

- In Paris in January 2015, two masked gunmen attacked the offices of the satirical newspaper "Charlie Hebdo." They killed 12 people and then escaped, but were killed in a standoff with police several days later.[11]
- In Nairobi, Kenya, in September 2013, gunmen attacked an upscale shopping mall, terrorizing shoppers and ultimately killing 67. The Islamist group Al-Shabaab (which is known to recruit from a large Somali population in Minnesota) claimed responsibility for the attack.[12]
- In Norway in July 2011, **lone wolf** terrorist Anders Breivik arrived at an island summer camp dressed as a police officer. He opened fire and killed 69 people—many of them children and teenagers—and injured more than 100.[13]

These and other attacks also demonstrated the need for the nation's law enforcement agencies to become much more knowledgeable about terrorists' methods here and abroad, how to predict and possibly prevent future attacks, and how to respond when terrorists do strike in the event of an attack, and to adopting a long-term broader view of protecting the homeland.[14]

Cyberterrorism—and the Asian Threat

According to INTERPOL, cybercrime is one of the fastest growing areas of crime and includes attacks against computer hardware and software, financial crimes and corruption, and abuse, in the form of grooming or "sexploitation," especially crimes against children. Cybercrime or cyberterrorism includes such activities as identity theft, attacks against computer data and systems, the distribution of child sexual abuse images, Internet auction fraud, and the penetration of online financial services, as well as the deployment of viruses, botnets, and various e-mail scams such as phishing.[15]

Unquestionably, many people around the world are now working full time in trying to hack into online data and perpetrate related crimes; these cyberattacks are not only becoming more frequent, but becoming more expensive to address as well; a recent study found that over a billion personal data records were breached in the United States in 2014—an increase of 78 percent over the previous year and, on average, an average of about 664,000 personal records per breach.[16]

The most challenging and potentially disastrous type of cybercrime—actually, cyberespionage—now being perpetrated against the United States is by Chinese hackers, who are estimated to be responsible for the theft of 50 to 80 percent of all American intellectual property and have compromised many of the nation's most sensitive advanced weapon systems, including missile defense technology and combat aircraft. It is believed that Chinese hackers have accessed designs for more than two dozen of the U.S. military's most important and expensive weapon systems (the cost to develop plans for one aircraft alone—the F-35 Joint Strike Fighter—was $1.4 trillion). Doing so enables China to understand those systems and be able to jam or otherwise disable them. The Pentagon recently concluded that another country's computer sabotage can constitute an act of war, which could eventually lead to use of military force by the United States. China's computer hacking targets also include corporate and business secrets, and there are also concerns about threats posed to U.S. nuclear reactors, banks, subways, and pipeline companies. The specter of electricity going out for days and perhaps weeks, the gates of a major dam opening

Mourners with sign saying "I am Charlie—for freedom of expression," in the aftermath of the 2015 killing of 12 people at the Charile Hebdo newspaper offices in Paris, France.
Dominique Faget/AFP/Getty Images.

suddenly and flooding complete cities, or pipes in a chemical plant rupturing and releasing deadly gas are nightmare scenarios that keep homeland security professionals awake at night.[17]

Bioterrorism

Another means of attack by terrorists involves the use of chemical/biological agents, or bioterrorism. Poisons have been used for several millennia; recent attacks using chemical/biological agents including toxins, viruses, or bacteria such as anthrax, ricin, and sarin have underscored their potential dangers and uses by terrorists today. Chemical weapons—including several types of gases—suffocate the victim immediately or cause massive burning.

Biological weapons are slower acting, spreading a disease such as anthrax or smallpox through a population before the first signs are noticed. Many experts believe it is only a matter of time before chemical/biological weapons are used like explosives have been to date. All that is required is for a toxin to be cultured and put into a spray form that can be weaponized and disseminated into the population. Fortunately, such dissemination is extremely difficult for all but specially trained individuals to make in large quantities and in the correct dosage; they are also difficult to transport because live organisms are delicate.[18]

LAW ENFORCEMENT STRATEGIES

Adapting and Evolving

Given the above nature of terrorism in all its forms, since 9/11 law enforcement agencies have certainly been compelled to adapt so as to anticipate and address such attacks. Next we discuss how the police role has changed in these regards.

Broadly speaking, the police have four means of addressing terrorism:

1. Gathering raw intelligence on the organization's structure, its members, and its plans (or potential for the use of violence).
2. Determining what measures can be taken to counter or thwart terrorist activities.
3. Assessing how the damage caused by terrorists can be minimized through rapid response and containment of the damage.
4. Apprehending and convicting individual terrorists and dismantling their organizations.[19]

More specifically, current federal, state, and local strategies for addressing terrorism would include:

- The Department of Homeland Security (DHS), which has as its founding mission the protection of the United States from terrorism, continues to work with domestic, international, and private sector partners to protect our nation against terrorist threats while simultaneously facilitating the trade and travel that is essential to our economic security. Following are more of those related efforts[20]:
  - ○ *National Terrorism Advisory System:* In 2011, the DHS replaced the color-coded alerts of the Homeland Security Advisory System with the National Terrorism Advisory System (NTAS), designed to more effectively communicate information about terrorist threats by providing timely, detailed information to the American public. It recognizes that Americans all share responsibility for the nation's security, and should always be aware of the heightened risk of terrorist attack in the United States and what they should do.[21]
  - ○ *Nationwide Suspicious Activity Reporting Initiative:* This is a collaborative effort by the U.S. Department of Homeland Security, the Federal Bureau of Investigation, and state, local, tribal, and territorial law enforcement partners to provide law enforcement with another tool to help prevent terrorism and other related criminal activity by establishing a national capacity for gathering, documenting, processing, analyzing, and sharing what is termed Suspicious Activity Reporting (SAR) information. To date, more than 229,000 frontline law enforcement personnel have received SAR training to recognize behaviors potentially related to terrorism.[22]
  - ○ The "If You See Something, Say Something" campaign, which emphasizes the importance of training frontline personnel.[23]

○ *Homeland Security Information Network (HSIN):* HSIN is a DHS-hosted tool that provides a secure, Internet-based network for real-time sharing of information between federal agencies and local first responders.[24]

○ *Grant Funding:* Since fiscal year 2003, DHS has awarded more than $36 billion in preparedness grant funding based on risk to build and sustain targeted capabilities to prevent, protect against, respond to, and recover from threats or acts of terrorism.

○ *Screening for Airline Passengers:* DHS has strengthened its in-bound targeting operations to identify high-risk travelers who are likely to be inadmissible to the United States and to recommend to commercial carriers that those individuals not be permitted to board a commercial aircraft through its Pre-Departure program.[25]

○ *Secure Flight:* DHS implemented the TSA Secure Flight program in 2010, under which DHS conducts passenger watch list matching for 100 percent of covered U.S. aircraft operator and foreign air carrier flights flying to, from, or within the United States to identify individuals who may pose a threat to aviation or national security and designate them for enhanced screening or, as appropriate, prohibit them from boarding an aircraft. TSA now vets over 14 million passengers weekly.[26]

The FBI lists terrorism as its highest priority and is the nation's lead federal law enforcement agency for investigating and preventing acts of domestic and international terrorism. It is the lead federal agency for investigating attacks involving weapons of mass destruction—those involving chemical, radiological, biological agents, or nuclear weapons. The FBI is also responsible for specific terrorism-related offenses, such as violence at airports, money laundering, attacks on U.S. officials, and others. The FBI also works closely with the Director of National Intelligence and other U.S. intelligence agencies to gather and analyze intelligence on terrorism and other security threats. It is the number one priority of the FBI to protect the United States and U.S. persons and interests around the world from terrorist attack.[27]

• *Joint Terrorism Task Forces (JTTFs):* Overseen by the FBI and located around the nation, **JTTFs** bring together more than 500 state and local agencies and 55 federal agencies (including the Department of Homeland Security, the U.S. military, Immigration and Customs Enforcement, and the Transportation Security Administration) into a single team dedicated to address terror threats of all kinds. JTTFs are essentially small cells of highly trained, locally based, investigators, analysts, linguists, and SWAT experts, who chase down leads, gather evidence, make arrests, provide security for special events, conduct training, collect and share intelligence, and respond to threats and incidents at a moment's notice.[28]

• *National Counterterrorism Center:* Within the federal government there also exists the **National Counterterrorism Center** (NCTC), which serves to integrate and analyze all intelligence pertaining to terrorism possessed or acquired by the U.S. government (except purely domestic terrorism). It then shares its knowledge, acting as a center for joint operational planning and joint intelligence, staffed by personnel from the various agencies. NCTC is staffed by personnel from multiple departments and agencies from across the Intelligence Community. NCTC is organizationally part of the Office of the Director of National Intelligence.[29]

The U.S. Department of Homeland Security promotes an "If You See Something, Say Something" campaign, which emphasizes the importance of training frontline personnel.

Courtesy Department of Homeland Security.

- *Fusion Centers:* State and major urban area **fusion centers** serve as focal points within the state and local environment for the receipt, analysis, gathering, and sharing of threat-related information between the federal government and state, local, tribal, and other agencies. Located in states and major urban areas throughout the country, fusion centers conduct analysis and facilitate information sharing while assisting law enforcement and homeland security partners in preventing, protecting against, and responding to crime and terrorism.[30]

OTHER APPROACHES IN THE LAW ENFORCEMENT TOOLKIT

Legislative Measures

Another tool in the police toolbox for addressing terrorism involves enacting legislation to assist in the effort. Discussed next are three such legislative enactments.

Immediately after the 9/11 attacks, Congress passed the **USA PATRIOT Act**. A number of new investigative measures were provided to federal law enforcement agencies through the enactment of the Uniting and Strengthening America by Providing Appropriate Tools Required to Intercept and Obstruct Terrorism Act of 2001 (known as the USA PATRIOT Act) shortly after the 9/11 attacks. The Act dramatically expanded the federal government's ability to investigate Americans without establishing probable cause for "intelligence purposes" and to conduct searches if there are "reasonable grounds to believe" there may be national security threats. Federal agencies such as the FBI and others are given access to financial, mental health, medical, library, and other records. The act was reauthorized in March 2006, providing additional tools for protecting mass transportation systems and seaports from attack, the "roving wiretap" portion and the "sneak and peek" section. The first allows the government to get a wiretap on every phone a suspect uses, while the second allows federal investigators to get access to library, business, and medical records without a court order. Then, in June 2015, Congress extended the Act through 2019, but amended it to stop the National Security Agency from continuing its mass phone data collection program.[31]

Also aiding the fight against terrorism is the **Military Commissions Act** (MCA), which allows the president to establish military commissions to try unlawful enemy combatants; the commissions are also authorized to sentence defendants to death, and defendants are prevented from invoking the Geneva Conventions as a source of rights during commission proceedings. The law contains a provision stripping detainees of the right to file habeas corpus petitions in federal court and also allows hearsay evidence to be admitted during proceedings, so long as the presiding officer determines it to be reliable. This law also allows the Central Intelligence Agency (CIA) to continue its program for questioning key terrorist leaders and operatives—a program felt by many to be one of the most successful intelligence efforts in U.S. history.[32]

Finally, while the **Posse Comitatus Act of 1878** prohibits using the military to execute the laws domestically, the military may be called on to provide personnel and equipment for certain special support activities, such as domestic terrorist events involving weapons of mass destruction. Furthermore, President George W. Bush directed the Department of Homeland Security secretary to develop and administer a National Incident Management System (NIMS). This system provides a consistent nationwide approach for federal, state, and local governments to work effectively together to prepare for, prevent, respond to, and recover from domestic incidents. All federal departments and agencies must adopt and use the NIMS, and its use by state and local agencies is a condition for federal preparedness assistance.[33]

Use of Unmanned Aerial Vehicles: How to Balance Security and Privacy

Another rapidly emerging issue in the fight against terrorism is the use of drones, also known as **unmanned aerial vehicles** (UAVs). These powered aerial vehicles are directed by a ground or airborne controller, do not carry human operators, and are designed to carry nonlethal payloads for reconnaissance, command and control, and deception. UAVs are available in a variety of shapes, sizes, and capabilities, from one that is about the size and appearance of a hummingbird and carrying a tiny camera to another the size of a jumbo airplane.[34] Drones are also proliferating;

you be the... JUDGE

Police Use of Drones

More local law enforcement agencies are using drones and only 14 states have passed privacy legislation regulating how such agencies can use drones (including requiring officers to obtain a search warrant before using drones for surveillance). Some observers describe the relative lawless time in which drone technology is emerging as a "wild west" for law enforcement.[37]

Assume you are an advisor to a presidential panel that is to make recommendations for police use of UAVs/drones, and respond to the following questions:

- Would you support police use of drones for surveillance purposes involving serious offenses? If so, for what crime-related purposes?
- Would you allow the police to use drones for Fourth Amendment (searches and seizures) types of operations, if legal conditions have been met?
- Do you endorse using drones for lower-level functions, such as catching traffic speeders?
- Would your panel be in favor of arming the drones with bullets or tear gas?
- Do you believe drones should be used, without prior consent from any courts or other oversight body, for killing persons whose "profile" indicates they are a dangerous threat to security?

indeed, nearly 300,000 drone owners registered their small aircraft in the first 30 days after the Federal Aviation Administration (FAA) introduced an online registration system in December 2015, for a mere $5 fee.[35]

Drones would seem to be tailor-made for seeking out and surveilling persons who are planning or involved in terroristic activities. However, the issue concerning use of drones came to the forefront in early 2013 during Senate confirmation hearings for President Obama's nominee to head the CIA, John Brennan. A U.S. Department of Justice (DOJ) memo came to light in which the DOJ supported Obama's legal authority to use drones as mentioned above—to target American citizens whose behavior conforms to a particular profile and are working with al-Qaeda—but with little or no oversight by Congress or the judicial system. What is evident from the hearings is that Americans are very suspicious of—and may demand that legal criteria be established for—the overflights of drones in this country as we have deployed them over Pakistan and other countries. Clearly these are vexing security and privacy issues that our government and society must resolve, and each day the U.S. criminal justice system is closer and closer to the day when it will likewise be embroiled in those same issues.[36]

THE ROLE OF LOCAL POLICE

Need for Vigilance

In March 2015, firefighters in a Western city responded to a report of a firebomb at a fast-food restaurant. Upon arrival, they observed a broken window, a flammable material inside, and the initials "ALF" written on a drive-through sign. Recognizing the signs of possible domestic terrorism (ALF are the initials of the Animal Liberation Front, at times a very violent group in its advocacy for anything they suspect involves animal cruelty), the firefighters immediately secured the scene and contacted the Federal Bureau of Investigation.

This incident clearly demonstrates the need of all public safety first responders—police, fire, medical, military, health, and so on—to be vigilant in identifying the signs of terrorism in today's post-9/11 society. Although the role of the federal Department of Homeland Security was discussed above, here a brief examination is provided of the role of local police (municipal police and county sheriff's personnel) in protecting the homeland—a very daunting task for a nation with 3.79 million square miles, about 3,000 counties, and 2,500 cities with 10,000 or more people.[38]

Notwithstanding the many acts of terrorism committed in the United States since 9/11, described above and shown in Table 4–1, most such acts are foiled, such as attempts to place bombs near public facilities or send harmful chemicals through the mail. This is not by accident; it is widely recognized that local police are key in terms of being the eyes and ears in the U.S. counterterrorism effort. New York City Police Chief William Bratton argues that local police also know which targets are more at risk and are best equipped to coordinate the first response to attacks. Furthermore, because they are experienced in conducting investigations, well schooled in community policing and problem solving, and thus possess a vast network of contacts in the community, local police are well positioned to deal with terrorist networks.[39]

Today's police agencies must not ask *whether* another terroristic attack will occur on U.S. soil, but rather *when* it will occur. They must consider the possibility of attacks by weapons of mass destruction (WMD), including biological, nuclear, or radiological devices. And, depending on their location, they must plan for the possibility that the risk of attack is high if their community has historically significant assets (e.g., Independence Hall in Philadelphia, the Alamo in San Antonio); is a center of tourism (e.g., Las Vegas); is a state capital or a major commercial, manufacturing, or financial center (e.g., Wall Street); is near a port of entry; is the site of animal research facilities; is near a large military base; or is a major site for petroleum refineries, nuclear facilities, or a transportation hub.[40]

Having Plans in Place

A primary need for local police agencies is to inculcate an organizational culture that will accept and respond to the need for terrorism preparedness so that the agency achieves a state of operational readiness. While each community stands alone in its needs and vulnerabilities and thus it is not possible to have a "cookie-cutter" approach to terrorism readiness, being prepared minimally involves activities in three categories: processes, resources, and personnel.

1. *Processes:* Terrorism preparedness involves putting in place necessary policies and procedures that address the need for communicating, planning, and training as they involve terroristic threats.
2. *Resources:* This entails acquiring the essential equipment, databases, and other assets for terrorism preparedness (while also avoiding unnecessary duplication of services and, often, joining with other agencies toward a regionalized approach).
3. *Personnel:* While it is important to emphasize that increasing personnel alone does not improve preparedness, the data analysis and related functions required for the above processes and resources functions require a minimal number of staffing in an agency.[41] In addition, police executive staff should ensure that intelligence data are collected and analyzed, limit access to and parking near critical facilities, have personnel and the community be alert for suspicious packages, monitor all municipal reservoirs and wastewater treatment plants, and ensure that such related assets as command posts, public information, officer shift modification and family assistance, and equipment are in place.[42]

Finally, when an attack does occur, local police must ensure that:

- Ingress and egress from the attack site are managed, so that emergency vehicles can get to and from the scene and victims can be evacuated.
- Community policing remains in place, not only so that officers can take the lead in coordinating efforts against vigilantism, but also to reach out to Islamic and Arabic communities for information or help in developing informants.
- Manage and share information (not only with the public, but also with other assisting police, fire, military, and medical units), and give accurate instructions.[43]

Engaging the Community and Using Social Media

There are no visual or physical cues—such as dress, location, or size—that automatically identify someone as a violent extremist to law enforcement. For instance, someone taking a picture may be plotting an attack, or they may be a tourist. However, community members are well situated to help counter this "blend" factor by recognizing things that are out of the ordinary. By providing programs that engage the community and raise their awareness of potential indicators of radicalization to violence and of the different ways they can contact authorities to report such situations, the community can contribute to enhancing safety and violent extremists will have a more difficult time blending in with the population. Civilians and volunteers within the department can provide law enforcement with valuable insight into ways to begin to reach out and engage the community.[44]

Community members can be made aware of the common indicators of radicalization to violence through educational campaigns and partnerships; when properly educated, parents, teachers, and peers will be in a better position to recognize early signs of radicalization to homegrown violent extremism.

Extremists also often try to recruit youth, whom they see to be the most vulnerable, for homegrown violent extremism. Thus, law enforcement's attempts to engage youth in positive relationships provide an opportunity to counter the message offered by homegrown violent extremism. Offering programs—such as police athletic leagues, youth police academies, and youth advisory councils—and sponsoring youth-specific events help law enforcement to potentially offset the allure of radicalization for some vulnerable youth.

THE ROLE OF COMMUNITY POLICING

Building Trust

Community policing could play an integral role in homeland security. As discussed in Chapter 2, community policing helps to build trust between the community and law enforcement, which allows officers to develop knowledge of the community and resident activity and can provide vital intelligence relating to potential terrorist actions. Problem-solving process typically used in community policing (discussed later, in Part III) are well suited for preventing and responding to possible terrorist activity. Using existing data sources, agencies can conduct target vulnerability assessments and develop risk management and crisis plans (see Exhibit 4–2).[45]

As early as 2002, a Markle Foundation Task Force report stated:

> Most of the real frontlines of homeland security are outside of Washington D.C. Likely terrorists are often encountered, and the targets they might attack are protected, by local officials—a cop hearing a complaint from a landlord, an airport official who hears about a plane some pilot trainee left on the runway, an FBI agent puzzled by an odd flight school student in Arizona, or an emergency room resident trying to treat patients stricken by an unusual illness.[46]

Exhibit 4–2	*Partnerships and Information Sharing: The Case of Khalid Ali-M Aldawsari*

The case of Khalid Ali-M Aldawsari demonstrates the necessity for partnerships and information sharing between law enforcement and private businesses. Aldawsari had attempted to purchase a toxic chemical from a company in North Carolina. Because of the quantity he sought to purchase, officials from the company were suspicious; in addition, the shipping address was that of a freight company in Texas. The chemical company reported the purchase to the local FBI office in Greensboro, North Carolina, while the freight company contacted the Lubbock (Texas) Police Department after receiving a call from Aldawsari. During the call, he indicated that a package would be arriving and requested that the company hold the package until he could pick it up. Employees noted that Aldawsari had no previous relationship of any kind with the company. Taking note of the frequency of law enforcement and private business contacts, a Joint Terrorism Task Force (JTTF) opened an investigation. Aldawsari later tried to order chemicals from a company in Georgia, but that company also became suspicious. JTTF was also able to confirm that Aldawsari was not a university student as he claimed to be; nor was he conducting research that would require the chemicals he was attempting to purchase. In short, his plot was foiled, and he was convicted by a federal jury in June 2012 of one count of attempted use of a weapon of mass destruction and sentenced to life in prison.[47]

In a more recent report, the Rockefeller Institute observed that "while much attention has been focused on the national government's efforts to address these [Homeland Security] problems, there has been less consideration of the role of state and local governments, which play a critical role in preventing and responding to terrorist attack."[48]

There are a number of community policing practices that can support efforts in homeland security. These practices include adopting the philosophy organization-wide, decentralizing decision making and accountability, fixing geographic and general responsibilities, and utilizing volunteer resources. Local law enforcement officers are most likely to come into contact with individuals who are either directly or indirectly involved in terrorist activities and are certain to be the first responders to any attack.

Empowering officers at lower levels with greater decision-making authority and responsibility for important decisions could be valuable in a crisis. During a terrorist event, there may be little time for decisions to move up the chain of command. Officers who are accustomed to making decisions and retaining authority may be better prepared to respond quickly and decisively to any event.

Developing Programs and Using Social Media

Many agencies have formally entered into the use of community policing to protect their own "homeland," by developing solid programs. Following are a few examples.

In Boston, Massachusetts, the PortWatch program is a collaboration between public and private stakeholders to ensure public safety in and around the Port of Boston. The program was established by the chief of the Massport Police (part of the Massachusetts State Police). Partners include federal, state, and local law enforcement and regulatory agencies; private corporate security stakeholders and other private companies; and community representatives. These entities share relevant information and intelligence, which includes current trends in local, national, and international criminal or terrorist activity that may be relevant to the Port and its surrounding areas; upcoming significant events; and any operations that may impact daily routines. Law enforcement also works with private security directors to develop security awareness programs that are tailored to each company that is a part of the program. In addition, PortWatch includes a training component, building on the federal "See Something, Say Something" campaign (discussed above). Employees of area hotels, restaurants, and other "soft targets" are taught how to recognize and assess suspicious behaviors, as part of enhancing the safety and security of the Port of Boston and surrounding communities.[49]

Another innovative approach has been collaboratively taken by the Los Angeles Police Department (LAPD) and the Los Angeles County Sheriff's Department (LASD), which together provide officers and deputies with some of the most comprehensive CVE training. All LAPD officers and LASD deputies are trained as Terrorism Liaison Officers, attending courses on criminal networks as they pertain to terrorism and money laundering schemes as well as extremist ideologies, in order to conduct critical analyses to help eliminate any inflammatory material and damaging instruction being taught about certain religions and individuals. The two agencies partnered with the Muslim Public Affairs Council to develop a training video for officers and deputies regarding Muslim contacts. In addition, all recruits must complete cultural competency courses that cover cultural sensitivities, common greetings in different languages, key principles and promising practices for law enforcement, and differences between religions and sects of the same religion. Furthermore, the LAPD partnered with regional representatives of the Anti-Defamation League to ensure that all of the training modules were developed with civil rights and civil liberties in mind. Site visits to places of worship are also conducted to further enhance law enforcement's understanding of the community and to build networks with attendees.[50]

Law enforcement agencies can also engage and communicate with residents through **social media**. Agencies can post questions and encourage comments as a way to solicit tips and feedback and engage in dialogue with community members. Agencies can encourage residents to play an active role in addressing crime and disorder in their neighborhood by disseminating information about unsolved crimes and crime trends in the community on social media sites, effectively creating force multipliers. More information can be obtained concerning how law enforcement can use social media to engage community members by visiting the IACP Center for Social Media at www.IACPSocialMedia.org.[51]

Summary

This chapter has described how and why, in stark terms, we are no longer safe in America. There are simply countless radical individuals, living both here and abroad, who wish at the least to do us harm and even see us dead. Their reasoning is either grounded in religion or politics: they wish to compel democratic countries such as the United States and its allies to withdraw their military forces from territories that terrorists view as their homeland. In addition, such radical militants do not like our culture, our freedom, our government, our incursions into other countries abroad to attempt to spread democracy, or anything about us, and they will use any means available to them to hurt us if they can.

The duty thus falls to law enforcement agencies at all levels to develop the knowledge, means, and ability to protect us from such individuals. This chapter has set forth in brief terms how those agencies are attempting to go about that task.

Key Terms and Concepts

Bioterrorism	Homegrown violent	Legislative measures	Posse Comitatus Act of 1878
Cyberterrorism	extremists	Lone wolf	Social media
Extremists	Joint Terrorism Task Forces	Military Commissions Act	Unmanned aerial vehicles
Fusion center	(JTTFs)	National Counterterrorism Center	USA PATRIOT Act

Items for Review

1. What is the definition of terrorism, per the FBI?
2. Explain why domestic, "lone wolf" extremists are of particular concern today.
3. Describe how a person becomes radicalized, using as an example the Zachary Chesser case study.
4. Review the kinds of activities cybercriminals engage in—and China's suspected role in cyberterrorism.
5. Explain why those who would use bioterrorism to attack the United States have thus far been largely unsuccessful.
6. Delineate law enforcement's four means of addressing terrorism.
7. What are some specific efforts employed by Department of Homeland Security, FBI, and Joint Terrorism Task Forces to combat terrorism?
8. What are fusion centers?
9. Describe the roles that are played by the USA PATRIOT Act, Military Commissions Act, and Posse Comitatus Act of 1878 in combatting terrorism.
10. Explain the roles that are played by each of the following in combatting terrorism:

    Drones
    Local police
    Community policing
    Social media.

Learn by Doing

1. Terrorists would prefer to attack critical targets—several of which exist in nearly any city or county. You, as a lieutenant in your local police agency, have been assigned to work in your countywide fusion center. The captain who oversees the unit informs you that your first task is to identify all critical targets; then, once identified, the center must consider responses for the time when a terrorist attack or other significant event occurs.
    a. What types or categories of critical infrastructure should concern you?
    b. What structures in your county do you feel should be listed as critical targets?
    c. Might local politics come into play when developing this list, especially if someone's business is (or is not) included? If so, how will you deal with it?
    d. What should your fusion center do once this list is compiled?
2. You are a small-town police chief. Early one morning—although you don't yet know it—a man rows his small fishing boat, containing a duffel bag and two fishing rods, down the remote side of a river that runs through your city. After a slow, 30-minute ride, the fisherman approaches the dam's spillway. He then removes four interconnected backpacks from the duffel bag and lowers them into the water along the sloping spillway. A button on a control device is depressed, and a large explosion is heard for miles. The underwater explosion blows a massive hole in the earthen wall, leading to a huge avalanche of water carving a wide chasm in the dam. Within minutes, the first call of the dam break reaches you; a frantic scramble ensues as media and emergency rescue teams begin to alert everyone living downstream. Reports are also quickly coming in about people drowning near the dam. People are in a state of panic and trying frantically to escape. Several miles of roads have been wiped out.

    Your task: Consider the kinds of advance planning that should have been done to prepare for such a situation. Also, what would be the initial duties and responsibilities of law enforcement and other first-response personnel? The types of technologies and equipment needed? Public information responsibilities? What multiagency coordination must be accomplished?
3. To better grasp the methods of, and problems confronted by, federal/state law enforcement agencies and local police departments, you

could do no better than to seek out and interview those individuals who work in these arenas on a daily basis. Better yet, if your interests are keen in any one of these areas, you could attempt to accomplish a university-sponsored internship with one of those agencies or,

perhaps, offer to volunteer your time at the agency (be forewarned, however: either of these latter objectives may not be accommodated by these agencies or, if so, would no doubt involve a thorough and lengthy background check prior to your being accepted).

Endnotes

1. Jack Dolan, Paul Pringle, and Stephen Ceasar, "San Bernardino Shooting Suspect Traveled to Saudi Arabia, Was Married, Appeared to Be Living 'American Dream,' Co-workers Say," *Los Angeles Times* (December 2, 2015), http://www.latimes.com/local/lanow/la-me-ln-syed-farook-had-traveled-to-saudi-arabia-married-appeared-to-live-american-dream-co-workers-say-20151202-story.html.

2. Federal Bureau of Investigation, "What We Investigate," https://www.fbi.gov/albuquerque/about-us/what-we-investigate.

3. 18 U.S.C. § 2331 states that international terrorism involves: violent acts or acts dangerous to human life that violate federal or state law; that appear to be intended (i) to intimidate or coerce a civilian population; (ii) to influence the policy of a government by intimidation or coercion; or (iii) to affect the conduct of a government by mass destruction, assassination, or kidnapping; and occur primarily outside the territorial jurisdiction of the U.S., or transcend national boundaries in terms of the means by which they are accomplished, the persons they appear intended to intimidate or coerce, or the locale in which their perpetrators operate or seek asylum.

    Domestic terrorism includes activities that: involve acts dangerous to human life that violate federal or state law; appear intended to intimidate or coerce a civilian population; to influence the policy of a government by intimidation or coercion; or to affect the conduct of a government by mass destruction, assassination, or kidnapping; and occur primarily within the territorial jurisdiction of the U.S.

4. See Michael Steinbach, Assistant Director, Counterterrorism Division, Federal Bureau of Investigation, *Statement Before the House Committee on Homeland Security, Washington, D.C.* (February 11, 2015), https://www.fbi.gov/news/testimony/the-urgent-threat-of-foreign-fighters-and-homegrown-terror; also see U.S. Department of Justice Office of Community Oriented Policing Services, *Awareness Brief: Homegrown Violent Extremism* (2014), http://ric-zai-inc.com/Publications/cops-w0738-pub.pdf.

5. Michael Morell, "The Gathering Threat," *Time* (May 25, 2015), pp. 20–21.

6. Peter Bergen, "Can We Stop Homegrown Terrorists?" *The Wall Street Journal* (January 23–24, 2016), pp. C1–C2.

7. U.S. Department of Homeland Security, "Remarks by Secretary of Homeland Security Jeh Johnson at the Canadian American Business Council at the Canadian American Business Council," October 1, 2014, http://www.dhs.gov/news/2014/10/01/remarks-secretary-homeland-security-jeh-johnson-canadian-american-business-council.

8. U.S. Department of Homeland Security, National Terrorism Advisory System, "Bulletin," December 16, 2015, https://www.dhs.gov/ntas/advisory/ntas_15_1216_0001.

9. Matthew Clark, "There's No Such Thing as a 'Self-Radicalized' Islamic Terrorist," American Center for Law and Justice (n.d.), http://aclj.org/jihad/self-radicalized-islamic-terrorist.

10. Majority and Minority Staff of the Senate Committee on Homeland Security and Governmental Affairs, *Zachary Chesser: A Case Study in Online Islamist Radicalization and Its Meaning for the Threat of Homegrown Terrorism* (Washington, D.C.: United States Senate, 2012).

11. "Terror in Paris: A Timeline," *CNN* (January 2015), http://www.cnn.com/2015/01/09/europe/charlie-hebdo-paris-shooting/.

12. Daniel Howden, "Terror in Westgate Mall," *The Guardian* (October 4, 2013), http://www.cnn.com/2015/01/09/europe/charlie-hebdo-paris-shooting/; see also Joyce Hackel, "In Minnesota, ISIS May Be Building on the Recruiting Networks Once Used by Other Terror Groups," *PRI* (March 27, 2015), http://www.pri.org/stories/2015-03-27/minnesota-isis-may-be-building-recruiting-networks-once-used-other-terror-groups.

13. Elisa Mala and J. David Goodman, "At Least 80 Dead in Norway Shooting," *The New York Times* (July 22, 2011), http://www.nytimes.com/2011/07/23/world/europe/23oslo.html.

14. For a comprehensive view of terroristic activities around the world, see U.S. Senate Armed Services Committee, *Worldwide Threat Assessment of the US Intelligence Community*, February 26, 2015, http://www.dni.gov/files/documents/Unclassified_2015_ATA_SFR_-_SASC_FINAL.pdf.

15. INTERPOL, "Cybercrime," http://www.interpol.int/Crime-areas/Cybercrime/Cybercrime.

16. Arjun Kharpal, "Year of the Hack? A Billion Records Compromised in 2014," *CNBC* (February 12, 2015), http://www.cnbc.com/2015/02/12/.

17. See "The World's Most Hacked," *Time* (June 8, 2015), p. 10; "Admit Nothing and Deny Everything," *The Economist* (June 8, 2013), http://www.economist.com/news/china/21579044-barack-obama-says-he-ready-talk-xi-jinping-about-chinese-cyber-attacks-makes-one (accessed June 13, 2013); Siobhan Gorman and Julian E. Barnes, "Cyber Combat: Act of War," *The Wall Street Journal* (May 30, 2011), http://online.wsj.com/article/SB10001424052702304563104576355623135782718.html (accessed June 13, 2013); Michael Riley and John Walcott, "China-Based Hacking of 760 Companies Shows Cyber Cold War," *Bloomberg Business* (December 14, 2011), http://www.bloomberg.com/news/2011-12-13/china-based-hacking-of-760-companies-reflects-undeclared-global-cyber-war.html.

18. Dana A. Shea and Frank Gottron, *Small-Scale Terrorist Attacks Using Chemical and Biological Agents: An Assessment Framework and Preliminary Comparisons*, Congressional Research Service, Report for Congress, May 20, 2004, http://www.fas.org/irp/crs/RL32391.pdf.

19. Edward J. Tully and E. L. Willoughby, "Terrorism: The Role of Local and State Police Agencies," National Executive Institute Associates, May 2002, http://www.neiassociates.org/terrorism-role-local-state-pol/.

20. See U.S. Department of Homeland Security, "Preventing Terrorism Overview," July 16, 2015, http://www.dhs.gov/topic/preventing-terrorism-overview.

21. U.S. Department of Homeland Security, "National Terrorism Advisory System," http://www.dhs.gov/national-terrorism-advisory-system.

22. Bureau of Justice Assistance, "The Nationwide SAR Initiative," https://nsi.ncirc.gov/?AspxAutoDetectCookieSupport=1.

23. U.S. Department of Homeland Security, "If You See Something, Say Something," http://www.dhs.gov/see-something-say-something.

24. U.S. Department of Homeland Security, Homeland Security Information Network (HSIN), September 23, 2015, http://www.dhs.gov/homeland-security-information-network-hsin.

25. See DHS, "Aviation Security," http://www.dhs.gov/aviation-security.

26. See ibid.; also see a TSA video of the Secure Flight program at https://www.tsa.gov/node/2271.

27. Federal Bureau of Investigation, "Frequently Asked Questions," https://www.fbi.gov/about-us/faqs.

28. Federal Bureau of Investigation, "Protecting America from Terrorist Attack: Our Joint Terrorism Task Forces," https://www.fbi.gov/about-us/investigate/terrorism/terrorism_jttfs.

29. See National Counterterrorism Center, "Who We Are," http://www.nctc.gov/; https://www.fbi.gov/about-us/investigate/terrorism.

30. U.S. Department of Homeland Security, "State and Major Urban Area Fusion Centers," http://www.dhs.gov/state-and-major-urban-area-fusion-centers.

31. Gary Peck and Laura Mijanovich, "Give Us Security While Retaining Freedoms," *Reno Gazette Journal* (August 28, 2003), p. 9A; also see "House Approves Patriot Act Renewal," http://www.cnn.com/2006/POLITICS/03/07/patriot.act.

32. Jurist: Legal News and Research, "Bush Signs Military Commissions Act," http://jurist.law.pitt.edu/paperchase/2006/10/bush-signs-military-commissions-act.php.

33. D. G. Bolgiano, "Military Support of Domestic Law Enforcement Operations: Working Within Posse Comitatus," *FBI Law Enforcement Bulletin* (December 2001), pp. 16–24.

34. Lev Grossman, "Drone Home," *Time* (February 11, 2013), pp. 26–33.

35. James Eng, "FAA Says Nearly 300,000 Drone Owners Have Registered in First 30 Days," *NBCNews.com* (January 22, 2016), http://www.nbcnews.com/tech/tech-news/faa-says-nearly-300-000-drone-owners-have-registered-first-n502201.

36. See "White House, Justice Officials Defend Drone Program After Release of Memo," Associated Press and Fox News, February 5, 2013, http://www.foxnews.com/politics/2013/02/05/senators-threaten-confrontation-with-obama-nominees-over-drone-concerns/.

37. Kaveh Waddell, "Few Privacy Limitations Exist on How Police Use Drones," *The National Journal* (February 5, 2015), http://www.nationaljournal.com/tech/few-privacy-limitations-exist-on-how-police-use-drones-20150205.

38. Michael P. Downing, "Policing Terrorism in the United States: The Los Angeles Police Department's Convergence Strategy," *The Police Chief* (February 2009), http://www.policechiefmagazine.org/magazine/index.cfm?fuseaction=display_arch&article_id=1729&issue_id=22009.

39. Graeme R. Newman and Ronald V. Clarke, *Policing Terrorism: An Executive's Guide* (Washington, D.C.: U.S. Department of Justice, Office of Community Oriented Policing Services, July 2008), http://www.popcenter.org/library/reading/pdfs/policingterrorism.pdf.

40. Ibid.

41. Jeremy W. Francis, "Increasing Terrorism Preparedness of Law Enforcement Agencies," *FBI Law Enforcement Bulletin* (December 2014), leb.fbi.gov/2014/december/increasing-terrorism-preparedness-of-law-enforcement-agencies.

42. Ibid.

43. Ibid.

44. See Jose Docobo, "Community Policing as the Primary Prevention Strategy for Homeland Security at the Local Law Enforcement Level," *Homeland Security Affairs* 1, Article 4 (June 2005), www.hsaj.org/articles/183.

45. Dennis J. Stevens, *Case Studies in Community Policing* (Upper Saddle River, N.J.: Prentice Hall, 2001); also see, generally, U.S. Office of Community Oriented Policing Services, "Homeland Security Through Community Policing," http://www.cops.usdoj.gov/Default.asp?Item=2472.

46. The Rockefeller Institute of Government, "The Federalism Challenge: The Challenge for State and Local Government," "The Role of 'Home' in Homeland Security: Symposium Series," Number 2, March 24, 2003.

47. Khalid Aldawsari, "Complaint Affidavit," *The Washington Post* (February 23, 2011), http://www.washingtonpost.com/wp-srv/world/documents/khalid-aldawsari-complaint-affidavit.html.

48. Matthew C. Scheider and Robert Chapman, "Community Policing and Terrorism," *Journal of Homeland Security* (April 2003), http://www.homelandsecurity.org/journal/articles/Scheider-Chapman.html.

49. From U.S. Department of Justice Office of Community Oriented Policing Services, *Using Community Policing to Counter Violent Extremism: 5 Key Principles for Law Enforcement* (2014), pp. 11–19, http://ric-zai-inc.com/Publications/cops-p299-pub.pdf.

50. Ibid.

51. Ibid., p. 13.

PART III

Problem-Solving Process, Programs, and Practices

This part consists of three chapters, which together set forth the formal approaches and strategies that form the community-oriented policing and problem-solving strategy now in practice by the police in the United States and abroad. Chapter 5 examines the model that has been developed for systematically engaging in problem solving; Chapter 6 looks at how the broad concept of crime prevention and its various programs and approaches can assist in problem-solving endeavors; and, finally, Chapter 7 describes the kinds of information technologies and tools that are in use for accomplishing problem-solving objectives.

Problem Solving:
A Process Model

LEARNING OBJECTIVES

As a result of reading this chapter, the student will understand:

- How and why problem solving was developed for the police, and how it changes the role of the street officer
- The four steps in the SARA problem-solving process, including their role, tools, and methods for each
- The potential difficulties with problem-solving efforts
- The different types of neighborhoods, and tailoring strategies for each

TEST YOUR KNOWLEDGE

1. Problem solving by police is new, with their only recently learning how to solve community problems.
2. It may be said that problem-oriented policing is a strategy that puts the philosophy of community policing into practice.
3. When engaged in problem solving, Goldstein argued that police should not conduct an extensive, uninhibited search for the most effective response to problems; doing so requires too much time and too many resources.
4. The heart of any problem-solving effort by police is analysis, which is critical to the success of any problem-solving effort.
5. All neighborhoods are essentially the same, so the same problem-solving efforts can be deployed anywhere.

Answers can be found on page 278.

The significant problems of our time cannot be solved by the same level of thinking that created them.

ALBERT EINSTEIN

INTRODUCTION

This chapter, in tandem with the discussion in Chapter 2 concerning community policing, represents the heart and soul of this book. We examine problem solving: its origin and operation, and the four-stage process that rests at its core. Included in this discussion is an overview of some possible difficulties that are involved with problem solving and how different types of neighborhoods require different approaches by the police in terms of overall strategies.

As we noted in Chapter 2, although the concepts of community-oriented policing and problem solving are often treated as separate and distinct entities, we maintain here and throughout the remainder of the book that they are complementary core components. Note also that there are several important adjuncts to community policing and problem solving, including situational crime prevention, crime prevention through environmental design (CPTED), technologies, crime analysis, and mapping. Those topics are addressed in Chapters 6 and 7.

PROBLEM SOLVING: RATIONALIZATION AND APPLICATION

Early Beginnings

Problem solving is not new; police officers have always tried to solve problems (we define the word "problem" for policing purposes below). The difference is that, in past eras of policing, officers who were dealing with problems did not have an in-depth understanding of the nature and underlying causes of those crime problems, nor receive much guidance, support, or sophisticated methods (e.g., crime analysis or mapping tools) to support their efforts. The routine application of problem-solving techniques is new. It is based on two facts: that problem solving can be applied by officers throughout the agency as part of their daily work and that routine problem-solving efforts can be effective in reducing or resolving problems.

Problem-oriented policing was grounded in principles different from community-oriented policing, but, again, they are complementary (see Figure 5–1). Problem-oriented policing is a strategy that puts the philosophy of community policing into practice. It advocates that police examine the underlying causes of recurring incidents of crime and disorder. The problem-solving process, discussed in later chapters, helps officers to identify problems, analyze them completely, develop response strategies, and assess the results.

Figure 5–1 highlights problem solving among the three key components of community policing and problem solving.

Community Partnerships
Collaborative partnerships between the law enforcement agency and the individuals and organizations they serve to develop solutions to problems and increase trust in police

Organizational Transformation
The alignment of organizational management, structure, personnel, and information systems to support community partnerships and proactive problem solving

Problem Solving
The process of engaging in the proactive and systematic examination of identified problems to develop and evaluate effective responses

FIGURE 5–1   Problem Solving Comprises One of the Three Key Components

Herman Goldstein is considered by many to be the principal architect of problem-oriented policing. His book, *Policing a Free Society* (1977),[1] is among the most frequently cited works in police literature. A later work, *Problem Oriented Policing* (1990),[2] provided a rich and complete exploration of the strategy. Goldstein first coined the term "problem-oriented policing" in 1979 out of frustration with the dominant model for improving police operations: "More attention [was] being focused on how quickly officers responded to a call than on what they did when they got to their destination."[3] He also bemoaned the linkage between the police and the telephone: "The telephone, more than any public or internal policy, dictates what a police agency does. And that problem has been greatly aggravated with the installation of 911."[4]

As a result, Goldstein argued for a radical change in the direction of efforts to improve policing—a new framework that should help move the police from their past preoccupation with form and process to a much more direct, thoughtful concern with substantive problems. To focus attention on the nature of police business and to improve the quality of police response in the course of their business, Goldstein argued that several steps must be taken[5]:

1. Police must be equipped to define more clearly and to understand more fully the problems they are expected to handle. They must recognize the relationships between and among incidents—for example, incidents involving the same behavior, the same address, or the same people.
2. The police must develop a commitment to analyzing problems. It requires gathering information from police files, from the minds of experienced officers, from other agencies of government, and from private sources as well. It requires conducting house-to-house surveys and talking with victims, complainants, and offenders.
3. Police must be encouraged to conduct an uninhibited search for the most effective response to each problem, looking beyond just the criminal justice system to a wide range of alternatives; they must try to design a customized response that holds the greatest potential for dealing effectively with a specific problem in a specific place under specific conditions.

John Eck and William Spelman advanced Goldstein's work by providing officers with a practical tool and process for analyzing and responding to recurring problems, termed **SARA** (for scanning, analysis, response, and assessment). In one of the first experiments problem solving occurred in Newport News, Virginia, SARA tested whether officers throughout a police agency could apply problem-solving techniques as part of their daily routine and whether problem-solving efforts were effective. Measurable outcomes showed that officers guided by the SARA process were successful in their responses to apartment burglaries, robberies, and theft from vehicles. These findings supported further experimentation and funding for agencies implementing problem-solving efforts.[6]

Basic Principles

In earlier chapters, we mentioned several limitations of traditional policing methods in trying to deal with incidents. The first step in problem solving, therefore, is to move beyond just handling each incident separately (see Figure 5–2) and recognizing that incidents are often merely overt symptoms of problems and require that officers take a more in-depth interest in incidents by acquainting themselves with some of the conditions and factors that cause them. Everyone in the department contributes to this mission, not just a few innovative officers or a special unit or function.[7]

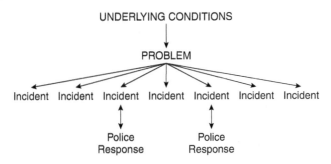

FIGURE 5–2 Incident-Driven Policing

Source: John E. Eck and William Spelman, *Problem-Solving: Problem-Oriented Policing in Newport News* (Washington, D.C.: U.S. Department of Justice, National Institute of Justice, 1987), p. 4.

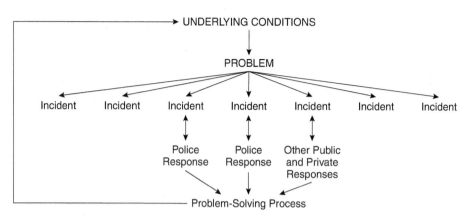

FIGURE 5–3   Problem-Oriented Policing

Source: John E. Eck and William Spelman, *Problem-Solving: Problem-Oriented Policing in Newport News* (Washington, D.C.: U.S. Department of Justice, National Institute of Justice, 1987), p. 4.

Figure 5–2 shows **incident-driven policing** as it attempts to deal with each incident. Like band-aid application, this symptomatic relief is valuable but limited. Because police leave unresolved the underlying condition that created the incidents, the incident is very likely to occur.

A problem-solving agency would respond as described in Figure 5–3. Officers use the information in their responses to incidents, along with information obtained from other sources, to get a clearer picture of the problem. Then they address the underlying conditions. As James Fyfe asked, "Can anyone imagine the surgeon general urging doctors to attack [a disease] without giving any thought to its causes?"[8] If successful, fewer incidents may occur; those that do occur may be less serious. The incidents may even cease.[9]

The problem-solving approach also addresses a major dilemma for the police: the lack of meaningful measures of their effectiveness in the area of crime and disorder. Crime rate statistics are virtually useless because they collapse all the different kinds of crime into one global category and are an imperfect measure of the actual incidence of criminal behavior (evaluating problem-solving initiatives is discussed in Chapter 11).[10] Goldstein also maintained that the police should "disaggregate" the different problems they face and then attempt to develop strategies to address each one.[11] Domestic disturbances, for instance, should be separated from public intoxication; murder should be separated from sexual assault. In this respect, problem-oriented policing is primarily a *planning process*.

A Broader Role for the Street Officer

A major departure of POP from the conventional style lies with its view of the line officer, who is given much more discretion and decision-making ability and is trusted with a much broader array of responsibilities. The problem-solving approach values thinking officers (see

Citizen input concerning crime and disorder is essential for successful community policing and problem solving.

Photographee.eu/Shutterstock.

Chapter 10, concerning training), urging that they take the initiative in trying to deal more effectively with problems in the areas they serve. This concept more effectively uses the potential of college-educated officers, "who have been smothered in the atmosphere of traditional policing."[12] It also gives officers a new sense of identity and self-respect; they are more challenged and have opportunities to follow through on individual cases, to analyze and solve problems, which will give them greater job satisfaction. We ought to be recruiting as police officers people who can "serve as mediators, as dispensers of information, and as community organizers."[13]

Under problem solving, officers continue to handle calls, but they also do much more. They use the information gathered in their responses to incidents together with information obtained from other sources to get a clearer picture of the problem. They then address the underlying conditions.

SARA: THE PROBLEM-SOLVING PROCESS

As mentioned above, a four-stage problem-solving process has been developed known as "SARA," for *scanning*, *analysis*, *response*, and *assessment*.[14] This process is depicted in Figure 5–4.

Scanning: Problem Identification

Scanning means problem identification. As a first step, officers should identify problems on their beats and then look for a pattern or persistent repeat incidents. A problem has been defined this way: A group of two or more incidents that are similar in one or more respects, causing harm and therefore being of concern to the police and the public. Identifying and defining policing problems requires more skilled analysis than might be apparent. Some policing problems present themselves quite clearly and obviously to the police, but others do not and can easily be missed without a structured approach to scanning the environment for problems.

There are a wide range of methods for identifying policing problems, each with its own advantages and disadvantages. Consider whether each method is reliably in place in your agency's operations and administrative systems.

- *High crime call periods:* Monitoring high-call time periods is important for detecting problems. Certain time periods are notorious for the police service demands they generate: bar closing time, work commuting times, school release times, alcohol-oriented festivals, etc.
- *Repeat offender lists:* A relatively few number of offenders commit a relatively high proportion of offenses, so police must identify the most active offenders within a jurisdiction across all types of offenses and give them some sort of special attention. Generating lists of repeat offenders of certain types of crimes will also assist.

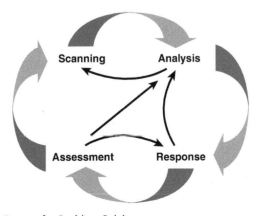

FIGURE 5–4   The SARA Process for Problem Solving

- *Repeat victim lists:* The same rationale pertains to repeat victims, but police agencies should also routinely scan their records for chronic victims who might merit some special attention to reduce their rate of victimization. As with repeat offenders and repeat call locations, they should consider generating multiple types of lists such as chronic victims of violent offenses, violence, theft, and so on.[15]

Community surveys will also be helpful in identifying problems, using a system called CHEERS which may be employed to define problems and to draw attention to the following elements of a problem:

1. *Community.* Members of the public must experience the harmful events. They include individuals, businesses, government agencies, and other groups. Only some not all or most community members need to experience the problem.
2. *Harmful.* People or institutions must suffer harm. The harm can involve property loss or damage, injury or death, serious mental anguish, or undermining the capacity of the police (as in repeat fraudulent calls for service). If such reports meet all the CHEERS criteria, they are problems.
3. *Expectation.* Some members of the community must expect the police to address the causes of the harm (their numbers do not have to be large). Expectation should never be presumed, but must be evident through processes such as citizen calls, community meetings, press reports, or other means. It is the role of analysis to uncover the causes.
4. *Events.* You must be able to describe the type of event that makes up the problem. Examples of events include a break-in at a home, one person striking another, two people exchanging money and sex, or a burst of noise. Most events are brief, though some may involve a great deal of time—some frauds, for example.
5. *Recurring.* These events must recur. Recurrence may be symptomatic of acute troubles or a chronic problem. Acute problems suddenly appear, as in the case of a neighborhood with few vehicle break-ins suddenly having many such break-ins. Chronic problems persist for a long time, as in the case of a prostitution stroll that has been located along one street for many years. Unless something is done, the events from chronic problems will continue to occur.
6. *Similarity.* The recurring events must have something in common. They may be committed by the same person, happen to the same type of victim, occur in the same types of locations, take place in similar circumstances, involve the same type of weapon, or have one or more other factors in common. Without common features, you have an arbitrary collection of events, not a problem.

CHEERS suggests that the following basic questions be answered during the scanning stage:

Who in the community is affected by the problem?

What are the harms created by the problem?

What are the expectations for the police response?

What types of events contribute to the problem?

How often do these events recur?[16]

Aggregating Incidents

It is also important to combine and examine what may appear to be isolated incidents. Looking to see if a cluster of similar incidents exists will lead to discovering a new and more effective strategy for dealing with it. Incidents may be similar in various ways:

- *Behaviors.* A pattern of behavior is the most frequent type of indicator and includes such activities as drug sales, robberies, thefts, and graffiti.
- *Locations.* Problems occur in hot spots, such as downtown cruising areas, housing complexes plagued by burglaries, and parks where gangs commit crimes.
- *Persons.* They can be repeat offenders or victims; both account for a high proportion of crime.

- *Times.* There may be a time pattern (e.g., seasonal, day of week, hour of day) due to traffic congestion, closing times for bars, or tourist activity.
- *Events.* Crimes may peak during such events as university spring breaks, rallies, and rock concerts.

At some point, a determination must be made concerning the appropriate level of aggregation at which to examine and address a public safety problem. For instance, assume that crime analysts detect a high number of burglaries occurring in a large apartment complex, and these burglaries have been occurring over a lengthy period of time. Here, a decision must be made concerning whether to analyze and address the burglary problem only in this particular apartment complex, or to examine burglaries in other apartment complexes in that area as well. Another judgment might have to be made concerning whether to limit the scope of the inquiry to apartment complex burglaries or to expand it to include all apartment, residential, or commercial burglaries. Many policing problems could be either expanded or contracted in scope so as to incorporate more than one type of troublesome behavior, more than one group of people affected, more than one location, or more than one time period.[17] Therefore, it is important at the outset to determine what will be the length and breadth of the problem-solving effort. This is similar to what is termed in the arena of research methodology as the unit of analysis. It is important to see the forest as well as the trees, and identify what the primary goals and objectives will be. In sum, the primary purpose of scanning is to conduct a preliminary inquiry to determine if a problem really exists and whether further analysis is needed. During this stage, priorities should be established if multiple problems exist and a specific officer or team of officers assigned to handle the problem. Scanning initiates the problem-solving process.

Analysis: The Heart of Problem Solving

The second stage, **analysis**, is the heart of the problem-solving process, so we will dwell on it at greater length. Comprehensively analyzing a problem is critical to the success of a problem-solving effort. Effective tailor-made responses cannot be developed unless people know what is causing the problem. Thus, the purpose of analysis is to learn as much as possible about problems in order to identify their causes; officers must gather information from sources inside and outside their agency about the scope, nature, and causes of problems.

PRINCIPLES OF ANALYSIS. A complete analysis includes identifying the seriousness of the problem, all the persons/groups involved and affected, and all the causes of the problem and then assessing current responses and their effectiveness. One might be tempted to circumvent or give only passing attention to the analysis phase of SARA, believing that the nature of the problem is obvious, succumbing to pressure to quickly solve the problem, or feeling that the pressure of CFS precludes their having time for detailed inquiries into the nature of the problem. Problem solvers must resist these temptations, or they risk addressing a problem that does not exist and/or implementing solutions that are ineffective in the long run.

There are several considerations to remember when planning and conducting problem analysis:

- *Analysis is based on common sense:* Although good analysis will include some statistical analysis and research methodology that are not typical law enforcement activities, the process also relies on the officer's experience and ability to determine what is known about the offender, offenses, locations, and victims.
- *There is no one way to do analysis:* Done appropriately, analysis will generate valuable knowledge about the problem and suggest potential responses. There are often many ways to produce such information, using multiple analytical approaches.
- *Individual problems require individual analysis:* Because an analysis plan was successful in one location does not guarantee that it will succeed elsewhere. Much can be learned from the experiences of other jurisdictions, so it is wise to consult agencies that have encountered similar problems.

Abandoned and neglected homes and neighborhoods can quickly lead to widespread crime and disorder— all of which must be identified in a thorough crime analysis.
Jon Bilous/Shutterstock.

- *Analysis requires creativity and innovation:* Many problem solvers limit their analysis to reported incidents. Other sources should be considered, however. Incident reports typically include only information about the offense, not about the general conditions surrounding the incident. Additional sources of information that can clarify the problem include changes in usage of target areas, property values, business profits, medical data, and building occupancy rates.
- *Analysis does not need to be complex:* In most cases, simple frequencies of events, percentages of various categories, and tables showing how characteristics relate to each other (e.g., type of burglary by time of day) are sufficient for adequate analysis.

TOOLS FOR ANALYSIS. A number of tools can assist in capturing data and other information about crime and disorder problems:

- *Crime analysts:* Crime analysts can provide a great deal of assistance in collecting and analyzing data and other information about specific crime and disorder problems.
- *Records management system:* Such systems can help police collect, retrieve, and analyze information about problems. In particular, the system should be able to quickly and easily help users identify repeat calls for service relating to specific victims, locations, and offenders.
- *Mapping/geographic information systems:* These systems can illuminate patterns, help identify problem areas, and show potential links between crime hot spots and other types of establishments (ATMs, liquor stores).
- *Technical assistance:* Criminal justice practitioners who specialize in using problem solving to address specific crime problems, such as auto theft, robbery, and street-level drug dealing, can provide valuable assistance to police and community members. In addition, noncriminal justice personnel with backgrounds in a variety of areas can also aid in problem-solving efforts. For example, a mental health expert may be able to assist in

Police survey and meet with business owners to help identify and analyze problems, develop responses to problems, and assess the effectiveness of their problem-solving efforts.
Jassada Watt/Shutterstock.

assessing a community's current response to people with mental illness and help improve that response.

- *Resident/business surveys:* Such surveys can help police and community-based entities identify and analyze problems, gauge fear levels, identify preferred responses, and determine the real and perceived effectiveness of problem-solving efforts. These surveys also can help determine general and repeat victimization rates, particularly for under-reported, low-level crimes.

SEEKING "SMALL WINS." Karl Weick explained that people often look at social problems on a massive scale.[18] The public, media, elected officials, and government agencies often become fixated on problems and define them by using the simplest term (gangs, homelessness, poverty, mental illness, violent crime, and so on). Viewing problems in this manner leads to defining problems on a scale so massive that they are unable to be addressed and people become overwhelmed in their attempts. For this reason, Weick introduced the "**small wins**" concept. One must understand that some problems are too deeply ingrained or too rooted in other complex social problems to be eliminated. Conversely, however, adopting the small wins philosophy helps people to understand the nature of an analysis and a response to problems.

As indicated above, the more appropriate response to these problems is to break them down into smaller, more controllable problems. Although an individual small win may not seem important, a series of small wins may have a substantial impact on the overall problem. Eliminating the harms (graffiti, drug sales, and so on) is a sensible and realistic strategy for reducing the impact of gang behaviors. Therefore, it makes sense to address a large problem at a level where there can be a reasonable expectation of success.

The idea of small wins is also helpful when prioritizing problems and working together in a group. We have discussed the benefits of collaborating with the community and other outside agencies to address problems. Small wins can help the group understand the problem better, select realistic objectives, and formulate more effective strategies. It also helps to build confidence and trust among group members.

USING THE PROBLEM ANALYSIS TRIANGLE. Generally, three elements are needed for a problem to occur: an offender, a victim, and a location. The **problem analysis triangle** helps officers visualize the problem and understand the relationship between these three elements. Additionally, it helps officers to analyze problems, it suggests where more information is needed, and it assists with crime control and prevention.

The relationship between these three elements can be explained as follows. If there is a victim and he or she is in a place where crimes occur but there is no offender, no crime occurs. If there is an offender and he or she is in a place where crimes occur but there is nothing or no one to be victimized, then no crime will occur. If an offender and a victim are not in the same place, there will be no crime. Part of the analysis phase involves finding out as much as possible about the victims, offenders, and locations where problems exist in order to understand what is prompting the problem and what can be done about it.

The three elements must be present before a crime or harmful behaviors—problems—can occur: an *offender* (someone who is motivated to commit harmful behavior), a *victim* (a desirable and vulnerable target must be present), and a *place* (the victim and offender must both be in the same place at the same time) (see Figure 5–5). (We discuss locations in more detail below.)

FIGURE 5–5 Problem Analysis Triangle
Source: U.S. Department of Justice, Bureau of Justice Assistance, *Comprehensive Gang Initiative: Operations Manual for Implementing Local Gang Prevention and Control Programs* (Draft, October 1993), p. 3.

FIGURE 5–6   Graffiti Problem Triangle

Source: Adapted from John E. Eck, "Police Problems and Research: A Short, Furious, Concise Tour of a Complex Field." Unpublished draft 1.2, January 20, 2002, p. 4; and U.S. Department of Justice, Bureau of Justice Assistance, *Comprehensive Gang Initiative: Operations Manual for Implementing Local Gang Prevention and Control Programs* (Draft, October 2003), pp. 3–11. Used with permission.

If these three elements show up over and over again in patterns and recurring problems, removing one of these elements can stop the pattern and prevent future harms.[19]

As an example, let us apply the problem analysis triangle to the issue of graffiti, using Figure 5–6. The place is marked buildings and areas immediately around them. The victims are the owners and users of the buildings; the offenders are the writers of the graffiti (see the inside triangle of Figure 5–6; the outside triangle is discussed below). Removing one or more of these elements will remove the problem. Strategies for removing one of these elements are limited only by an officer's creativity, availability of resources, and ability to formulate collaborative responses.

Some jurisdictions, for example, are using nonadhesive paint on buildings and property (protecting locations) to discourage taggers ("offenders"). Other jurisdictions have contemplated outlawing the sale of spray paint or limiting the sale of broad-tip markers to juveniles, while still others have enacted graffiti ordinances to help business owners ("victims") to keep their locations graffiti-free.

Police engaged in problem solving need to also be aware of three types of third parties that can either help or hinder the problem-solving effort by attempting to act on behalf of one or more of the three elements discussed above in the problem analysis triangle. We will again use examples and Figure 5–6 to explain the role of third parties:

1. *Handlers.* There are people who, acting in the best interests of the potential offenders, try to prevent them from committing crimes. **Handlers** of gang members might be parents, adult neighbors, peers, teachers, and employers. However, these youths may live in a poor one-parent home or not be attending school or working. Controllers can often restrict the tools used by gang members, such as putting spray cans in locked bins, restricting the wearing of colors, and passing laws obstructing the sale of semiautomatic and automatic weapons.[20]

2. *Guardians.* There are people or things that can exercise control over each side of the triangle so that crime is less likely and are called **guardians**. For instance, if the crime problem is drug dealing in a house and the offender side of the triangle includes dealers and buyers, then a list of guardians would include police, parents of dealers/buyers, probation and parole officers, landlords, city codes, health and tax departments, and neighbors. Tools used by guardians can include crime prevention techniques.[21]

3. *Managers.* People who oversee locations are called **managers**. For example, apartment managers can help prevent or solve problems by installing security equipment in their buildings, screening tenants carefully, and evicting troublemakers or criminals. Conversely, where managers are absent or lax, risks will be higher.[22]

Police should constantly look for ways to improve the effectiveness of third parties, as these groups of individuals have the authority to deal with the problem. There will always be the temptation on the part of society to use the police as handlers, guardians, or managers. Although this may be effective for a short time, there are rarely enough officers to control a recurring problem in the long run.

We conclude our discussion of this critical analysis stage of the SARA process by noting that in Chapter 7 we examine additional technological tools—such as mapping, GPS, CompStat, and computer-aided dispatch systems—that can also be brought to bear on the analysis of crime problems.

Response: Formulating Tailor-Made Strategies

After a problem has been clearly defined and analyzed, the officer confronts the ultimate challenge in problem-oriented policing: the search for the most effective way of dealing with it. This stage of the SARA process focuses on developing and implementing a **response** to the problem. Before entering this stage, an agency must overcome the temptation to implement a response prematurely and need to be certain that it has thoroughly analyzed the problem; attempts to fix problems quickly are rarely effective in the long term.

To develop tailored responses, problem solvers should review their findings about the three sides of the crime triangle—victim, offender, and location—and develop creative solutions that will address at least two sides of the triangle.[23] It is also important to remember that the key to developing tailored responses is making sure the responses are very focused and *directly linked* to the findings from the analysis phase of the project.

Responses may be wide-ranging and often require arrests (but apprehension may not be the most effective solution), referral to social service agencies, or changes in ordinances. Potential solutions to problems can be organized into five groups.[24]

1. *Totally eliminating the problem.* Effectiveness is measured by the absence of the types of incidents that this problem creates. It is unlikely that most problems can be totally eliminated, but a few can.
2. *Reducing the number of incidents the problem creates.* A reduction of incidents stemming from a problem is a major measure of effectiveness.
3. *Reducing the seriousness of the harms.* Effectiveness for this type of solution is demonstrated by showing that the incidents are less harmful.
4. *Dealing with a problem better.* Treating participants more humanely, reducing costs, and increasing the effectiveness of handling incidents are all possible choices. Improved victim satisfaction, reduced costs, and other measures can show that this type of solution is effective.
5. *Removing the problem from police consideration.* The effectiveness of this type of solution can be measured by looking at why the police were handling the problem originally and the rationale for shifting the handling to others.

Box 5–1 provides an explanation of the possible range of responses to problems. Furthermore, because problem-solving officers must often seek the assistance of the community, other city departments, businesses, private, and social service organizations. Box 5–2 is a guide to collaboration—developing networks with people and other agencies in developing appropriate responses.

Any effort to reduce crime may result in unintended consequences. Displacement and diffusion of benefit are two issues that must be considered when responding to crime conditions and assessing results. These two issues are discussed in more detail in Chapter 6.

Assessment: Did Responses Diminish the Problem?

Finally, in the **assessment**, officers evaluate the effectiveness of their responses. During assessment, several questions should be answered: Did the problem decline? If so, did the response cause the decline? Did the response occur as planned? Did the problem decline enough for you to end the effort and apply resources elsewhere? (If the problem did not decline substantially, then the job is not done, and the police may have to reanalyze the problem and develop a new response.) In summary, the police begin planning for an evaluation when they take on a problem. The evaluation builds throughout the SARA process, culminates during the assessment, and provides findings that help to determine if they should revisit earlier stages to improve the response.[25]

A number of measures have traditionally been used by police agencies and community members to assess effectiveness. These include numbers of arrests, levels of reported crime, response times, clearance rates, citizen complaints, and various workload indicators, such as CFS and the number of field interviews conducted.[26]

BOX 5–1
Range of Possible Response Options

1. *Concentrate attention on the individuals accounting for a disproportionate share of the problem.* A relatively small number of individuals usually account for a disproportionate share of practically any problem, by causing it (offenders), facilitating it (controllers, managers, guardians), or suffering from it (victims).

2. *Connect with other government and private services.* A thorough analysis of a problem often leads to an appreciation of the need for (a) more effective referrals to existing governmental and private services, (b) improved coordination with agencies that exert control over some of the problems or individuals involved in the incidents, and (c) initiative for pressing for correction of inadequacies in municipal services and for development of new services.

3. *Use mediation and negotiation skills.* Often the use of mediation and negotiation teams can be effective responses to conflicts.

4. *Convey information.* Relating sound and accurate information is one of the least used responses. It has the potential, however, to be one of the most effective for responding to a wide range of problems. Conveying information can help (a) reduce anxiety and fear, (b) enable citizens to solve their own problems, (c) elicit conformity with laws and regulations that are not known or understood, (d) warn potential victims about their vulnerability and advise them of ways to protect themselves, (e) demonstrate to people how they unwittingly contribute to problems, (f) develop support for addressing a problem, and (g) acquaint the community with the limitations on government agencies and define realistically what can be expected of those agencies.

5. *Mobilize the community.* Mobilizing a specific segment of the community helps implement a specific response to a specific problem for as long as it takes to deal with the problem.

6. *Make use of existing forms of social control.* Solve problems by mobilizing specific forms of social control inherent in existing relationships—for example, the influence of a parent, teacher, employer, or church.

7. *Alter the physical environment to reduce opportunities for problems to recur.* Adapt the principles of crime prevention through environmental design and situational crime prevention to the complete range of problems.

8. *Increase regulation, through statutes or ordinances, of conditions that contribute to problems.* An analysis of a specific problem may draw attention to factors contributing to the problem that can be controlled by regulation through statutes or ordinances.

9. *Develop new forms of limited authority to intervene and detain.* Examination of specific problems can lead to the conclusion that a satisfactory solution requires some limited authority (e.g., to order a person to leave) but does not require labeling the conduct criminal so that it can be dealt with through a citation or a physical arrest followed by a criminal prosecution.

10. *Make more discriminate use of the criminal justice system.* Use of the criminal justice system should be much more discreet than in the past, reserved for those problems for which the system seems especially appropriate, and used with much greater precision. This could include (a) straightforward investigation, arrest, and prosecution; (b) selective enforcement with articulated criteria; (c) enforcement of criminal laws that, by tradition, are enforced by another agency; (d) more specific definitions of behavior that should be subject to criminal justice prosecution or control through local ordinances; (e) intervention without making the arrest; (f) use of arrest without the intention to prosecute; and (g) new conditions attached to probation or parole.

11. *Use civil law to control public nuisances, offensive behavior, and conditions contributing to crime.* Because most of what the police do in the use of the law involves arrest and prosecution, people tend to forget that the police and local government can initiate a number of other legal proceedings, including those related to (a) licensing, (b) zoning, (c) property confiscation, (d) nuisance abatement, and (e) injunctive relief.

Source: Adapted from Herman Goldstein, *Problem-Oriented Policing* (New York: McGraw-Hill, 1990), pp. 140–141. Used with permission of McGraw-Hill.

Several of these measures may be helpful in assessing the impact of a problem-solving effort; however, a number of nontraditional measures will shed light on whether a problem has been reduced or eliminated.[27]

- Reduced instances of repeat victimization.
- Decreases in related crimes or incidents.
- Neighborhood indicators (including increased profits for businesses in the target area, increased usage of the area, increased property values, less loitering and truancy, and fewer abandoned cars).
- Increased citizen satisfaction regarding the handling of the problem, determined through surveys, interviews, focus groups, electronic bulletin boards, and so on.
- Reduced citizen fear related to the problem.

Assessment is obviously key in the SARA process; knowing that we must assess the effectiveness of our efforts emphasizes the importance of documentation and baseline measurement. Supervisors can help officers assess the effectiveness of their efforts.

BOX 5–2
Problem Solving: Guide to Collaboration

General Background

1. Develop personal networks with members of other agencies who can give you information and help you with problems on which you may be working.
2. Become familiar with the workings of your local government, private businesses, citizen organizations, and other groups and institutions that you may need to call on for help in the future.
3. Develop skills as a negotiator.

Getting Other Agencies to Help

1. Identify agencies that have a role (or could have a role) in addressing the problem early in the problemsolving process.
2. Determine whether these other agencies perceive that there is a problem.
   a. Which agency members perceive the problem and which do not?
   b. Why is it (or isn't it) a problem for them?
   c. How are police perceptions of the problem similar to and different from the perceptions of members of other agencies?
3. Determine whether there is a legal or political mandate for collaboration.
   a. To which agencies does this legal mandate apply?
   b. What are the requirements needed to demonstrate collaboration?
   c. Who is checking to determine whether collaboration is taking place?
4. Look for difficulties that these other agencies face that can be addressed through collaboration on this problem.
   a. Are there internal difficulties that provide an incentive to collaborate?
   b. Are there external crises affecting agencies that collaboration may help address?
5. Determine how much these other agencies use police services.
6. Assess the resource capabilities of these agencies to help.
   a. Do they have the money?
   b. Do they have the staff expertise?
   c. Do they have the enthusiasm?

7. Assess the legal authority of these other agencies.
   a. Do they have special enforcement powers?
   b. Do they control critical resources?
8. Determine the administrative capacity of these agencies to collaborate.
   a. Do they have the legal authority to intervene in the problem?
   b. What are the internal procedures and policies of the stakeholders that help or hinder collaboration?

Working with Other Agencies

1. Include representatives from all affected agencies, if possible, in the problem-solving process.
2. Look for responses to the problem that maximize the gains to all agencies and distribute costs equitably.
3. Reinforce awareness of the interdependence of all agencies.
4. Be prepared to mediate among agencies that have a history of conflict.
5. Develop problem information sharing mechanisms, and promote discussion about the meaning and interpretation of this information.
6. Share problem-solving decisions among stakeholders, and do not surprise others with already-made decisions.
7. Develop a clear explanation as to why collaboration is needed.
8. Foster external support for collaborative efforts, but do not rely on mandates to further collaboration.
9. Be prepared to negotiate with all involved agencies as to their roles, responsibilities, and resource commitments.
10. When collaborating with agencies located far away, plan to spend time developing a working relationship.
11. Try to create support in the larger community for collaborative problem solving.

When Collaboration Does Not Work

1. Always be prepared for collaboration to fail.
2. Have alternative plans.
3. Assess the costs and benefits of unilateral action.
4. Be very patient.

Source: Adapted from John E. Eck, "Implementing a Problem-Oriented Approach: A Management Guide," mimeo, draft copy (Washington, D.C.: Police Executive Research Forum, 1990), pp. 69–70.

If the responses implemented are not effective, the information gathered during analysis should be reviewed. New information may need to be collected before new solutions can be developed and tested.[28]

It is also important to distinguish between evaluation and assessment. Evaluation is an overarching scientific process for determining if a problem declines and if the solution caused the decline; it begins at the moment the problem-solving process begins and continues throughout the effort. Though assessment is the final stage of both evaluation and problem solving, critical decisions about the evaluation are made throughout the process.

Figure 5–7 shows the relationship between the problem-solving process and critical evaluation questions that should be asked at each stage. The left side of the figure shows the SARA process while the right side lists critical questions to address to conduct an evaluation. We discuss assessment (evaluation) in greater depth in Chapter 4.

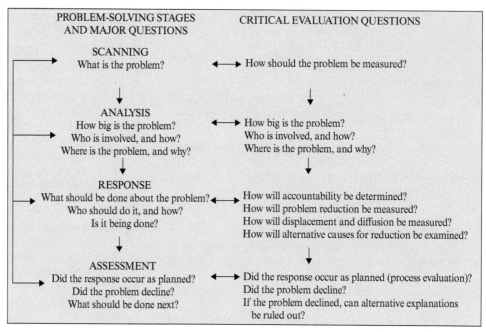

FIGURE 5–7   The Problem Solving Process and Evaluation

Source: John Eck, *Assessing Responses to Problems: An Introductory Guide for Police Problem Solvers* (Washington, D.C.: U.S. Department of Justice, Office of Community Oriented Policing Services, 2004), p. 6.

DIFFICULTIES WITH PROBLEM-SOLVING EFFORTS

Notable community policing and problem-solving researcher and author John Eck has bluntly offered a number of caveats with respect to problem solving. Given his pioneering involvement with and stellar reputation in the field, his musings are certainly worthy of mention.

First, Eck argues that problem solving suffers from appearing to be simple—beginning with the term "problem solving" itself. It is one of those ubiquitous terms that are used in countless business, mathematics, computer, psychology, and many other books. Another problem is that the term suggests that for every difficulty there is a solution that is easy, cheap, permanent, and 100 percent effective.[29]

Eck also bluntly maintains that several explanations have been offered for why problem-solving efforts are not always successful. Most of these explanations (but not all, he argues) are inadequate[30]:

- *Police officers do not have the analytical skills required to analyze problems.* Eck believes that while more problem-solving training certainly could be given to officers, it should not be assumed that we even know *how* to train police in problem solving, especially in its nuances. (See, however, Chapter 10 on training for problem solving, which includes discussion of the new Police Training Officer [PTO] program.)
- *Police managers and supervisors do not know how to foster problem solving.* Eck believes this is probably true. Can supervisors discriminate between quality problem solving and superficial problem solving? The answer is no.
- *Police agencies resist change.* Eck argues that despite a large body of literature on policing and problem solving, there is little practical advice that research can provide to police executives. Resistance to change is to be expected if research cannot provide practical guidance on how to behave with a new approach.
- *Police workloads prevent anything but superficial analysis.* One thing is clear: Problem solving—which requires days, weeks, even months—has a different time frame than responding to calls, which is measured in minutes and hours. Eck is of the opinion that difficulty with time is not how much time is available but how much time the police are willing to devote.
- *There is too little involvement of communities.* There is also merit to this argument. Neighborhoods usually cover much larger areas than most problems, even the most

engaged communities are aware of problems, and citizens are often in the dark about how to systematically analyze and fix problems, Eck states.

- *Little is known about what works under what circumstances.* Eck believes this statement is also true. He says that the police and community can therefore experiment with solutions or systematically record and organize their problem-solving experiences; then they can share them with each other. Neither approach is adequate, however. Experimentation is a slow process, while few problem-solving efforts result in a formal evaluation.

TAILORING STRATEGIES TO NEIGHBORHOODS

Which Strategy Where?

Some interesting research has been done on whether or not problem-oriented policing can work in different types of neighborhoods; one study suggests that this strategy should have similar benefits in different types of neighborhoods.[31] Furthermore, a theoretical framework has been developed by Nolan et al. to help police decide which type of problem-solving strategy to employ in specific neighborhoods.[32] First, it is important to remember—as noted in Chapter 3 discussions of communitarianism, social capital, mobilization, and alliances—that the level of responsibility for neighborhood safety and problem solving is important and relates to a community's level of crime. Some authors have termed this as "collective efficacy": the cohesion among residents combined with shared expectations for the social control of public space that predicts both crime and disorder.[33] Some researchers argue that neighborhood-level collective efficacy is the most significant predictor of crime.

In a related vein, research has indicated that a neighborhood can exist in one of the three identifiable stages[34]:

1. *Dependence.* Community members depend on the police to solve problems related to public order, and officers are willing to do so. Most residents view officers as competent and respect them, and officers view the neighborhood as unable or unwilling to care for itself.
2. *Conflict.* Here, officers cannot address community problems or provide safety because residents have become dissatisfied with the police and with each other; they see the police as having primary responsibility for order maintenance in the neighborhoods but consider the police to be ineffective. In defending themselves, officers may initiate high-visibility foot or bicycle patrols or other methods in order to appease residents. To move out of this stage, officers must give up the notion that they alone can address crime and disorder in neighborhoods.
3. *Interdependence.* Once the police and the community have come to recognize their mutual responsibilities for restoring order and safety, development of social networks begins to occur. Officers play a less prominent role in order maintenance and develop a more trusting relationship with the community.

Differing Types of Neighborhoods

Obviously, neighborhoods will differ in their ability to move along these stages of development. Some are stronger than others and have more resources to help them evolve. There are four basic types of neighborhoods, which are briefly discussed next[35]:

1. *Strong.* Strong communities experience low levels of crime and have residents who interact or organize themselves on issues of community disorder.
2. *Vulnerable.* Vulnerable neighborhoods also have low rates of crime and disorder, but they have minimal levels of development as well. Residents depend on the police to deal with disorder.
3. *Anomic.* Anomic communities have high rates of crime and disorder and low levels of neighborhood development. Residents are dependent on officers to take care of safety problems and are dissatisfied because of the officers' lack of success.
4. *Responsive.* Responsive neighborhoods have high levels of crime and disorder, but residents work with the police to resolve problems.

| Exhibit 5–1 | Global Perspective: New Zealand's Awards for Problem-Oriented Policing Efforts |

Each year a national award is given in Christchurch, New Zealand, recognizing the best problem-oriented policing efforts. Known as the POP Award, the award recognizes police agencies for excellence in addressing long-term sustainable crime prevention and reduction.

Applicants for the award are held to very high standard and are divided into three newly added categories: excellence in achieving collective impact, excellence in reducing harm from the drivers of crime, and excellence in reducing repeat victimization. With the addition of these new award categories, there are nearly 20 applications each year.

Candidates must demonstrate a diverse range of initiatives from changing the way police work with victims to raising awareness concerning crime drivers.[36]

Effective policing involves not only reducing crime and disorder but also facilitating neighborhood development. The police must strive to move the community along two dimensions: low levels of crime and disorder, and high levels of integration and collective efficacy (interdependence). Therefore, matching the policing style to the neighborhood type represents only the first step in the process (see Exhibit 5–1).

IN SUM. . .

To pull together all of the foregoing descriptions of the elements contributing to problem-solving policing, see Figure 5–8. It visually portrays how community policing and problem-oriented policing together constitute a philosophy that promotes organizational strategies that support the systematic use of partnerships and problem-solving techniques to proactively address the immediate conditions that give rise to public safety issues.

YOU BE THE PROBLEM SOLVER: THE CASE OF THE LATE-NIGHT DELIVERY ROBBERIES

To illustrate problem-oriented policing and SARA in action, it would be helpful for you to walk through a case study as a problem solver and see how a problem might be scanned, analyzed, and addressed.

For the following problem, after reading the facts (i.e., scanning and analyzing it), and prior to reading the responses provided, consider how you might go about responding to it. (Note that three other excellent examples of problem-oriented policing for addressing crime and disorder are provided in Appendix I.)

Assume the following crime situation:

> In an eastern city of 35,000, with a relatively low crime rate, there have been occurring a number of robberies of food delivery drivers. The robberies are occurring at a rate of one per month. Hearing news of the robberies and knowing their drivers are very fearful, several pizza and other fast-food stores refuse deliveries to a mostly low-income and predominantly black neighborhood where many of the robberies are taking place. On the other side, many elderly residents of this neighborhood are complaining about the lack of delivery service and petition the city to reverse the policy.

Stakeholders (in addition to the police) would include:

- Potential home delivery customers in "no-delivery" neighborhood.
- Signers of the petition.
- Fast-food delivery people and restaurant management.
- National pizza delivery chains.
- Local NAACP chapter, legislators, and media.

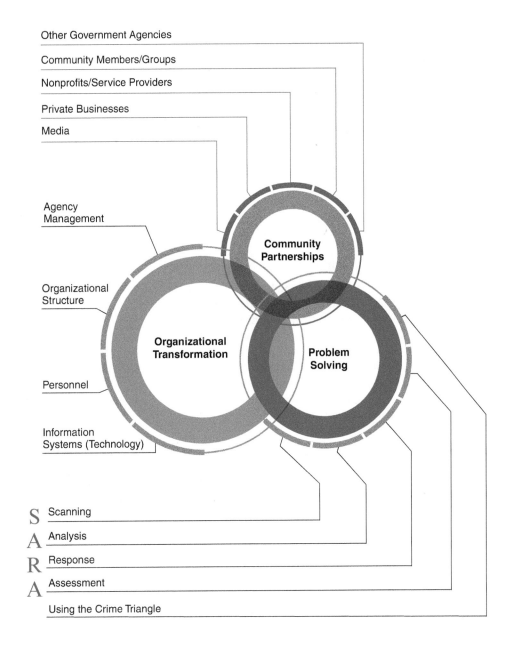

FIGURE 5–8   The Primary Elements of Community Policing

During scanning, what are some of the kinds of questions about the robbery problem that, at minimum, the police should be asking? Consider the following:

Victims

1. Who were the victims (age, race, gender)? For whom were they working? What was the nature of the attacks?
2. What time of day were the victims attacked?
3. Have any food delivery people been attacked more than once? Have delivery people from certain restaurants being attacked more often than others?
4. What areas do they fear most? Do they have any suggestions on ways to make their job safer? Are they issued any security devices or provided with safety training?

Locations

1. Where are the robberies occurring?
2. Are the delivery people robbed near their vehicle or away from it? Is their vehicles identified as for fast-food delivery?

3. What routes do delivery people take?

4. Are there any environmental patterns to the robberies (lighting, shrubbery, isolated or blind areas)?

Offenders

1. What is the method of attack, and are any patterns evident? What weapons have been used and in how many attacks?

2. How do the offenders appear to select their victims, and why are some victims more attractive than others?

3. Do offenders place orders to lure delivery people to them or randomly meet their victims?

4. How much money did offenders steal during a typical incident? Is anything else being stolen?

5. Do the offenders live in the neighborhood(s) where the robberies are occurring?

During analysis, assume that the following information is uncovered:

- Large outdoor parties, mostly attended by youth in their late teens, are held each weekend night in several common areas near residential units.
- The party areas are in the vicinity of the robberies.
- Alcohol is served at the parties, and there are indications of underage drinking at the parties.
- Fast-food delivery staff recalls that a number of the robberies were committed by teenagers who appeared to have been drinking, and several drivers also recall seeing or passing a group of teenage partiers on foot before they were robbed.
- In 11 of the robberies, the offenders stole less than $40. In the other three robberies, between $40 and $60 was stolen.

Given this information, what kinds of tailored responses might be developed? To begin:

- The two most victimized stores might be asked to stop delivery at midnight and require customers to pick up their take-out between midnight and 2 AM.
- The stores could ask customers what bill denomination will be used to pay for the food, so that delivery people could carry the minimum amount of change required (exact change would be requested, but not required).
- The stores might refuse to deliver an order if it means walking by a large crowd that is loitering in the area.

One common response might be to increase patrol car or foot patrols in the problem area on weekend nights between the hours of 10 PM and 2 AM. However, this response would have been relatively costly to the police department. Another common response is to increase lighting in the problem area; however, unless the robberies have occurred in areas that are dimly lit, this strategy probably would have little effect on the fast-food robbery problem.[37]

Summary

As noted in the introduction, this chapter and the discussion of community policing in Chapter 2 constitute the heart and soul of this book and have set out the basic principles and strategies of the community policing and problem solving concepts. We believe, unequivocally, that the best philosophy and strategy for the future of policing lies with problem-oriented policing, for a comprehensive approach to providing quality police service.

It is essential for the reader (and police practitioners) to have a firm, fundamental understanding of problem solving, as this information will lay the foundation for what follows in the remaining chapters. Subsequent chapter topics elaborate on this strategy and include a large number of examples of problem solving in real-life situations. Furthermore, some chapters, particularly those addressing such topics as crime prevention, information technology, and crime analysis, bear heavily on the SARA problem-solving process.

Key Terms and Concepts

Analysis	Incident-driven policing	Problem solving	Scanning
Assessment	Manager	Response	Small wins
Guardian	Problem analysis triangle	SARA (problem solving	
Handler	Problem-oriented policing	process)	

Items for Review

1. Explain what is meant by problem oriented policing and how it differs from traditional reactive, incident-driven policing.
2. Briefly describe the four steps of the SARA problem-solving process.
3. Review in detail what kinds of activities are involved in the *analysis* stage of the SARA process, as well as tools that are available for performing an in-depth analysis.
4. Delineate the three elements of the problem analysis and graffiti problem triangles.
5. List the three types of roles of third parties in the problem analysis triangle.
6. List the five potential solutions to problems.
7. Describe five potential difficulties with problem solving.
8. Provide an example of how problem oriented policing might function in a situation involving night-time robberies of delivery trucks.
9. Review some of the considerations in tailoring problem-solving strategies to neighborhoods.

Learn by Doing

1. Assume that for the past six months a small neighborhood market in the western part of the city has generated dozens of calls for service about drug dealing because of several drug dealers and users frequenting the area. Part I ("Index") crimes are beginning to increase in the area as well. A nearby drug house contributes heavily to the problem, and a T-shaped alley behind the store provides easy ingress and egress for buyers, both on foot and in vehicles. The lighting is poor, and pay telephones in front of the store are constantly in use by traffickers. You are assigned to initiate a problem-oriented policing initiative at this location that will bring long-term results. What kinds of information would you collect about the area and the drug problem? What kinds of responses might be considered? What types of assessment would you perform?

2. Using media reports or local crime data (oftentimes available from your local police agency Web site), identify a particularly crime-ridden neighborhood, beat, or area of your jurisdiction. Then, using techniques described in this chapter, including the problem analysis triangle and SARA, explain what your approach would be to restoring order to that neighborhood through the use of a problem-solving exercise.

Endnotes

1. Herman Goldstein, *Policing a Free Society* (Cambridge, Mass.: Ballinger, 1977).
2. Herman Goldstein, *Problem-Oriented Policing* (New York: McGraw-Hill, 1990).
3. Herman Goldstein, "Problem-Oriented Policing." Paper presented at the National Institute of Justice Conference on Policing: State of the Art III, Phoenix, Arizona, June 12, 1987.
4. Ibid., p. 4.
5. Ibid., pp. 5–6.
6. See John E. Eck and William Spellman, *Problem-Solving: Problem-Oriented Policing in Newport News* (Washington, D.C.: Police Executive Research Forum, 1979), https://www.ncjrs.gov/App/publications/abstract.aspx?ID=111964.
7. John E. Eck and William Spelman, "A Problem-Oriented Approach to Police Service Delivery," in Dennis Jay Kenney (ed.), *Police and Policing: Contemporary Issues* (New York: Praeger, 1989), pp. 95–111.
8. Quoted in Roland Chilton, "Urban Crime Trends and Criminological Theory," in Chris W. Eskridge (ed.), *Criminal Justice: Concepts and Issues* (Los Angeles: Roxbury, 1993), pp. 47–55.
9. Ibid., p. xvii.
10. Samuel Walker, *The Police in America: An Introduction* (2nd ed.) (New York: McGraw-Hill, 1992), p. 177.
11. Goldstein, *Problem-Oriented Policing*, pp. 38–40.
12. Goldstein, "Toward Community-Oriented Policing: Potential, Basic Requirements, and Threshold Questions," *Crime and Delinquency* 33 (1987):6–30.
13. Ibid., p. 21.
14. Ibid., pp. 43–52.
15. Michael S. Scott and Stuart Kirby, *Implementing POP: Leading, Structuring, and Managing a Problem-Oriented Police Agency* (Washington, D.C.: Center for Problem-Oriented Policing, 2012), p. 36.
16. Adapted from Ronald V. Clarke and John E. Eck, *Crime Analysis for Problem Solvers in 60 Small Steps* (Washington, D.C.: Office of Community Oriented Policing Services, U.S. Department of Justice, 2015), pp. 40–41.
17. Michael S. Scott, *Identifying and Defining Policing Problems* (Washington, D.C.: Office of Community Oriented Policing Services, 2015), p. 41.
18. Karl E. Weick, "Small Wins: Redefining the Scale of Social Problems," *American Psychologist* 39(1) (1984):40–49.

19. John Eck, *A Dissertation Prospectus for the Study of Characteristics of Drug Dealing Places* (Dissertation, College Park, Md.: University of Maryland–College Park, 1992).

20. Marcus Felson, "Linking Criminal Career Choices, Routine Activities, Informal Control, and Criminal Outcomes," in Derek Cornish and Ronald Clarke (eds.), *The Reasoning Criminal: Rational Choice Perspectives on Offending* (New York: Springer-Verlag, 1986).

21. Lawrence E. Cohen and Marcus Felson, "Social Change and Crime Rate Trends: A Routine Activity Approach," *American Sociological Review* 44 (August 1979):588–608.

22. Eck, *A Dissertation Prospectus for the Study of Characteristics of Drug Dealing Places*, p. 5.

23. Rana Sampson, "Problem Solving," in *Neighborhood-Oriented Policing in Rural Communities: A Program Planning Guide* (Washington, D.C.: U.S. Department of Justice, Office of Justice Programs, Bureau of Justice Assistance, 1994), p. 4.

24. William Spelman and John E. Eck, "Problem-Solving," *Research in Brief* (January 1987):6.

25. John E. Eck, *Assessing Responses to Problems: An Introductory Guide for Police Problem Solvers* (Washington, D.C.: Office of Community Oriented Policing Services, 2015), pp. 4–5.

26. Ibid.

27. U.S. Department of Justice, Office of Community Oriented Policing Services, *Problem Solving Tips*, p. 20.

28. Sampson, "Problem Solving," p. 5.

29. John E. Eck, "Why Don't Problems Get Solved," in Wesley G. Skogan (ed.), *Community Policing: Can It Work?* (Belmont, Calif.: Wadsworth, 2004), pp. 185–206.

30. Ibid., pp. 190–193.

31. R. J. Sampson and S. W. Raudenbush, "Systematic Social Observation of Public Spaces: A New Look at Disorder in Urban Neighborhoods," *American Journal of Sociology* 105(3) (1999):603–651.

32. See W. G. Skogan, S. M. Hartnett, J. DuBois, J. T. Comey, M. Kaiser, and J. H. Lovig, *Problem Solving in Practice: Implementing Community Policing in Chicago* (Washington, D.C.: U.S. Department of Justice, National Institute of Justice, 2000).

33. Ibid.

34. Ibid, pp. 3–4.

35. Ibid., pp. 4–5.

36. New Zealand Police, "Top POP Cops Head to Christchurch for Final," June 23, 2015, http://www.police.govt.nz/news/release/top-pop-cops-head-christchurch-final.

37. Adapted from *Problem-Solving Tips: A Guide to Reducing Crime and Disorder Through Problem-Solving Partnerships* (2nd ed.) (Washington, D.C.: Office of Community Oriented Policing Services, July 2011).

Crime Prevention:
Programs and Practices

LEARNING OBJECTIVES

As a result of reading this chapter, the student will understand:

- How the crime prevention concept evolved
- How the concept of community and crime prevention relate to problem-oriented policing
- The meaning and functions of crime prevention through environmental design (CPTED)
- The meaning and value of situational crime prevention
- The roles of the contemporary crime prevention officer
- How to evaluate the outcomes of crime prevention initiatives
- The nature of crime displacement
- How to conduct a crime prevention publicity campaign
- Which crime prevention strategies work, do not work, and hold promise

TEST YOUR KNOWLEDGE

1. A criminal justice system adage holds that it is far better than to investigate, solve, arrest, and prosecute someone for committing a criminal offense than to prevent the crime from occurring in the first place.
2. Crime prevention today largely rests on the contemporary view that you should either "lock it or lose it."
3. At its heart, problem-oriented policing is about preventing crime.
4. We know that the proper design and use of the environment can lead to a reduction in the fear and incidence of crime as well as an improvement in the quality of life.
5. Studies show that, in general, Neighborhood Watch, boot camp, "Scared Straight," home detention, and gun buyback programs do not significantly reduce or prevent crime.

Answers can be found on page 278.

He who cures a disease may be the skillfullest, but he who prevents it is the safest physician.
—THOMAS FULLER

Crime and bad lives are the measure of a State's failure; all crime in the end is the crime of the community.
—H. G. WELLS

INTRODUCTION

Probably most if not all criminal justice students and practitioners learn early on in their careers that it is far cheaper to *prevent* a crime from occurring in the first place, rather than trying to reactively investigate it and then try to arrest, prosecute, and incarcerate the offender. Take, for example, the multimillion dollar hotel/convention center complex that was constructed in the middle of a large Midwestern city. Immediately upon its completion, police begin receiving reports of rapes in the parking garage, robberies in dark hallways, and all manner of other crimes. The parking garage, hallways, lighting, and security system—indeed, much of the facility—had to be retrofitted to prevent such an onslaught of crimes, at a major cost to the owners. The police department commander who headed up the agency's crime prevention bureau later lamented to one of the authors that:

> They [the hotel chain building the complex] came to town and talked with the architects, the health department, the street department, the zoning department, the fire department, and everyone else—but they never came to see me.[1]

Until relatively recently, such was often the angst of one whose career revolved around *preventing* crimes—a time when perhaps only a few, if any, officers were engaged in such activities, and they primarily gave out advice and brochures on target hardening the home, "lock it or lose it," and so forth. [Indeed, if one wishes to see how advanced and sophisticated the study of crime prevention has become, all he or she need do is to visit the website of the National Crime Prevention Council.][2] Thankfully, that simplistic era is now long gone, and today's crime prevention professionals are engaged in much more sophisticated—and appreciated—work.[3]

This chapter begins with a brief history of how crime prevention evolved, and then we discuss how crime prevention works hand-in-glove with the community-oriented policing and problem solving. Two very important components of crime prevention are then analyzed: **crime prevention through environmental design (CPTED)** and **situational crime prevention (SCP)**. Following that, we briefly review several issues and problems that can accompany crime prevention efforts: the role of the crime prevention officer, conducting a crime prevention publicity campaign, the displacement of crime, and the evaluation of initiatives. Finally, we view which crime prevention strategies have been shown to work, to not work, and to hold promise. The chapter concludes with a summary, review questions, and several scenarios and activities that provide opportunities for you to "learn by doing."

The underlying theme of this chapter, as demonstrated in Chapter 2, is that the police alone cannot prevent crime and disorder; the community *must* be engaged in a collaborative effort if the physical and social problems that plague the community are to be reduced or eliminated.

A BRIEF HISTORY

Crime prevention may be defined as:

> A pattern of attitudes and behaviors directed both at reducing the threat of crime and enhancing the sense of safety and security to positively influence the quality of life in our society and to help develop environments where crime cannot flourish.[4]

Crime prevention is not a new idea. Humans have long known that crime is not simply a matter of motivation; it is also a matter of opportunity. Indeed, for as long as people have been victimized, there have been attempts to protect one's self and family. The term "crime prevention," however, has only recently come to signify a set of ideas for combating crime.[5]

Our earliest ancestors maximized lighting from the sun and moon and employed defensive placement of homes on the side of cliffs, with only one entrance and exit.[6] Cave dwellers established ownership of a space by surrounding it with large boulders; later the Romans developed and enforced complex land laws. Walled cities and castles exist throughout the world. It is a natural human impulse to claim and secure an area to prevent problems.[7]

A more contemporary form of early preventive action was the Chicago Area Project (CAP), based on the research of Shaw and McKay in the 1930s and 1940s, which concerned the altering of the social fabric. Crime and delinquency were concentrated in the central areas of Chicago. Identifying a high level of transiency and an apparent lack of social ties in these areas as the root cause of the problems, Shaw and McKay labeled the problem as "social disorganization," meaning that the constant turnover of residents resulted in the inability of the people to exert any informal social control over the individuals in the area. Consequently, offenders could act with some degree of impunity in these neighborhoods.[8] Shaw's proposed solution to the problem was to work with the residents to build a sense of pride and community, thereby prompting people to stay and exert control over the actions of the people in the area. CAP was founded in 1931 and generated community support by using volunteers and existing neighborhood institutions.[9]

The 1970s saw the rise of community-based crime prevention programs, such as the Neighborhood or Block Watch. These programs used the same premise as physical design approaches: potential offenders will not commit a crime if they perceive citizen activity, awareness, and concern in an area. The focus is on citizen surveillance and action (such as cutting back bushes, installing lighting, removing obstacles to enhance sight lines, organizing security surveys, and distributing crime and crime prevention news). Signs of resident activity and cohesion should work to protect the neighborhood. The police also recognized that they could not stop crime or solve problems on their own; they needed the help of the citizenry.[10]

Crime prevention experienced perhaps its biggest boost, however, with the emergence of physical design as a topic of debate. Led by the work of Oscar Newman in 1972, flaws in the physical environment were identified as causes of, or at least facilitators for, criminal behavior. In 1969, Newman first coined the term "defensible space," which in his mind did not mean ugly fortress-like buildings where occupants were prisoners. (Table 6–1 depicts Newman's suggestions for defensible space.) Rather, buildings that are properly designed promote a sense of safety and power to their occupants, making them less afraid and vulnerable.[11]

Newman, an architect, argued that the physical characteristics of an area have the potential to suggest to residents and potential offenders either that the area is well cared for and protected or it is open to criminal activity. Design features conducive to criminal behavior—allowing offenders to commit a crime and escape with minimal risk of detection—would include common entrances for a large number of people, poorly placed windows inhibiting casual surveillance of grounds and common areas, hidden entrances, easy access for illegitimate users, and isolated buildings.[12]

Then in the 1970s and 1980s, theories of crime were developed that gave added importance to the role of **crime opportunity**. L. E. Cohen and M. Felson's **routine activity theory** seeks to explain how physical and social environments create crime opportunities by bringing together in one place at a particular time a "likely" offender, a "suitable" target, and the absence of a "capable guardian" against crime (e.g., a police officer or security guard).[13] Routine activity theory was used to explain how large increases in burglary rates occurred in the United States in

---

TABLE 6–1   Oscar Newman's Defensible Space Suggestions

1. Reduce the size of a housing estate or block.
2. Reduce the number of dwellings sharing an entrance way.
3. Reduce the number of stories in a building block.
4. Arrange dwellings in groups to encourage social contact.
5. Minimize the degree of shared public space inside and near blocks.
6. Make the boundaries between public and private space very clear.
7. Make public areas clearly visible to nearby housing.
8. Use external rather than internal corridors in blocks of housing so that they are visible.
9. Make entrances flush with the street rather than set back.
10. Do not have entrances facing away from the street because they are not open to surveillance.
11. Avoid landscaping and vegetation that impede surveillance.
12. Reduce escape routes (elevators, staircases, and multiple exits) for criminals.

Source: U.S. Department of Housing and Urban Development, *Crime Prevention Brief,* "Crime Prevention Through Environmental Design" (no date), p. 2.

Under community policing and problem solving, crime prevention strategies are highly comprehensive and sophisticated—going well beyond the Neighborhood Watch campaign that began developing in the mid-1960s.

shalunts/Shutterstock.

the 1960s and 1970s because (1) home electronic goods became lighter, and (2) women increasingly entered the labor force, resulting in more empty homes during the day that could be entered by burglars.

Another opportunity theory is the **rational choice** perspective, which holds that all crime is purposive behavior designed to benefit the offender.[14] In committing an offense, the offender makes the choice to balance the effort, risks, and rewards with the costs and benefits of alternative legal means of achieving an end.

James Q. Wilson and George Kelling's 1982 **"broken windows" theory** extended Oscar Newman's focus on housing projects to entire neighborhoods. "Broken windows" refers to physical signs that an area is unattended: There may be abandoned vehicles and buildings in the area, trash and litter may be present, and there may be broken windows and lights and graffiti.[15] In addition to these physical indicators are social manifestations of the same problems, such as loitering youths, public drunkenness, prostitution, and vagrancy. Both the physical and social indicators are typically referred to as signs of "incivility" that attract offenders to the area.[16]

The most recent movements in crime prevention focus efforts and interventions on attacking specific problems, places, and times. Ronald V. Clarke proposed "situational crime prevention" as "measures directed at highly specific forms of crime that involve [environmental changes that] reduce the opportunities for crime and increase its risk."[17] Examples of situational crime prevention include the installation of surveillance equipment in a parking lot experiencing vandalism, erecting security screens in banks to stop robberies, altering traffic patterns in a drug market neighborhood, using electronic tags for library materials, and

Signage and displays often make natural surveillance difficult or impossible, and can contribute to a location's being a target for offenders.

John Keeble/Getty images.

using caller ID for obscene phone calls.[18] The physical environment as it relates to crime prevention is discussed shortly. Next we discuss the contemporary crime prevention-based philosophy.

PROBLEM-ORIENTED POLICING, COMMUNITY, AND CRIME PREVENTION: A SYMBIOTIC RELATIONSHIP

Community-oriented policing and problem solving argues that the police and the community must stop treating the symptoms of the problem. This strategy thus requires a new age of prevention—as well as improvement of prevention efforts.

Altering physical designs of buildings, for example, is not in itself generally sufficient for altering the level of crime; physical design changes cannot stop a truly motivated offender. Furthermore, altering the physical environment does not guarantee that residents will become involved and take action. Direct efforts to enhance active citizen involvement are necessary.[19]

Close Companions

Crime prevention and the problem-solving process are therefore close companions, attempting to define a problem, identify contributing causes, seek out the proper people or agencies to assist in identifying potential solutions, and work as a group to implement the solution. The problem drives the solution.[20]

At its heart, then, community policing and problem solving is about preventing crime. Crime prevention efforts provide information and skills that are essential to community policing. Furthermore, crime prevention and police problem solving have six major points in common[21]:

1. *Each deals with the health of the community.* They acknowledge the many interrelated issues that contribute to crime.
2. *Each seeks to address underlying causes and problems.* Although short-term and reactive measures (such as personal security and response to calls for service) are necessary, they are insufficient if crime is to be significantly reduced. Looking beyond symptoms to treat the causes of community problems is a strategy that both, at their best, share in full measure.
3. *Each deals with the combination of physical and social issues that are at the heart of many community problems.* An abandoned building may attract drug addicts; bored teens may become area burglars. Both approaches examine the broadest possible range of causes and solutions.
4. *Each requires active involvement by community residents.* Both have the chief task of enabling people to make themselves and their communities safer by helping them gain appropriate knowledge, develop helpful attitudes, and take useful actions.
5. *Each requires partnerships beyond law enforcement to be effective.* Both efforts can and have involved schools, community centers, civic organizations, religious groups, social service agencies, public works agencies, and other elements of the community.
6. *Each is an approach or a philosophy rather than a program.* Neither is a fixed system for delivery of a specific service; instead, each is a way of doing business and involves the development of an institutional mindset.

The community's role is also exceptionally important in crime prevention, as has been the common theme throughout this book. In fact, community policing should be the foundation of any general crime prevention approach. And while simply engaging the community alone will not reduce crime, community engagement can provide important inputs to help focus crime reduction strategies. Community members provide information about crime and disorder problems, and help to solve specific crimes. Indeed, a central idea in community policing is to engage residents so that they can exert more control over situations and dynamics that contribute to their own potential for victimization. Police departments should strive to develop similar working relationships not only with individual residents, but also with local businesses, social service agencies, and other criminal justice organizations.[22]

Furthermore, the more disparate types of individuals and groups that can be brought together, for crime prevention, the better chance for CPTED efforts to succeed. Such groups

| Exhibit 6–1 | Auburn Boulevard Revitalization Project, Sacramento, California |

A section of Auburn Boulevard in Sacramento, California, had long been notorious for criminal activity. In response, local agencies and community groups, including the Sacramento County District Attorney's Office, the city's environmental management division and departments of building, probation, child protective services, and animal control and fire, and the local utility company, joined to form a Nuisance Response Team (NRT).

This eclectic group worked together to focus their resources more effectively. As a result, the Sacramento Housing and Redevelopment Agency (SHRA) was able to develop several affordable housing and other projects. In addition, the sheriff's department dedicated two officers to implement problem-oriented policing practices and the district attorney's office trained code enforcement officers on evidence collection to improve cases against property owners. Finally, Sacramento County Code Enforcement issued code violations on particularly troubling nuisance properties. With SHRA's help, residents formed a neighborhood watch group and a homeowners association. The presence of these different agencies enabled the NRT to address multiple problems simultaneously, creating more effective pressure on property owners to make improvements. As a result, incidence of crime and property problems declined significantly, and SHRA has been able to increase its redevelopment efforts and encourage reputable businesses to move into the area.[24]

might include law enforcement, architects, engineers, planners, public health professionals, designers, code enforcement, community stakeholders, and others who wish to prevent crime by designing a physical environment that positively influences human behavior.[23]

Exhibit 6–1 demonstrates how such a collective effort can work.

The Community's Role in Preventing Crime and Restoring Anchor Points

The recent revelation in Cleveland, Ohio, that three young women had been kidnapped by Ariel Castro and held captive for 10 years in a quiet neighborhood home termed the "house of horrors"[25] raises important questions about how neighborhoods and residents function. Two neighbors intervened and rescued the three young women after hearing screams from the house. Although the kidnapper certainly shoulders all of the blame for the taking and treatment (to include multiple rapes) of these women, one is forced to wonder why it took so long for the neighborhood to uncover and react to the crimes. Did residents not know each other? Were they isolated from each other? Did they never observe any suspicious behavior at the household? For the persons who called the police, what compelled them to do so, and to care about safety and crime prevention? Why do any of us act concerning a problem within our neighborhoods?

The answers to these questions depend on how cohesive the neighborhood's citizens are, and how the citizens perceive their role in developing and sustaining crime control efforts. Certainly, a feeling of belongingness, camaraderie, neighbors coming together to meet each other, and working on small projects like a neighborhood cleanup are essential.

As suggested in Chapter 1, the police can encourage neighborhood cohesion by conducting beat meetings where citizens can contribute directly to local-level decision making by creating a list of crime and safety problems, prioritizing two or three problems on the list, and pooling their information to analyze the problems. They can decide what to do and who will do it, and then assess the effectiveness of their responses. If their efforts are successful, they can move on to other problems; if not, they can develop different approaches to deal with the problems.

Neighbors do not necessarily need to become friends, but they do need to identify shared concerns, and eventually, strategies to address these concerns. For cohesion to occur and problem-solving efforts to succeed, there must be clear incentives and immediate rewards. Strong leadership, good communication, and recognition of volunteers' efforts are also important to ensure continued involvement.[26]

KEEPING KIDS
CO⊕L&
C⋆NFIDENT

AND OUT OF **GANGS**

2012-13 CRIME PREVENTION MONTH KIT

The National Crime Prevention Council assists police by providing hundreds of different types of brochures and crime-prevention resources to citizens.
Courtesy National Crime Prevention Council.

Also important to social cohesion are neighborhood "**anchor points**"—schools, libraries, parks, medical facilities, grocery stores, child care centers, commercial stores, churches, and so on, which are important for social, physical, and spiritual survival and where residents interact, share information, and form social ties.

However, anchor points can also be crime generators, such as a park where drug sales occur, homeless people sleep, or gangs hang out. Certain retail establishments (bars, pawn shops, liquor stores, fast-food restaurants), public transportation centers, and other types of establishments become hot spots of crime (hot spots are defined by Sherman as "small places in which the occurrence of crime is so frequent that it is highly predictable, at least over a 1-year period").[27] Many problem-oriented policing efforts involve identifying these areas and projects take steps to address the factors producing crime.[28]

CRIME PREVENTION THROUGH ENVIRONMENTAL DESIGN

Designing Out Crime

Crime prevention through environmental design (CPTED) is defined as the "proper design and effective use of the environment that can lead to a reduction in the fear and incidence of crime, and an improvement in the quality of life."[29] At its core are three principles that support problem-solving approaches to crime[30]:

1. *Access control.* Access control uses elements such as doors, shrubs, fences, and gates to deny admission to a crime target and to create a perception among offenders that there is a risk in selecting the target.
2. *Natural surveillance.* Natural surveillance includes the proper placement of windows, lighting, and landscaping to increase the ability of those who care to observe intruders as well as regular users, allowing them to challenge inappropriate behavior or report it to the police or the property owner.
3. *Territorial reinforcement.* Using such elements as sidewalks, landscaping, and porches helps distinguish between public and private areas and helps users exhibit signs of "ownership" that send hands-off messages to would-be offenders.
4. *Maintenance.* Maintenance attends to the maintenance and management of space by proper upkeep of lawns, trimming trees, landscaping, repairing broken windows, and painting over graffiti.[31]

Ironically, in the past the police were not involved in design planning, whereas fire departments have promulgated and enforced national fire codes for about a half-century. Today, in cities such as Tempe, Arizona, if the police are not involved in the preliminary stages of planning a building, they often become very involved afterward, when crimes are committed in or around the structure.[32]

Cities such as Tempe have become leaders in expanding policing's new role in **designing out crime**. In the late 1900s, Tempe enacted an ordinance requiring that no commercial, park, or residential building permit be issued until the police department had approved it, ensuring that the building fully protected its occupants.

Electronic gates, signage, alarms, and other forms of asset protection let would-be burglars and thieves know that their efforts to gain entry will be met with resistance.
Hans Engbers/Shutterstock.

Tempe's CPTED officers advocate that walls around the perimeter of a building be at least eight feet high to make them more difficult to scale. River rocks are banned from parking lots, as they can be used as weapons. Natural surveillance, which can be obtained from proper lighting and window placement, helps people to oversee nearby activities. Transparent fences are better than walls to monitor activities. Light switches in rest rooms should be keyed or remotely controlled to prevent tampering, thus perhaps facilitating a possible hiding place for an attacker; rest rooms should not be located at the ends of hallways where they are isolated. Defensive architecture includes "target hardening" through quality deadbolts and other mechanical means and includes proper landscaping (e.g., thorny bushes help to keep burglars away).[33]

At least six types of information may be considered for CPTED planning[34]:

1. **Crime data:** included are calls for service, distribution of crime, temporal distribution of crime, and offenders' modus operandi.
2. **Population characteristics:** this should include age, gender, race and ethnicity, family and household demographics.
3. **Institutional and Organizational Relationships:** included are neighborhood associations such as neighborhood watch, schools, clubs, and hospitals.
4. **Land use and development:** this area addresses neighborhood stability, property values and land use legislation and policies.
5. **Traffic systems:** this category may include transportation networks, traffic routes and transit systems, and neighborhood related complaints.
6. **Resident/user surveys or stakeholder interviews:** this includes surveys or interviews that focus on community issues of concern including victimization and fear.

Second-Generation CPTED

As emphasized in Chapter 2 and stated by Greg Saville and Gerry Cleveland, "what really counts is a sense of community."[35] In that vein, while the first-generation of CPTED focused on all spaces having a clearly defined and designated purpose and being routinely cared for and monitored, a **second-generation CPTED** has more recently been developed that, again in the words of Saville and Cleveland, "recognizes that the most valuable aspects of a safe community lie not in structures of the brick and mortar type, but rather in structures of family, of thought, and, most importantly, of behavior."[36]

In addition to the basic elements such as access control and natural surveillance, second-generation CPTED looks at several *social* aspects of how neighborhoods work[37]:

- ***Size of the district, population density, and differentiation of buildings.*** There is an environmental influence on social interaction. We have relied for too long on large systems for survival. It is difficult to get to know one's neighbors when the neighborhood consists of 100 homes, an apartment building has over 300 units, a high school has more than 3,000 students. Size can affect the alienation of a place. We need to live in smaller, locally based neighborhoods, near where we work, go to school, and socialize. We must develop ways to encourage more local contacts for social, economic, and political interaction. (This brings us full circle to the Chicago studies of the 1930s, discussed above.)
- ***Urban meeting places.*** Providing meeting places is an absolute necessity in neighborhoods, and the lack thereof can make urban spaces empty and dangerous—which is why regional shopping malls fail to become places of community gathering.
- ***Youth clubs.*** Again, the creation of youth clubs has been a crime prevention and community-building strategy since the aforementioned Chicago Area Project of the 1930s and can provide activities, meeting places, and life skills training.

Second-generation CPTED also involves the idea of an ecological threshold, or what is called the neighborhood "tipping point." The fundamental idea is that a neighborhood, just like a natural ecosystem, has the capacity to contain only so much; too much of something and the system will collapse.

A study of neighborhood bars and taverns serves as an example. For those persons who are harmed by alcohol-related behavior, for the police who respond to alcohol-related calls for service, and other municipal officials who attempt to control these establishments, too many bars in too small an area can create an excessive amount of crime and disorder. The bars can lead to a

| **Exhibit 6–2** | Breaking Down CPTED Functions and Activities |

Following are some examples of actual CPTED activities, reported by the federal Office of Community Oriented Policing Services, that demonstrate how it works. Note that for each example, asking *why here?* compels the person(s) examining the situation to consider the motivations behind the activities, as well as the environmental conditions related to the location. Solving a problem thus requires a detailed understanding of both crime and place, and the response should consider one of the three objectives of CPTED: control access, provide opportunities to see and be seen, or define ownership and encourage the maintenance of territory.

Case #1: Custodial workers routinely find evidence of smoking, drinking, and vandalism in a high school lavatory.

Why here? The lavatory is in an isolated area of the building, adjacent to a ticket booth and concession stand that are active only during athletic events. The school's open lunch policy allows students to eat anywhere on campus, while monitors are assigned only to the cafeteria.

CPTED response: A lock is installed on the lavatory door, and it remains locked unless there is an athletic event. The open lunch policy has been revised: Students are still allowed to leave the cafeteria but must eat in designated areas, and a faculty member is charged with patrolling these areas during lunch periods.

Case #2: The back wall of a building in an office center is repeatedly tagged with graffiti.

Why here? The taggers have selected an area that is out of the view of passers-by: a rear corner location where two buildings come together at the end of a poorly lit service lane. Visibility is further reduced by hedges at the site's perimeter. Businesses in the office center are open from 9 AM to 5 PM during the week; however, the tagged building is next to a roller skating rink where activity peaks at night and on weekends.

CPTED response: Hedges are trimmed and wall-mounted light fixtures installed along the service lane, with motion detection lighting in the problem area. The skating rink agrees to change to a "no re-admission" policy to keep skaters inside the building and away from the office property.

Case #3: ATM patrons at a bank are being robbed after dark.

Why here? The bank is situated along a commercial strip in a neighborhood with vacant properties and abandoned businesses. The ATM is in the front corner of the bank building, and the drive-through teller windows are at the side of the building, around the corner from the ATM. Robbers hide in the darkened drive-through teller area and attack unsuspecting ATM users after they complete a transaction.

CPTED response: The bank installs a fence at the corner of the building, creating a barrier between the ATM and the drive-through teller area.

Source: Diane Zahm, *Using Crime Prevention through Environmental Design in Problem Solving* (U.S. Department of Justice, Office of Community Oriented Policing Services), August 2007, pp. 1–3, http://www.popcenter.org/tools/cpted/.

---

drain on municipal services, especially the police, and the neighborhood may reach its tipping point. Studies show that the number of bar seats located in a neighborhood has a multiplier effect on the police calls for service, and at some point the police, social services, and city resources become exhausted, and the situation can no longer be tolerated.[38] More research is certainly warranted concerning this tipping point concept (see Exhibit 6–2 for related examples).

SITUATIONAL CRIME PREVENTION

Situational crime prevention (SCP) draws from the aforementioned rational choice and routine activities theories and departs radically from most criminology in its orientation. It is often referred to as a problem-solving approach to crime prevention. It is focused on the settings for crime and the prevention of crime rather than on persons committing criminal acts. It seeks to forestall the occurrence of crime rather than to detect and sanction offenders. It seeks not to eliminate criminal or delinquent tendencies through improvement of society or its institutions but merely to make criminal action less attractive to offenders.[39] Simply, it seeks to eliminate crime opportunities.

SCP is a targeted means of reducing crime. It provides an analytical framework for strategies to prevent crime in varying settings. It is an "environmental criminology" approach that seeks to reduce crime opportunity by making settings less conducive to unwanted or illegal activities, focusing on the environment rather than the offender.[40] The commission of a crime requires not merely the offender but, as every detective story reader knows, also the opportunity for crime.[41]

Because "opportunity makes the thief," seven principles of crime opportunity have been developed, some of which draw on the above theories[42]:

1. Opportunities play a role in all crime.
2. Crime opportunities are highly specific (e.g., the theft of cars for joyriding has a different pattern of opportunity than theft for car parts).
3. Crime opportunities are concentrated in time and space (dramatic differences are found from one address to another, even in high-crime areas, and shift by time, hour, and day of week).
4. Crime opportunities depend on everyday movements of activity (e.g., burglars visit houses in the daytime when occupants are away).
5. One crime produces opportunities for another (e.g., a successful burglary may encourage the offender to return in the future, or a youth who has his bicycle stolen may feel justified in stealing someone else's).
6. Some products offer more tempting crime opportunities (e.g., easily carried items such as electronic equipment and jewelry are attractive).
7. Social and technological advancements produce new opportunities (products are most sought after in their new "mass-marketing" stages, when demand for them is greatest; most products reach a saturation stage where most people have them and they are unlikely to be stolen).

Although the concept of SCP was British in origin, its development was influenced by two independent, but nonetheless related, strands of policy research in the United States: defensible space and crime prevention through environmental design—both of which preceded SCP and were discussed earlier in the chapter. Because of the trans-Atlantic delay in the dissemination of ideas, however, there was no stimulus for the development of SCP.[43]

SCP is a problem-oriented approach that examines the roots of a problem and identifies a unique solution to the problem. Experience has shown that successful SCP measures must be directed against specific crimes and must be designed with a clear understanding of the motives of offenders and their methods. SCP relies on the rational choice theory of crime, which asserts that criminals choose to commit crimes based on the costs and benefits involved with the crime. For example, a potential offender will commit a high-risk crime only if the rewards of the crime outweigh the risks.[44]

Although by now largely taken for granted, glass-enclosed stairwells and elevators provide natural surveillance for users and reduce opportunities for victimization.

Gary Friedman/Los Angeles Times/Getty Images.

Ronald V. Clarke divided crime prevention goals into five primary objectives, each of which is designed to dissuade the criminal from committing the offense by making the crime too hard to commit, too risky, or too small in terms of rewards to be worth the criminal's time.[45] We discuss each of these five objectives:

1. *Increasing the effort needed to commit the crime.* Crimes typically happen because they are easy to commit. A person might see an easy opportunity to commit a crime and do so. Casual criminals are eliminated by increasing the effort needed to commit a crime. Following are different methods for increasing the effort needed to commit a crime:

   a. *Hardening targets.* Install physical barriers (such as locks, bolts, protective screens, and mechanical containment and antifraud devices to impede an offender's ability to penetrate a potential target).

   b. *Controlling access.* Install barriers and design walkways, paths, and roads so that unwanted users are prevented from entering vulnerable areas.

   c. *Deflecting offenders.* Discourage crime by giving people alternate legal venues for their activities (such as decreasing littering by providing litter bins or separating fans of rival teams after athletic events).

   d. *Controlling facilitators.* Facilitators are accessories who aid in the commission of crimes. Controlling them is achieved by universal measures (such as firearms permit regulations) and specific measures (metal detectors in community centers).

2. *Increasing the risks associated with the crime.* Increasing the risks associated with a crime reduces the incidence of that crime, because criminals believe they will not be caught; offenders who believe that they will be caught are less likely to offend. For example, if a video camera monitors all entrances and exits to a convenience store or bank, potential robbers who know of such surveillance will be less likely to rob such establishments.

   a. *Entry and exit screening.* Screening methods include guest sign-ins or a required display of identification; they ensure that residents and visitors meet entrance requirements.

   b. *Formal surveillance.* Using security personnel and hardware (such as CCTV and burglar alarms) is a deterrent to unwanted activities.

   c. *Informal surveillance.* The presence of building attendants, concierges, maintenance workers, and attendants increases site surveillance and crime reporting.

   d. *Natural surveillance.* The surveillance can be provided by people as they go about their daily activities, making potential offenders feel exposed and vulnerable.

3. *Reducing the rewards.* Reducing the rewards from crime makes offending not worthwhile to offenders. Methods of reducing rewards include making targets of crime less valuable by the following means:

   a. *Removing targets.* Eliminate crime purposes from public areas. Examples include having a no-cash policy and keeping valuable property in a secure area overnight.

   b. *Identifying property.* Use indelible marks, establishing ownership and preventing individuals from reselling the property.

   c. *Removing inducements.* Related to target removal, this involves removing temptations that offenders have not targeted in advance but that are likely to become the targets of a spontaneous crime (such as vacant houses or other living units or broken windows and light fixtures).

4. *Reducing the provocations.* The environment or manner in which places are managed (e.g., busy bars and unmonitored drinking) may provoke crime and violence. Studies show that certain lighting improves people's mood and morale in the workplace. Additional seating and soothing music, measures to avoid long waiting lines, and other such options may reduce people's frustrations in crowded public places.

5. *Removing the excuses.* Many offenders say, "I didn't know any better" or "I had no choice." This strategy involves informing individuals of the law and rules and offers them alternatives to illegal activity by eliminating their excuses for committing crime. For example, a "no trespassing" sign is enforceable if posted. It also involves rule setting, such as clearly stating the rules of a housing development, which establish the procedures of punishment for violators. Such methods prevent offenders from excusing their crimes by claiming ignorance or misunderstanding.

TABLE 6–2 Situational Crime Prevention Matrix

Increase the Effort	Increase the Risks	Reduce the Rewards	Reduce the Provocations	Remove the Excuses
1. *Harden targets* immobilizers in cars antirobbery screens	6. *Extend guardianship* cocooning Neighborhood Watch	11. *Conceal targets* gender-neutral phone directories off-street parking	16. *Reduce frustration and stress* efficient queueing soothing lighting	21. *Set rules* rental agreements hotel registration
2. *Control access to facilities* alley gating entry phones	7. *Assist natural surveillance* improved street lighting Neighborhood Watch hotlines	12. *Remove targets* removable car radios; prepaid public phone cards	17. *Avoid disputes* fixed cab fares; reduce crowding in pubs	22. *Post instructions* "No parking" "Private property"
3. *Screen exits* tickets needed electronic tags for libraries	8. *Reduce anonymity* taxi driver IDs "How's my driving?" signs	13. *Identify property* property marking; vehicle licensing	18. *Reduce emotional arousal* controls on violent porn; prohibit pedophiles working with children	23. *Alert conscience* roadside speed display signs "Shoplifting is stealing"
4. *Deflect offenders* street closures in red light district separate toilets for women	9. *Utilize place managers* train employees to prevent crime support whistleblowers	14. *Disrupt markets* checks on pawn brokers licensed street vendors	19. *Neutralize peer pressure* "Idiots drink and drive" "It's OK to say no"	24. *Assist compliance* litter bins public lavatories
5. *Control tools/weapons* toughened beer glasses; photos on credit cards	10. *Strengthen formal surveillance* speed cameras CCTV in town centers	15. *Deny benefits* ink merchandise tags; graffiti cleaning	20. *Discourage imitation* rapid vandalism repair; V-chips in TVs	25. *Control drugs/alcohol* Breathalyzers in pubs; alcohol-free events

Source: Ronald V. Clarke and Derek Cornish, "Opportunities, Precipitators, and Criminal Decisions: A Reply to Wortley's Critique of Situational Crime Prevention." In M. Smith and D. B. Cornish (eds.), Theory for Situational Crime Prevention. *Crime Prevention Studies*, Vol. 16 (Monsey, N.Y.: Criminal Justice Press, 2003).

Table 6–2 presents a situational crime prevention matrix for CPTED, specifically for the five CPTED objectives discussed. Included are organized (procedural measures), mechanical (provision or removal of certain physical objects), and natural (use of native aspects of the environment) means of facilitating each.

OTHER CRIME PREVENTION CHALLENGES

Next we look at four challenges that come into play with crime prevention operations that must be taken into account if the strategy is to function properly: the role of the **crime prevention officers' roles**, crime displacement and diffusion of benefit, properly publicizing crime prevention campaigns, and the evaluation of results.

Officers' Roles

What do crime prevention officers do? In broad terms, the mission of the crime prevention officer is to solve problems. By using all resources—city agencies, social services, the fire department, power companies, and landlords—the crime prevention effort builds a sense of partnership with other city and community agencies. It is proactive work, investigating suspicious people and activities. It is police work that recognizes the importance of community input and involves officers trying to solve community problems even if they are not criminal in nature.

Today's crime prevention officers are also specifically engaged in the following activities:

- Obtaining useful information concerning hot spots, crime patterns, and individuals of interest.
- Using resources to put an end to ongoing problems and reduce the number of calls for service that require officer intervention, so as to free up patrol time and afford officers more time to be proactive.
- Acting as liaisons for Neighborhood Watch participants along with conducting public relations events, thus giving the department a human face and improving relationships between the police and the citizens.
- Obtaining and using grant money and other donations to fund programs allow the department to use budgeted funds for other needed activities.[46]

It has also been said that every police officer needs to know at least as much as the criminal knows. The problem-solving process discussed in Chapter 5 illustrates the importance of officers understanding of crime prevention, especially during analysis and response steps. Certainly, the knowledge to commit criminal acts is not limited to a few; such information now is widely available on the Internet. For example, the Open Organization of Lockpickers, or TOOOL (www.toool.nl), is an organization dedicated to the so-called sport of lock picking. Although most TOOOL enthusiasts are generally law-abiding people who are interested in the intricacies of locks and keys, that information is available to those with criminal designs as well. Another site where such information proliferates is YouTube, where videos now explicitly show how to open padlocks with a tool made from a soft drink can, and how to get drinks and food from vending machines without paying. Obviously the police must monitor such sites and be aware of what the "bad guys" know, are doing, and are using as tools.[47]

Conducting a Publicity Campaign

Crime prevention **publicity campaigns** target two main audiences: potential victims and offenders. Police agencies should decide which audience to target based on the nature of the problem. For example, if a police department notices there are numerous preventable property crimes in an area, perhaps a short campaign to remind residents about the importance of securing their belongings could be beneficial. On the other hand, if local youths routinely vandalize cars in a parking lot, a campaign threatening police apprehension would be more effective. A dual approach can also be used, whereby two campaigns run simultaneously, one to reduce the number of potential victims, and the other to deter offenders. Many agencies utilize their police volunteers to distribute crime prevention materials throughout the community such as libraries, public buildings, and community centers.

Victim-Oriented Campaigns

Efforts to reach victims can take one of two forms: police can try to provide general information to residents concerning crime and its prevention, or they can advertise a specific community program they are undertaking. These campaigns often involve cooperation between the police department and the community in conducting home security surveys, obtaining steering-wheel locks, or providing classes on various security-enhancing measures. Fliers and newsletters demonstrating techniques to make cars and houses "burglar-proof" are common in these "target-hardening" campaigns.

Offender-Oriented Campaigns

Offender-oriented crime prevention strategies rely on the notion that offenders are rational individuals who seek to maximize their rewards while minimizing their potential costs. With that premise, giving offenders information about the risks of crime becomes an important component of crime reduction efforts. Publicity campaigns that threaten an increased risk of arrest can be more effective in reducing offending.

Offender campaigns are successful not when they threaten later punishment, but when they threaten detection and arrest. Offender campaigns are more efficient when they target specific crime types and focus on a clearly defined geographic area. For offenders to take the message

TABLE 6–3	Managing Victim- and Offender-Oriented Publicity Campaigns

Publicity directed at VICTIMS can advertise:

- Self-protection techniques
- New ways to report crime
- Locations of police facilities or resources
- Dangerous areas
- Offenders living in the area (e.g., sex offenders)
- Neighborhood crime problems.

Publicity directed at OFFENDERS can advertise:

- Police techniques or future police crackdowns
- Penalties or the risk of apprehension for certain crimes
- Results of past crackdowns or police operations
- Knowledge of an illicit market or drug trade
- Legislative changes

Source: U.S. Department of Justice, Office of Community Oriented Policing Services, Center for Problem Oriented Policing, "Police Publicity Campaigns and Target Audiences," http://www.popcenter.org/responses/crime_prevention/2 (Accessed September 22, 2010).

seriously, they need to feel as though the campaign targets them directly. For example, a police initiative to reduce car vandalism after school hours can include posting signs around town stating that "Vandalism is a Misdemeanor," but a more focused approach might include posters in the problem area with messages such as "Smile: Undercover Officers are Watching You," or "Our Officers Have Arrested 12 Students for Vandalism This Month – Will You Be Next?"[48]

Table 6–3 provides the primary considerations when developing both victim- and offender-oriented campaigns.

Displacement of Crime and Diffusion of Benefit

An issue that emerges in any serious discussion of crime prevention is **crime displacement**, which refers to the idea that rather than eliminating crime, interventions simply result in the movement of crime to another area, shift offenders to new targets in the same area, alter the methods used to accomplish a crime, or prompt offenders to change the type of crime they commit.[49] Displacement has, therefore, been the Achilles' heel of crime prevention in general. Efforts to control drug dealing and crime in neighborhoods and places are often criticized for having displaced the offending behavior instead of reducing it. If crime or drug dealing has only been moved around without any net reduction in harmful behavior, then that would be a valid criticism.

Research indicates, however, that displacement is not inevitable but is contingent on the offender's judgments about alternative crimes. If these alternatives are not viable, the offender may well settle for smaller criminal rewards or for a lower rate of crime. Few offenders are so driven by need or desire that they have to maintain a certain level of offending, whatever the cost. For many, the elimination of easy opportunities for crime may actually encourage them to explore noncriminal alternatives.[50] There are six commonly recognized types of displacement[51]:

1. *Time.* Offenders change the time when they commit crimes (e.g., switching from dealing drugs during the day to dealing at night).
2. *Location.* Offenders switch from targets in one location to targets in other locations (e.g., a dealer stops selling drugs in one community and begins selling them in another community).
3. *Target.* Offenders switch from one type of target to another type (e.g., a burglar switches from apartment units to detached single-family homes).
4. *Method.* Offenders change the way they attack targets (e.g., a street robber stops using a knife and uses a gun).

5. *Type.* Offenders switch from one form of crime to another (e.g., from burglary to check fraud).
6. *Perpetrator.* New offenders replace old offenders who have been removed by police enforcement (e.g., a dealer is arrested and a new dealer begins business with the same customers).

A review of the evidence for displacement shows that when attempts to detect displacement have been made, it is often not found, and if found, it is far less than 100 percent. John Eck found that of 33 studies that looked for displacement effects, only 3 found evidence of much displacement.[52] Eck concluded, "There is more reason to expect no displacement than a great deal. A reasonable conclusion is that displacement can be a threat, but that it is unlikely to completely negate gains due to an enforcement crackdown or a crime prevention effort."[53]

Research has shown that offenders generally begin offending at places they are familiar with and explore outward into increasingly unfamiliar areas.[54] If opportunities are blocked (by increased enforcement, target hardening, or some other means) close to a familiar location, then displacement to other targets close to familiar areas is most likely. Displacement usually occurs in the direction of familiar places, times, targets, and behaviors. Offenders may desist for varying periods of time, or they may even stop offending, depending on how important crime is to their lives.[55]

Although studies have indicated that displacement may not pose a major threat to crime prevention efforts, it is still a phenomenon that police officials must take into account. Ignoring this problem can lead to inequitable solutions to problems; this is particularly true of problem-solving tactics designed to displace offenders from specific locations. Efforts must be made to track those individuals to ensure that they do not create a problem somewhere else.[56]

Diffusion of benefits is the opposite of crime displacement. Diffusion is positive crime reductions that occur in areas outside the areas of targeted crime prevention efforts. For example, police may target prostitution in a three-block area and learn that strong armed robberies and car burglaries were reduced in areas near but outside their zone of prostitution efforts. Diffusion effects are often referred to as Halo, free rider, and multiplier effects. Simply put, it is a positive effect on crime that does not require that police expend resources in those areas affected.

Evaluating Crime Prevention Initiatives

The field of crime prevention generally suffers from the same shortcoming and criticisms that many other interventions suffer from: poor or nonexistent **evaluation**. The evaluation component of many initiatives is often poorly conceived, marginally funded, and short-lived. A useful form of evaluation is an outcome or impact evaluation to determine whether the intervention accomplished the expected result. Assessments of this nature require more planning and effort, and consideration must be given to the selection of comparison groups, time frames, outcome variables, potential confounding factors, and analytic techniques.[58] (We will discuss such higher levels of evaluation in Chapter 11.)

For now, we will briefly note that evaluations not only provide the police with valuable information, but also give community leaders and residents an indication of the success or failure of crime prevention efforts.[59] That point hopefully will be made as we look at the following discussion of what works and does not work in crime prevention.

CRIME PREVENTION: WHAT WORKS AND WHAT DOESN'T

Many crime prevention programs work; others do not. Most programs have not yet been evaluated with enough scientific evidence to draw conclusions. Enough evidence is available, however, to create tentative lists of **what works**, what does not work, and what is promising.

Following are the major conclusions of a report to Congress, based on a systematic review of more than 500 scientific evaluations of crime prevention practices by the University of Maryland's Department of Criminology and Criminal Justice.[60] This is the first major evaluation of crime prevention programs, resulting in much attention and debate in the field. There are some surprising findings, particularly in the list of programs that do not hold promise—several of which have become pet projects of police agencies and political leaders.

What Prevents or Reduces Crime

The following are programs that researchers believed with reasonable certainty would prevent crime or reduce risk factors for crime. These programs are thus likely to be effective in preventing some form of crime:

- Providing extra police patrols in high-crime hot spots.
- Monitoring known high-risk repeat offenders to reduce their time on the streets and returning them to prison quickly.
- Arresting employed domestic abusers to reduce repeated abuse by these suspects.
- Offering rehabilitation programs for juvenile and adult offenders that are appropriate to their risk factors to reduce their rates of repeat offending.
- Offering drug treatment programs to prison inmates to reduce repeat offending after their release.

What Does Not Appear to Be Successful

Sufficient evidence indicated to the University of Maryland researchers that the following programs failed to reduce crime or reduce risk factors:

- Gun buyback programs failed to reduce gun violence in cities (as evaluated in St. Louis and Seattle).
- Neighborhood Watch programs organized with police failed to reduce burglary or other target crimes, especially in higher-crime areas where voluntary participation often fails.
- Arrests of unemployed suspects for domestic assault caused higher rates of repeat offending over the long term than nonarrest alternatives.
- Increased arrests or raids on drug markets failed to reduce violent crime or disorder for more than a few days, if at all.
- Storefront police offices failed to prevent crime in the surrounding areas.
- Police newsletters with local crime information failed to reduce victimization rates (as evaluated in Newark, New Jersey, and Houston, Texas).
- Correctional boot camps using traditional military training failed to reduce repeat offending after release compared to similar offenders serving time on probation and parole, for both juveniles and adults.
- "Scared Straight" programs that bring minor juvenile offenders to visit maximum-security prisons to see the severity of prison conditions failed to reduce the participants' reoffending rates and may increase crime.
- Shock probation, shock parole, and split sentences, in which offenders are incarcerated for a short period of time at the beginning of the sentence and then supervised in the community, did not reduce repeat offending compared to the placement of similar offenders only under community supervision, and they increased crime rates for some groups.

Although adult and juvenile military-style boot camps multiplied in the 1990s as a tough-on-crime measure, their use dropped off rapidly when studies revealed they accomplished little in reducing recidivism.
Richard Smith/Alamy Stock Photo.

- Home detention with electronic monitoring for low-risk offenders failed to reduce offending compared to the placement of similar offenders under standard community supervision without electronic monitoring.
- Intensive supervision on parole or probation did not reduce repeat offending compared to normal levels of community supervision.

What Holds Promise

Researchers determined that the level of certainty for the following programs is too low for there to be positive generalizable conclusions, but some empirical basis exists for predicting that further research could show positive results:

- Problem-solving analysis is effective when addressed to the specific crime situation.
- Proactive arrests for carrying concealed weapons in gun crime hot spots, using traffic enforcement and field interrogations, can be helpful.
- Community policing with meetings to set priorities reduced community perceptions of the severity of crime problems in Chicago.
- Field interrogations of suspicious persons reduced crime in a San Diego experiment.
- Gang offender monitoring by community workers and probation and police officers can reduce gang violence.
- Community-based mentoring by Big Brothers/Big Sisters of America substantially reduced drug abuse in one experiment, although evaluations of other similar programs showed that it did not.
- Battered women's shelters were found to reduce at least the short-term (six-week) rate of repeat victimization for women who take other steps to seek help.

Many more impact evaluations using stronger scientific methods are needed before even minimally valid conclusions can be reached about the impact of programs on crime. Again, as previously noted, there is much debate in the field about the research findings. The Maryland report to Congress, however, has raised the consciousness of the crime prevention discipline and will, it is hoped, bring about much more needed research and inquiry.

Summary

It is clear that the field of crime prevention has matured from its earlier forms, originally involving strategic placement of rocks by early cave dwellers and until recently having to do primarily with target hardening one's home with better locks. This chapter has shown its various elements as well as the results of research efforts concerning what good can occur when measures are taken to prevent crimes. The police realize that they alone cannot prevent or address crime and disorder and that a partnership with the community is essential if the physical and social problems that plague communities are to be reduced or eliminated.

Key Terms and Concepts

Anchor points
Crime displacement
Crime opportunity
Crime prevention officers'
 roles

Crime prevention through
 environmental design
 (CPTED)
Designing out crime
Diffusion of benefit

Evaluation
Publicity campaign
Second-generation CPTED
Situational crime prevention
 (SCP)

"What works" (in crime
 prevention)

Items for Review

1. Describe briefly the history of crime prevention.
2. Explain the relationship between community, crime prevention and problem-oriented policing, and how each can identify and address crime in so-called "anchor points."
3. Define what is meant by CPTED, how it functions, and the focal points of its first, second, and third generations.
4. Explain the crime prevention officer's roles.

5. Describe what is meant by situational crime prevention, and list its five goals.
6. Review some of the primary considerations for conducting a crime- and victim-oriented publicity campaign.

7. Explain what is meant by crime displacement and how it relates to crime prevention.
8. Discuss some crime reduction or prevention activities have been shown by researchers to work, to not work, and to hold promise.

Learn by Doing

1. As part of a class group project, you and a fellow criminal justice student have been assigned to determine what research shows concerning "what works, what doesn't work, and what has promise." You contact the research, planning, and analysis unit of your local police agency and ask for their input. What will they say does, in fact, "work" in policing, and what initiatives have been shown to not work?
2. Your criminal justice professor assigns your class the following individual or group task: identify the hot spots for crime within a

particularly crime-prone neighborhood in your city. Next, identify the anchor points that exist within that neighborhood, and which of them tend to contribute to the crime problems. Finally, focusing on those anchor points, identify what kinds of collective activities might jointly be undertaken by the police and citizens to reduce crime and disorder in order to reclaim them.
3. Your criminal justice professor asks you to prepare an essay defining crime prevention, CPTED, and situational crime prevention. What will be your responses?

Endnotes

1. Major Richard Mellard, Wichita, Kansas, Police Department, personal communication (August 1, 1983).
2. See National Crime Prevention Council, http://www.ncpc.org/.
3. Ronald V. Clarke, *Situational Crime Prevention: Successful Case Studies* (2nd ed.) (Monsey, N.Y.: Criminal Justice Press, 1997), p. 2.
4. Crime Prevention Coalition of America, *Crime Prevention in America: Foundations for Action* (Washington, D.C.: National Crime Prevention Council, 1990), p. 64.
5. Steven P. Lab, "Crime Prevention: Where Have We Been and Which Way Should We Go?" in Steven P. Lab (ed.), *Community Policing at a Crossroads* (Cincinnati, Ohio: Anderson, 1997), pp. 1–13.
6. Cynthia Scanlon, "Crime Prevention Through Environmental Design," *Law and Order* (May 1996):50.
7. U.S. Department of Housing and Urban Development, "Crime Prevention Through Environmental Design," in *Crime Prevention Brief* (Washington, D.C.: Author, n.d.), p. 2.
8. Lab, "Crime Prevention," p. 5.
9. Ibid.
10. Ibid., p. 7.
11. Scanlon, "Crime Prevention Through Environmental Design," p. 50.
12. Lab, "Crime Prevention," p. 6.
13. L. E. Cohen and M. Felson, "Social Change and Crime Rate Trends: A Routine Activity Approach," *American Sociological Review* 44 (1997):588–608.
14. D. B. Cornish and R. V. Clarke, *The Reasoning Criminal: Rational Choice Perspectives on Offending* (New York: Springer-Verlag, 1986).
15. James Q. Wilson and George Kelling, "Broken Windows," *The Atlantic Monthly* 211 (1982):29–38.
16. Lab, "Crime Prevention," p. 6.
17. Ronald V. Clarke, "Situational Crime Prevention: Its Theoretical Basis and Practical Scope," in Michael Tonry and Norval Morris (eds.), *Crime and Justice: An Annual Review of Research* (Vol. 4) (Chicago, Ill.: University of Chicago Press, 1983), pp. 225–256.
18. Lab, "Crime Prevention," pp. 8–9.
19. Lab, "Crime Prevention," p. 6.
20. Ibid., p. 8.
21. U.S. Department of Justice, Bureau of Justice Assistance, *Crime Prevention and Community Policing*, p. 3.
22. Anthony Braga, "Crime and Policing Revisited," Harvard Kennedy School (Washington, D.C.: National Institute of Justice, September 2015), pp. 17–18.
23. National Crime Prevention Council, *Crime Prevention Through Environmental Design Training Program*, http://www.ncpc.org/training/training-topics/crime-prevention-through-environmental-design-cpted-.
24. Association of State and Territorial Health Officials, "Crime Prevention Through Environmental Design," (Arlington, Va.: Author, n.d.).
25. "Ohio Kidnapping Survivors Recount Captivity, Escape from Horror," NPR, April 29, 2015, http://www.npr.org/2015/04/29/403035591/ohio-kidnapping-survivors-recount-captivity-escape-from-horror.
26. Sharon Chamard, "Community Cohesion and Empowerment," in Kenneth J. Peak (ed.), *Encyclopedia of Community Policing and Problem Solving* (Thousand Oaks, Calif.: Sage, 2013), pp. 34–37.
27. Lawrence Sherman, quoted in Keith Harries, *Mapping Crime: Principle and Practice*, National Criminal Justice Reference Service, December 1999, https://www.ncjrs.gov/html/nij/mapping/ch4_9.html.
28. Craig D. Uchida, Marc L. Swatt, Shellie E. Solomon, Sean Varano, "Data-Driven Crime Prevention: New Tools for Community Involvement and Crime Control" (Washington, D.C.: U.S. Department of Justice, March 2014), Document No. 245408, unpublished, pp. 1–2.
29. C. R. Jeffrey, *Crime Prevention Through Environmental Design* (Beverly Hills, Calif.: Sage, 1971), p. 117.
30. National Crime Prevention Council, *Designing Safer Communities: A Crime Prevention Through Environmental Design Handbook* (Washington, D.C.: Author, 1997), pp. 7–8.
31. National Crime Prevention Council, *Best Practices for Using Crime Prevention Through Environmental Design in Weed and Seed Sites*, December 2009, http://www.ncpc.org/

resources/files/pdf/training/Best%20Practices%20in%20 CPTED%20-2.pdf.

32. "Building a More Crime-Free Environment: Tempe Cops Have the Last Word on Construction Projects," *Law Enforcement News* (November 15, 1998):7.

33. Scanlon, "Crime Prevention Through Environmental Design," pp. 51–52.

34. Diane Zahm, *Using Crime Prevention Through Environmental Design in Problem-Solving* (Washington, D.C.: U.S. Department of Justice, Center for Problem-Oriented Policing, August 2007), pp. 18–24, http://www.popcenter.org/tools/ pdfs/cpted.pdf.

35. Greg Saville and Gerry Cleveland, "2nd Generation CPTED: An Antidote to the Social Y2K Virus of Urban Design," Paper presented at the Third Annual International CPTED Conference, Washington, D.C., December 14–16, 1998.

36. Ibid., p. 1.

37. Ibid.

38. Gregory Saville, "New Tools to Eradicate Crime Places and Crime Niches," Paper presented at the Conference of Safer Communities, Melbourne, Australia, September 10–11, 1998, pp. 9–10.

39. Clarke, "Situational Crime Prevention," p. 230.

40. U.S. Department of Housing and Urban Development, "Situational Prevention," *Crime Prevention Brief* (Washington, D.C.: Author, n.d.), p. 1.

41. Clarke, "Situational Crime Prevention," p. 231.

42. U.S. Department of Justice, Center for Problem-Oriented Policing, "The 10 Principles of Crime Opportunity," http://www.popcenter. org/about-situational.htm.

43. Clarke, "Situational Crime Prevention," p. 236.

44. Ibid.

45. Ibid.

46. Adapted from Ron Francis and Jeff Wamboldt, "Making Crime Prevention a Priority," *The Police Chief* (January 2010), p. 40, http://www.policechiefmagazine.org/magazine/index. cfm?fuseaction=display_arch&article_id=1989&issue_id=12010.

47. Jeffrey Dingle, "Thinking Like a Thief Is the Key to Crime Prevention," *The Police Chief* (January 2010), p. 30, http://www. policechiefmagazine.org/magazine/index.cfm?fuseaction=display_ arch&article_id=1986&issue_id=12010.

48. Ibid., pp. 5–11.

49. Lab, "Crime Prevention," p. 12.

50. Clarke, "Situational Crime Prevention," p. 237.

51. Robert Barr and Ken Pease, "Crime Placement, Displacement, and Deflection," in Michael Tonry and Norval Morris (eds.), *Crime and Justice: A Review of Research* (Vol. 12) (Chicago, Ill.: University of Chicago Press, 1990), pp. 146–175.

52. John E. Eck, "The Threat of Crime Displacement," *Criminal Justice Abstracts* 25 (3) (1993):529.

53. Ibid., pp. 534–536.

54. Ibid., p. 537.

55. Ibid.

56. Ibid., pp. 541–542.

57. Kate Bowers and Shane Johnson, "Measuring the Geographical Displacement and Diffusion of Benefit Effects of Crime Prevention Activity." *Journal of Quantitative Criminology* 19(3) (2003):275–301.

58. John E. Eck, "The Threat of Crime Displacement," *Criminal Justice Abstracts* 25 (3) (1993):529.

59. William Spelman and John Eck, "Problem Solving: POP in Newport News," *National Institute of Justice Research in Brief* (January 1987), p. 8.

60. Lawrence W. Sherman, Denise C. Gottfredson, Doris L. MacKenzie, John Eck, Peter Reuter, and Shawn D. Bushway, "Preventing Crime: What Works, What Doesn't, What's Promising." *National Institute of Justice Research in Brief* (1998), pp. 1–27.

61. Adapted from European Crime Prevention Network, "What Does EUCPN Do?" http://eucpn.org/about/network.

Tools for Problem Solving:
Using Information Technology

LEARNING OBJECTIVES

As a result of reading this chapter, the student will understand:

- How information technology came to policing, how it has evolved, and the role police chief executives believe it plays
- The conceptual framework underlying use of IT for problem-oriented policing
- The role in, and contributions of, crime analysis to problem solving
- How to determine which IT tools to use for particular police operations
- The basics of crime mapping functions and real-time crime centers
- Four crime management strategies: CompStat, intelligence-led policing, predictive policing, and smart policing
- How social media and civic apps are being applied to crime fighting

TEST YOUR KNOWLEDGE

1. Common use of computers in patrol cars—mobile computing—should come to policing in about a decade.
2. Hacking for public purposes—known as civic hacking—can actually be a benefit to police.
3. Information technology is the backbone of problem-oriented policing.
4. Crime analysts are commonly hired from interviews at high school career fairs and immediately put to use primarily to plot the places where crimes occur.
5. Police have little or no—and some say will never have—the ability to predict where and what types of crimes will occur.

Answers can be found on page 278.

Everything we do is driven by data.
—WESTERN SHERIFF

INTRODUCTION

Although by now it sounds rather cliché, since the Great Recession forced the funding spigots to compress for most police agencies, they have had to learn to operate smarter and more affordably. One obvious way to do so is to use technology in more efficient ways. And while many police administrators may find it difficult to afford or justify new or existing technologies in the current fiscal environment, it can also be argued that it is certainly unwise to cut **information technology** (IT) investments and staffing; indeed, nowhere is technology needed more than in the realm of problem-oriented policing, where IT can serve as a "force multiplier" and give police agencies a distinct advantage in combating crime and disorder; as a RAND report noted, it can improve the effectiveness of operations and generate cost savings.[1] And as policing budgets begin to increase, it would be wise to likewise increase the agency's IT capabilities to the extent possible.

Many agencies are already using an array of databases, cameras, gunshot location devices, automated license plate readers, social media for allowing citizens to text crimes and other functions, and operational intelligence centers in efforts to obtain real-time crime data and feed it to the officers on the street in order to better respond to incidents. Even patrol cars are tracked so that officers can be deployed faster and where they are needed most.[2]

This chapter elaborates on those capabilities and explains the importance and application of tools and technologies used for police in their problem-solving efforts. It begins by briefly tracing how technologies came into policing, with assistance of the federal government, and how IT is now indispensable in addressing crime. Next we review the conceptual framework and rationale for using IT in problem-oriented policing, and then focus on analysis—the fundamental step of the SARA problem-solving model (discussed in Chapter 5)—and include the various functions and contributions of **crime analysis and analysts**. After looking at some means of determining which IT tools to use for different police functions, we then consider the major contributions of crime mapping and real-time crime centers. Then we examine four strategies that police managers can now deploy for addressing crime: **CompStat**, intelligence-led policing, predictive policing, and smart policing. The chapter concludes by considering how civic apps are used in fighting crime, how social media are being used, and how private corporations are providing the essential software used in problem solving.

A number of examples of IT applications are disseminated throughout the chapter, as are four exhibits. The chapter concludes with a summary, review questions, and several scenarios and activities that provide opportunities for you to "learn by doing."

Note that we will not endeavor to list or describe all of the technologies and tools that are available for, or adaptable to, problem-oriented policing purposes; the IT that is now available is simply too widespread and varied in role, nature, and application for us to attempt to do so. Therefore, here we will only cover the basics.

FIRST THINGS FIRST: IT COMES TO POLICING

Early Federal Stimulus

First, although it is a term that is used quite broadly, it would be beneficial to define a key term. IT is "anything related to computing technology, such as networking, hardware, software, the Internet, or the people that work with these technologies."[3] It may well be said that IT has become the backbone of problem-oriented policing.

The federal Law Enforcement Assistance Administration (LEAA) program lasted but 13 years, being abolished in 1982 after spending about $7.5 billion on all manner of criminal justice programs. Although the good that LEAA accomplished in light of those amounts of time and expenditures will be long debated, the agency nevertheless helped to educate and train thousands of criminal justice personnel while implementing new and worthwhile projects and paving the way for academics and practitioners to master new skills for criminal justice planning, analysis, and coordination. During its time, police departments began to invest in computers and eventually apply them to more sophisticated tasks, helped by LEAA-funded software via a series of grants.[4]

Later, in the 1990s, a national survey found that the use of computers was growing and police agencies were using them for increasingly diverse purposes; indeed, by 1993, two-thirds of local police departments were using computers, compared to half in 1990. More importantly, many agencies were using computers not only for routine record keeping, but also for relatively sophisticated functions such as criminal investigations, crime analysis, budgeting, and manpower allocation.[5]

Chief Executives' Views

Computers would later become essential in the development of Automated Fingerprint Identification Systems (AFIS). The development of 911 came next, and the introduction of computers into community policing came into being at the outset of the third and current era in American policing, the community policing era (discussed in Chapter 1). The value of computers for community policing and problem solving quickly became evident. As one major city police chief put it:

> The use of high-technology equipment and applications is essential to the efficient practice of community policing. Without high technology, officers would find it difficult to provide the level and quality of services the community deserves. Computer-aided dispatching, computers in patrol cars, automated fingerprinting systems, and online offense-reporting systems are but a few examples of the pervasiveness of technology in agencies that practice community policing.[6]

An example of those perceived applications is the Charlotte-Mecklenburg, North Carolina, Police Department's development of a $10 million "knowledge-based community-oriented policing system" that will focus "on the needs of the problem-solving officer in the streets."[7] Notably, the current class of police chiefs have a belief that computer technology is crucial to successful police work. As one chief put it, "My vision is that when an officer comes through the academy, we give him his weapon, we give him his radio, and we give him his laptop computer."[8] Indeed, many experts believe that the dominant transformation in policing has been the one in computing. So much of the criminal justice system can be seen as an information-processing system—dealing with information about events, about individuals. We are starting to see, still in a surprisingly limited way, the diffusion of that (computer) technology so that even fairly small police departments today have at least their own computers.

IT FOR PROBLEM-ORIENTED POLICING: A CONCEPTUAL FRAMEWORK

Rational for IT

To do their jobs effectively, law enforcement professionals at all levels depend on information. According to one estimate, "roughly 92% of an officer's time is spent acquiring, coalescing, or distributing information in one form or another."[9] While exact estimates of such percentages are difficult to make, access to and use of accurate and timely information is clearly critical to effective law enforcement. Even in traditional approaches to policing, responses to calls for service (CFS) and decisions on whether to detain individuals required access to the right data to ensure that actions are appropriate. More modern, sophisticated policing approaches (such as CompStat, predictive policing, and smart policing, discussed below) are even more information intensive and dependent. They involve not just information on crimes and perpetrators, but also data on community conditions, priorities, and other factors that could shape crime prevention and responses.

Systems for Acquiring Crime Information

Traditionally, users of police crime information and types of analysis could consult information that was drawn from three sources[10]:

- *Operations information systems:* These include the police radio, police records, NCIC, mobile computers, cellular phones, and so on; these were designed to supply police officers and detectives with raw data on such topics as CFS, persons, property, and vehicles. [**Mobile computing** has become the catchall phrase for outfitting an officer's vehicle or person with the technology that allows him or her to be a "mobile office." Mobile computing allows officers to access, receive, create, and exchange information wirelessly in the field. Officers can proactively query local, state, and national databases; receive and initiate CAD events; view unit status; send e-mail; prepare and file incident reports; issue citations; capture field interview information; access department policies and procedures; research penal codes; and perform many other functions.][11]
- *Command and control systems:* These include the above operations information system components plus 911, **computer-aided dispatching (CAD)**, vehicle locator systems, and other equipment designed to aid supervisors and middle managers in directing and

controlling their subordinates, especially patrol officers. [CAD is indispensable for policing, from processing emergency CFS to managing officer-initiated car stops. CAD automates the call-taking and dispatching functions; is used with systems that track patrol vehicle status; can help to prioritize CFS; and makes recommendations for unit and resource dispatching based on beats, zones, closest resources, repeat CFS, and/or current unit activities.][12]

- *Management information systems:* MIS consists of various databases pertinent to the internal management of the police organization, such as officer productivity, citizen complaints, and inventory, designed to aid managers and executives in carrying out their administrative duties. [MIS captures, maintains, and analyzes all police agency and incident-related information and is vital for tracking and managing criminal and noncriminal events, investigations, and personnel information. It can automate the daily practice of entering, storing, retrieving, retaining, archiving, viewing, and exchanging records, documents, data, information, or files related to persons, vehicles, incidents, arrests, warrants, traffic accidents, citations, pawn tickets, civil process papers, gun registration investigations, property, and evidence.][13]

Community policing and problem solving requires adjustments to each of these three types of information systems. For example, rather than obtaining raw crime data, front-line problem-solving officers require more geographically based information, more information about problems (not just isolated incidents), and more in-depth analysis products. Furthermore, MIS needs to focus less on efficient incident handling and accountability for each minute of an officer's time, and more on effective problem solving and on accountability for conditions in geographic areas of responsibility.

In addition, problem-oriented policing requires at least three other general types of police information systems:

- *Geographic information systems:* Crime data must be related to locations that result in maps and other products pertinent to identifying and analyzing geographically based problems and conditions, and the way they change over time.
- *Problem-solving information systems:* Databases and systems must capture information about completed and ongoing problem-solving efforts in order to aid officers and citizens in identifying, analyzing, and responding to substantive problems in communities.
- *External information systems:* Officers must be able to obtain data and information from other organizations and from the public, which also aid those entities in obtaining information from the public.[14]

Exploiting the Young Officer's Flair for IT

As discussed in Chapter 3, many police executives are noticing the technological skills that many young officers (of the Millennial generation) bring to their departments. One example, provided by a Western police chief:

> About six months ago I was out on patrol and I stopped to back up one of our officers, who is 23 years old. He was on his smartphone, and I learned that he had written his own application to access criminal records and photographs of inmates booked into the county jail. He had written it himself. We took that application and spread it throughout the organization, and it didn't cost us anything. Another officer is working on an app so that we can look on our smartphones and watch the real-time GPS tracking of offenders on probation or parole. We also have an app under development to map restraining orders, and have automated our crime mapping process, so every day the crime maps are updated automatically.[15]

CRIME ANALYSIS: REVISITING SARA

What It Is, and How It Works

Crime analysis may be defined as:

> The qualitative and quantitative study of crime and law enforcement information in combination with socio-demographic and spatial factors to apprehend criminals, prevent crime, reduce disorder, and evaluate organizational procedures.[16]

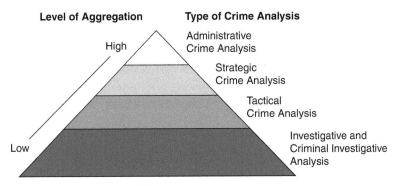

FIGURE 7–1 The Crime Analysis Model

Source: Rachel Boba, Introductory Guide to Crime Analysis and Mapping (U.S. Department of Justice, Office of Community Oriented Policing Services (November 2001), p. 15.)

Crime analysis has been used in many different policing philosophies and strategies. From its initial application to investigations and solving crimes and reporting statistics, crime analysis is now well integrated into many of the strategies being practiced by police departments in the twenty-first century. Some of the more common ones, in addition to problem-oriented policing, include CompStat, predictive policing, and intelligence-led policing (discussed below). All have different foci but are data-driven.

For community policing and problem solving, crime analysis techniques and processes can be integrated at many levels. Crime analysts can identify problems that need to be worked, assist with collecting and analyzing the data, help inform the team on the best responses, and assess the results of problem-solving efforts. Crime analysis is also important in producing and sharing information with stakeholders, both internal and external to the department.

Figure 7–1 depicts how the four types of crime analysis relate to one another in terms of the level of aggregation of the information:

1. *Administrative* crime analysis is the presentation of findings of crime research and analysis based on legal, political, and practical concerns to inform audiences within police administration, city government/council, and citizens.
2. *Strategic* crime analysis is the study of crime and police information integrated with socio-demographic and spatial factors to determine long term "patterns" of activity, to assist in problem solving, as well as to research and evaluate responses and procedures.
3. *Tactical* crime analysis examines characteristics such as how, when, and where criminal activity has occurred to assist in problem solving by developing patterns and trends, identifying investigative leads/suspects, and clearing cases.
4. *Criminal* investigative analysis is the study of serial criminals, victims, and/or crime scenes and physical, sociodemographic, psychological, and geographic characteristics to develop patterns for linking together and solving current serial criminal activity.[17]

What Crime Analysts Do

Specially trained crime analysts perform a variety of functions, including the following[18]:

- Review daily all police reports to identify patterns and trends as they emerge. If a burglar starts targeting drug stores in an officer's jurisdiction, a crime analyst will likely let him or her know after the second incident. Trend analyses provide officers with the who, what, when, where, how, and why of emerging crimes, toward developing effective tactics and strategies for preventing victimization and reducing crime.
- Research and analyze long-term problems that every police department faces, from a park that has been a drug dealing hot spot for 20 years to a street that has a high number of car accidents to crime and disorder at budget motels. Crime analysts can explore its dimensions, and help the police department come up with long-term solutions.
- Develop and link local intelligence concerning criminals and criminal organizations: their goals, their activities, their chains of command, how money and goods flow through them, what they're planning, and so on.

Finally, crime analysts make the police department look good. Personnel are informed about a crime pattern before the press hears about it. And when someone wants crime information—a politician, reporter, another agency, or citizen—it can be provided completely and quickly.

New York City Police Commissioner William Bratton has said that:

> The heart and soul of any department's success in its principal obligation of crime control is first rate crime analysis—a field of endeavor that has been growing in leaps and bounds, thankfully . . . chiefs need to understand just how essential this area is to successful crime control.[19]

Acquiring the Ability to Analyze Crimes

Effective problem solving obviously requires a thorough analysis of a problem to understand its causes or contributing factors; therefore, problem analysis is most likely to be that aspect of problem-oriented policing that poses the greatest challenge to perform and requires the greatest amount of effort and technologies. Some agencies will no doubt find the ability to analyze crime problems to be a daunting, if not impossible, task.

Therefore, a necessary first step for the agency toward performing analyses for problem solving is to determine whether it possesses, or needs, the expertise required for effective problem analysis. Few sworn police officers or even managers or executives bring to the job the requisite knowledge, skills, and abilities necessary to perform advanced problem analysis. Indeed, a minimum of a baccalaureate degree (and, preferably, a master's) level of training is required. Without an in-depth understanding of statistics and research methods, analyses may be improperly conducted and conclusions improperly drawn.

There are several options available for hiring a qualified analyst(s):

- *Hire your own analyst:* The ideal option is to hire analysts with the proper background, training, skills, and orientation for problem analysis as permanent police agency employees. An unscientific rule of thumb is that there should be one problem-solving analyst for every 100 sworn officers in your agency. Having fewer than this will make it difficult to conduct much problem analysis.
- *Enlist an external analyst:* If there is a college or university nearby, one or more professors and their students (preferably graduate level) might be available to perform some problem analysis for the agency. The chief's or sheriff's city or county government, or the federal government, might also have available analysts. Some state departments of justice or law enforcement have analysts on staff to work on law enforcement-related issues. As a last resort, a chief executive might explore hiring on a contract basis another police agency's analyst to work on specific analysis tasks for the agency.[20]

To further describe the kinds of abilities a crime analyst must possess and tasks to be able to perform, Exhibit 7–1 provides a job description for this position. It will be seen that this is a very demanding and challenging position.

| Exhibit 7–1 | Crime Analyst Job Description |

Per the Mesa, Arizona, Police Department, a job description for a crime analyst would include the following responsibilities, qualifications, and abilities.[21]

Responsibilities: Performs crime analysis work for the Police Department. Duties include:

▶ Performing difficult statistical and analytical research involving the use of computer applications, random statistical samplings, correlation and regression analysis, and probability studies.

▶ Gathering and analyzing crime data for crime pattern detection, suspect–crime correlations, target-suspect profiles, and crime forecasting; preparing reports on crime data and trends for police personnel.

▶ Making presentations to police personnel, members of the community, and outside agencies.

▶ Coordinating the automatic scheduling process for the Police Department.

▶ Managing the analysis for a Patrol District or for CompStat.

Minimum Qualifications:

▶ Any combination of training, education, or experience equivalent to graduation from an accredited college or university with a Bachelor's degree.

▶ Successful completion of a background investigation and polygraph.

▶ A pre-employment or pre-placement alcohol, drug, and/or controlled substance testing as outlined in city policy and procedures.

▶ Prefer that candidates have coursework in quantitative methods and program languages, and experience in statistical research and analysis using automated systems/records, geographic information systems (GIS), statistical analysis system (SAS) or statistical product and service solutions (SPSS), and general programming abilities.

Manual/Physical Abilities:

▶ Enter, search, and retrieve information utilizing a terminal or personal computer (PC) in order to collate and analyze crime statistics, maintain histories of crime information, and compile crime bulletins.

▶ Sort, separate, arrange, and file police reports, crime statistics, bulletins, and articles to maintain a history of crime-related statistics and perform crime analyses.

▶ Draw or letter charts, schedules, graphs, and maps to illustrate crime patterns/trends and statistical findings utilizing computer-aided graphics.

▶ Observe, compare, and monitor data including departmental reports and computer-generated statistics to determine compliance with crime analysis procedures. Inspect and monitor computer software for proper operation.

WHICH IT TOOLS TO USE? LOOK AT TYPE OF POLICE FUNCTION INVOLVED

One way to view what technologies can do for policing is to categorize police activities by types of functions performed; such a classification was developed by Hoey[22] (1998), whose three broadly defined areas were as follows:

- *Support* functions, including communication, coordination, administrative, and oversight functions, such as dispatch, personnel management, surveillance, and in-service training. Specific types of IT investments supporting these functions include:
  - *Administrative systems*, including records management.
  - *Communications systems*, including computer-aided dispatch systems and in-car mobile data terminals.
  - *Surveillance systems*, including CCTV and gunshot detection systems.
- *Reactive* policing functions, including responding to citizens' CFS, responding to emergencies, and conducting investigations. Specific types of related IT investments included systems intended to help law enforcement with *crime investigations*, such as the agency having ownership of an Integrated Automated Fingerprint Identification System terminal.
- *Proactive* policing functions, including intelligence-driven operations, such as hot spot patrols, community-oriented engagement, and data sharing with other federal and state agencies, businesses, and partner organizations.

These three categories reflect key differences in strategies. They also demonstrate that before a police agency can realize any value from its IT investments, it must first understand the kinds of activities those tools are intended to assist.

This is most readily seen with proactive policing techniques: for example, while IT-based community interaction tools might be valuable for a department deeply involved in community policing, a department that either chooses or must only engage in reactive answering of calls for service would find such an investment to be a waste of scarce resources. Therefore, the above classification scheme allows agencies to separate activities by the different potential effects of IT in terms of desired outcomes, and also to determine whether benefits would even be expected from particular IT investments, given departmental strategies and officer allocation decisions.[23]

CRIME MAPPING

Certainly all of the aforementioned police strategies (CompStat, and so on) rely heavily on knowing where crimes occur; the influence of geography not only informs criminals about where to commit their crimes, but the task then falls to the police to try to anticipate and shift resources to those places.

A Long-Standing Practice

Conclusive evidence from clay tablets found in Iraq proves that maps have been around for several thousand years—perhaps tens of millennia.[24] More recently, the value of mapping was established in London in the mid-nineteenth century, when cholera became a horrific disease that brought tremendous death and suffering. Determining that the disease appeared to be concentrated in specific neighborhoods, Dr. John Snow, a physician who attempted to establish a pattern for the deadly disease, plotted the location of cholera deaths on a map of central London. Believing that contaminated water caused cholera, he also marked the locations of the area's 11 water pumps and noticed on the map that they concentrated near a pump on Broad Street. Dr. Snow had the handle of the Broad Street pump removed, and the cholera epidemic came to an abrupt halt after having taken more than 500 lives.[25]

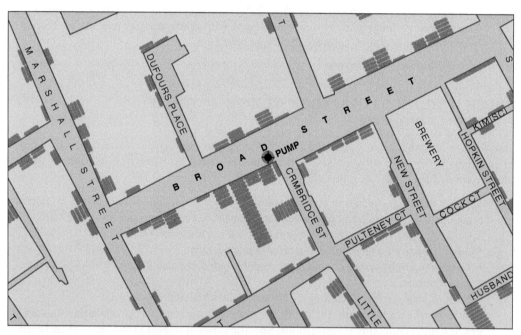

The value of mapping was established in London in the mid-19th century, when Dr. John Snow established a pattern for the deadly disease of cholera and showing that water was its cause.
theguardian.com

Policing Looks at Crime and Place

As with this case involving disease, geography also has a major influence on crime. In fact, the idea of mapping crime can also be traced back to the 1800s, in France, where an ethnographer and a lawyer, using crime statistics and census data, developed maps of crimes against property and persons. However, these efforts did not sustain the interest in **crime mapping** (probably because of the large amount of time and effort required to manually collect data), so it was not until the 1930s in Chicago that crime mapping was again used, here, to determine the location and distribution of gangs.[26] Automated crime mapping emerged in the 1960s, and of course the advent of the computer and Internet have allowed the field to grow dramatically.[27]

Combining geographic data with police report data and then displaying the information on a map is an effective way to analyze where, how, and why crime occurs. The features and characteristics of cityscapes and rural landscapes can make it easier or more difficult for crime to occur. The placement of alleys, buildings, and open spaces, for example, affects the likelihood that a criminal will strike. Problem solving thus looks to simultaneously address the relationship between people and their environments—particularly those places with social ills that cause real problems. Geographic analysis can help to reveal crime patterns in places, such as examining where past victims and offenders lived and where crimes occurred.[28]

Computerized crime maps became more commonplace with the introduction of desktop computing and software programs called **geographic information systems (GIS)**. Analysts map where crime occurs, combine the resulting visual display with other geographic data (such as location of schools, parks, and industrial complexes), analyze and investigate the causes of crime, and develop responses. Recent advances in statistical analysis make it possible to add more geographic and social dimensions to the analysis.[29]

Computerized crime mapping combines geographic information from global positioning satellites with crime statistics gathered by the department's CAD system and demographic data provided by private companies or the U.S. Census Bureau. The result is a picture that combines disparate sets of data for a whole new perspective on crime. Although it is known that crime does not occur evenly over time and has fluctuations, maps can paint a picture for analysts, who in turn inform officers where they need to focus their patrols. For example, if analysts discern a clustering of crimes in a part of the city during the month of May, officers can focus in that area—and analysts would expect to see a decline in crime in the targeted area if the tactic is working.

Maps of crimes can be overlaid with maps or layers of causative data: unemployment rates in the areas of high crime, locations of abandoned houses, population density, reports of drug activity, or geographic features (such as alleys, canals, or open fields) that might be contributing factors. Furthermore, the hardware and software are now available to nearly all police agencies for a few thousand dollars.

The National Institute of Justice's (NIJ) Mapping and Analysis for Public Safety (MAPS) program supports research that helps agencies use GIS to enhance public safety. The program examines:

- How to use maps to analyze crime.
- How to analyze spatial data.
- How maps can help researchers evaluate programs and policies.
- How to develop mapping, data sharing, and spatial analysis tools.

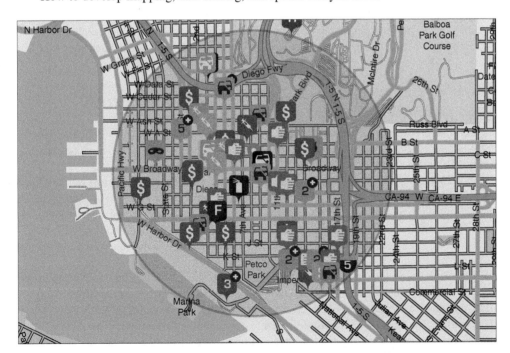

The ARJIS crime mapping system of San Diego County enables citizens to view regional crime maps and get automated e-mail alerts of crimes in their neighborhoods.
Courtesy ARJIS Crime Mapping Research Center.

REAL-TIME CRIME CENTERS

Related to crime mapping and analysis is another relatively new approach, the **real-time crime center** (RTCC), which has the purpose of using technologies to reduce officers' reliance on paper reports and nonintegrated databases to identify crime patterns. A number of police agencies are finding that these facilities—which gather and use vast amounts of crime-related data, such as arrest records, mug shots, and warrant information and provide it rapidly to officers and investigators in the field—can help in crime investigations and protect officer safety. Soon, RTCCs will hopefully become as ubiquitous as CompStat and other tech-based strategies.

Essentially, with RTCC police use a new information hub containing many years of voice, video, and crime data, which is translated into actionable intelligence that shows criminal activity unfolding in real time. Resembling a "mission control" center, it allows crime analysts and commanders to track the police calls as they are occurring citywide. The RTCC allows staff to notice patterns and spikes in certain activity so that commanders can deploy patrol officers and detectives where they're most needed at any given time.[30]

Seattle, Washington, Police Chief Kathleen O'Toole calls RTCC "agile policing," combining the work of police officers and civilian crime analysts to adapt to the changes in the city's criminal activity at all times.[31] The initiative can also include daily morning meetings among neighboring police agencies to share information on what anomalies or spikes they're observing. Commanders and crime analysts look at a dashboard illuminating a large screen on the wall that shows how many calls police are responding to, the priority level of each call, the nature of the calls, and where on a city map each call is coming from. The information is drawn from 911 dispatch calls, crime data, radio traffic, and vehicle information data. It allows the staff to visualize the call data so that commanders can make operational decisions on how to deploy police in the city. Agencies hope this practice will allow police to halt crime sprees as they happen, and to hopefully stop crimes and incidents before they become more serious.[32]

Patrol officers and detectives receive information from the RTTC via radio and the computers in their cars. The crime center consolidates the agency's Criminal Intelligence Section, Data Driven Policing Section, and Crime Analysis detectives into a new Intelligence and Analysts Section.[33]

The New York Police Department's RTCC system, launched in 2005 (and recently expanded to include robberies, rapes, missing persons, and other serious crimes beyond homicides and shootings), can comb through 120 million New York City criminal complaints, arrests, and 911 call records dating back a decade; five million criminal records and parole files maintained by the state of New York; and more than 31 million records of crime committed nationwide. RTCC also made it possible for officers to receive photographs of individuals via handheld devices, and the technology to transmit photographs to the police car laptops also became available.[34]

Exhibit 7–2 describes how the Houston Police Department established and uses RTCC.

| **Exhibit 7–2** | Houston Sets Up Real-Time Crime Center[35] |

Houston, the largest city in Texas, has more than 2.1 million people and a police department (HPD) of about 5,200 sworn officers and 1,300 civilian employees. HPD officers patrol approximately 656 square miles.

For 15 years, HPD maintained a data warehouse containing historic crime data, fed daily with information collected by the various police divisions across the city. Every four hours, that data—along with related maps—was migrated to a database containing nearly 900 fields about victims and suspects. However, officers lacked the ability to regularly and quickly employ that database. As a result, analysis remained the exclusive purview of specialists. Another challenge was to make the crime center real time.

The department worked with a private concern to establish design, build, and deploy a real-time crime center (RTCC) that makes critical information—derived from crime, jail booking, probation, and other databases—immediately available to officers responding to calls. Now, when a call comes in, integration technologies feed the incident information to the RTCC crime analysts. A report is run, pulling related historical information from the various law enforcement databases. Analysts then cross-reference that information with the details of emergency calls. Additional data on persons, vehicles, and property is pulled from internal officers' notes, as well as external government databases. All this information can then be communicated to the responding officers while they are en route to the crime scene. For example, officers sent to a domestic violence incident will know if the husband is a repeat offender, has spent time in prison for similar crimes, or is a permitted to carry a concealed weapon—all of which will impact the way the officer responds.

To improve the timeliness of information provided to police managers, the platform includes a dashboard for tracking crime statistics and trends. Previously, captains would be provided with crime reports on a monthly basis and were thus outdated and not very actionable. Now, police managers and crime analysts can more closely monitor occurrences of violent crimes such as murders, rapes, robberies, and aggravated assaults and nonviolent crimes like burglaries, thefts, and auto thefts. Information is refreshed every four hours, and can be viewed in tabular or graphical format, by day or shift, or by specific districts or beats.

As a result of RTCC, a significant decline in crime rates has been observed in recent years. Although this approach is not the only contributing factor to that decline, a key factor is the strategic use of technology, specifically the solutions that help support the real-time crime center.

STRATEGIES AND TOOLS FOR CRIME MANAGEMENT

It will be seen below that, with the advent of CompStat in the mid-1990s as a police management tool for analyzing crime data, several other interrelated strategies have followed—albeit with varying goals and methods—that examine (and attempt to predict) crimes and criminals, and provide feedback on those strategies to determine what works and produces results. Next we discuss those four interrelated strategies.

CompStat

A crime management process used in the problem-solving process is known as CompStat—for comparative or computer statistics—which is designed for the collection and feedback of information on crime and related quality-of-life issues. Since introduced by the New York City Police Department in 1994, CompStat has been widely adopted: a national survey found that 58 percent of large agencies (those with 100 or more sworn officers) either had adopted or were planning to implement a CompStat-like program.[36] The key elements of CompStat are as follows:

- Specific objectives.
- Accurate and timely intelligence.
- Effective tactics.
- Rapid deployment of personnel and resources.
- Relentless follow-up and assessment.[37]

CompStat pushes all precincts to generate weekly or monthly crime activity reports. Crime data are readily available, offering up-to-date information that is then compared at citywide, patrol, and precinct levels.

At CompStat meetings, police officials discuss crime patterns in their assigned area(s) and brainstorm about tactics and resources that might be used to address them.
Courtesy Washoe County, Nevada, Sheriff's Office.

Under CompStat, police begin proactively thinking about ways to deal with crime in terms of suppression, intervention, and prevention. Commanders must proactively respond to crime problems, and explain what tactics they have employed to address crime patterns, what resources they have and need, and with whom they have collaborated. Follow-up by top brass further ensures accountability.

Intelligence-Led Policing

Intelligence-led policing (ILP) originated in Great Britain, where police believed that a relatively small number of people were responsible for a comparatively large percentage of crimes; they believed that officers would have the best effect on crime by focusing on the most prevalent offenses occurring in their jurisdiction.[38]

The word "intelligence" is often misused; the most common mistake is to consider "intelligence" as synonymous with "information." Information is not intelligence; rather, "information plus analysis equals intelligence," and without analysis, there is no intelligence. Intelligence is what is produced after collected data are evaluated and analyzed by a trained intelligence professional.[39]

Exhibit 7–3 explains the views of the federal Bureau of Justice Assistance (BJA) concerning the need for, and the development and functions of, ILP.

Exhibit 7–3   Intelligence-Led Policing: Origins and Functions, Per BJA

ILP, while a relatively new concept in the United States, was an outcome of British efforts during the late 1990s to manage law enforcement resources efficiently and to respond effectively to serious crime. In 2000, the National Criminal Intelligence Service published the National Intelligence Model (NIM) that established the following priorities for British police service:

▶ Target prolific offenders through overt and covert means.
▶ Manage crime and disorder hot spots.
▶ Identify and investigate linked series of crime or incidents.
▶ Apply prevention measures that include working with a broad range of other disciplines.

NIM priorities were grounded in experience and solid research. Several authoritative longitudinal projects, in America and the United Kingdom, have convincingly demonstrated that a small minority of offenders commit a majority of crimes. It is well known that crime reports and service calls often cluster predominately at specific locations; research has shown that violent crime and neighborhood disorder can be reduced by focused, multiagency efforts in which law enforcement plays an important, if not exclusive role.

ILP does not replace the concepts of problem-solving policing or the community involvement and neighborhood maintenance theories [broken windows], nor the police accountability and information sharing practices [CompStat]. It builds on these concepts to keep pace with changes in society, technology, and criminal behavior. ILP encourages greater use of criminal intelligence, attends to offenders more than offenses, and offers a more targeted, forward-thinking, multijurisdictional and prevention point of view to the business of policing.

As such, successful adoption of ILP will generally involve the following practices:

▶ Information collection is part of the organizational culture—led by the chief executive, supervisors, and managers encourage line officers and investigators to regularly collect and forward intelligence.
▶ Analysis is indispensable to tactical and strategic planning—**records management systems** are robust, analysts are well trained and equipped, and actionable intelligence products are regularly produced to inform both tactical and strategic decisions.
▶ Enforcement tactics are focused, prioritized by community harm assessments, and prevention-oriented; operations are mounted against repeat or violent offenders; serious organized (gang, trafficking, etc.) groups are identified and dismantled; and traffic violations are enforced at dangerous intersections or roadways.

Source: Adapted from Office of Justice Programs, Bureau of Justice Assistance, "Intelligence-Led Policing," http://www.ojp.usdoj.gov/BJA/topics/ilp.html.

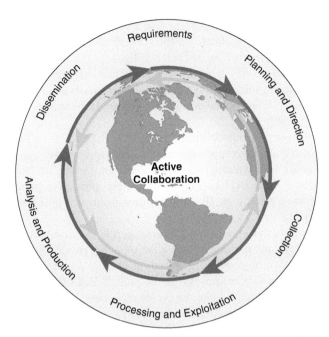

FIGURE 7–2 The FBI intelligence cycle develops unrefined data into polished intelligence by taking information through six steps. This graphic shows the circular nature of the cycle.
Courtesy Federal Bureau of Investigation.

To better comprehend what is meant by ILP, break it down into its core components. For example, many police agencies have both crime analysts and intelligence analysts. Crime analysts keep their fingers on the pulse of crime in the jurisdiction: which crime trends are up, which ones are down, where the hot spots are, what type of property is being stolen, and so on. Intelligence analysts, on the other hand, are likely to be more aware of the specific *people* responsible for crime in the jurisdiction—who they are, where they live, what they do, who they associate with, and so on (see Exhibit 7–3). Integrating these two functions—crime analysis and intelligence analysis—is essential for obtaining a comprehensive grasp of the crime picture. *Crime analysis* allows police to understand the "what, when, and where," while *intelligence analysis* provides an understanding of the "who"—crime networks and individuals.

Shown in Figure 7–2, is the six-step "intelligence cycle" as promulgated by the Federal Bureau of Investigation (see https://www.fbi.gov/about-us/intelligence/intelligence-cycle).[40]

Predictive Policing

Many people believe that **predictive policing** is the future of law enforcement. The reason is that it represents a replication of the operations of private businesses and corporations, which for decades have used data analysis to anticipate market conditions or industry trends and drive sales strategies. Walmart, for example, learned through analysis that when a major weather event is in the forecast, demand for three items rises: duct tape, bottled water, and strawberry Pop-Tarts. Armed with this information, stores in the affected areas can ensure their shelves are fully stocked to meet customer needs.[41] Police can use a similar data analysis to help make their work more efficient. The idea is being called "predictive policing," and some in the field believe it has the potential to transform law enforcement by enabling police to anticipate and prevent crime instead of simply responding to it.

Have you ever logged onto a Web site to purchase an item and seen something like "other customers who placed similar orders also ordered these items"? Or entered an online auction service and been provided with some items you might also be interested in bidding on? Essentially, in these instances private businesses are harnessing social sciences to predict human behavior. The processes used in predicting your shopping behavior are the same ones used to determine criminal behavior, only they are using different data sets (bearing in mind, however, that private industry may be able to use more personal data than a police agency can).[42]

Welcome to the world of predictive analysis, where the next generation of police problem solving could combine existing technologies like computers, crime analysis, and police reports with a few newer technologies such as artificial intelligence. The future may well bring a system that can predict crimes before they happen—with predictive analytics acting as a force multiplier that are focused on problem solving.[43] Of course, high-tech tools alone cannot solve crimes, but when trained crime analysts and police management combine the tools with their ingenuity, anything is future in this high-tech world.

The term predictive policing, according to the U.S. Department of Justice (DOJ), is a relatively new concept that "integrates approaches such as cutting-edge crime analysis, crime-fighting technology, intelligence-lead policing, and more to inform forward thinking crime prevention strategies and tactics."[44] The DOJ states that, ultimately, predictive policing is intended as a framework to advance strategies like community policing, problem-oriented policing, intelligence-led policing, and hot spot policing.[45]

The police have always known that robberies surge near check-cashing businesses, that crime spikes on hot days and plummets during the rain, that residential burglaries often occur on Sunday mornings (while people are attending church services), and that Super Bowl Sunday is usually the slowest crime day of the year.[46] But officers' minds can store and remember only so much data. So when the police monitor crime data and query a computer system for historical and real-time patterns, they can predict, more systematically, over a bigger area, and across shifts and time spans, where crimes are likely to occur. More importantly, the crime analysis software does not forget details, get sick, take vacation, or transfer to a different precinct.

So if commercial robberies were high in, say, March 2015, their software will predict another spike in March 2016, and the police can then look at the types of businesses that were hit, their locations, and time of day. The system can even analyze a robber's modus operandi—what was said, type of weapon used, and so on.[47]

How might predictive policing work for the street officer? Imagine that you are dispatched to a domestic dispute that involves a man and woman. You arrive at the home, knock on the door, are escorted into the living room, and all is going as it has at such calls a thousand times—but now you are engaged in a struggle for your life. As indicated above with RTCC, you might have approached this call differently if, upon being given the call, your mobile computer had informed you that the subject you would confront has been previously arrested for assaulting officers in another jurisdiction and was recently arrested for driving under the influence. This is just one example of how predictive policing can be applied—simply by looking at patterns of behavior—to the patrol officer in addition to crime analysts.

Smart Policing: Combining the Above

Vestiges of each of the above three strategies can be found in what is now generally termed as **smart policing initiatives (SPI)**, which were first grant-funded in June 2009 by the federal BJA; proposals were solicited that would identify or confirm effective, crime reduction techniques that were efficient and easy for other agencies to replicate. Perhaps the most unique aspect of SPI is the research partnership. Significantly, BJA emphasized police and criminal justice scholar partnerships for these efforts, working together to test solutions that were informed by crime science theories and assessed with sound evaluation methods. Since its inception, BJA has funded more than $12.4 million for agency projects in dozens of cities.

Because the initial SPI did not prescribe any particular policing model or approach, but stressed the importance of in-depth problem analysis and definition to guide their later efforts, an impressive array of strategies and tactics were developed and implemented by the local SPI sites. For example, while some sites focused primarily on hot spot and place-based policing strategies, others focus primarily on offender-based approaches (e.g., focused deterrence through identification of prolific offenders and strategic application of suppression and social support strategies). Some first identified hot spots and then pinpointed the prolific offenders within them. Some sites began with a distinct problem-oriented policing approach (e.g., application of the SARA model, while others focused on community policing with emphasis on community and victim engagement); several sites have implemented initiatives with a strong predictive analytic approach, others incorporated elements of intelligence-led policing, and still others adopted technological approaches (e.g., strategic use of surveillance cameras, enhanced crime analysis capabilities, enhancements to "real-time crime centers," or enhanced predictive analytic capabilities).[48]

Findings thus far also suggest that SPI can significantly reduce violent crime (Philadelphia), involve creative use of crime analytics and problem solving to reduce crime in historically violent police districts (Los Angeles), prevent violence in chronic hot spots (Boston), and reduce service calls and property crime at troubled high-traffic convenience stores (Glendale, Arizona). Other SPI projects now underway seek to examine patrol officer body-worn camera testing (Phoenix, Arizona and Las Vegas, Nevada), explore the links between traffic violations/vehicle crashes and other criminal activity (Shawnee, Kansas and York, Maine) and video camera surveillance of high-density, order-maintenance areas (Pullman, Washington), and test intelligence-led policing (Columbia, South Carolina) and predictive policing (Cambridge, Massachusetts and Indio, California).[49]

Exhibit 7–4 shows some of Germany's efforts in IT for better policing, specifically as it relates to community policing, police shootings, and neighborhood crime control.

Exhibit 7–4   Global Perspective: Germany's Unique View of IT and Neighborhood Crime Control

German police observe the actions of their U.S. counterparts closely. For example, following multiple high-profile shootings of unarmed black men by police officers in the United States in 2015–2016, several agencies put all of their officers in body-worn cameras (discussed in Chapter 3). However, the goal of the cameras is different in Germany: rather than protecting citizens from police abuse, they are aimed at deterring violence against officers. Indeed, German police use their firearms much less frequently than their American colleagues. They fatally shoot fewer than 10 people per year, compared with more than 400 across the United States.[50] Furthermore, the German police are known to be experimenting with 3D plastic guns to see if they can be adapted to police uses.[51]

Like other European nations, community policing in Germany has existed for several decades and is largely an outgrowth of a community concept of crime prevention. After a surge in crime in the 1980s, the government opted to focus on neighborhood crime prevention while police developed new strategies at the local levels. Crime prevention is viewed as the duty of society as a whole, thus bringing together all government and social service agencies, schools, churches, trade unions, businesses, youth programs, and others.

Germany is federalized—and thus highly decentralized—with 16 separate states, most of which have their own Crime Prevention Council. Focusing on community policing has succeeded: by the mid-2000s, Germany had about 820 homicides in a population of over 82 million residents, or a ratio of 1 homicide for every 100,000 population. Also, German states have experimented with various policing approaches over the past two decades.

However, Germany rejects the highly regarded American policing philosophies of "zero tolerance" or "broken windows," as do nearly all the member states of the European Union. These strategies are felt to only masquerade as true community policing and not reduce crime in the long term. Therefore, community policing in Germany is not a single organizational feature of German police forces, but rather an applied philosophy that can be used in specific neighborhoods, in specific instances, and for achieving clearly defined results. Its structure is determined by each state separately and is fixed by the individual state government. In others, it is delegated to the towns and cities to decide at local level.

In most states, police either take the initiative in organizing community policing boards or councils in their town or city, or cooperate with the mayor or city council by participating on a local Crime Prevention Council. In addition, a federal-level commission acts as a research and development bureau for specific areas of work. It disseminates research studies and "how to" manuals to the various states and local police departments in the prevention of narcotics sales and abuse, robbery and blackmail, personal violence, endangering youth, youth crime, and domestic violence.[52]

APPLYING SOCIAL MEDIA: LESSONS FROM BOSTON'S MARATHON BOMBING

On April 15, 2013, during Boston's annual marathon, two bombs exploded near the finish line, killing three people and injuring more than 260 others. What ensued was an extraordinary manhunt as well as massive use of **social media** by law enforcement to keep the media and frightened citizens accurately informed about what was going on. In this way, misinformation was quickly corrected by the BPD from its official Twitter account. In sum, the practice was very simple and yet effective.[53]

Today, some police agencies employ full-time civilian personnel who are in charge of social media and direct public relations through the various channels—Twitter, Facebook, YouTube—in a real-time manner. Formerly press releases would only reach the mainstream media; now, they are available to anyone in the community who follows the police via social media.

The scope of social media continues to grow, with some police agencies having thousands of followers. Social media also allows police to have two-way conversations with the community, to include receiving messages from citizens about crime and disorder (including anonymous tips). It can also be used to conduct virtual "ride-alongs," with live tweeting during an entire shift from an officer's patrol car. This gives the public a view of what police do and a better understanding of what's going on.[54]

Four out of five police agencies now also use social media for investigations. The most common uses include evidence collection (people bragging about their actions on social media sites); location of suspects (investigators "friend" suspects and track their locations); and criminal network investigations (again, gangs are prone to boast about their actions on social media sites).

Of course, using social media has its challenges as well. As with any nonverbal form of communication, the message can be distorted as it gets passed along. Also, police executives must establish policies concerning who controls the information.

Following are some additional examples of police of social media:

- The Los Angeles Police Department (LAPD) has used social media to help with special events such as the NBA All Star Game in 2011 and the Stanley Cup playoffs in 2012. Here, the department tracked large-scale parties and other gatherings throughout the city, and deployed teams of building inspectors, police officers, and fire department officials to ensure the events were legal and safe. The department also monitored social media to keep tabs on "trending" topics, such as whether large crowds of people planned to head downtown, and adjusted deployment plans accordingly. Officers also send out messages of their own, to encourage law-abiding behavior and show good faith on the part of the department in managing major events peacefully; they wanted people to know how many officers were deployed.[55]
- The Albuquerque Police Department works with private security partners to monitor tweets containing certain keywords, in order to intercept rival gangs; in one instance, police prevented the gangs from causing disruptions at a major amusement park.[56]

CIVIC APPS USED TO FIGHT CRIME

In 2011, the City of Chicago released to the public a large amount of city data for public consumption, including up-to-date crime incident data. This release of data into the public realm helped citizens to merge data with the police, toward bringing together the needs of safe communities with law enforcement's efforts to fight crime and improve public safety.

"Hacking" has understandably become a dirty word for most Americans and governments; however, in this context, hacking is actually a positive approach to problem solving. Here, **civic hacking** for the public's benefit is defined as:

> hands-on, citizen-driven action which produces civic innovation—it could be contributing code to an open-source civic app . . . or conducting a workshop with city officials to discuss how new policy could improve a neighborhood.[57]

In 2013, Chicago city officials sponsored a "safe communities" hackathon, where participants were to use new methods to query crimes, wanted lists, and mug shots, as well as graffiti problems, vacant building code violations, and even police beat boundaries. The result was a wave of apps that Chicagoans could use to track crime and improve public safety. The success of this crime hackathon spawned other such practices, some of which included contests for the best civic app. One of the winners was a mobile app that allows an injured or lost person to send out a distress notice to anyone designated as a recipient. A second companion app sends out continuous updates on the location of the individual in trouble.[58]

In Redlands, California, city officials have worked with a software firm to create an app that serves as a first step toward an eventual 311 call center for residents to report problems and complaints. In Philadelphia, the city's mobile messaging platform for public safety helps police access difficult-to-reach population groups, lets neighbors know to secure their doors if their block is getting targeted for burglaries, and reports on someone's parole. Moreover, the Virginia State Police launched a crime reporting app that is a suspicious-activity reporting tool to connect individuals, police agencies, and regional fusion centers and collects and analyzes intelligence on criminals and terrorists. Citizens are encouraged to report suspicious photography, vehicles, or people in places that just look out of place.[59]

DEDICATED SOFTWARE FOR PROBLEM-SOLVING TASKS

The need for police agencies to get smarter—and more high-tech—has not gone unnoticed by private, for-profit corporations. They provide a tremendous service, using esoteric knowledge—which is definitely known only to a few—to develop integrated software for problem-oriented policing, to identify and address everything from crime hot spots to traffic tie-ups, security breaches, and other emergencies. These IT industries can assist police with synchronizing and analyzing information that is gathered from diverse data collection systems and looking for patterns so as to anticipate—rather than just react to—problems. Communications workers can dispatch first responders quicker to the scene.[60]

Another useful software program used by many police agencies and researchers in the United States is Windows-based and is used with crime mapping. The program includes more than 100 statistical approaches to spatial analysis of crime and other incidents. It inputs incident locations (e.g., robbery locations) using either spherical or projected coordinates, calculating distances between incidents (including neighbor analysis), various hot spot analyses, relationships between time and space, crime forecasts, behaviors of a serial offender, and regression modeling (analyzing the relationship between a dependent variable and one or more independent variables).[61]

Summary

This chapter has demonstrated why, as its title suggests, having and utilizing information technologies is an essential prerequisite for problem-oriented policing. Since computers first came to the field in the 1970s, their use and potential for crime fighting has grown exponentially, and it would seem that their future use is only limited by the budgets and creativity of police managers. Certainly just a few years ago, one could not have conceived of police software and practices where crimes could be predicted (based on past trends) to the extent they are today.

And, as amounts of data and numbers of available databases continue to increase, the police will only become more astute in addressing crime and disorder. Soon, the real-time crime centers, discussed in this chapter, will be as commonplace as computers in patrol cars and officers with smartphones. Certainly, IT—along with the ability of officers to use their creativity with the SARA problem-solving process and other tools—makes this a most exciting time to be in the field of law enforcement.

Key Terms and Concepts

Civic hacking
Command and control
  systems
CompStat
Computer-aided dispatch
  (CAD)

Crime analysis/analyst
Crime mapping
Geographic information
  system (GIS)
Information technology
Intelligence-led policing

Management information
  systems
Mobile computing
Operations information
  systems
Predictive policing

Real-time crime center
Records management
  systems
Smart policing initiatives
  (SPI)
Social media

Items for Review

1. How did information technology come to policing, and what role does it play today in problem-oriented policing?
2. How would you describe the purposes of the three primary systems used for obtaining crime information: command and control systems, management information systems, and records management system?
3. What benefits are accrued from thorough crime analysis? What is the minimal training—and duties—of a professional crime analyst?

4. Which IT tools are proper for use with *proactive* police operations?
5. What benefits are provided by crime mapping?
6. What are the role and functions of real-time crime centers?
7. How would you briefly describe the four management strategies for addressing crime: CompStat, intelligence-led policing, predictive policing, and smart policing?
8. How is social media being used to address crime and disorder? Civic apps?

Learn by Doing

1. This chapter included an example of how one police executive valued the "flair" for IT by young Millennial officers who created their own programs and apps for problem solving. Given your knowledge of IT, expand on that discussion and describe additional ways in which young officers' knowledge of IT might be beneficial for addressing crime and disorder.
2. Assume that a major motorcycle rally of approximately 100,000 bikers is coming to your jurisdiction soon. These rallies are known

to be frequented by opposing gang members, which has resulted in violence in other cities. Your police chief executive has tasked you with taking the lead on the intelligence-led policing and planning efforts so that your agency might be prepared and staffed for the bikers' arrival. Accordingly, what kinds of information would you want to obtain, databases would you consult, and outside agencies would you contact in order to develop a strategy for policing this large gathering?

Endnotes

1. Brian A. Jackson, Victoria A. Greenfield, Andrew R. Morral, and John S. Hollywood, *Police Department Investments in Information Technology Systems* (Santa Monica, Calif.: Rand Corporation, 2014), p. 2.
2. Tod Newcombe, "Forecasting the Future for Technology and Policing," *Government Technology* (September 26, 2014), http://www.govtech.com/public-safety/Forecasting-the-Future-for-Technology-and-Policing.html?utm_source=related&utm_medium=direct&utm_campaign=Forecasting-the-Future-for-Technology-and-Policing.
3. TechTerms, "IT Definition," http://techterms.com/definition/it.
4. Seaskate, Inc., "The Evolution and Development of Police Technology," http://www.police-technology.net/id59.html#.
5. Ibid.
6. Lee Brown, quoted in ibid.
7. Dennis Nowicki, quoted in ibid.
8. Ibid.
9. Mary Maureen Brown, "The Benefits and Costs of Information Technology Innovations: An Empirical Assessment of a Local Government Agency," *Public Performance and Management Review* 24(4) (June 2001), pp. 351–366.
10. Terence Dunworth, Gary Cordner, Jack Greene, Timothy Bynum, Scott Decker, Thomas Rich, Shawn Ward, and Vince Webb, *Information Systems Technology Enhancement Project (ISTEP)* (Washington, D.C.: Abt Associates and Office of Community Oriented Policing Services, 2000).
11. Heath J. Grant and Karen J. Terry, *Law Enforcement in the 21st Century* (Boston, Mass.: Allyn & Bacon, 2005), pp. 329–330.
12. Timothy C. O'Shea and Keith Nicholls, *Crime Analysis in America: Findings and Recommendations* (Washington, D.C.: U.S. Department of Justice, Office of Community Oriented Policing Services, March 2003), p. 7.

13. Grant and Terry, *Law Enforcement in the 21st Century*, p. 330.
14. Dunworth et al., *Information Systems Technology Enhancement Project (ISTEP)*.
15. Albuquerque, New Mexico Police Chief Ray Schultz, quoted in Police Executive Research Forum, *Future Trends in Policing* (Washington, D.C.: Office of Community Oriented Policing Services, 2014), p. 37.
16. Rachel Boba, *Introductory Guide to Crime Analysis and Mapping* (U.S. Department of Justice, Office of Community Oriented Policing Services, November 2001), p. 9.
17. Ibid., pp. 11–15.
18. International Association of Crime Analysts, "What Crime Analysts Do," http://www.iaca.net/dc_analyst_role.asp; also see ibid., "What is Crime Analysis?" http://www.iaca.net/dc_about_ca.asp.
19. Ibid.
20. Michael S. Scott and Stuart Kirby, *Implementing POP: Leading, Structuring, and Managing a Problem-Oriented Police Agency* (U.S. Department of Justice, Office of Community Oriented Policing Services, September 2012), pp. 37–38.
21. Adapted from City of Mesa, Arizona, Police Department, "Crime Analyst Job Description," http://apps.mesaaz.gov/jobdescriptions/documents/JobDescriptions/cs4509.pdf.
22. Quoted in Jackson et al., *Police Department Investments in Information Technology Systems*, p. 7.
23. Ibid., p. 9.
24. U.S. Department of Justice, National Institute of Justice, *Crime Mapping and Analysis by Community Organizations in Hartford, Connecticut* (Washington, D.C.: Author, March 2001), p. 1.
25. David Weisburd and Tom McEwen (eds.), *Crime Mapping and Crime Prevention* (Monsey, N.Y.: Willow Tree Press, 1998), p. 1; see also Keith Harries, *Mapping Crime: Principle and Practice* (Washington, D.C.: Office of Justice Program, December 1999).

26. Ibid., pp. 6–9.

27. Ibid.

28. National Institute of Justice, "Mapping and Analysis for Public Safety" (May 22, 2013), http://www.nij.gov/topics/technology/maps/pages/welcome.aspx.

29. Ibid.

30. Lynsi Burton, "New SPD 'Crime Center' Shows City's Activity Unfolding in Real Time," *Seattlepi.com* (October 7, 2015), http://www.seattlepi.com/local/crime/article/New-SPD-crime-center-shows-city-s-activity-6556969.php.

31. Quoted in ibid.

32. Ibid.

33. Ibid.

34. Joseph D'Amico, "Stopping Crime in Real Time," *The Police Chief*, November 2015, http://www.policechiefmagazine.org/magazine/index.cfm?fuseaction=display&article_id=995&issue_id=92006.

35. Information Builders, "Houston Police Department Creates Real-Time Crime Center," n.d., http://www.informationbuilders.com/applications/houston.

36. Daniel DeLorenzi, Jon M. Shane, and Karen L. Amendola, "The CompStat Process: Managing Performance on the Pathway to Leadership," *The Police Chief* (September 2006), http://www.Theiacp.org/foundation/Foundation.htm.

37. Grant and Terry, *Law Enforcement in the 21st Century*, pp. 329–330.

38. U.S. Department of Justice, Office of Justice Programs, Bureau of Justice Statistics, *Intelligence-Led Policing: The New Intelligence Architecture* (Washington, D.C.: Author, 2005), p. 9.

39. Ibid., p. 3.

40. See U.S. Department of Justice, Federal Bureau of Investigation, "Intelligence Cycle," https://www.fbi.gov/about-us/intelligence/intelligence-cycle.

41. Beth Pearsall, "Predictive Policing: The Future of Law Enforcement?" (Washington, D.C.: National Institute of Justice, June 23, 2010), http://www.nij.gov/journals/266/pages/predictive.aspx; see also Charlie Beck, "Predictive Policing: What Can We Learn from Wal-Mart and Amazon about Fighting Crime in a Recession?" *The Police Chief* (November 2009), http://www.policechiefmagazine.org/magazine/index.cfm?fuseaction=display_arch&article_id=1942&issue_id=112009.

42. Eric Mills, "An Ounce of Prevention," *Law Enforcement Technology* (September 2009), pp. 60–64.

43. Ibid., p. 63.

44. Ibid., pp. 12–13.

45. Ibid., pp. 10–11.

46. U.S. Department of Justice, "Predictive Policing: A National Discussion," http://blogs.usdoj.gov/blog/archives/385; see also U.S. Department of Justice, National Institute of Justice, "Predictive Policing Symposium: Agenda."

47. U.S. Department of Justice, National Institute of Justice, "Predictive Policing Symposium: The Future of Prediction in Criminal Justice," http://www.ojp.usdoj.gov/nij/topics/law-enforcement/predictive-policing/symposium/future.htm.

48. Information concerning the origins and initial grant-funded test sites for SPI was obtained from the following sources: James R.

Coldren Jr., Alissa Huntoon, and Michael Medaris, "Introducing Smart Policing: Foundations, Principles, and Practice," *Police Quarterly* 16(3) (September 2014): 275–286; Nola M. Joyce, Charles H. Ramsey, and James K. Stewart, "Commentary on Smart Policing," *Police Quarterly* 16(3) (September 2014): 358–368. This special issue of *Police Quarterly* contains a number of other, site-specific articles that discuss SPI.

49. For another successful Smart Policing initiatives, see U.S. Department of Justice, Bureau of Justice Assistance, "Los Angeles, California Smart Policing Initiative Reducing Gun-Related Violence through Operation LASER" (October 2012), p. 2, http://www.smartpolicinginitiative.com/sites/all/files/spotlights/LA%20Site%20Spotlight%20FINAL%202012.pdf.

50. German police happy to wear body cameras, *The Local* (April 10, 2015), http://www.thelocal.de/20150410/german-police-happy-to-wear-body-cameras.

51. Shaunacy Ferro, "German Police to Experiment with 3-D Printed Guns," *Popular Science* July 24, 2013, http://www.popsci.com/technology/article/2013-07/german-police-agencies-invest-3-d-printers-play-around-weapons.

52. Adapted from Los Angeles Community Policing, "Community Policing in Europe: Structure and Best Practices in Sweden, France, Germany," http://www.lacp.org/Articles%20-%20Expert%20-%20Our%20Opinion/060908-CommunityPolicingInEurope-AJ.htm.

53. Tod Newcombe, "Social Media: Big Lessons from the Boston Marathon Bombing," *Government Technology* (September 24, 2014); see also Edward F. Davis III, Alejandro A. Alves and David Alan Sklansky, *Social Media and Police Leadership: Lessons from Boston* (Washington, D.C.: National Institute of Justice, 2014).

54. Ibid.

55. Police Executive Research Forum, "Social Media and Tactical Considerations for Law Enforcement" (May 2013), http://www.policeforum.org/assets/docs/Free_Online_Documents/Technology/social%20media%20and%20tactical%20considerations%20for%20law%20enforcement%202013.pdf.

56. Ibid.

57. Jake Levitas, "Defining Civic Hacking," *Code for America* (June 7, 2013), http://www.codeforamerica.org/blog/2013/06/07/defining-civic-hacking/.

58. Tod Newcombe, "Civic Apps: Can They Help Fight Crime?" Government Technology (September 25, 2014), http://www.govtech.com/public-safety/Civic-Apps-Can-They-Help-Fight-Crime.html.

59. Ibid.

60. See, for example, IBM Corp., *Integrated Law Enforcement: A Holistic Approach to Solving Crime* (2014), http://www.redbooks.ibm.com/redpapers/pdfs/redp5116.pdf; also see ibid., http://www.ibm.com/smarterplanet/us/en/public_safety/ideas/.

61. See Ned Levine, *CrimeStat: A Spatial Statistics Program for the Analysis of Crime Incident Locations (v 4.02)* (Houston, Tex.: Ned Levine & Associates and the National Institute of Justice, January 26, 2015), http://www.nij.gov/topics/technology/maps/pages/crimestat.aspx.

PART IV

Needed: Organizational Foundation for Problem Solving

This part consists of four critical approaches that together form what might be termed the infrastructure that allows community policing and problem solving to succeed. Chapter 8 generally examines how the police culture, leadership, and overall workforce must be adapted to this strategy. Chapter 9 describes what are often overlooked but key elements for this strategy: its planning and implementation; problem-oriented policing cannot "just happen," and it must be planned and implemented in such a way as to overcome resistance and become the agency's philosophy in order to succeed. Then, in a similar vein, Chapter 10 sets forth the kinds of training and mentoring that must be afforded to personnel under this strategy; it is key that adult-based learning and technologies be geared to this undertaking. Finally, we discuss in Chapter 11 the highly important tasks of determining whether or not problem-solving efforts worked by using evaluation and assessment methods. This—the all too often lack of measurement of outcomes—is a major criticism of problem-oriented policing, and it must be addressed.

Changing Agency Culture:
Toward Constitutional and Legitimate Policing

LEARNING OBJECTIVES

As a result of reading this chapter, the student will understand:

- What is meant by a police organization's "culture"
- How and why the police are considering "new" means of becoming professional
- Several essential elements for cultural change in contemporary policing, including engaging in constitutional policing and police legitimacy
- How the use of force and responses to mass demonstrations must be modified under the new culture
- How a police organization can change from being "good" to "great" and what is meant by "moments of truth"
- The importance and challenges of recruiting quality officers, to include the Millennial generation
- The roles of police leaders in seeing that all of the above are accomplished in order to modify the agency culture as necessary

TEST YOUR KNOWLEDGE

1. The term "constitutional policing" means training police officers so that they memorize the key parts of the Bill of Rights as they apply to the field.

2. Experience has shown that police should always make a show of force at public demonstrations.

3. Policing today has an extremely challenging time recruiting and achieving an applicant pool and in maintaining a stable workforce.

4. Changing the police agency's culture in regard to its use of force actually begins with recruits in the academy—training them to be problem solvers, not as soldiers.

5. It is established that the most challenging aspect of changing the culture of a police agency lies in changing the attitudes and beliefs of first-line supervisors (i.e., sergeants).

Answers can be found on page 278.

We live in a moment of history where change is so speeded up that we begin to see the present only when it is already disappearing.
—R. D. LAING

INTRODUCTION

"The post-Ferguson environment is one of the most unusual situations in policing in the last 30 years. There has been a crisis, and many people have lost trust in the police. But on the plus side, we have some of the strongest leadership that I have ever seen in policing. So we have the capacity to make changes to strengthen our relationships with the community. The challenge for us is to make sure that relationships between police and community get better and, at the same time, that crime rates go down. We owe this to the communities we serve."

—Director Ronald L. Davis,
Office of Community Oriented Policing Services[1]

COPS Office Director Davis set the tone for this chapter concerning what police executives must do in confronting "one of the most unusual situations" policing is experiencing over the course of the past three decades.

Because community policing is now so entrenched in U.S. policing, the meaning of "changing the culture" of the organization in order to accommodate this strategy and bringing police and community together has itself changed from what it meant a few years ago; then, it meant how to transition the organization; announce the shift to this philosophy; obtain buy-in from middle managers, first-line supervisors, and patrol officers; how to adapt the performance evaluation and promotional systems; and so on.

In this current climate of policing, however, changing the culture requires a return to the basics, strengthening relationships with the community. Thus, this chapter will focus on needs and methods for doing so—which still involves, to a large extent, changing the agency's culture—as is needed for community policing. Police executives often speak of their role as being "agents of change" with respect to community policing, and as we will see below, never before has managing change been a larger element of their jobs.

In Chapter 2, which concerned developing community partnerships, we discussed several aspects of contemporary policing that need to be put in place and would fit well in this chapter, i.e., shifting to a "guardian" mindset, the "New Professionalism." Here, we take these preliminary goals farther, looking at remaining measures that are needed to effect a fully community-oriented policing organization.

Many people would like to see today's police having a "guardian" mindset, rather than acting as "soldiers," under a "new professionalism."
Scott Olson/Getty Images.

This chapter begins with a look at new directions many police agencies and personnel are undertaking in order to focus on being more professional. At its root, of course, a police agency's culture is determined by its *people*; therefore, this chapter gives considerable attention to several aspects of human resources under community policing and problem solving. We begin with several discussions that serve to lay the foundation for today's challenges. First is a look at what actually constitutes a police organization's culture, and then how police leaders create a "new professional" and bring about a greater reliance on what are termed constitutional policing and legitimacy. Next is a discussion of how leaders can transform their organizations from being "good" to "great" and then examine a number of contemporary challenges with recruiting quality people into community police service (to include problems with obtaining an applicant pool and the coming Millennial generation divide). After an overview of the roles of key leaders in transforming the **culture of policing**, the chapter concludes with a summary, review questions, and several scenarios and activities that provide opportunities for you to "learn by doing." Six exhibits provide unique perspectives related to changing culture.

FIRST THINGS FIRST: WHAT IS A POLICE ORGANIZATION'S "CULTURE"?

As one person described it, in its simplest form, a police culture means "This is how we do things around here."[2] At a more complex level, a police organization's culture is derived from its mission, values, customs, and rituals, all of which are drawn from the organization's history and how its members interact with one another and with those outside of the organization. Organizational culture is also influenced by how leaders reward, recognize, or discipline behaviors.[3]

This is why a few organizations are highly professional and respected, while a few are constantly receiving citizens' complaints, being sued for excessive force, and so on. And, while some police chiefs can be consumed with departmental integrity and ethics, this message must be conveyed (and rewarded) on the street, lest the officers do something altogether different on the street.

This is also why it is imperative that each organization develop and publicize its values and mission statements, such as those shown in Exhibit 8–1.

Exhibit 8–1	Mission and Values Statements, St. Louis County, Missouri, Police Department[4]

MISSION STATEMENT

The mission of the St. Louis County Police Department is to work cooperatively with the public, and within the framework of the Constitution to enforce the laws, preserve the peace, reduce fear, and provide a safe environment in our neighborhoods.

STATEMENT OF VALUES

The St. Louis County Police Department exists to serve the community by protecting life and property, by preventing crime, by enforcing the laws, and by maintaining order for all people.

Central to our mission are the values that guide our work and decisions. These help us contribute to the high quality of life in St. Louis County.

The public trust and confidence given to those in the police service requires the adoption and compliance of stated values, which are the foundation upon which our policies, goals, and operations are built.

In fulfilling our mission, we need the support of citizens and elected officials in order to provide the quality of service our values commit us to providing.

We, the men and women of the St. Louis County Police Department, value:

Human life: We value human life and dignity, as guaranteed by the Constitution.

Integrity: We believe that integrity is the basis for community trust.

Laws and Constitution: We respect the principles that are embodied in the Constitution of the United States. We recognize the authority of federal, state, and local laws.

Excellence: We strive for personal and professional excellence.

Accountability: We are accountable to the people in the community, and each other.

Cooperation: We believe that cooperation with the community and the members of our organization will enable us to combine our diverse backgrounds, skills, and styles to achieve common goals beneficial to the community and the St. Louis County Police Department.

Problem solving: We are most effective when we can identify and solve community problems.

Ourselves: We are dedicated, caring, and capable people who are performing important and satisfying work for the people of St. Louis County.

REVISITING THE "NEW PROFESSIONAL"

A New Mindset

Given the contemporary problems that exist between the police and the communities they serve-particularly minorities—there has been movement from within the police service to bring itself back to an earlier time when they were indeed seen as true protectors of the community, without bias or favor. As noted above, in Chapter 2 we had a brief discussion of the contemporary need for a new police professionalism and legitimacy. We expand on that discussion here.

The many drawbacks of policing that existed during the professional era were discussed in Chapter 1. Suffice it to say that citizens had little influence in crime control, and police were reactive, accomplished little in the way of long-term problem solving, and were the "thin blue line." Citizens were no longer encouraged to go to "their" neighborhood police officers or districts, and officers passed by and drove patrol cars randomly through streets while their productivity was judged by the numbers of arrests they made or the number of miles they drove during a shift. The crime rate became the primary indicator of police effectiveness.

Today, however, police organizations across the United States are striving for what might be termed a New Professionalism, one that includes stricter *accountability* in terms of their effectiveness and conduct, while also increasing their *legitimacy* in the eyes of those they serve, and to encourage continuous *innovation* in police practices. These three goals suggest a fourth element as well: a *national coherence*. Next we discuss these four principles in greater detail.

1. A commitment to *accountability* means having an obligation to account for police actions—not only internally but also to civilian review boards (discussed below), city councils and county commissioners, state legislatures, and courts. Also, there is a greater accountability for dealing with crime (in later chapters, we discuss such methods as CompStat, intelligence-led policing, predictive policing, and smart policing). Police agencies might also conduct public surveys in order to learn about crime and disorder and fear of crime. It is also hoped that the New Professionalism will bring reductions in the use of force as police departments become more proficient in analyzing events leading up to use-of-force incidents to determine if the officers were justified in using such tactics.

2. A commitment to *legitimacy* includes a determination to engage in police activities with the consent, cooperation, and support of the community. The New Professionalism emphasizes professional integrity and public trust. Traditionally, police often measured their legitimacy in terms of the numbers of civilian complaints that were lodged against them. This measure is highly problematic, because relatively few people actually make a formal complaint. Legitimacy is discussed more below.

3. A commitment to *innovation* means actively experimenting with new ideas and changing policies and procedures accordingly. Such agencies look for practices that work as they attempt to both prevent crimes and solve problems. Knowledge—its creation, dissemination, and practical application—is essential to genuine professionalism. Police must measure their outcomes, encourage independent evaluations of their policies and tactics, and design experiments that rigorously test new ideas. In sum, police departments need to become learning organizations.

4. *National coherence* means that agencies exemplifying the New Professionalism participate in national conversations about professional policing. They are training their officers, supervisors, and leaders in successful practices and theories. Such organizations as the Police Foundation, the Police Executive Research Forum, the federal COPS Office, the Office on Violence Against Women, the Office of Justice Programs, the Major Cities Chiefs Association, and other professional associations have helped by nurturing national conversations among practitioners and researchers.[5]

Again, "Guardians" or "Soldiers"?

The discussion in Chapter 3 of policing in a diverse society centered on the historical and contemporary chasm between police and minorities, and the question of whether or not the police have become too militarized. Here we merely note that much of that discussion revolves around how the police are now too often being seen as "soldiers" or "warriors." Certainly, the recent killings by police of young African-American men and others have caused many people to ask whether or not there exists within the police culture a "warrior mindset."[6] It is time for the police to consider the sort of image they project to the public and to minority communities in particular.

TWO ESSENTIALS FOR THIS ENVIRONMENT: CONSTITUTIONAL POLICING AND PROCEDURAL JUSTICE

The Constitution as "Boss"

As noted above, several race-related events led to a careful review of police practices and calls for reform. Then, however, subsequent uses of police force in other cities kept policing practices at the forefront of the national consciousness.

At the heart of this issue are questions of race relations, and as a result many police agencies are now looking at their agency's culture in a new light. These protests have centered on the experiences of minority communities and questions of disparate treatment, particularly with respect to the use of deadly force. Police chief executives are becoming much more heavily involved in constitutional policing, to be used as a cornerstone of their community policing efforts. When a police agency develops policies and practices that advance the constitutional goals of protecting citizens' rights and providing equal protection under the law, then, as New Haven (Connecticut) Police Chief Dean Esserman put it, "The Constitution is our boss. We are not warriors, we are guardians. The [police] oath is to the Constitution."[7]

Many police agencies now look at their agency's culture in a new light, developing policies and practices that advance constitutional goals, protect citizens' rights, and provide equal protection under the law.

Billion Photos/Shutterstock.

Constitutional policing, then, forms the foundation of community policing. Police agencies cannot form positive and productive relationships with the citizens they serve if those communities do not trust the police or if the communities do not believe that the police see their mission as protecting civil rights as well as public safety. Too often, concerns with constitutional aspects of policing occur only after the fact—when police officials, community members, and the courts look at an officer's actions to determine whether or not laws, ordinances, or agency policies were violated. Now, there is a growing recognition among police leaders that constitutional policing should be on the minds of all agency members on an everyday basis.[8]

Greater Cooperation Through Legitimacy

A related yet different concept is that of police **legitimacy**: the extent to which the community believes that police actions are appropriate, proper, and just.[9] If the police have a high level of perceived legitimacy in a community, members of the community tend to be more willing to cooperate with the police and to accept the outcome of their interactions with the police.

Legitimacy is reflected in several ways. First, people want to have an opportunity to explain their situation or tell their side of the story to a police officer. Second, people want the police authorities to be neutral—make decisions based on consistently applied legal principles and the facts of an incident, not an officer's personal opinions and biases. Third, people want to be treated with dignity and politeness, and have their rights respected. Finally, people focus on cues that indicate trustworthiness—the belief that their police are benevolent, caring, and sincerely trying to do what is best for the people with whom they are dealing.[10]

A good case study in which legitimacy was especially pertinent involved the recent "stop and frisk" policy in New York City and other cities (e.g., Philadelphia). Proponents of this practice argued that large numbers of stops help police to get guns and drugs off the streets (and in some cases, stops did result in arrests). Opponents argued that the large majority of street stops did not yield either guns or drugs, but instead often resulted in the repeated stopping and humiliation of innocent people, which damages police–community relationships. Even the U.S. Department of Justice argued in a formal "Statement of Interest" that there was "significant evidence that unlawfully aggressive police tactics are not only unnecessary for effective policing, but are in fact detrimental to the mission of crime reduction. The public's trust and willingness to cooperate with the police are damaged when officers routinely fail to respect the rule of law."[11]

The issue came to a head in August 2013, when the U.S. District Court handed down its ruling in a lawsuit brought by a group of African-American and Hispanic persons who said they were stopped by police without a legal basis in violation of Constitution. Judge Shira A. Sheindlin said that the argument that NYPD's stop-and-frisk practices was effective in reducing crime was irrelevant; rather, the practice was unconstitutional, and ... each stop is also a demeaning and humiliating experience. No one should live in fear of being stopped whenever he leaves his home to go about the activities of daily life". And, according to a report by the Cambridge Review Committee, "Those who are routinely subjected to stops are overwhelmingly people of color, and they are justifiably troubled to be singled out when many of them have done nothing to attract the unwanted attention. A judge can determine if a police action was lawful, and a police supervisor can determine whether an officer acted within the bounds of departmental policy. But citizens will form their own opinions about whether they view the actions of an officer as measured or excessive, as impartial or discriminatory. In short, did the officer exercise his or her discretion in a fair manner?"[12]

In sum, to address the question of the legitimacy of the police and of policing practices among members of the public, police need to think about their role in a new way, focusing on the influence that their values, mission, policies, and practices have on public views about their legitimacy—how citizens view police practices and deem as appropriate, reasonable, and just.

Angst from Hot Spot Policing and Other Strategies

Closely related to goals of constitutional policing and procedural justice is the use of police crime reduction strategies. Indeed, much of the anger in many communities is likely the result of police crime-fighting tactics actually alienating citizens. Some police methods can be interpreted as oppressive, and while police agencies nationwide have produced remarkable successes in crime reduction over the last two decades, that success may have come at a high price due to the unintended consequences of certain policing strategies that focused on what has been termed a "culture of data," in which agency successes are measured in terms of their number of stops conducted, arrests made, the number of searches that result in the seizure of guns, and so on.

It is ironic that one of the primary differences said to exist between the professional era and today's community era of policing is that the latter took policing way from their near-total obsession with numbers and quantitative "successes." However, there is now in many police agencies a new emphasis on the range of data that are analyzed, and the overreliance on data can have a negative impact on police–community relationships. Under constitutional policing and legitimacy, officers learn that large numbers of stops, arrests, seizures, and so on is no longer the path to success in the department.

Similarly, police must be sensitive to the appearance of oppressiveness and racial bias in their focusing of police resources on crime "hot spots" (discussed in Chapter 6). These concentrations of crime often are found in poor neighborhoods and areas with significant minority populations, and when agencies engage in "zero tolerance" crime-fighting tactics they need to consider how that feels for community members.

Chief Cathy Lanier of the Metropolitan Police Department of the District of Columbia provides an example of how police operations can alienate community members in high-crime neighborhoods:

> We'd send all of these cops down to high-crime areas during the afternoon after roll call. The first officer would lock up a guy who runs a stop sign and whose permits were expired by 30 days. Then another officer would see a 55-year-old woman on her front porch with a beer in her hand step off of her porch to talk to a neighbor. He'd lock her up for drinking in public.[13]

Later, Chief Lanier explained, the officers were back at the station processing these low-level arrestees, and "guess what happens in the neighborhood where they just were: carjackings, home invasions, armed robberies." Chief Lanier believes police must remember that hot-spot neighborhoods are home not only to the most crime but also to the most victims and witnesses. Therefore, police must be responsive to the concerns that residents express, whether they are about serious crimes in their neighborhood or less serious "quality-of-life" issues, such as abandoned cars.[14]

Use of Force in the New Culture of Policing

The police agency's culture in regard to its use of force actually begins with recruit training in the academy. "In Boston, we don't train our recruits to be a military force. I want my officers to come out as problem-solvers, not an occupying force." Thus stated Boston Police Commissioner William Evans. And, as Kansas City, Missouri, Chief Terry Zeigler put it, "For a long time, the police academy has been based on a military boot camp type of philosophy. That is missing the point. Policing is mostly about manners and courtesy."[15]

Responding to Mass Demonstrations

The rage and violence involved in several of the 2014–2015 riots and protests in many cities also changed how many police agencies react to **mass demonstrations**; as Pittsburgh, Pennsylvania Police Chief Cameron McLay stated, "How you approach a crowd of demonstrators will determine what you will get back from the crowd."[16] As part of the application of constitutional policing and in consideration of police legitimacy, a "soft" approach is now recommended in dealing with demonstrations, beginning with police communicating with protest leaders before and during the event to deter any violence by agitators and ensure that protests can be conducted peacefully. In sum, police responses are to be measured and proportional to what is happening during a demonstration. As Boston Police Commissioner William Evans said, "If we go looking for a fight with demonstrators, that's what we'll get."[17]

Also under recent consideration is the "optics" of a police response. This means police should avoid bringing heavy equipment to the scene of a demonstration or wearing protective riot gear if there is no indication that a demonstration will be violent. Also, police have learned through trial and error that interacting with people—such as asking them kindly to move along if necessary—is much more effective.[18]

The Nashville Police Department emphasized the "we're not looking for a fight" approach when engaging protesters during a protest following Ferguson when demonstrators marched for a couple of miles to police headquarters. Police met them not with numerous officers in riot gear, but with three officers and coolers full of ice water. On another occasion, when there were protests following the grand jury decision in Ferguson, it was cold outside, so police met them with hot chocolate and coffee.[19]

MOVING FROM A "GOOD" TO "GREAT" POLICE ORGANIZATION

Flowing from the above discussion of changing police culture to one that is "guardian" in nature and making related adaptations and modifications of police policy and practices, the work of Jim Collins, making a "good" organization and making it "great" is also highly relevant.

The "Level 5 Leader"

Certainly community policing and problem solving requires that the police organization be as innovative, efficient, and effective as it can be. In that vein, Jim Collins authored two books[3] that were the result of his organizational studies and looked at how organizations could move from being "good" to becoming "great."[20]

First, regarding their leadership, Collins coined the term "**Level 5 leader**" to describe the highest level of executive capabilities. Level 5 executives' ambitions are directed first and foremost to the organization and its success, not to personal renown. Such leaders, Collins stressed, are "fanatically driven, infected with an incurable need to produce results."[21] They are also self-effacing, quiet, reserved, and even shy.

Collins also uses a bus metaphor when talking about transforming from good to great:

> The executives who ignited the transformations…did not first figure out where to drive the bus and then get people to take it there. No, they *first* got the right people on the bus (and the wrong people off the bus) and *then* figured out where to drive it (emphasis his).[22]

Collins wrote, "The main point is not about assembling the right team—that's nothing new."[23] Rather, the main point is that great leaders assemble their teams *before* they decide where to go; the right people will be self-motivated. Good-to-**great organizations**, Collins found, also have a "culture of discipline" in which employees show extreme diligence and intensity in their thoughts and actions, always focusing on implementing the organizations mission, purpose, and goals.[24]

Therefore, people are not an organization's most important asset; rather, the *right* people are. Collins states that picking the right people and getting the wrong people off the bus are critical. "*By whatever means possible, personnel problems have to be confronted in an organization that aspires to greatness.*"[25]

Of course, Collins was not writing about the transition to community policing and the inherent change in agency culture; however, his viewpoints are certainly apropos in this regard—particularly when considering that there are some people who will not be in the right seat on the community policing bus, and there are younger officers waiting in the wings who are in need of the challenge and training inherent in this strategy—and for the purpose of accepting the mantle of leadership in this type of organization when the current baby boomers retire.

Certainly, the kinds of issues and challenges discussed in this textbook—particularly in such areas as crime analysis, CompStat, intelligence-led policing, predictive policing, and technologies where higher levels of cognitive ability are necessary—demand that succession planning (discussed in Chapter 15, concerning the future development of police leadership) be part of the organizational fabric.

"Moments of Truth"

Jan Carlzon, former president of Scandinavian Airlines, wrote a book entitled *Moments of Truth* in which he defined the moment of truth in business as follows: "Anytime a customer comes into contact with any aspect of a business, however remote, is an opportunity to form an impression."

Moments of truth are anywhere that someone has an opportunity to make a lasting impact on others. Certainly such opportunities present themselves each day in policing—and are unequivocally a part of the fabric of community policing. Every contact an officer makes with a citizen—from the way the officer looks in his or her uniform, to the tone of voice used—provides an opportunity for them to make a lasting impact—for good or for bad.[26]

Although most if not all officers probably understand that they can have such an impact, the Scottsdale, Arizona, Police Department (SPD) has taken the moment-of-truth concept to a higher level, realizing that, as one police executive stated, "Safe communities are developed and maintained through community partnerships. The public's willing cooperation to help prevent crime and disorder is the cornerstone of the agency's system of policing."[27]

Realizing that police leaders play the most critical role in changing an agency's culture and adopting a customer service orientation, an article in SPD's monthly employee newsletter explained the theory, history, and advantages of moments of truth. All employees were encouraged to submit for publication examples of employees proving enhanced customer service through moments of truth; meanwhile, command staff discussed and reinforced moments of truth with employees at squad briefings, manager meetings, and employee forums. Almost immediately, supervisors began to submit examples of positive moment of truth encounters through their chains of command to underscore personnel performance. Soon, employees at all levels and across all bureaus began to draw attention to the many examples of moments of truth carried out by their peers and manifested through enhanced customer service. Moments of truth are now part of the department's vernacular and culture. These published moments of truth can be accessed at http://www.scottsdaleaz.gov/Police/about/Customer/MOT.asp.

RECRUITING QUALITY OFFICERS FOR COMMUNITY POLICING

The Applicant Pool

Community policing increases the number of functions police undertake, particularly for larger departments. Working with citizen groups to address crime and disorder proactively requires time and resources that are in addition to those needed for traditional police responsibilities, such as responding to calls for service, crime prevention, and traffic enforcement. However, these are very challenging times for police agencies in terms of human resources. Of course, problems with their ability to obtain a satisfactorily large pool of applicants for police positions are nothing new; many people who indicate such interest simply wash out quickly in the preliminary application or background investigation stage due to criminal, financial, drug, or other problems. However, the recent Great Recession—and ongoing retirements of Baby Boomer employees—has exacerbated this difficulty. In fact, in early 2009, when the recession was in full swing and $1 billion in Congressional appropriations to spend on police hiring, the Office of Community Oriented Policing Services received a staggering 7,272 applications for the program, requesting $8.3 billion to fill more than 39,000 sworn-officer positions throughout the United States. Obviously, the need for police officers is great, while the ability of cities and counties to pay for more officers is limited.[28]

Exhibit 8–2 describes how a number of changes in the levels of violence, crime, and terrorism in France served to foment changes in its culture of government and policing over the past two decades.

Exhibit 8–2	Global Perspective: France Changes Police—and Community—Culture

Over the past two decades, France has undergone a number of wrenching social changes, including an increase in violence and property crimes as well as acts of terrorism. The French national government, aware that its hard-nosed national police were making matters worse, appointed a committee to study the psychology of violence, the effects of improved urban planning on crime, and the influence of economic opportunity on crime and violence.

Ultimately, the committee criticized the traditional structure of French top-down bureaucracy, which had become secretive and unresponsive to the public; it was recommended that more power be given to communities to determine their own crime prevention and security programs, and to involve key neighborhood persons and organizations in coming up with workable solutions.

A part of that effort was recruiting local elected officials such as mayors and city councils, school teachers and principals, social service directors, youth and sports counselors, police, magistrates, and members of local communities. This inclusion prompted the national police, as well as the judiciary (prosecutors, investigating magistrates, parole, and probation officers), to form their own council for crime prevention. Then, in August 2002, the French Parliament enacted legislation creating the Local Security and Crime Prevention Councils, which fully integrated crime prevention with crime suppression techniques, leaving the important decision-making powers with the local communities.

While all of the foregoing was occurring, France also enhanced the recruiting and training of local beat officers in community policing skills. This strategy has spread throughout the country and resulted in a number of innovative outreach techniques that proved effective in reducing crime while improving community feelings of safety and participation in an interactive program.

Some serious problems remain in France, such as the government remaining very centralized and a deep gulf existing between the police and the citizens in France (with police still tending to adopt new policies without even notifying the public or inviting input). And, to be sure, the fear of terroristic attacks remains due to the growth of local terrorist support cells (particularly after the January 2015 attacks at a Paris newspaper office, killing 20, and multiple simultaneous attacks in Paris in November 2015 that killed 130).

But the French remain optimistic, and community policing is still evolving and bringing about many crime prevention innovations. Much work remains, however, particularly in bridging the gap between police and ordinary citizens who are, in the view of too many officers, not qualified to "tell them what to do."[29]

Much of the difficulty police agencies face in sustaining their workforce is also due to employee attrition. Although attrition can be positive—such as losing individuals who are not suited to the occupation—attrition can be a problem when it occurs in waves. Some jurisdictions hire large numbers of officers at one time, not anticipating that large numbers will also retire at about the same point in time and thus making it difficult to hire and maintain the necessary workforce of officers.

Officers of the Baby Boom generation are beginning to retire, and the number of such retirements is likely to increase in the near future as the number of officers eligible for retirement increases significantly. Retention also changes with generations of employees. Younger generations of workers might have less organizational commitment than older ones, with many changing careers often. Furthermore, the lack of promotional opportunities, low salaries and benefits, the attraction of lucrative private-sector careers, and the negative image of policing will result in even fewer qualified recruits and less retention. Simply put, if agencies do not seek to aggressively employ targeted **recruitment** strategies—especially for women and minorities—and "sell themselves" when recruiting, they will suffer in numbers even more (Exhibit 8–3 describes how the federal government is attempting to help in this regard).

Exhibit 8–3   The Federal Community Policing Hiring Program: How to Allocate $126 Million

The federal Office of Community Oriented Policing Services (COPS Office) Hiring Program has a nice annual problem: how to determine where to allocate about $126 million of funding when nearly $426 million in hiring funds is requested from police agencies.

In a recent year, using an online application system, approximately 3,500 agencies requested 3,469 officer positions for $425,734,755 in federal funding. Therefore, the COPS Office had to focus on several priority areas for additional consideration, including:

- ▶ Current commitment to community policing.
- ▶ Reported crime for the previous three years.
- ▶ Planned community policing activities.
- ▶ Changes in budget for law enforcement agencies and revenues for local governments.
- ▶ Poverty and unemployment rates.

Current hiring priority areas also included homeland security and trust problems. "Homeland security issues" include protecting critical infrastructures, information/intelligence concerns, and other homeland security problems. Addressing trust problems category includes such activities as regularly distributing crime and disorder information to community members, routinely seeking input from the community to identify and prioritize neighborhood problems (through regular community meetings, annual surveys, and so on), and collaborating with local government agencies, nonprofit organizations, neighborhood groups, and local businesses in problem solving.[30]

Although new hire officer positions were not required to be military veterans, applicants who committed to hiring or rehiring at least one veteran received additional consideration. Similarly school resource officer positions for community policing emphasis also received additional consideration. The applicants have to provide objective and verifiable indicators, to include how applicants planned to form community partnerships, financial need (as measured by economic and fiscal health questions), and crime in the jurisdiction. Although very time consuming, the COPS Office checked and verified all such information provided to it, to ensure that information was accurate and reliable. A minimum score was established for the community policing portion of the application.

Due to the high demand and limited funding available, only 215 (17 percent) of the 1,296 requests were funded. By law, half of all hiring funds were awarded to agencies serving populations of more than 150,000 and half to those serving populations of 150,000 or less.[31]

A police agency's commitment to changing its culture will often begin with recruitment, giving due consideration to applicants' race, generation (e.g., Millennials), sex and gender identity or expression, national origin, and so on.
RosaIreneBetancourt 9/Alamy Stock Photo.

Attracting Candidates: Strategies

Following are some strategies that police agencies are urged to consider when setting out to hire quality community policing officers[32]:

- *Integrate the community in the hiring process:* Including community input can allow citizens to help ensure that hiring reflects not only community needs but also community characteristics. For example, St. Paul, Minnesota, as part of a program to reduce racially biased policing, worked with the community to determine a list of characteristics (e.g., enthusiastic, fair, possessed of good judgment, tenacious, respectful, compassionate, and unafraid to engage the community) that ideal candidates should possess.

- *Use internal recruiting strategies:* The best police recruiters for a police agency are often its own personnel. The use of employee referral networks—referrals by family, friends, and employees—can strongly influence individual decisions to apply for careers in public service; this approach also works for dispelling myths about police work.
- *Assess internal employee engagement strategies:* Although police agencies cannot adopt Google's employee engagement strategies—which include on-site dry cleaning, a wine club, and yoga classes—they can offer such benefits as flexible work hours, vacation benefits, workout areas, and health counseling. Police executive should place themselves in the applicant's position and ask themselves, "Why would I want to work for this department?" This is a crucial step in department marketing and outreach efforts.
- *Use "word of mouse":* Social networking, traditional job fairs, and proactive community partnerships work well, and getting the word out via social media reaches more people.
- *Brand your department:* The agency message that is transmitted through advertising represents the "brand" that applicants see and its identity. For example, the Los Angeles police recruitment video series includes a variety of images, including a black female police sergeant, a diverse workforce of Hispanic and Asian officers, and fast-paced and adventurous police work. Segments also display officers attempting to calm disputes, dealing with family problems, and working closely with community members in emotionally charged situations as much as they display traditional "crime-fighter" images, which is intended to resonate with Internet-savvy and video-oriented applicants who are seen as socially aware, brand loyal, and susceptible to cause branding.
- *Target second-career applicants, and train them appropriately:* With the recent Great Recession came an increase in laid-off applicants seeking a second career in policing, emerging from many diverse career fields. Although providing a sizeable pool of applicants, these individuals often present unique challenges by having differential training needs and abilities, previous work experiences, levels of commitment, competing work values, preconceived notions of salary and benefits, and concepts of professionalism.

Exhibit 8–4 discusses another internal recruiting issue: whether or not relaxing recruitment standards is advisable.

| **Exhibit 8–4** | Relaxing Qualifications for Hiring: A Good Idea? |

Given the aforementioned problems with finding qualified people to work as community policing officers, some agencies have decided to "open the floodgates" by eliminating some of the traditional restrictions. Relaxing requirements in order to "fill empty seats on test day" can prove to be politically volatile and attract criticism. For example, relaxing residency restrictions can lead to public criticism that the applicants have little knowledge of the community. Some agencies have also eased educational requirements, which will only serve to rekindle the long-standing debate about the desirability of degreed candidates as officers.

Some agencies have relaxed minimum age requirements to attract more candidates, raising concern about the readiness of younger applicants for police work. Some agencies have become more tolerant of experimental drug use, bad credit history, and minor arrest records to attain larger numbers of applicants.

Relaxing such restrictions can interfere with the department's ability to build community confidence in the quality of its officers. Therefore, because of the potential organizational, political, and social ramifications of relaxing restrictions, before doing so departments should carefully consider the overall effect on recruiting, officer quality, and the message that is sent concerning hiring standards.

Workforce of the Future: From Baby Boomers to Millennials

As noted above, the retiring Baby Boomer generation of police officers has stressed the ability of police agencies to maintain a stable workforce. Indeed, between now and the late 2020s, 10,000 baby boomers a day will reach retirement age.[33] As this baby boom generation begins to retire, police departments will experience a changing workforce as well, with the rise of the **Millennials** or Generation Y, born roughly between 1982 and 2000 and the largest generation since the Baby Boom. In fact, Millennials, with a population of 83.1 million, now outnumber Baby Boomers at 75.4 million; in 2015, they also surpassed Generation X (those born between 1965 and 1979), to become the nation's largest workforce. According to the Pew Research Center, more than one in three American workers is a Millennial.[34] This new workforce will obviously present several new challenges. For that reason, federal agencies and universities are convening workshops to discuss a number of recruitment and retention issues. These new hires are technically savvy, enthusiastic, and service-oriented, and also tend to carry high expectations. As a whole, they may be more eager for quick advancement and higher starting salaries. In addition, while police officers have traditionally stayed in the same career field and even agency for their entire careers, workers in general are now more likely to switch jobs and employers after just a few years.

How can police agencies hire and retain Millennials? Obviously, they cannot compete with the private sector, where one study found the following perks had recently been given to Millennials by employers as rewards for their efforts:

- A $25,000 guided trip to Mt. Everest base camp.
- World Series tickets.
- Trapeze lessons.
- Kayaking trips.
- Stand-up comedy lessons.
- Chanel shopping spree with a personal stylist (value: $5,000).
- Aerobatic flight in an air races plane.[35]

A number of suggestions have been offered for recruiting and retaining the Millennials. First is the importance of offering them opportunities for specialization and training. In addition, agencies may need to rethink annual performance evaluations, moving to more individual, informal, and frequent feedback from supervisors.

Regarding retention of Millennials, a compressed work week and job sharing to allow for more flexibility for officers with young families is recommended. Some agencies are experimenting with a sabbatical program, allowing employees to leave the department to try a new job or career with the option to return.[36]

Exhibit 8–5 discussed one agency's approach to its personnel concerns as it transitioned to a problem-oriented approach.

Exhibit 8–5	Hayward, California: Hiring, Training, and Evaluation of Personnel[37]

After making the decision to change its policing philosophy, a systems change was required that would greatly affect personnel. Therefore, the initial focus was on personnel systems such as recruiting, hiring, training, performance appraisals, and promotability guidelines. To transform the recruiting and hiring processes, the Hayward, California, Personnel Department and Police Department began exploring the following three questions:

1. Overall, what type of candidate, possessing what types of skills, should be recruited?
2. What specific knowledge, skills, and abilities reflect the community policing philosophy—particularly regarding problem-solving abilities and sensitivity to community needs?
3. How can these attributes best be identified in the initial screening process?

The department also analyzed the city's demographics, finding that it had a diverse ethnic composition. To promote cultural diversity and sensitivity to the needs of the community, a psychologist was employed to develop a profile of an effective community policing officer in Hayward. These considerations became an integral part of the department's hiring process.

Next the training and performance evaluation systems were reappraised. All personnel, both sworn and civilian, had to receive problem-solving training to provide a clear and thorough understanding of the history, philosophy, and transition to this strategy. The department's initial training was directed at management and supervisory personnel and was designed to assist these employees in accomplishing the department's goals of reinforcing community policing's values, modifying the existing police culture, strategically transitioning the organization from traditional policing to the new philosophy, and focusing on customer relations. Rank-and-file officers were given 40-hour blocks of instruction.

Performance and reward practices for personnel were modified to reflect the new criteria. Emphasizing quality over quantity (e.g., arrest statistics, number of calls for service, and response times), new criteria included an assessment of how well a call for service was handled and what type of problem-solving approach was used to reach a solution for the problem. Other mechanisms were developed to broadcast and communicate successes, including supervisors' logs, a newsletter, and city-wide recognition of extraordinary customer service efforts.

The department's promotional process was also retooled; a new phase was added to the department's promotional test—the "promotability" phase—to evaluate the candidate's decision-making abilities, analytical skills, communication skills, interpersonal skills, and professional contributions.

ROLES OF KEY LEADERS

In previous chapters (and in several to follow), we discussed the new and challenging role of the patrol officer under community policing and problem solving. Here, we examine the roles of their leaders—chief executives, middle managers (e.g., captain, lieutenants), and first-line supervisors (i.e., sergeants).

Beware the "Toxic Leader"

A dynamic that might occur in any of the following rank levels is that of toxic leadership, which can spell the demise of any agency's community policing efforts, where the key to success lies in the relationship between the patrol officers and the neighborhoods they serve. As Karl Bickel put it, "**Toxic leaders** that poison the workplace environment, demoralize personnel, create disincentives, produce unnecessary stress, stifle creativity, decrease risk taking, and promote themselves on the backs of the rank and file, while they present an obstacle to organizational transformation and the institutionalization of community policing."[38]

Such leaders may be arrogant and possess a perfectionist attitude, lack in self-confidence, be shallow and condescending toward subordinates, engage in bullying, and cause rifts among staff members; such attitudes in a community policing organization may well kill all efforts to engage in long-term problem solving and the related aspects (e.g., training, evaluation, community meetings, and so on) that accompany that effort. Such leaders can also severely impair employee morale and job satisfaction on the part of enthusiastic officers who enjoy the challenges of problem solving and the long-term benefits it affords. This, in turn, can ultimately lead to a more toxic organizational culture, described above. Therefore, if an agency displays symptoms of toxic leadership—low morale, disgruntled employees, high rates of sick leave use and turnover, citizen complaints, and so on—the problem must be dealt with sooner than later (in order to avoid the "rotten apple spoiling the barrel" dynamic). Jim Collins' view that the right people must be on the bus (discussed above) applies here as well, as demotions, transfers, even terminations (where legitimately documented and provided in applicable personnel regulations) may be in order.

Chief Executives

Of course, the police **chief executive** is ultimately responsible for all of the facets of this philosophy and practice, from implementation to training to evaluation. Therefore, what is needed are chief executives who are willing to do things that have not been done before, or as one writer put it, "risk takers and boat rockers within a culture where daily exposure to life-or-death situations makes officers natural conservators of the status quo."[39] These are chief executives who become committed to getting the police and neighborhoods to work together to attack the roots of crime. For them, "Standing still is not only insufficient ... it is going backwards."[40]

Therefore, as noted earlier, a police executive must be a viable **change agent**. In any hierarchy, the person at the top is responsible for setting both the policy and tone of the organization. Within a police agency, the chief or sheriff has the ultimate power to make change, particularly one as substantive as community policing. The chief executive must be both visible and credible and must create a climate conducive to change. Under this philosophy, chief executives must focus on the vision, values, mission, and long-term goals of policing in order to create an organizational environment that enables officers, government officials, and community members to work together. By building consensus, they can establish programs, develop timelines, and set priorities. They should honor the good work done in the past but exhibit a sense of urgency about implementing change while involving people from the community and the department in all stages of the transition. The chief executive's roles and responsibilities include the following:

- Articulating a clear vision to the organization.
- Understanding and accepting the depth of change and time required to implement the methods and practices.
- Assembling a management team that is committed to translating the new vision into action.
- Being committed to removing bureaucratic obstacles whenever possible.

Many police organizations boast talented and creative chief executives who, when participating in the change process, will assist in effecting change that is beneficial and lasting. James Q. Wilson put it this way:

> The police profession today is the intellectual leadership of the criminal justice profession in the United States. The police are in the lead. They're showing the world how things might better be done.[41]

Middle Managers

Middle managers also play a crucial role in this philosophy. The emphasis on problem solving necessitates that middle managers draw on their familiarity with the bureaucracy to secure, maintain, and use authority to empower subordinates, helping officers to actively and creatively confront and resolve issues, sometimes using unconventional approaches on a trial-and-error basis.

There are many really significant contributions middle managers can make to the changing culture of the agency to embrace and sustain it. First, they must build on the strengths of their subordinates, capitalizing on their training and competence.[42] They do so by treating people as individuals and creating talented teams.[43] They must "cheerlead," encouraging supervisors and patrol officers to actually solve the problems they are confronting.[44] It is also imperative that middle managers *not* believe they are serving the chief executive's best interests by preserving the status quo. The lieutenants are the gatekeepers and must develop the system, resources, and support mechanisms to ensure that the officers, detectives, and supervisors can perform to achieve the best results. The officers and supervisors cannot perform without the necessary equipment, resources, and reinforcement.[45]

Middle managers, like their subordinates, must be allowed the freedom to make mistakes—and good middle managers protect their subordinates from organizational and political recrimination and scapegoating when things go wrong. Put another way, middle managers cannot stand idly by while their people are led to the guillotine, and they must protect their officers from the political effects of legitimate failure.[46] They must not allow their problem-solving officers to revert to traditional methods. They must be diplomats and facilitators, using a lot more persuading and negotiating (toward win-win solutions) than they did under the traditional "my way or the highway" management style.[47]

The roles and responsibilities of middle managers during the changeover include the following:

- Assuming responsibility for strategic planning.
- Eliminating red tape and bottlenecks that impede the work of officers and supervisors.
- Conducting regular meetings with subordinates to discuss plans, activities, and results.

The position of middle managers in a community policing environment was well described by Kelling and Bratton:

> The idea that mid-managers are spoilers, that they thwart project or strategic innovation, has some basis in fact. Mid-managers improperly directed can significantly impede innovation. Yet, ample evidence exists that when a clear vision of the business of the organization is put forward, when mid-managers are included in planning, when their legitimate self-interests are acknowledged, and when they are properly trained, mid-managers can be the leading edge of innovation and creativity.[48]

First-Line Supervisors

It is widely held that the most challenging aspect of changing the culture of a police agency lies in changing the attitudes and beliefs of **first-line supervisors**. The influence of first-line supervisors is so strong that their role warrants special attention.

The primary contact of street officers with their organization is through their sergeant, so the quality of an officer's daily life is often dependent on his or her immediate supervisor. Most officers do not believe their sergeants are sources of guidance and direction but rather are authority figures to be satisfied (by numbers of arrests and citations, manner in which reports are completed, officer's ability to avoid citizen complaints, and so on). There is just cause for the reluctance of first-line supervisors to avoid change. Herman Goldstein stated it this way:

> Changing the operating philosophy of rank-and-file officers is easier than altering a first-line supervisor's perspective of his or her job, because the work of a sergeant is greatly simplified by the traditional form of policing. The more routinized the work, the easier it is for the sergeant to check. The more emphasis placed on rank and the symbols of position, the easier it is for the sergeant to rely on authority—rather than intellect and personal skills—to carry out [his or her] duties…. [S]ergeants are usually appalled by descriptions of the freedom and independence suggested in problem oriented policing for rank-and-file officers. The concept can be very threatening to them. This … can create an enormous block to implementation.[49]

Supervisors must be convinced that this approach makes good sense in today's environment, and they should possess the characteristics of a good problem-oriented supervisor; see Exhibit 8–6.

Exhibit 8–6	*Characteristics of a Good Problem-Oriented Supervisor*

1. Allowing subordinates freedom to experiment with new approaches.
2. Insisting on good, accurate analyses of problems.
3. Granting flexibility in work schedules when requests are appropriate.
4. Allowing subordinates to make most contacts directly and paving the way when they are having trouble getting cooperation.
5. Protecting subordinates from pressures within the department to revert to traditional methods.
6. Running interference for subordinates to secure resources, protect them from criticism, and so forth.
7. Knowing what problems subordinates are working on and whether the problems are real.
8. Knowing subordinates' beats and important citizens in it, and expecting subordinates to know it even better.
9. Coaching subordinates through the process, giving advice, helping them manage their time.
10. Monitoring subordinates' progress and, as necessary, prodding them along or slowing them down.
11. Supporting subordinates even if their strategies fail, so long as something useful is learned in the process and the process was well thought through.
12. Managing problem-solving efforts over a long period of time; not allowing efforts to die simply because they get sidetracked by competing demands for time and attention.

13. Giving credit to subordinates and letting others know about their good work.
14. Allowing subordinates to talk with visitors or at conferences about their work.
15. Identifying new resources and contacts for subordinates and making them check them out.
16. Stressing cooperation, coordination, and communication within the unit and outside it.
17. Coordinating efforts across shifts, beats, and outside units and agencies.
18. Realizing that this style of policing cannot simply be ordered; officers and detectives must come to believe in it.

Source: Police Executive Research Forum, "Supervising Problem-Solving" (Washington, D.C.: Author, training outline, 1990).

The roles and responsibilities of first-line supervisors include the following:

- Understanding and practicing problem solving.
- Managing time, staff, and resources.
- Encouraging teamwork.
- Helping officers to mobilize stakeholders.
- Tracking and managing officers' problem solving.
- Providing officers with ongoing feedback and support.

Summary

The focal point of this chapter has been about police cultural change. Certainly the problems confronting policing today, described in earlier chapters, have driven this chapter's discussion points. Those challenges are even more daunting when adding the problems of public image, the need for becoming more "constitutional" and "legitimate," addressing use of force and handing public demonstrations, with recruiting new officers while making the field attractive to a new generation of employees whose wants and abilities are quite different from those of earlier generations.

This chapter has underscored the importance and means of changing the culture of the police agency, from recruit to chief, to accommodate the new philosophy and the operation of community policing and problem solving. Also called for is the inherent need for each agency to examine its mission and values, for each chief executive to take their organization from being "good" to being "great," and for all employees, sworn and civilian, to support the cultural changes needed within the organization.

Key Terms and Concepts

Change agent	First-line supervisor	Mass demonstrations	Recruitment (for community policing)
Chief executive	"Great" organizations	Millennials	
Constitutional policing	Legitimacy	Middle manager	Toxic leader
Culture of policing	Level 5 leader	"Moments of truth"	

Items for Review

1. How would you describe the primary elements of a police organization's "culture"?
2. What constitutes "new" means of becoming professional in policing?
3. How can constitutional policing and possessing more legitimacy serve to change police culture?
4. Explain why such a successful strategy as hot-spot policing can cause angst among citizens.
5. In what ways might the use of force—including responses to mass demonstrations—be modified to bring about a new police culture?
6. How might a police organization change from being "good" to "great"?
7. Why is obtaining a satisfactory police applicant pool so challenging, and what means might be used to do so?
8. In what ways is/will the Millennial generation demand change in policing culture?

Learn by Doing

1. You are special events coordinator in your municipal police department, where what is publicized as a large peaceful demonstration against animal research is being planned. This group sponsoring the protest is known to become agitated and, at times, violent. What kinds of information would you provide to your officers concerning how to address the demonstrators?

2. Assume that you are part of a classroom group that is studying police administration, and you are to make a five-minute presentation on ways of assisting a "good" police organization in becoming "great." What would be the major points of your presentation, per Collins?

3. You are the officer assigned to recruit officers into your agency who have strong community policing abilities. What approaches will you use (and avoid)?

Endnotes

1. Quoted in Police Executive Research Forum, *Constitutional Policing as a Cornerstone of Community Policing* (Washington, D.C.: Police Executive Research Forum, 2015), p. 1, http://ric-zai-inc.com/Publications/cops-p32F4-pub.pdf.

2. Chris Braiden, "Cliché Policing: Answer Before Question," Unpublished paper, n.d.

3. Bob Vernon, "Organizational Culture," *Law Officer* (July 31, 2008), http://www.lawofficer.com/articles/print/volume-4/issue-8/leadership/organizational-culture.html.

4. St. Louis County, Missouri, Police Department, "Values: Our Mission Statement and Codes of Ethics," http://www.stlouisco.com/LawandPublicSafety/PoliceDepartment/AboutUs/Values.

5. Christopher Stone and Jeremy Travis, *Toward a New Professionalism in Policing* (National Institute of Justice and Harvard Kennedy School, March 2011), pp. 2–19, https://www.ncjrs.gov/pdffiles1/nij/232359.pdf.

6. Seth Stoughton, "Police Warriors or Community Guardians?" *Washington Monthly* (April 17, 2015), http://www.washingtonmonthly.com/ten-miles-square/2015/04/police_warriors_or_community_g055130.php.

7. Quoted in Police Executive Research Forum, *Constitutional Policing as a Cornerstone of Community Policing*, p. 2.

8. Ibid., p. 3.

9. Ibid.

10. See T. R. Tyler, *Why People Obey the Law: Procedural Justice, Legitimacy, and Compliance.* (Princeton, N.J.: Princeton University Press, 2006); also see J. Sunshine and T. R. Tyler, "The Role of Procedural Justice and Legitimacy in Shaping Public Support for Policing," *Law and Society Review* 37(3) (2008): 555–589.

11. Police Executive Research Forum, *Constitutional Policing as a Cornerstone of Community Policing*, pp. 16–17.

12. "Judge Rejects New York's Stop-and-Frisk Policy." *The New York Times* (August 12, 2013), http://www.nytimes.com/2013/08/13/nyregion/stop-and-frisk-practice-violated-rights-judge-rules.html?hp&_r=1&; also see "Statement of Interest of the United States," in *Floyd v. The City of New York*, U.S. District Court for the Southern District of New York, filed June 12, 2013, http://www.justice.gov/crt/about/spl/documents/floyd_soi_6-12-13.pdf. Also see Police Executive Research Forum, *Legitimacy and Procedural Justice: A New Element of Police Leadership*, March 2014, p. 29, http://www.policeforum.org/assets/docs/Free_Online_Documents/Leadership/legitimacy%20and%20procedural%20justice%20-%20a%20new%20element%20of%20police%20leadership.pdf.

13. Quoted in Police Executive Research Forum, *Constitutional Policing as a Cornerstone of Community Policing*, p. 18.

14. Ibid.

15. Ibid., p. 26.

16. Ibid., p. 30.

17. Ibid., p. 28.

18. Ibid.

19. Ibid.

20. Jim Collins, *Good to Great: Why Some Companies Make the Leap...And Others Don't* (New York: HarperCollins, 2001); Jim Collins, *Good to Great and the Social Sectors: A Monograph to Accompany Good to Great* (New York: HarperCollins, 2005).

21. Jim Collins, *Good to Great: Why Some Companies Make the Leap...And Others Don't*, p. 5.

22. Quoted in Wexler et al., *Good to Great: Application of Business Management Principles in the Public Sector*, p. 5.

23. Ibid.

24. Ibid., p. 22.

25. Ibid.

26. *Moments of Truth: New Strategies for Today's Customer-Driven Economy* (New York: Ballinger, 1987), p. 24.

27. Sean Duggan, "Moments of Truth in Policing," *The Police Chief* (June 2010), http://www.policechiefmagazine.org/magazine/index.cfm?fuseaction=display&article_id=2114&issue_id=62010.

28. Jeremy M. Wilson, Erin Dalton, Charles Scheer, Clifford A. Grammich, *Police Recruitment and Retention for the New Millennium: The State of Knowledge* (Santa Monica, Calif.: Rand Center on Quality Policing, 2010), p. 1.

29. Adapted from Los Angeles Community Policing, "Community Policing in Europe: Structure and Best Practices in Sweden, France, Germany," http://www.lacp.org/Articles%20-%20Expert%20-%20Our%20Opinion/060908-Community-PolicingInEurope-AJ.htm.

30. Office of Community Oriented Policing Services, *COPS Office Application Attachment to SF-424*, May 2015, http://www.cops.usdoj.gov/pdf/2015AwardDocs/Standard-Application.pdf.

31. Office of Community Oriented Policing Services, "COPS Hiring Program (CHP)—How Decisions Were Made to Allocate the $123 Million When More than $425 Million Was Requested," http://www.cops.usdoj.gov/pdf/2014AwardDocs/CHP/2014CHP-Methodology.pdf.

32. Wilsom et al., *Police Recruitment and Retention for the New Millennium*, pp. 83–85.

33. Pew Research Center, "Baby Boomers Retire," December 29, 2010, http://www.pewresearch.org/daily-number/baby-boomers-retire/.

34. Nancy Trejos, "Millennials Help Drive Change in the Hotel-Stay Experience," *USA Today* (November 23, 2015), http://www.usatoday.com/story/travel/hotels/2015/11/23/hotels-marriot-target-millennials-over-baby-boomers/76093970/.

35. Marco Della Cava, "For Millennials, Gift Cards Are a Snooze," *USA Today* (October 18, 2015), http://usatoday.newspaperdirect.com/epaper/viewer.aspx.

36. Office of Community Oriented Policing Services, "Today's Officer, Tomorrow's Chief: Police Recruitment and the Millennial Generation," *Community Policing Dispatch* (December 2008), http://cops.usdoj.gov/html/dispatch/December_2008/police_recruitment.htm.

37. Adapted from Joseph E. Brann and Suzanne Whalley, "Community Policing and Problem Solving: The Transformation of Police Organizations," in *Community Oriented Policing and Problem Solving* (Sacramento, Calif.: California Department of Justice, Attorney General's Office, Crime Prevention Center, 1992), p. 72.

38. Quoted in Office of Community Oriented Policing Services, "Are Toxic Leaders Derailing Your Community Policing Efforts?" *Community Policing Dispatch* (March 2014), http://cops.usdoj.gov/html/dispatch/03-2014/toxic_leaders_derailing_your_cp.asp.

39. Mike Tharp and Dorian Friedman, "New Cops on the Block," *U.S. News and World Report* (August 2, 1993), p. 23.

40. Ibid.

41. James Q. Wilson, "Six Things Police Leaders Can Do About Juvenile Crime," *Subject to Debate* (September/October 1997), p. 1.

42. William A. Geller and Guy Swanger, *Managing Innovation in Policing: The Untapped Potential of the Middle Manager* (Washington, D.C.: Police Executive Research Forum, 1995), p. 105.

43. Ibid., p. 131.

44. Ibid., p. 131.

45. Ibid., p. 109.

46. Ibid., p. 112.

47. Ibid., pp. 137–138.

48. George L. Kelling and William J. Bratton, "Implementing Community Policing: The Administrative Problem," *Perspectives on Policing* 17 (1993):11.

49. Herman Goldstein, *Problem-Oriented Policing* (New York: McGraw-Hill, 1990), p. 29.

Planning and Implementation:
Keys to Success

LEARNING OBJECTIVES

As a result of reading this chapter, the student will understand:

- How individuals engage in strategic planning for major decision making
- The primary elements and importance of strategic thinking and strategic planning
- How approaches to strategic policing have been affected by the recent recession
- The importance of developing and applying a planning document
- The roles of chief executives, middle managers, first-line supervisors, detectives, patrol officers, and labor unions in planning and implementing community policing and problem solving
- Several ways in which one can undermine the implementation of this strategy
- How to recognize and cope with resistance to change in the organization using force field analysis
- Some major considerations involved when one is assigned to engage in a major problem solving project

TEST YOUR KNOWLEDGE

1. Private individuals have no opportunity—or need—to engage in strategic planning for living their own lives.
2. Strategic planning for government agencies must always be complex, thus it is best to outsource those efforts.
3. A forward-thinking perspective for police agencies' strategic planning efforts would include considering such areas as hiring, budgeting, transportation, technology, and the law.
4. A police agency's transitioning to community-oriented policing and problem solving strategy only involves higher ranking, sworn personnel with the department.
5. A particularly useful technique for analyzing sources of support and resistance for change is the force field analysis.

Answers can be found on page 278.

ALICE:	*Cheshire Puss, would you tell me, please, which way I ought to go from here?*
CHESHIRE CAT:	*That depends a good deal on where you want to get to.*
ALICE:	*I don't much care where . . .*
CHESHIRE CAT:	*Then it doesn't matter which way you go.*
	—*Lewis Carroll*, in Alice's Adventures in Wonderland (1865, Chapter 6)

INTRODUCTION

As Lewis Carroll wrote, above, if we do not care what road we must travel in order to get from Point A to Point B, then it really does not matter which one we take to get there. However, for better or worse, we humans (and police executives) strongly prefer to map out our lives, time, and activities. This chapter discusses how we can best get to "Point B"—strategically planning for and implementing community-oriented policing and problem solving.

To hopefully make this chapter's topics more comprehensible, it begins with a look at how individuals can and probably do engage in strategic planning when making major life choices. Next is the general need for strategic thinking and planning, particularly as they concern police executives and their organizations. Then we shift to the implementation of community policing and problem solving *per se*, considering four of that function's principal components: leadership and administration, human resources, field operations, and external relations. We then review several general obstacles to implementation and by delineating 10 ways that problem-oriented policing (POP) can be undermined. The chapter concludes with what we hope will provide the reader with a hands-on, real-world flavor. The reader is invited to consider some of the major considerations that would come into play if someone were assigned to developing a plan for transitioning their police agency to this approach; following that, you are to deliberate on some of the considerations that would ensue if someone were to be assigned to a major problem-solving project. Then the chapter concludes with a summary, review questions, and several scenarios and activities that provide opportunities for you to "learn by doing."

The bottom line for this chapter is that police personnel of all ranks long ago passed the point where they only needed to "plan ahead to five o'clock on Friday," engage in major changes haphazardly and with little planning and forethought, and not have to be concerned with the repercussions of those changes. This chapter provides a rational and formal approach for police personnel of all levels to transition to community policing and problem solving. But first, it might be interesting to see how *you* might go about doing so in your own life.

Figure 9–1 graphically depicts the kinds of organizational transformations with regard to organizational management, structure, personnel, and information systems that must be made in order to support community partnerships and proactive problem solving.

FIGURE 9–1   Alignment of organizational systems to support community partnerships and proactive problem-solving

PERSONAL PERSPECTIVE: STRATEGICALLY PLANNING *YOUR* FUTURE

This chapter's content may well seem, at first blush, to be highly abstract, incomprehensible, and perhaps even unnecessary for the "average" reader; most of us probably don't often perceive ourselves as engaging in strategic thinking or planning, or develop a written "document" that maps out one's life. Therefore, to put the chapter into perspective, we might do well to first discuss how an individual does in fact engage in strategizing at major junctures in his or her life. Doing so might well have saved countless students from changing their academic goals (majors) one or more times while engaged in postsecondary education, and thus having to devote far more time and money than necessary to that phase of their lives to prepare for a career.

Take, for example, a high school senior who is pondering where to attend a college or university. Some preliminary questions to ponder for helping set life goals and priorities would include: Where am I now, intellectually? What are my aptitudes and interests (e.g., am I inclined to want to work with other people, in retail or social-science related fields? In physical sciences, technology, engineering, or math? As a teacher?). Given that, what sort of career do I wish to have and could I succeed in? How do I get there—and how will I know when I have arrived?

Once such fundamental decisions have been made about life goals (and an academic major), certainly finances will play a major role in this strategic thinking: Can I afford to go to an out-of-state school? Are scholarships available to me? Will I have to work part- or full-time while in school? Can I get family help? Will I be able to afford (or even need) a car while in school? How will I pay for books, tuition, housing, and other living expenses?

Having thought through and planned for these challenges, the prospective student will at least have a much better set of goals—and objectives for reaching those goals—than if he or she just wandered blindly into the academic world without any notion of how to achieve one's life aims. Of course, there will be some tough choices involved, and the student must be very honest in assessing his or her strengths, weaknesses, likes/dislikes, and so on. In addition, it would be good to commit this strategic plan to writing; it does not have to be overly complex, but it should include how and when major milestones are expected to be achieved. Even a very basic strategic plan will help to better understand one's overall approach.

Then, at the end of this long and arduous process (of obtaining a college degree), the measure of that success will hopefully be one's diploma in hand.

This exercise is not unlike that of a police executive who wishes to have some better plan of taking the agency where it needs to go. Strategic planning thus means seeing both the big picture and its operational implications. As Herocleous observed, the purpose of strategic thinking is to discover novel, imaginative strategies "that can rewrite the rules of the competitive game and to envision potential futures significantly different from the present."[1]

Strategic thinking is, therefore, compatible with strategic planning. Both are required in any thoughtful strategy-making process and strategy formulation. Thus, both strategic thinking and strategic planning are necessary, and neither is adequate without the other for effective strategic management.[2] Herocleous also stated:

> It all comes down to the ability to go up and down the ladder of abstraction, and being able to see both the big picture and the operational implications, which are signs of outstanding leaders and strategists.[3]

As you read through this chapter, reflect back on this exercise in order to better understand the material; hopefully doing so will help to put the material in clearer perspective.

STRATEGIC PLANNING: BASIC ELEMENTS

Strategic planning is a leadership tool and a process; it is primarily used for one purpose: to help an organization do a better job—to focus its energy, ensure that members of the organization are working toward the same goals, and assess and adjust an organization's direction in response to a changing environment. In short, strategic planning is a disciplined effort to produce fundamental decisions and actions that shape and guide what an organization is, what it does, and why it does it, with a focus on the future.[4]

The history of strategic planning begins in the military, in which strategy is the science of planning and directing large-scale military operations. Although our understanding of strategy as applied to management has been transformed, one element remains: aiming to achieve competitive advantage. Strategic planning also includes the following elements[5]:

- It is oriented toward the future and looks at how the world could be different 5–10 years in the future. It is aimed at creating the organization's future.
- It is based on thorough analysis of foreseen or predicted trends and scenarios of possible alternative futures.
- It thoroughly analyzes the organization, both its internal and external environment and its potential.
- It is a qualitative, idea-driven process.
- It is a continuous learning process.
- When it is successful, it influences all areas of operations, becoming a part of the organization's philosophy and culture.

Excellent examples of strategic planning abound; for example, see the strategic plan of the U.S. Department of Justice at: https://www.justice.gov/sites/default/files/jmd/legacy/2014/02/28/doj-fy-2014-2018-strategic-plan.pdf.[6]

For police leaders, strategic planning holds many benefits. It can help an agency anticipate key trends and issues facing the organization, both currently and in the future. The planning process explores options, sets directions, and helps stakeholders make appropriate decisions. It facilitates communication among key stakeholders who are involved in the process and keeps organizations focused on outcomes while battling daily crises. Planning can be used to develop performance standards to measure an agency's efforts. Most important, it helps leaders facilitate and manage change (which was the subject of Chapter 8).

FIRST AND FOREMOST: A FORWARD-THINKING PERSPECTIVE FOR NAVIGATING THE FUTURE

This chapter is about planning for the future. Unfortunately, we do not possess a crystal ball (and cannot put much faith in Ouija boards to assist us); so the police must engage in unaided futures thinking in order to anticipate and better be able to address the problems that will be faced in the future. In short, a futurist perspective will benefit police administrators in making decisions on a variety of different issues confronting police departments, including several that have implications for the future of the profession in at least five areas[7]:

1. ***Recruiting and hiring:*** In previous chapters, we emphasized the need to properly recruit and adequately train personnel for problem solving; in sum, we need to understand the dynamics of the current pool of candidates, as well as the impact of other trends (such as the arrival of the Millennials) upon the work environment. The capacities and potentials of those we select, train, and educate will need to respond to a dynamic operational environment. The Information Age is changing the nature of policing in many ways, so each new hire who is not, or cannot become, information-savvy is a drain on the workforce and can return but little of the investment made in him or her. Remember, too, that this endeavor is like fishing: police recruiters must go where the best candidates will be found. They are not reading want ads in newspapers, nor are they watching television or mailing in job applications. They are on the Web, participating in social networks, texting their buddies, and using Google, and police leaders must learn to capitalize upon that in recruiting.
2. ***Budgeting:*** As indicated above, most police jurisdictions will continue to operate under budgetary pressures, facing ongoing budget shortfalls. Strategically developing and using community partnerships with citizens and community business interests will be a good beginning toward "doing more with less." Rapid developments in technology will require

more flexible financing, because as crime becomes more and more technologically based, budgetary needs will continue to expand in order to develop employees who can provide professional services to citizens.

3. *Technology:* The world increasingly depends on information for a comfortable, informed existence and for accountability. Related to this is the contemporary public outcry for the police to purchase and use body-worn cameras (see Chapter 3). Furthermore, the physical changes of robotics, nanotechnology, virtual reality, and the byproducts of genomic research will soon require additional skills for detection and interpretation of evidence. Crimes of cyberspace will force the police to decide how to deal with crimes based on Internet transactions. The amount of cybercrime that can be perpetrated against citizens is virtually limitless. Furthermore, hacking, bomb-making, identity theft, and other criminal information is readily available to those who wish to use it. Police must also anticipate the effects of social networking and the shift toward data theft and sales that lead to identity fraud in multiple venues (theft, cover for illegal immigrant employment, false identities concealing other crimes, and so on).

4. *Case and statutory law:* Dealing with the above (to include immigration as well as that pertaining to drones and all manner of technologies) has already expanded to the point where traditional training of officers in law is not working well. As the preceding discussions indicate, the rapid expansion of technology also greatly alters the landscape of law. For example, Internet crime is criminal, but it also reaches to communications (regulatory) law, privacy concerns, and others. As cyberspace begins to redefine citizenship, it may also tilt the balance toward a redefinition of law.

5. *Transportation:* America's infrastructure needs will also greatly impact policing and police budgets. For example, any casual drive across the U.S. (or even a portion of it) will indicate that the mid-2014 report that 63,000 bridges need significant repairs[8] was not taken lightly by federal and state governments. Money for such repairs and for new highway systems will likely put great strains on federal, state, and local law enforcement budgets. Furthermore, many municipal governments are outsourcing major portions of traffic enforcement to private agencies that maintain speed and red-light camera systems. Another major budgetary hit on police budgets may well be the ongoing maintenance and upkeep of highways and streets.

THE CHANGING FACE OF POLICING—IN A DIRE ECONOMY

Certainly, the Great Recession from 2007 to 2009 greatly affected (and may affect forever) the manner in which police organizations plan and are conducting business, and we would be remiss in not mentioning the financial aspect of policing in discussing program planning and implementation.

This is, simply put, an unprecedented time in the history of policing. For the first time in a field known for being stable and recession-proof and affording a high degree of job security, the economy has altered policing such that some agencies are closing precincts, merging with other departments, and even shutting down completely. In some jurisdictions, recruits who have been hired are being released while in, or upon graduating from, the training academy.

Certainly agencies have had to prioritize their efforts. As a report by the federal Office of Community Oriented Policing Services put it:

> Police service delivery can be categorized into three tiers. The first tier, emergency response, is not going to change. Tier two is nonemergency responses, where officers respond to calls after the fact, primarily to collect the information and statements necessary to produce reports. These calls, while an important service, do not require rapid response—the business has already been vandalized and the bike already stolen. Tier three deals with quality of life issues, such as crime prevention efforts or traffic management duties. They help make our communities better places to live, but they are proactive and ongoing activities. The second and third tiers of police service delivery have always competed for staffing and financial resources, but as local budgets constrict, that competition becomes fiercer. The public expects that both tiers are addressed, and agencies with shrinking payrolls are faced with finding new ways to make sure that can happen.[9]

Inherent in this discussion is the compelling need for police agencies to work with their communities in their crime-fighting efforts—underscoring the community partnerships discussion in Chapter 2.

To compensate for shrinking budgets, many agencies have had to focus on what can be sacrificed from their normal level of service in order to offset the reduction in available spending. While families can adjust to shrinking budgets by, say, sacrificing their annual summer vacation or changing their shopping habits, police agencies must still maintain the same quality of service that they always have provided despite a severe reduction in available resources. Therefore, to successfully deliver the same high levels of protection and emergency responsiveness, these agencies have had to develop new and innovative techniques to address the needs of their communities in cost-effective ways. Adapting to this new economic reality is more important than ever, as is developing strategic management practices to ensure the effective and efficient delivery of police services.[10]

THE PLANNING DOCUMENT: A GUIDE FOR IMPLEMENTATION

Strategic planning is both a document and planning process. The strategic plan should be set forth in a written document or plan, to assist with organizing key objectives and to serve as a guide for those persons involved in the **implementation** process.

Following are some format and content issues for the planning process and the development of a **planning document**:

1. Develop statements of vision, mission, and values:
    a. Vision is a scenario or description of how the agency and community will change if the plan is successful.
    b. Mission defines the "business" of problem-oriented policing. The statement can be expected to include both traditional aspects of policing (such as public safety, enforcement, "protect and serve") and aspects of this philosophy (community engagement, shared responsibility for public safety).
    c. Values guide decisions and actions. Prioritize and develop a short list of key principles that people who are involved in problem-solving implementation should consider.
2. Identify primary objectives that define critical outcomes anticipated from the change to problem-oriented policing.
3. Select strategies from various options outlined during the process that clearly outline the primary avenues and approaches that will be used to attain objectives.
4. Set goals that are general statements of intent. They are the first step in translating a mission statement into what can realistically be attained. Goals should be obtainable and measurable, often beginning with such phrases as "to increase," "to reduce," or "to expand."
5. Set objectives, specific statements of what must be done to achieve a goal or desired outcomes. Usually, several objectives are developed for each goal. A meaningful and well-stated objective should be:
    a. *Specific:* Stating precisely what is to be achieved.
    b. *Measurable:* Answering how much, how many, and how well.
    c. *Time-bound:* Indicating when results will be achieved.
6. Set activities, detailed steps necessary to carry out each strategy; they should be time-framed and measurable.
7. Identify a responsible person for every task.
8. Set timelines for the completion of tasks.

Exhibit 9–1 briefly describes the strategic planning efforts of the Durham, New Hampshire Police Department.

KEY LEADERS AND COMPONENTS

Since community policing and problem solving came into existence, most police executives have implemented the strategy throughout the entire agency; some executives, however, still attempt to implement the concept by introducing it in a small unit or in an experimental district and often in a specific geographic area of the jurisdiction.

| Exhibit 9–1 | Small Town, Large Strategic Planning Effort: Durham, New Hampshire |

The Durham, New Hampshire, Police Department has 19 sworn officers and serves about 12,000 residents, but it is also home to the University of New Hampshire, with 12,000 students. Concerns arose when it was discovered that residents saw the department as distant from the people in the community; the decision was made to launch a strategic planning initiative.

The first step was to conduct a community survey wherein citizens could rate the department.

Questions were developed that would answer three questions:

1. How do our customers perceive crime in the community?
2. How does crime affect them?
3. How does the community perceive the police department?

An internal survey of officers and staff was also developed, invited personnel to write narrative explanations of the ratings and make suggestions for improving the department in response to questions such as the following:

1. What would you change about this function if you were the chief of police?
2. What challenges does this function currently face and what challenges will it face in the future?

Next, a one-day strategic planning session was conducted, bringing together officers, community leaders, and other citizens for a frank discussion about contemporary and future police services. Presentations were made by officers concerning drug enforcement, juvenile investigations, school resource officers, training, patrol, and accreditation. Officers also led a tour of the police facility and a discussion about the department's future plans. Citizens shared feedback on police services and offered their views on the department's goals.

Armed with findings from the surveys and this session, the department set out to draft its strategic plan, which evolved into seven long-term objectives—maintaining accredited status, reducing crime, increasing quality of service and customer satisfaction, obtaining grants and other funding, replacing equipment as needed, maintaining an acceptable workload for officers, and providing high-quality training for all personnel. Each objective had a performance indicator, target dates, and strategies for achieving it. Copies of the plan were disseminated to the town council and key session participants as well as made available for public viewing. The community and department now have a better understanding of the police mission, values, goals, and strategies.[11]

It is strongly argued that this strategy be implemented on a department-wide basis because the introduction of a "special unit" seems to exacerbate the conflict between community policing's reform agenda and the more traditional outlook and hierarchical structure of the agency. A perception of elitism is created—a perception that is ironic because problem-oriented policing is meant to close the gap between patrol and special units and to empower and value the rank-and-file patrol officer as the most important functionary of police work.

There is no "golden" or "bright line" rule or any universal method to ensure the successful adoption of problem-oriented policing. Two general propositions are important, however, for consideration in implementing the concept: the role of the rank-and-file officer and the role of the environment (or "social ecology") in which this strategy is to be implemented.[12] The social ecology of problem solving includes both the internal/organizational and external/societal environments. Both of these factors are discussed later in the chapter.

Moving an agency to problem-oriented policing is a complex endeavor. Four principal components of implementation profoundly affect the way agencies do business: leadership and administration, human resources, field operations, and external relations.[13] Figure 9–2 ties together these four key areas—leadership and administration, human resources, field operations, and external relations—illustrating the principal components of implementation.

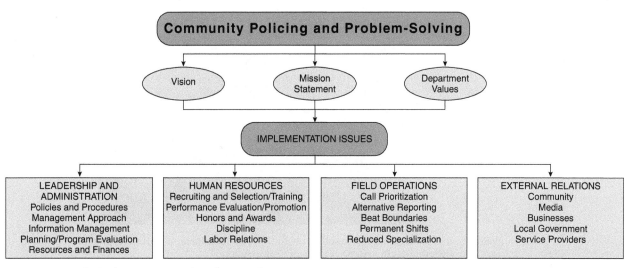

FIGURE 9–2   Principal Components of Implementation

Leadership and Administration

MANAGEMENT APPROACHES.   At minimum, problem-oriented policing requires changing the philosophy of leadership and management throughout the entire organization. This begins with the development of a new vision/values/mission statement, as noted earlier. Leadership should be promoted at all levels, and a shift in management style from controller to facilitator is necessary. The organization should invest in information systems that will assist officers in identifying patterns of crime and support the problem-solving process.

CHIEF EXECUTIVES.   First, it is essential that chief executives communicate the idea that problem-oriented policing is department-wide in scope. To get the whole agency involved, the chief executive must adopt four practices as part of the implementation plan[14]:

1. Communicate to all department members the vital role of problem solving in serving the public. Executives must describe why handling problems is more effective than simply handling incidents.
2. Provide incentives to all department members to engage in this strategy. This includes a new and different personnel evaluation and reward system as well as positive encouragement.
3. Reduce the barriers to problem solving that can occur. Procedures, time allocation, and policies all need to be closely examined.
4. Show officers how to address problems. Training is a key element of implementation. The executive must also set guidelines for innovation. Officers must know they have the latitude to innovate.

Challenging the pull of tradition in the organization can be an awkward process. The remedy lies in the personal commitment of the chief and his or her senior managers and supervisors.[15]

MIDDLE MANAGERS.   In the early twentieth century, a powerful midlevel management group emerged that extended the reach of chiefs throughout the department and became the locus of the practice and skill base of the occupation. As such, middle managers—captains and lieutenants—became the leading edge in the establishment of decentralized control over police departments' internal environment and organizational operations.[16] Furthermore, in the past one of the basic functions and practices of middle managers was to forestall creativity and innovation.

Times have changed in this regard, however; today these middle managers play a crucial role in planning and implementing community policing and problem-solving as well as encouraging their officers to be innovative, to take risks, and to be creative.[17] As George Kelling and William Bratton observed, "Ample evidence exists that when a clear vision of the business of the

Police chief executives must constantly communicate and reinforce to staff that community policing and problem solving is the agency's philosophy and practice.
VladKol/Shutterstock.

organization is put forward, when mid-managers are included in planning, when their legitimate self-interests are acknowledged, and when they are properly trained, mid-managers can be the leading edge of innovation and creativity."[18]

FIRST-LINE SUPERVISORS.   Research has provided additional information for leaders to consider when implementing a problem-oriented policing philosophy. To begin, first-line supervisors and senior patrol officers seem to generate the greatest resistance to community policing, largely because they have long-standing working styles cultivated from years of traditional police work and because these officers can feel disenfranchised by a management system that takes the best and brightest out of patrol and (they often believe) leaves them behind. The press of 911 calls also makes it difficult to meet the need for community outreach, problem solving, and networking with other agencies. Officers may become concerned about the size of the area for which they are responsible; community policing beats are typically smaller than those of radio patrols.

The organization should conduct an in-depth analysis of the existing departmental rank structure, which itself can be a principal obstacle to the effective communication of new values and philosophy throughout the organization. A large metropolitan police force may have 10 or more layers of rank. The chief executive must talk with the officers; therefore, it is necessary to ensure that the message not be filtered, doctored, or suppressed.[19]

The role of middle managers and first-line supervisors is covered in greater detail in Chapter 8, on changing the culture of the organization.

Human Resources

As shown in Chapter 8, which dealt with agency culture, human resources constitute the basis of organizational culture. Developing problem-oriented policing as a part of daily police **modeling behaviors** and practices presents a major challenge. To accomplish this requires that the mechanisms that motivate, challenge, reward, and correct employees' behaviors comport with the principles of this strategy. They include recruiting, selection, training, performance evaluations, promotions, honors and awards, and discipline, all of which should be reviewed to ensure that they promote and support the tenets of police problem solving.

LABOR RELATIONS.   Another challenge for leadership and administration in the implementation of problem-solving policing centers on its labor unions. Unions or collective bargaining units are often viewed by administrators and the public as a negative force, focusing only on financial gain and control over administrative policy making without regard for the department or community.

Does problem-oriented policing conflict with the philosophy of police unions? It is understandable that this approach could be construed as antithetical to union interests. For example, officers will be asked to assume a proprietary interest in the neighborhoods where they work and to be flexible and creative in their work hours and solutions to problems. This approach often conflicts with collective bargaining contracts in which unions have negotiated for stability of work hours and compensation when working conditions are altered. The idea of civilianization, reductions of rank, and decentralized investigations can also be viewed as a threat to officers' lateral mobility, promotional opportunities, and career development. Labor organizations are also concerned with any proposed changes in shifts, beats, criteria for selection, promotion, discipline, and so on.

It is wise to include labor representatives in the planning and implementation process from the beginning. When the unions are excluded from the planning process, officers perceive the implementation of problem-oriented policing as a public relations gimmick in management's interests. It is also important that union leaders understand management's concerns and collaborate in planning an agency's future.

Remember, too, that police problem-solving efforts are important from both the labor and management perspectives. Both sides are interested in creating a quality work environment for employees. This translates to a healthy and productive workforce. Problem-oriented policing provides officers the opportunity to use their talents, and it removes layers of management and quota-driven evaluations that are often opposed by officers.

Field Operations

DECENTRALIZED SERVICES. The need for available time to engage in problem solving presents a supervisory challenge that begins with managing CFS. This may well require comprehensive workload and crime analyses, including call prioritization, civilianization of some services, and alternative means of handling calls. This information helps an agency when its managers are considering a decentralized approach to field operations that involves assigning officers to a beat and shift for a minimum of one year to learn more about a neighborhood's problems. It is also helpful in reconstructing beat boundaries to correspond more closely with neighborhoods.

Decentralized service is an important part of the general scheme of this strategy. When the chief executive says to the officer, "This area is yours, and nobody else's," the territory becomes personalized. The officer's concern for the beat does not end with a tour of duty; concerned officers will want to know what occurred on their beat while they were off duty and will often make unsolicited follow-up visits, struggling to find causes of incidents that would otherwise be regarded as inconsequential.[20]

DETECTIVES. Detectives may view the introduction of problem-oriented policing as a matter strictly for the patrol officers—that "Our job is still to investigate and solve crimes"[21]—and thus have to be incorporated into this philosophy (see Exhibit 9–2). Valuable intelligence information gained by detectives through investigations can be fed to the patrol division. Also, detectives must believe that crime prevention is their principal obligation and not the exclusive responsibility of the patrol force.

Detectives also have opportunities to establish and enhance positive working relationships with victim advocacy groups, civic organizations, police district advisory councils, and other stakeholders in the system. Detectives, like patrol officers, attend regular community meetings and impart valuable knowledge relating to criminal activities, trends, and patterns; in addition, quicker, easier investigative responses can be realized. After analyzing the problem—and examining the environment of the offenses, including victims' family situations, economics, and social pressures involved in lack of prosecutions—detectives can work with the patrol division to encourage victims to follow through with prosecutions, engage in follow-up investigations, and even devise a rudimentary witness protection unit, with impressive outcomes.

TOP PRIORITY: PATROL PERSONNEL. There is one very important positive aspect of considering whether to implement a problem-oriented policing philosophy, one that all chief executives should remember: It encourages many of the activities that patrol officers would like to do, that is, to engage in more inquiry of crime and disorder and get more closure from their work.

| Exhibit 9–2 | Investigations in the Community Policing and Problem-Solving Context |

One problematic issue for police departments that are implementing community policing and problem-solving is the appropriate organization of investigative functions. How can agencies structure investigations to best support these approaches? Who in the organization should conduct which types of investigations? Should agencies decentralize investigative functions? Should there be a separate command structure for detectives?

A group of chiefs leading organizations through the change process first identified this whole issue. The National Institute of Justice will fund a research project surveying 900 law enforcement agencies, all those serving populations of at least 50,000 and having at least 100 sworn personnel. The Police Executive Research Forum will ask these agencies about their status with respect to community policing and problem-solving, as well as detailed questions about the structure of their investigative functions. Researchers will then develop several models of the investigative function in the community policing and problem-solving context.

Source: Workshop presentation, Mary Ann Wycoff, Police Executive Research Forum, "The 8th Annual International Problem Oriented Policing Conference: Problem Oriented Policing 1997," November 16, 1997, San Diego, California.

When asked why they originally wanted to enter policing, officers consistently say that they joined in order to help people.[22] By emphasizing work that addresses people's concerns and giving officers the discretion to develop a solution, this strategy helps make police work more rewarding.

External Relations

In Chapter 2, we discussed the various stakeholders and partners that police will find in the community for assistance in the problem-oriented policing initiative. Enlisting the assistance of the community is often a more complex undertaking than one might assume.

Collaborative responses to neighborhood crime and disorder are essential to the success of this strategy. This requires new relationships and the sharing of information and resources among the police and community, local government agencies, service providers, and businesses. Also, police agencies must educate and inform their external partners about police resources and neighborhood problems using surveys, newsletters, community meetings, and public service announcements. The media also provide an excellent opportunity for police to educate the community. Press releases about collaborative problem-solving efforts should be sent to the media, and news conferences should be held to discuss major crime reduction efforts.

Letting officers devise creative problem-solving responses—and have the time to work on and resolve neighborhood problems—will improve morale by making the job more rewarding.
Reuters Pictures.

A number of cities have chosen to facilitate the expansion of external relations by creating a comprehensive neighborhood services organization: for example, Detroit's Neighborhood Services Organization is described at http://www.nso-mi.org/index.php; the same for the City of Phoenix, Arizona, is at https://www.phoenix.gov/nsd.

Elected officials must also provide direction and support through policy development and resource allocation. They must realize that the police exercise considerable discretion, and can and should do more than merely enforce the laws, such as mobilizing the community (as witnesses), requesting that citizens exercise greater informal social control over one another (e.g., parents over children, teachers over students, landlord over tenants, and so on), using mediation skills to resolve disputes, altering the physical environment to reduce crime opportunities, intervening short of arrest (e.g., issuing warnings, placing people in temporary custody), enactment of new laws, and concentrating on those repeat offenders who account for a disproportionate share of crime problems.[23]

TEN WAYS TO UNDERMINE COMMUNITY POLICING AND PROBLEM SOLVING

Exhibit 9–3 offers, to the tradition-bound police chief, John Eck's "ten things you can do to undermine" community policing and problem solving—a prescription for preventing this strategy from gaining a foothold for many years to come.[24] Many of these tactics are being practiced today, sometimes out of ignorance and sometimes intentionally. With apologies to the U.S. Surgeon General, we issue a prefatory warning: "Practicing these techniques in a police department may be hazardous to the health of community policing and problem solving."

Exhibit 9–3	Ten Ways to Undermine Community Policing and Problem-Solving

1. *Oversell it:* Community policing and problem solving should be sold as the panacea for every ill that plagues the city, the nation, and civilization. Some of the evils you may want to claim community policing and problem-solving will eliminate are crime, fear of crime, racism, police misuse of force, homelessness, drug abuse, gangs, and other social problems. Community policing and problem-solving can address some of these concerns in specific situations, but by building up the hopes and expectations of the public, the press, and politicians, you can set the stage for later attacks on community policing and problem-solving when it does not deliver.

2. *Don't be specific:* This suggestion is a corollary of the first principle. Never define what you mean by the following terms: community, service, effectiveness, empowerment, neighborhood, communication, problem solving. Use these and other terms indiscriminately, interchangeably, and whenever possible. At first, people will think the department is going to do something meaningful and won't ask for details. Once people catch on, you can blame the amorphous nature of community policing and problem-solving and go back to what you were doing before.

3. *Create a special unit or group:* Less than 10 percent of the department should be engaged in this effort, lest community policing and problem-solving really catch on. Since the "grand design" is possibly the return to conventional policing anyway (once everyone has attacked community policing and problem-solving), there is no sense in involving more than a few officers. Also, special units are popular with the press and politicians.

4. *Create a soft image:* The best image for community policing and problem-solving will be a uniformed female officer hugging a small child. This caring and maternal image will warm the hearts of community members suspicious of police, play to traditional stereotypes of sexism within policing, and turn off most cops.

5. *Leave the impression that community policing and problem-solving is only for minority neighborhoods:* This is a corollary of items 3 and 4. Since a small group of officers will be involved, only a few neighborhoods can receive their services. Place the token community

policing and problem-solving officers in areas like public housing. With any luck, racial antagonism will undercut the approach. It will appear that minority, poor neighborhoods are not getting the "tough on crime" approach they need.

6. *Divorce community policing and problem-solving officers from "regular" police work:* This is an expansion of the soft image concept. If the community policing and problem-solving officers do not handle calls or make arrests, but instead throw block parties, speak to community groups, walk around talking to kids, visit schools, and so on, they will not be perceived as "real" police officers to their colleagues. This will further undermine their credibility and ability to accomplish anything of significance.

7. *Obfuscate means and ends:* Whenever describing community policing and problem-solving, never make the methods for accomplishing the objective subordinate to the objective. Instead, make the means more important than the ends, or at least put them on equal footing. For example, to reduce drug dealing in a neighborhood, make certain that the tactics necessary (arrests, community meetings, etc.) are as important as, or more important than, the objective. These tactics can occupy everyone's time but still leave the drug problem unresolved. Always remember: The means are ends, in and of themselves.

8. *Present community members with problems and plans:* Whenever meeting with community members, officers should listen carefully and politely and then elaborate on how the department will enforce the law. If the community members like the plan, go ahead. If they do not, continue to be polite and ask them to go on a ride-along or witness a drug raid. This avoids having to change the department's operations while demonstrating how difficult police work is, and why nothing can be accomplished. In the end, they will not get their problems solved, but will see how nice the police are.

9. *Never try to understand why problems occur:* Do not let officers gain knowledge about the underlying causes of the problems; community policing and problem-solving should not include any analysis of the problem and as little information as possible should be sought from the community. Keep officers away from computer terminals; mandate that officers get permission to talk to members of any other agency; do not allow community policing and problem-solving officers to go off their assigned areas to collect information; prevent access to research conducted on similar problems; suppress listening skills.

10. *Never publicize a success:* Some rogue officers will not get the message and will go out anyway and gather enough information to solve problems. Try to ignore these examples of effective policing and make sure that no one else hears about them. When you cannot ignore them, describe them in the least meaningful way (item 2). Talk about the wonders of empowerment and community meetings. Describe the hours of foot patrol, the new mountain bikes, or shoulder patches. In every problem solved, there is usually some tactic or piece of equipment that can be highlighted at the expense of the accomplishment itself. When all else fails, reprimand the community policing and problem-solving officer for not wearing a hat.

Source: John E. Eck, "Helpful Hints for the Tradition-Bound Chief," *Fresh Perspectives* (Washington, D.C.: Police Executive Research Forum, June 1992), pp. 1–7.

RESISTANCE TO CHANGE: USING FORCE FIELD ANALYSIS

One particularly popular and useful technique for analyzing sources of support and resistance is called **force field analysis**, developed in 1943 by Kurt Lewin, a German social psychologist.[25]

Lewin believed that participation and communication are keys to change, and collaborative strategies are preferred to conflict strategies. The force field analysis technique is based on an analogy to physics: a body will remain at rest when the sum of forces operating on it is zero. When forces pushing or pulling in one direction exceed forces pushing or pulling in the opposite one, the body will move in the direction of the greater forces. In planned change, we are dealing with social forces rather than physical ones. Generally, we want to try to reduce resistance to change.

Such a change as transitioning to problem-oriented policing and thus transforming the culture of the police agency will involve one of three options: (1) increasing forces in support of change; (2) decreasing forces against change (usually creates less tension and leads to

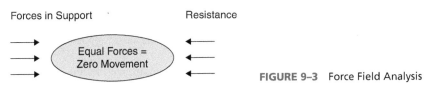

FIGURE 9–3   Force Field Analysis

fewer unanticipated consequences); or (3) doing both in some combination. There is always resistance to change. At best, there is inertia that the **change agent** must anticipate and overcome. Force field analysis is a valuable tool for doing this. Generally, we focus on reducing resistance.

Three steps are involved in conducting a force field analysis:

1. *Identifying driving forces* (those supporting change) and restraining forces (those resisting change).
2. *Analyzing the forces* identified in step 1. Assess (for each):
   - *Amenability to change* (how likely is it that this force can be changed?).
   - *Potency* (how much impact would reducing this source of resistance have on moving the intervention forward?).
   - *Consistency* (does this force remain stable or change over time?).
3. *Identifying alternative strategies* for changing each force identified in step 1. Focus on reducing sources of resistance.

To engage in a force field analysis for a problem-solving initiative, you might begin by drawing the diagram as shown in Figure 9–3, and then drawing a line down the middle of the page; you then put the idea or situation to be considered above the top of the line. Write "for" and "against" on either side of the line. Next, determine the existing forces for and against the change, writing these on the appropriate side of the line. Show the significance of these forces with an arrow, where the length indicates the size of the force.

Now, study the diagram, considering the forces identified, and ask questions such as:

- What is the overall force, for and against?
- How can you tip the balance?
- How can you neutralize forces against?
- How can you increase the "for" forces?

Finally, draw your conclusions. You now have a good idea of those forces that will be in support and resistant to the proposed change to problem solving, an analysis of those forces, and possible alternative strategies for reducing sources of resistance.

YOU BE THE CHANGE AGENT: SOME HANDS-ON ACTIVITIES

To "put some meat on the bones" of **strategic thinking** and planning, next we add a real-world flavor to the matter using two case study activities which will engage you in the process. A number of questions are posed and new concepts are discussed for each.

First is an exercise on transforming the police agency from one that is primarily traditional and reactive, to one that practices the problem-oriented policing philosophy; second is "Opening a POP Project," in which problem-oriented policing is already established and practiced in your agency, and you must use the philosophy to address a problem of crime and disorder.

I. You Lead the Transition to Problem-Oriented Policing

Assume that you are a middle manager in your local police department and have been tasked with laying the foundation for launching this philosophy throughout your agency. You must develop an action plan, taking into account all kinds of preliminary requirements and activities for the transition.

- What kinds of training—for both sworn and nonsworn personnel—will be necessary (first, peruse Chapter 10)?

- What kinds of technologies (Chapter 7) must be obtained for performing the necessary crime analyses?
- How much regular and overtime staffing will be required, particularly during the initial phase of the initiative? What forms, Web sites, brochures, and other informational and communications resources will be required?
- If there are not enough funds available locally, how will the additional funding needed be obtained? What resource providers exist (e.g., social services, other organizations that can provide funding assistance or in-kind services)?

Other possible funding sources include:

a. *Local, state, or federal government agencies:* Federal agencies are most likely to have specific grant announcements; local (city or county) agencies are most likely to fund specific programs that address their mission.

b. *Governmental funds designated for special purposes:* Find out if city, state, or federal agencies have designated specific funds for certain programming areas (e.g., crime prevention, drug awareness education, violence prevention, etc.).

c. *User fees:* In some cases, nominal fees may be charged to the clients, although these fees are usually far less than actual program costs. In many criminal justice programs, such "user fees" are not popular, but we have seen more creative user fees in recent years (e.g., an intensive supervision probation program charges a daily fee to all participants, which helps to offset program costs).

d. *Private and nonprofit agencies:* For example, nonprofit agencies such as the MacArthur Foundation, the United Way, and the Pugh Foundation provide funding for programs which address their mission statements.

e. *Donations from businesses:* Many large corporations and even many small community businesses have become increasingly involved in providing resources for programs that address community needs. In addition to "giving something back to the community," many businesses may qualify for tax breaks by making donations of equipment, goods, services, or money.

f. *Volunteers:* Many programs make extensive use of volunteers to provide some of the program's services (e.g., tutoring and mentoring in after-school delinquency prevention programs).

g. *Fundraising projects:* Special projects may occasionally be undertaken to raise money for the program's services.

- How will you inform and train your **elected officials**, including those in other government agencies, and all members of your police agency about the transition to problem-oriented policing?
- By which dates will the above and other implementation tasks be accomplished, and responsibilities assigned to staff members for carrying out the tasks? This is a very important task at this stage—developing a timeline, and your **Gantt chart** (see Figure 9–4) should specify the following:

   1. All the specific implementation activities that need to be accomplished.
   2. Assignment of responsibility for each specific task to one or more individuals.
   3. A specific date by which each task is to be completed.

Without a specific plan that incorporates all three elements listed above, the program is likely to experience difficulty (or even mortality) before it gets off the ground.

- What mechanisms will you develop to ensure that progress is being made, to monitor staff performance, and enhance communication, including procedures for orienting participants, coordinating activities, and managing resistance and conflict?
- What sources of resistance to change should you anticipate, and how will you address them (see the force field analysis, above)?

PROGRAM/POLICY IMPLEMENTATION. At some point, you should attempt to find out if the transition is being implemented properly. *Monitoring* refers to the collection of information to determine to what degree the program/policy design or blueprint is being carried out as planned.

	TASK	Start	End	Duration	Jan	Feb	Mar	Apr	May	Jun	Jul	Aug	Sep	Oct	Nov	Dec
1	Assemble implementation team; develop mission & goals statements; meet with key union, first-line, mid-management and outside agency personnel	1/1/2017	3/3/2017	60	█	█										
2	Determine technologies and related funding required for analysis	1/1/2017	2/7/2017	30	█											
3	Develop new recruiting literature, employee testing/selection/evaluation processes	1/1/2017	5/7/2017	120	█			█								
4	Develop training programs for sworn & non-sworn personnel	4/1/2017	6/27/2017	90				█		█						
5	Conduct COPPS training for all personnel	7/1/2017	9/28/2017	90							█		█			
6	Train key external agency personnel and elected officials	10/1/2017	11/27/2017	45										█		█
7	Evaluate outcomes of the above; adjust as necessary	11/17/2017	1/1/2018	45											█	█

FIGURE 9-4 Gantt Chart

The purpose is to identify gaps between the program/policy on paper (design) and the program/policy in action. Adjustments are made to revise either the design of the intervention (e.g., program components) or to make what is being done conform to the intended design. Major activities include:

- Design monitoring instruments to collect data.
- Designate responsibility for data collection, storage, and analysis.
- Develop information system capacities.
- Provide feedback to staff, clients, and stakeholders.

II. Opening a POP Project

In addition to many of the same activities described in the above section, transitioning to problem-oriented policing, there are some unique tasks that might well be undertaken when becoming involved in an actual problem-oriented policing initiative, as will be seen in this section.

Assume that you are a member of a police agency that adopted the problem-oriented policing approach many years ago. Upon being informed of a potentially serious neighborhood problem of crime and disorder in your sector, further assume that you have performed the scanning and analysis stages of the SARA problem-solving process, and that you have established that there is indeed a problem. You now realize that tailor-made responses (per stage three of SARA) must be developed, to include obtaining citizen input and feedback from other governmental/social services agencies, and thus you must open a problem-solving project.

Following are some additional measures that are to be carried out: (1) setting goals and objectives and (2) planning and carrying out some interventions.

SETTING GOALS AND OBJECTIVES.   Every criminal justice intervention attempts to achieve some kind of outcome (i.e., some change in the problem). Many expensive and otherwise well-designed interventions fail due to their inadequately defining the desired outcomes of the intervention.

Major activities at this stage include:

- Seeking participation from different individuals and agencies in goal setting.
- Writing goal statements specifying the general outcome to be obtained. Goals should be broad in nature, perhaps not more than a sentence or two in length. An example might be "To significantly reduce criminal victimization involving bank properties."
- Writing specific outcome objectives for each goal. Goals should be quantifiable (and attainable), such as, "Reduce the incidents of weekend ATM robberies in Beat X by 50 percent during the next year." These should include a time frame for measuring impact, and a specific measure of impact.
- Specifying an impact model: how the intervention will act upon a specific cause so as to bring about a change in the problem.
- Identifying compatible and incompatible goals in the larger system: where do values of different stakeholders overlap or conflict?
- Identifying needs and opportunities for interagency collaboration. For example, police and property managers need to collaborate to make landlord–tenant laws work.

OTHER ACTIVITIES CONCERNING THE PROGRAM OR POLICY DESIGN.   Next it would be helpful to specify, in as much detail as possible, who does what to whom, in what order, and how much? It is the guts of the initiative, including its staff, its services, and its clients. While the planning steps for programs and policies are generally similar, at the design stage we find it best to distinguish activities for programs and policies separately.

Major activities for *program design* include:

- Defining the target population: who is to be served, or changed? Would it be best to perform a community or neighborhood survey? Other than providing order maintenance in the area, what other needs exist that must be addressed (e.g., level of fear of crime among residents) and what are the characteristics of intended clients (e.g., age, gender, and geographic residence).

- Defining program components: the precise nature, amount, and sequence of services provided must be specified. Who does what to whom, in what order, and how much?
- Determining what we need to know: are there POP Guides (see Chapters 3 and 4) covering this particular problem that will provide insight concerning causes and possible solutions for this problem? Are other activities required, for example, a series of neighborhood meetings, steering a neighborhood, or graffiti cleanup?
- Determining whether new legislation is going to be required, such as new laws concerning curfew, cruising, or loitering laws; problem-solving training, education concerning laws pertaining to juveniles; and so on.
- Determining who will write job descriptions for the officers who will have their "boots on the ground," and which kinds of knowledge, skills, and abilities they must possess for the particular problem(s) to be addressed.
- Establishing how many and what kind of staff are required to operate the problem-solving intervention: What specific duties will they carry out? What kinds of qualifications do they need? How much money is needed for regular as well as overtime deployment?[26]

A TOOL FOR MEASURING AGENCY IMPLEMENTATION: CP-SAT

In Chapter 8, which concerns program and policy evaluation, we will be discussing the Community Policing Self-Assessment Tool, known as CP-SAT, that was developed by the federal Office of Community Oriented Policing Services, the Police Executive Research Forum, and ICF International (a management, technology, and policy consulting firm) that allows agencies to assess, among many other things, their implementation of problem-oriented policing. CP-SAT operationalized the philosophy of police problem solving across different ranks and provides resources that assist agencies' efforts to determine their strengths and gaps in several areas discussed in this chapter, including problem solving, partnerships, and organizational transformation; see http://www.cops.usdoj.gov/Default.asp?Item=2584.

EXAMPLES OF PLANNING AND IMPLEMENTATION

Exhibit 9–4 provides an excellent example of how one agency (Concord, California) engaged in strategic planning and implementation for community policing and problem solving, while including many of the considerations discussed earlier in this chapter. Another excellent example of a police agency's strategic plan—for Columbia, South Carolina—may be found at https://www.columbiasc.net/depts/headlines/cpd_strategicplan_2015-2019_web.pdf.

Exhibit 9–4	A Case Study in Planning and Implementation in Concord, California[27]

Concord, California, is 40 miles west of San Francisco and 65 miles south of Sacramento.

Thirty square miles in size, Concord is geographically fairly small, with a population of about 112,000, to include a police department of 155 sworn officers and 61 full-time nonsworn personnel.

Until putting problem-oriented policing into practice, the department had taken pride in using traditional policing strategies, which were described as a "kick ass and take names" approach. However, seeing the futility of that approach, the CPD began planning a redirection of the agency by creating a Participative Management Task Force to develop a strategy for implementing community policing. For two years, task force members evaluated the department's underlying philosophy, its mission, vision, and values, while also researching community policing and developing a training strategy for officers. The task force presented its plan, and the department began agencywide community policing training which consisted of visits by officers to other police departments with a national reputation for excellence in community policing. At the same time, the department began surveying the Concord community to understand the public's priorities for police services. Soon the CPD was viewed as a national model in community policing, receiving grants and awards. Following is description of how problem-oriented policing was put into effect.

First, all CPD officers were expected to use problem-oriented policing (POP) techniques. In the police academy, recruits received training in problem solving, and during field training, they received hands-on experience. More experienced officers were trained (or retrained) by the Police Executive Research Forum and other consultants hired through the COPS Office. Every officer was encouraged—in some cases required—to complete up to three problem-solving projects a year. Some officers would cover other officers' calls for service to free their time for such projects. The CPD also began evaluating district commanders by the number and quality of problem-solving projects in their districts, which put additional pressure on sergeants, corporals, and sub-beat officers to engage in and document POP projects.

Concord's problem-solving capabilities were enhanced by crime-analysis system upgrades that enabled the capture of crime statistics all the way down to the beat level, assisting officers to scan for problems and assess their efforts to solve them. Officers could view the top five locations for calls for service in their areas, and the number of index crimes reported by crime type. They could compare their sub-beat's most current crime statistics with those of prior weeks and with those for the rest of the city.

The department formally partnered with the district attorney's office, a local battered women's shelter, the chamber of commerce, and probation and parole in joint efforts to reduce crime and domestic-violence problems. Indeed, CPD valued community partnerships, and was promoting community oriented government citywide. District partnership committees fostered formal partnerships between city departments, other public agencies, and community-based organizations, bringing stakeholders together to discuss neighborhood problems and to develop effective responses and resources.

The district commanders facilitated monthly meetings in each district. Typically, department representatives served as members while city's representatives came from organizations such as Housing, Parks, Neighborhood Preservations and Code Enforcement, Public Works, Traffic Engineering, and the city attorney's office. Furthermore, to increase its responsiveness to citizen needs and priorities, the police department administered annual citizen and business surveys which focused on quality of life, satisfaction with police, fear of crime, effectiveness of police strategies, and perceptions of crime and disorder. The CPD also used media to reach out to the community, producing Street Smart, a crime-prevention television program broadcast twice monthly on a local public access channel. The show focused on neighborhood crime problems and crime-prevention techniques. Residents could call in to ask officers questions, and program hosts announced "Concord's Most Wanted." A city survey indicated that 25 percent of Concord's residents had watched the program.

Neighborhood and business watch programs and a citizens' police academy were also established, with crime watch programs serving as a way for community members to gather to discuss local safety and law enforcement issues, and the academy affording the public an insider's view of the agency.

Organizational change became the norm, in order to support problem-oriented policing. The command structure was modified and a new beat system was adopted; field offices sprung up in each district, staffed with part-time civilians. The CPD sharply increased the number of civilians working there, and community service officers (CSO) worked at district offices, taking reports from citizens who walked in to report a crime (and giving sworn officers more time to perform community policing and problem solving). The Volunteers in Police Service program was created, with sixty volunteers working a required minimum of 16 hours a week in offices and on neighborhood patrols.

The CPD's police union had resisted civilianization, particularly the volunteer program. Our interviews led us to conclude that union management may have generated some of the anxiety among officers about civilians taking over their jobs. To help counter those worries and to build good working relationships, volunteers were posting photographs of themselves, hosting coffee-and-bagel breakfasts for sworn officers, and organizing potluck dinners where officers and volunteers could get acquainted. CPD's administrators found they could decentralize the investigations unit so as to instill a sense of geographic ownership in the investigators and to strengthen the relationship between investigations and patrol.

The department also explored the possibility of formalizing its relationship with Concord's neighborhood associations, in order to foster a stable, more reliable working relationship.

Summary

This chapter has shown how both common citizens and police executives must think and plan strategically, and provided examples of how to implement community policing and problem solving and develop a planning document. Four keys to successful implementation—leadership and administration, human resources, field operations, and external relations—were examined, and we considered how one must expect and be prepared to address and formally analyze resistance to change.

The reader was also given an opportunity to "be" the person in the trenches, looking at the kinds of planning and implementation questions and issues might arise for both transitioning an agency to this strategy as well as launching a problem-solving project. This exercise demonstrates that there are many preliminary steps to be taken prior to entering into any form of change.

It should be quite evident—particularly when looking at the chapter *en toto* as well as the 10 ways to undermine community policing—that there is no substitute for having a well-thought-out, well-laid-out plan of implementation for this philosophy. As with any new venture, there must be a "road map" to show the executive and the agency how to travel the "highway" in order to reach the ultimate destination.

Key Terms and Concepts

Change agent	Force field analysis	Implementation	Strategic planning
Decentralized services	Gantt chart	Planning document	Strategic thinking

Items for Review

1. Explain how you might engage in strategic thinking and strategic planning when setting out to make major life choices. Give examples.
2. Explain the roles of chief executives, middle managers, and first-line supervisors in the planning and implementation of problem-oriented policing.
3. Review the roles of detectives and patrol personnel in its planning and implementation.
4. Describe Lewin's force field analysis, and how it functions in anticipating and planning for resistance to change.
5. Delineate some of the major considerations that would come into play if you were to be assigned with developing a plan for transitioning your police agency to a problem-oriented policing strategy.
6. Delineate some of the major considerations that would come into play if you were to be assigned to address a major problem-solving project.

Learn by Doing

1. Assume that you are sitting as an assessor for another police agency's promotional board, which is interviewing candidates for the director's position with its Research and Analysis division. Some of the questions to be posed of all candidates concerns (1) what they know about strategic planning, (2) how they would go about engaging in developing a strategic plan, and (3) how the economy has affected planning in general. What key answers would you look for the candidates to provide for each of these three items?

2. Your agency is nationally known for its community policing and problem-solving efforts and has won a Herman Goldstein Award for innovative problem solving. You are consulting with an agency in another state that is only half-heartedly engaged in problem-solving activities; it now wishes to transform the entire agency so as to fully embrace that philosophy. What will you attempt to "teach" them regarding the many requirements for a successful transition?

Endnotes

1. Loizos Heracleous, "Strategic Thinking or Strategic Planning?," *Long Range Planning* 31 (1998):481–487.
2. Ibid.
3. Heracleous, "Strategic Thinking or Strategic Planning?," p. 482.
4. Internet Nonprofit Center, "What Is Strategic Planning?" (San Francisco, Calif.: Author, 2000), p. 1.
5. "Brief History of Strategic Planning," http://www.des.calstate.edu/glossary.html, p. 2.
6. U.S. Department of Justice, "Information Technology Strategic Plan," https://www.justice.gov/sites/default/files/jmd/legacy/2014/02/28/doj-fy-2014-2018-strategic-plan.pdf.
7. Adapted from Richard Myers, Joseph Schafer, and Bernard H. Levin, *Police Decision-Making: A Futures Perspective*, Police Futurists International, Futures Working Group White Paper Series, Vol. 1, No. 2, September 2010, pp. 20–26.
8. Ashley Halsey III, "U.S. Has 63,000 Bridges that Need Significant Repairs: Local Governments Turn to Congress," *The Washington Post* (April 25, 2014), https://www.washingtonpost.com/local/trafficandcommuting/us-has-63000-bridges-that-need-significant-repairs-local-governments-turn-to-congress/2014/04/24/17137338-cb24-11e3-a75e-463587891b57_story.html.

9. Bernard K. Melekian, quoted in *The Impact of the Economic Downturn on American Police Agencies* (Washington, D.C.: U.S. Department of Justice, Office of Community Oriented Policing Services, 2011), p. 2.

10. Ibid., p. 34.

11. David Kurz, Strategic Planning: Building Strong Police-Community Partnerships in Small Towns (Alexandria, Va.: International Association of Chiefs of Police, n.d.), pp. 1–5; also see Drew Diamond and Deidre Mead Weiss, *Community Policing: Looking to Tomorrow* (Washington, D.C.: U.S. Department of Justice, Office of Community Oriented Policing Services, 2009); also see Michael S. Scott and Stuart Kirby, *Implementing POP: Leading, Structuring, and Managing a Problem-Oriented Police Agency*, September 2012, http://www.popcenter.org/library/reading/pdfs/0512154721_Implementing_POP_FIN_092019.pdf; for an excellent example of an agency's approach to strategic planning, also see Will Davis and Debra Allemang, "Scottsdale Police Department: Strategic Planning as a Management Philosophy," *The Police Chief* (December 2006), http://www.policechiefmagazine.org/magazine/index.cfm?fuseaction=display_arch&article_id=1066&issue_id=122006.

12. Gregory Saville and D. Kim Rossmo, "Striking a Balance: Lessons from Community-Oriented Policing in British Columbia, Canada" (Unpublished manuscript, 1993), pp. 29–30.

13. Ronald W. Glensor and Kenneth J. Peak, "Implementing Change: Community-Oriented Policing and Problem Solving," *FBI Law Enforcement Bulletin* 7 (July 1996):14–20.

14. John E. Eck and William Spelman, *Problem-Solving: Problem-Oriented Policing in Newport News* (Washington, D.C.: Police Executive Research Forum, 1987), pp. 100–101.

15. Malcolm K. Sparrow, "Implementing Community Policing," *Perspectives on Policing* 9 (November 1988):2–3.

16. George L. Kelling and William J. Bratton, "Implementing Community Policing: The Administrative Problem," *Perspectives on Policing* 17 (July 1993): 4.

17. Ibid., p. 9.

18. Ibid., p. 11.

19. Sparrow, "Implementing Community Policing," p. 5.

20. Ibid., p. 6.

21. Ibid., p. 7.

22. Jesse Rubin, "Police Identity and the Police Role," in Thomas J. Sweeney and William Ellingsworth (eds.), *Issues in Police Patrol: A Book of Readings* (Kansas City, Mo.: Kansas City Police Department, 1973); John Van Maanen, "Police Socialization: A Longitudinal Examination of Job Attitudes in an Urban Police Department," *Administrative Science Quarterly* 20 (1975): 207–228.

23. Adapted from Joel B. Plant and Michael S. Scott, *Effective Policing and Crime Prevention: A Problem-Oriented Guide for Mayors, City Managers, and County Executives* (Washington, D.C.: U.S. Department of Justice, Office of Community Oriented Policing Services, 2009), pp. 13–14.

24. John E. Eck, "Helpful Hints for the Tradition-Bound Chief," in *Fresh Perspectives* (Washington, D.C.: Police Executive Research Forum, June 1992), pp. 1–7.

25. Kurt Lewin, "Defining the Field at a Given Time," *Psychological Review* 50 (1943):292–310.

26. Some of the materials for this chapter section were adapted from Wayne N. Welsh and Phillip W. Harris, Criminal Justice Policy and Planning (3d ed.) (Cincinnati: Anderson, 2008), Chapters 2–4.

27. Adapted from Edward Maguire and William Wells (eds.), *Implementing Community Policing: Lessons from 12 Agencies* (Washington, D.C.: U.S. Department of Justice, Office of Community Oriented Policing Services, July 2009).

Training for Problem Solving: "Learning by Doing"

LEARNING OBJECTIVES

As a result of reading this chapter, the student will understand:

- How training for community-oriented policing and problem solving can be structured so as to emphasize constitutional policing, procedural justice, and fair and impartial policing
- The basic methods of delivering training and mentoring to police officers
- The value of higher education for problem-solving police officers
- How to involve the community in the training process
- The philosophy and use of adult- and problem-based learning, and how to apply them to problem-oriented policing training
- The characteristics of a learning organization, and why it is important for police agencies to become as such
- Some training technologies now in use, such as avatars, e-learning, and distance learning
- A model curriculum for problem-solving training

TEST YOUR KNOWLEDGE

1. Formally training sworn police officers, nonsworn personnel, and the community about problem-oriented policing is largely unnecessary, as the strategy is mostly learned on-the-job.
2. Higher (college and university) education, too, serves little purpose in training for problem-oriented policing.
3. E-learning may be said to represent a new "educational revolution" for police training.
4. Using training technologies and techniques that mirror electronic video games has been found to be a waste of time with problem-solving training.
5. Adult-based learning should maximize problem-solving exercises and minimize lectures.

Answers can be found on page 278.

> *Perhaps the most valuable result of all education is the ability to make yourself do the thing you have to do, when it ought to be done, whether you like it or not; however early a man's training begins, it is probably the last lesson that he learns thoroughly.*
> —Thomas H. Huxley

> *A man can seldom—very, very seldom—fight a winning fight against his training: the odds are too heavy.*
> —Mark Twain

INTRODUCTION

The late Helen Thomas, journalist and longtime White House correspondent, said,

> Everyone with a cell phone thinks they're a photographer. Everyone with a laptop thinks they're a journalist. But they have no training, and they have no idea of what we keep to in terms of standards, as in what's far out and what's reality. And they have no dedication to truth.[1]

As harsh as that may sound, it contains more than a kernel of truth. Training and education are what keeps our civilization and way of life intact because, as famed educator John Dewey put it, "Education is not preparation for life; education is life itself."

And so it is with the community policing and problem-solving strategy. In order to transform an entire police organization, other related governmental units, and the community in the philosophy and practice of this concept, police trainers must understand how to instruct, what to instruct, and what technologies are available for these purposes. This training is particularly critical in today's society, with many people having distanced themselves from the police and following a wave of protests across the country due to police use of force being at the forefront of the national consciousness. However, this challenge also presents an opportunity for police to both effect positive change via training sessions and find new ways to bring police and their communities closer together.

We begin this chapter with a look at how Seattle, Washington, is approaching today's training challenge; included in this discussion is a section on training for **constitutional policing** and procedural justice (discussed in Chapter 8). Next is a review of training and mentoring new officers and the four basic methods of training delivery (e.g., the recruit academy) and the benefits of higher education for problem-solving police officers. Following that is a review of the unique challenges of training older, adult learners and the use of problem-based learning, as well as the need to create a learning organization. Next we consider the technologies that might be employed for providing problem-based training to today's officers, to include the use of gaming, e-learning, and distance education. The chapter concludes with a listing of several web-based resources, a summary, review questions, and several scenarios and activities that provide opportunities for you to "learn by doing."

Also note that on a related topic, we include in Appendix II a *Model Academic Curriculum for Problem-Oriented Policing*, as espoused by the U.S. Department of Justice, Center for Problem-Oriented Policing Services.

TRAINING POLICE FOR TODAY'S SOCIETY: THE SEATTLE EXAMPLE

Today's police training for community-oriented policing and problem solving must take into account the milieu in which the police function. As noted in Chapter 8, there is now a push for the police to become more like "guardians," as opposed to "soldiers." Certainly, what police are taught, and how, must be reflective of that emphasis.

A police training academy in Seattle recently broke with many years of tradition, shifting away from a military model and instead having a goal of training "guardians" of communities. The class of 29 recruits was still taught the basics of police work—interviewing, report writing, use of firearms, and so on—but the instruction also included an increased emphasis on expressing empathy, adhering to constitutional requirements, and treating citizens with respect and dignity. The entire academy put a premium on verbal skills and de-escalation techniques, as well as using communication and behavioral psychology as a tool to gain control and compliance; the underlying assumption was that the best control tactic is to get voluntary compliance.[2]

Sue Rahr, a former county sheriff who administers the state training commission that oversees the academy, wanted the training to be grounded in the Constitution and developed the overall theme of the guardian model.[3] Rahr found support in Plato's book *The Republic* where he describes guardians of the state who are gentle with citizens but fierce with enemies, excel at judging what is true and best, and responsible for the management of society. Plato proposed the establishment of an additional class of citizens, the guardians who were philosophical and responsible for management of the society itself. Such special people would be specially tested and trained for determining whether they were qualified to do so.[4] As part of this Washington training, training sessions include recruits spending time candidly sharing their personal stories, or oral biographies, while embracing the guardian concept. The class chose "Guardians of the Gate" and "We the People" as its mottos—even having T-shirts made with those inscriptions.[5]

HOW TO TRAIN FOR CONSTITUTIONAL POLICING AND PROCEDURAL JUSTICE

Changing the Culture of Training

In Chapter 8 we discussed how today's police agency culture should be changed so as to be more constitutional in nature. As noted, the task confronting police agencies in a time where concerns about police/public relationships are at the forefront is to retool officers' training to provide constitutional and **procedural justice** training as well as policing strategies and policies that the community perceives as legitimate.

As a report by the Police Executive Research Forum put it, this process involves having "open and honest conversations with the community, re-examining past practices, training officers in de-escalation techniques to prevent the need to use force, and responding to the diverse needs of community members."[6] It also means examining new technologies, procedures, and practices to ensure that they reflect the needs and rights of the community and that they retain that community's consent.

Training and changing police culture must also include modifications regarding race relations. In many police agencies, training instructors and senior officers are reluctant to talk about racial issues in policing; this reluctance can contribute to problems between the police and the community. Chief Harold Medlock of the Fayetteville Police Department stated:

> Police agencies spend a lot of money doing psychological background checks on people to make sure that we're hiring the most "normal" people out there. Then we put them in a training academy and turn them completely abnormal. We change who they are through the academy process.[7]

Obviously it is essential in today's policing environment, where the cultural mosaic of communities broadens as a result of immigration (see Chapter 2), that police receive initial and ongoing training in cultural diversity, communication, behavioral psychology, de-escalation, and other related areas of fair and impartial policing, as discussed next.

Fair and Impartial Policing Training

"**Fair and Impartial Policing**" is among the new training initiatives on race that police departments have introduced. The training is intended to show that implicit or unconscious bias can impact what people perceive and do, even among people who consciously hold nonprejudiced attitudes.[8]

Traditionally, policing training sessions regarding cultural and racial bias have simply conveyed the message that officers must, "stop being prejudiced." In Fair and Impartial Policing training programs, however, the emphasis is on the idea that even officers who do not think of themselves as prejudiced may exhibit unconscious bias. For example, in a call for service where two parties have a dispute, even an officer who considers himself unprejudiced might unconsciously give slightly greater credence to the party who is white man rather to the other party, who is African American.[9]

TRAINING AND MENTORING NEW OFFICERS

Assume the following scenario: a young police recruit enters academy training but does not appear to be taking seriously the minimal responsibilities and requirements for successful graduation (e.g., not taking classroom notes or preparing for weekly examinations, and so on). In fact, she asks academy staff why she is expected to organize her notes and study during the evening hours. When the staff explains that after-hours work is needed in order to keep up with daily materials and prepare for the quizzes and exams, she provides several reasons why she does not need to do so. Of course, this recruit quickly earns a reputation for doing the minimum amount. Several of her more seasoned classmates meet her to discuss their concerns, her frequently challenging what is expected, and so on. She says, "I don't understand why you think I have to do all this work and spend all of this time." The instructors and classmates feel frustrated because the recruit is very vocal about not agreeing with the demands and expectations placed on recruits.[10]

Unfortunately, there is very little in the research to suggest what teaching strategies work with the Millennials, or Generation Y. What is known, however, is that this age cohort has unique characteristics that affect learning in both positive and negative ways. First and foremost, trainers must understand that these students cannot be forced into the mold of past generations. Rather, it is important to understand that their differences are not necessarily weaknesses.[11]

First, as indicated above (and in Chapter 8), Millennials are technologically savvy, so trainers need to stay abreast of new technologies and incorporate them into teaching. Successful strategies will involve hands-on teaching with simulations and group discussion.

Collaborative learning coupled with immediate feedback within a practical context is key. Teachers should thus minimize lectures as a primary teaching method. When lectures are used, they should incorporate multimedia presentations or bring in applied, hands-on role-playing for problem-solving exercises and discussions. Trainers should also involve community members in sessions that involves neighborhood crime and disorder problem solving (this topic is discussed more below).[12]

Also note that Millennials may well inappropriately multitask with their technology. This group is accustomed to using technology when they should be studying or are in class, and they typically do not understand how such multitasking may be perceived as rude or distracting. Clear rules about multitasking are thus essential. For example, they need to understand that sending texts via smartphone during class is distracting to instructors and other students.[13]

Mentoring is a related training concept that is certainly related to leadership and professional development—as well as training—of Millennials in the workplace. Mentor was the name of the man charged with providing wisdom, advice, and guidance to King Odysseus's son in the ancient Greek epic *The Odyssey*. Later, in a nonfictional sense, during the Middle Ages boys served as apprentices to masters in a craft or trade while gaining skills to qualify as a master.[14]

In today's context, the very fabric of organizational culture is affected and transmitted by mentoring. De Pree[15] termed it "tribal storytelling." Every police agency has its very own historical context, value system, and stories that give employees a unique sense of organizational pride. "Tribal elders," or agency employees with the most seniority, must routinely share these stories and their significance with others so the culture remains vibrant and purposeful. Effective mentors can and should be these tribal storytellers. Mentoring is even more important when one considers that an entire generation of seasoned officers, supervisors, and command staff is retiring at an accelerated rate. This is creating a void of experienced leadership, which also means that younger officers stepping in to fill these vacancies will most likely occupy formal leadership positions for many years.[16]

It is therefore very important that younger officers have a sense of the organization's artifacts (e.g., history, organizational structure, dress code, acceptable language, and standards of ethical behavior) and espoused beliefs (e.g., ideologies or organizational values).[17]

Mentors have the following responsibilities, all of which are key to both the individual being mentored as well as the organization:

- Encouraging and modeling value-focused behavior.
- Sharing critical knowledge and experience.
- Listening to personal and professional challenges.
- Setting expectations for success.
- Offering wise counsel.
- Helping to build self-confidence.
- Offering friendship and encouragement.
- Providing information and resources.
- Offering guidance, giving feedback, and cheering accomplishments.
- Discussing and facilitating opportunities for new experiences and skill building.
- Assisting in mapping a career plan.[18]

Generation Y trainees want to have a close relationship with instructors, and feel that instructors care about them personally. In sum, they want to feel special, preferring to work with superiors who are approachable, supportive, good communicators, and good motivators. Millennials are discussed more below.

FOUR TRAINING DELIVERY METHODS

Police training may be obtained through four primary means—recruit academy, post academy field training/police training officer, in-service training, and roll call training—in addition to the many excellent conferences and workshops that also now exist to provide problem-solving training. Each is extremely important for imparting values and information concerning this philosophy.

Recruit Academy

Academy training (the recruit or cadet phase) sets the tone for newly hired officers. It is at the **recruit academy** that new officers begin to develop a strong mind-set about their role as police. Ideally, academy training will provide comprehensive instruction in the two primary elements of problem-oriented policing—community engagement and problem solving—if the proper philosophical mind-set for recruits is to be formed. In many cases, this will require that traditional courses, such as those in history, patrol procedures, police-community relations, and crime prevention, be revamped to include the topics and information recommended in this chapter; this information will teach officers to be more analytical and creative in their efforts to address community crime and disorder. A primary emphasis on the nature of crime and disorder and problem-solving methods should be the foundation for this training.

In 1996, Maryland became the first state in the nation to initiate a community policing academy with the goal of providing such training to officers in every local police agency. The academy serves as a central resource for providing agencies with continuing education as well as training in resource development and community involvement.

Exhibit 10–1 shows what a training academy in New Jersey is doing to instruct recruits on the basics of community policing in the classroom—and applying their problem-solving knowledge in their neighborhoods.

Exhibit 10–1	Community Policing in the Academy and Beyond[19]

The Somerset County, New Jersey, Police Academy developed a recruit program in which community policing was the underlying foundation. That's not usual. Today, however, this academy stands apart in its promotion of partnerships and problem solving, both inside and outside the classroom. In the classroom, police recruits learn the fundamentals of community policing. But the centerpiece of the six-month program is a Capstone Project, which requires the recruits to work with members of the community to identify a problem or community concern. Senior citizens, educators, community members, business leaders, and representatives of the faith community are invited to the academy to participate in the project. Community members, referred to as "community facilitators" are recommended by their local police chiefs and agency heads and then paired with recruits based on either common interests or jurisdictions. These community facilitators work with recruits as they implement the SARA process to identify and develop responses to actual community problems.

Part of the project involves recruits writing a detailed analysis of the identified issue which often results in a 25–40 page paper. Many Capstone Projects lead to the development of handbooks, curriculum, and/or strategic plans that recruits can take with them when they embark on their new careers. At the end of the academy, each Capstone team gives an oral presentation, sharing how they addressed their community problem. Since the program was established, approximately 800 recruits have successfully completed a Capstone Project and received their community policing certification.

The recruit police academy is the optimal place for officers to begin learning the history, philosophy, and methods of community policing and problem solving.
Mario Tama/Getty Images.

Field Training Officer and Police Training Officer Programs

The next phase of training for newly hired officers is the **field training officer (FTO)** program, which is provided immediately on leaving the academy. The field training program was begun in the San Jose, California, Police Department in 1972, and assists recruits in their transition from the academy to the streets while still under the protective arm of a veteran officer.[20] Most FTO programs consist of an introductory phase (where the recruit learns agency policies and local laws), training and evaluation phases (the recruit is introduced to more complicated tasks confronted by patrol officers), and a final phase (the FTO may act strictly as an observer and evaluator while the recruit performs all the functions of a patrol officer). This last phase of the recruit's training can obviously have a profound effect on his or her later career based on whether or not the neophyte officer is allowed to learn and put this strategy into practice.

Many police executives have come to believe, however, that the traditional FTO approach that was implemented in 1972 is not relevant to the challenges of contemporary policing, especially those agencies that have adopted problem-oriented policing. Therefore, many police agencies are retooling their FTO programs to emphasize community policing and to better meet the needs of their officers with what is termed the **police training officer (PTO)** program.

The Reno, Nevada, Police Department—with assistance and about a half million dollars in funding from the Police Executive Research Forum and the federal Office of Community Oriented Policing Services—recently developed a model PTO program that recognizes the importance of problem-solving skills and critical thinking. PTO uses a number of tools that embrace the aforementioned adult- and problem-based learning concepts as well as a learning matrix that shows core competencies, which are specific knowledge, skills, and abilities that are essential for community policing and problem solving. A comprehensive explanation of the program and its learning competencies may be viewed at http://www.reno.gov/government/departments/police/divisions-units/administration/training/pto-program.

In-Service Training

In-service training provides an opportunity to impart information and to reinforce new skills learned in the academy and FTO or PTO program. In-service classes are useful for sharing officers' experiences in applying problem-solving techniques to a variety of problems as well as for their collaboration with other city agencies, social service organizations, or the community. In-service training is also one of the primary means of changing the culture and attitudes of personnel.[21]

In-service training for police officers is often required by state law, specifying the minimum number of hours of such training to be received annually and, often, special topics (e.g., domestic violence, hazardous materials) to be covered.

Courtesy Boca Raton, Florida, Police Department.

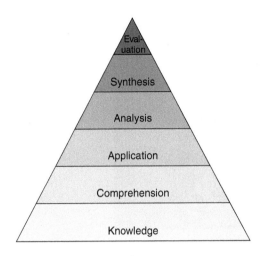

The PTO program, developed with federal assistance, uses a number of tools and involves specific knowledge, skills, and abilities that are essential for community policing and problem solving.

Community Oriented Policing Services, U.S. Department of Justice.

Obviously, a tremendous challenge for large police departments is providing this training for all of the many hundreds or even thousands of officers and civilians. Some large agencies have used videotaped or computer-assisted training. Many departments, using drug forfeiture funds, have also purchased high-technology equipment for use with training. In addition to courses and orientations, departmental newsletters can disseminate information to personnel on a regular basis.

Roll Call Training

Roll call training is that period of time—from 15 to 30 minutes prior to the beginning of a tour of duty—in which supervisors prepare officers for patrol. Roll call sessions usually begin with a supervisor assigning the officers to their respective beats. Information about wanted and dangerous persons and major incidents on previous shifts is usually disseminated. Other matters may also be addressed, such as issuing officers court subpoenas, explaining new departmental policies and procedures, and discussing shift- and beat-related matters.

Roll call meetings afford an excellent opportunity for supervisors to update officers' knowledge and to present new ideas and techniques. This is particularly advantageous for small police agencies that have limited training staff and resources. For example, videotapes or problem-solving case studies can be used at briefing sessions to provide relevant information.

NOT TO BE DISCOUNTED: THE VALUE OF HIGHER EDUCATION

Certainly a feature of the problem-oriented policing strategy concerns **higher education** for officers. To begin with, from 1967 to 1986 every national commission that studied crime, violence, and policing in America was of the opinion that a college education could help the police to do their jobs better.[22] Advocates of higher education for the police maintain that it improves the quality of policing by making officers more tolerant of people who are different from themselves; in this view, educated officers are more professional, communicate better with citizens, are better decision makers, and have better written and verbal skills.

A ringing endorsement for higher education for the police came in 1985, when a lawsuit challenged the Dallas, Texas, Police Department's requirement that all applicants for police officer positions possess 45 credit hours and at least a C average at an accredited college or university. The Fifth Circuit Court of Appeals and eventually the U.S. Supreme Court upheld the educational requirement. The circuit court—in language that could be speaking of police problem solving—said:

> A significant part of a police officer's function involves his ability to function effectively as a crisis intervenor, in family fights, teen-age rumbles, bar brawls, street corner altercations, racial disturbances, riots and similar situations. Few professionals are so peculiarly charged with individual responsibilities as police officers. Mistakes of judgment could cause irreparable harm to citizens or even to the community. The educational requirement bears a manifest relationship to the position of police officer. We conclude that the district court's findings ... are not erroneous.[23]

Certainly higher education is desirable for future and current police officers who will be engaged in community policing and problem solving.
Carlos E. Santa Maria/Shutterstock.

There is abundant empirical evidence indicating that college-educated police officers are better officers, including the fact that these officers have more favorable attitudes toward community policing.[24] Certainly the kinds of analytical abilities that are required for officers to work through the SARA process (described in Chapter 5), as well as the skills needed by officers to communicate with citizens and to deal with them with respect and cooperation, would seem to result from having officers who have received higher education.

INVOLVING THE COMMUNITY IN THE TRAINING PROCESS

Another means of changing police agency culture so as to build legitimacy involves inviting community groups to make presentations in training sessions. Doing so with academy training can accomplish several goals: it establishes the importance of relationship-building in policing; it helps officers to learn the skills to interact with citizens; it provides citizens and new officers a chance to get to know one other; and it allows both citizens and officers an opportunity to become personally invested in the community and its problems.[25]

In several cities, representatives are being invited from the LGBT community, the faith community, immigrant-rights, and other groups, which are each given one- to two-hour blocks of time on the training calendar. Agencies are also conducting scenario training with community members, using them as role players in simulated crime and disorder problems (Exhibit 10–2 provides an example of such training in Chicago).

Exhibit 10–2   *Chicago Trains in the "Guardian" Program[26]*

In 2012, Chicago sought to remodel its police training program so as to put officers on the street who could deal with tense situations with empathy while also respecting the impact of their actions and being responsive, impartial, respectful, and fair. By 2014, more than 8,000 academy graduates had attended the new curriculum.

Proponents of the training strategy say it not only reduces tensions between police and the community, but improves public safety by making citizens more likely to obey laws and cooperate with police. Adopting the training strategy by Sue Rahr of Washington State's police training commission, the program dispenses with military-style boot-camp model in favor of coursework focusing on communication and conflict resolution. Recruits take courses in behavioral psychology and are encouraged to talk problems out rather than simply respond to barked orders.

The program is challenging. In one exercise, recruits are doused twice in the face with pepper spray and asked to complete a series of tasks that frequently includes reciting the federal and state statutes governing the use of force. The purpose of the exercise is to demonstrate to officers that they can focus, think, problem solve, defend themselves, and even deescalate a situation while under extreme duress.

ORGANIZING AND CONDUCTING ADULT TRAINING AND EDUCATION

The traditional view of police training is one of an academy that approaches a boot camp, being quasimilitaristic, and requiring a high degree of physical conditioning, drills, and vocational preparation. While those elements are necessary to some extent in any academy, today's professional trainers realize that basic police training also requires a comprehensive, multisensory learning, and educational process that goes well beyond those historical approaches.[27]

The Two Dimensions of Training

Basic police training, at its root, involves two dimensions: the **curriculum** (shown in Appendix II for problem-oriented policing) and its instructional methodology.[28] Therefore, to understand what works best in training police officers in the context of problem-oriented policing, it is important to understand what methodologies for training adults is best; thus, we will first briefly discuss adult learning, problem-based learning, and the learning organization.

Knowles' Andragogy: Educating Adult Learners

In order for adult training to succeed, the certain conditions for **adult learning** to occur should be borne in mind:

- Adults must be partners in their own educational plans and evaluations.
- The material must be relevant.
- Adult learning should be problem centered rather than content oriented.

Based on these ends, the writings of Malcolm Knowles and Benjamin Bloom are important. Knowles's theory of **andragogy** (the theory and practice of educating adults) was developed specifically for adult learners. Andragogy emphasizes that adults are self-directed and need to be free to direct themselves; teachers must actively involve class participants in the learning process and serve as facilitators for them through such means as allowing presentations and group leadership. Knowles wrote that adults are characterized by the following[29]:

- Adults have life experiences and knowledge that may include work-related activities, family responsibilities, and previous education. They need to connect learning to this base, so try to draw out their experience and knowledge that are relevant to the topic.
- Adults are goal oriented and appreciate an educational program that is organized and has clearly defined elements. Instructors should explain how their course assists participants in obtaining their goals.
- Adults are relevancy oriented and must see a reason for learning something; learning must be applicable to their work or other purposes to be of value to them. Therefore, when possible, allow participants to choose projects that reflect their own interests.
- Adults need to be shown respect, and teachers should treat them as equals in experience and knowledge and allow them to voice their opinions freely in class.

Under Knowles' andragogy, adult learning is to be relevant and problem centered.

Courtesy Washoe County, Nevada, Sheriff's Office.

Bloom's Taxonomy

Benjamin **Bloom's taxonomy**[30] is also helpful. Bloom argued that learning occurs within three domains: the cognitive (knowledge and understanding), psychomotor (i.e., skills training, such as police weaponless defense, evidence collection, fingerprinting, and so on), and affective (feelings and emotions).[31] Although the cognitive and psychomotor domains are commonly seen in police training academies, the latter has generally been absent; little attention has been paid to the officers' "feelings" in the training setting. Bloom believed that learning cannot occur without human emotions, and that feelings are expressed in the trainee's attitudes, interests, appreciations, values, and emotional sets or biases. Therefore, setting the proper climate for learning is critical, and is influenced by both the physical and psychological environments. Certainly, the instructor's attitude will also have a major role in setting the proper tone and climate for learning. His or her attitude will directly influence the recruit's attitude and receptiveness to learning.[32]

Problem-Based Learning, Generally

Problem-based learning (PBL) is a learning process that also has application to training in problem-oriented policing, as it stimulates problem solving, critical thinking, utilization of nontraditional resources, and team participation. Like the adult learning theory discussed above, the purpose of PBL is to make learning relevant to real-world situations. In PBL, the trainee engages in self-teaching; trainees begin with a problem rather than follow the traditional approach whereby a class is given a problem to solve at the end of the class.[33]

Under PBL, the students are guided by instructors and facilitators so that they can ultimately learn what they are supposed to learn. PBL departs from traditional learning models by beginning with the presentation of a real-world problem that the trainee must attempt to solve. The trainee follows a path of inquiry and discovery whereby he or she expresses initial ideas about how to solve the problem, lists known facts, decides what information is needed, and develops a course of action to solve the problem. This approach to learning teaches the trainees to look at problems from a broader perspective. It encourages trainees to explore, analyze, and think systemically, while they also collaborate with peers, open lines of communication, and develop resources for solving future problems.

Adult learning and PBL are both essential for creating a learning organization, which is discussed next.

THE LEARNING ORGANIZATION

Peter Senge's concept of **learning organizations** certainly applies to training in problem-oriented policing and is very important for training adult learners. Senge felt that the organization must allow its employees to continually expand their capacity to nurture new and expansive patterns of thinking, and continually learn to see the whole picture.

In his book that popularized the concept, *The Fifth Discipline*,[34] Senge states:

> Learning organizations are those where people continually expand their capacity to create the results they truly desire, where new and expansive patterns of thinking are nurtured, where collective aspiration is set free, and where people are continually learning to see the whole together.[35]

Three indicators will determine if an organization can be identified as a learning organization:

1. How do individuals view their current assignment? If they attend staff meetings and are only concerned about how decisions affect their area of responsibility, it is not; if, however, they view the organization as a system where decisions affect all of its parts, it is open to learning new methods.
2. How do individuals in the organization view their co-workers? There must be a balance between competition and cooperation; without those aspects of work, there will be no dialogue, and without dialogue, new ideas will not be raised, and only the views of the command staff will prevail.
3. How does the individual view change the process in the organization? The "we've always done it this way" or, "if it ain't broke, don't fix it" mentality has no place in a learning organization, and consideration must be given to external forces of change as well as internal.[36]

TECHNOLOGIES FOR THE TASK

As stated unequivocally in the introduction, police training is too important to be left to "flying blind" kinds of methods. It must be accomplished in a formalized, and even expensive, manner that is efficacious for, and appeals to, today's recruits. This section discusses several highly effective technologies that are in use for this task. Of course, not all agencies can afford to obtain and use such methods, but it is important to know advanced technologies are available and being utilized.

The International Criminal Police Organization, or INTERPOL, based in Lyon France and composed of 190 member countries,[37] has teamed with the United States' Federal Law Enforcement Training Center to examine the best technologies, create competencies, and respond to the demands of the Generation X learner.[38]

Using "Gamification"

Contemporary police training that seeks to keep pace with the times may wish to engage in "gamification," or the use of video-gaming techniques. This approach offers the potential to provide police training that is economical, meaningful, interactive, asynchronous, and enjoyable.

First, INTERPOL argues that one of the best training technologies is simulation gaming. Now in use for training in interviewing skills, criminal investigations, firearms training, and other courses, for Millennial students in particular, the use of gaming/simulation technologies may even be critical, as it allows them to interact with the instructor, obtain an assessment of their performance in a timely manner to either reinforce decisions and actions or provide remediation for the future.

Furthermore, using a simulation game is challenging, while allowing the student to go back and try another one. The player must choose from available options and deal with obstacles that are in the way. And while failure in a gaming simulation is possible, it can be translated to experiential learning. Gaming also plays into the Millennial's naturally competitive instincts, as it may be programmed to allow to achieve a score or surpass a personal score, or to repeat successes and optimize performance through repeated efforts, thus reinforcing correct behaviors.[39]

Utilizing Avatars

Such training is utilized at the Federal Law Enforcement Training Center (FLETC), known as Avatar-Based Interview Training (ABIS). ABIS, the first simulator of its kind, is used as a tool to help students become better interviewers. Training police officers in effective interviewing requires practice; however, finding practice time—and a proper role-play setting—is difficult at best. In addition, the cost of acquiring role players and additional instruction hours can be daunting. Furthermore, the vast majority of FLETC basic students are from the X and Y generations, which grew up much more tech-savvy than previous generations of trainees. Therefore, in making these students more effective as interviewers, it seemed sensible to allow the students to learn with technology.[40]

The ABIS simulation is programmed to show physical distress—adding realism to the interview. Students must respond accordingly with empathy and appropriate questions. It permits free-flowing conversation utilizing speech recognition, a computer synthesized voice, and a virtual avatar to create a realistic interactive training experience. Students complete the simulation in a mock condominium to simulate the actual interview location.[41]

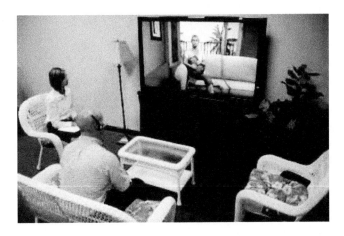

The Avatar-Based Interview Training (ABIS) program is programmed for students to conduct interviews using techniques they are taught. ABIS simulations include physical distress, which adds realism to the training.

Courtesy Federal Law Enforcement Training Center.

ABIS could prove useful in offering other training topics. As FLETC research and experience indicate, training that is offered in different learning styles will reach more students effectively.

AN "EDUCATIONAL REVOLUTION": E-LEARNING AND DISTANCE LEARNING

The **e-learning** concept was first identified by name in October 1999 during a computer-based training (CBT) seminar in Los Angeles. The term was meant to indicate a way learning based on the use of new technologies and online, interactive, and personalized training.

This approach to training represented a major leap forward in the field, linked with other advancements such as reading and writing, the emergence of the teaching profession, the development of moveable type (print technology), and the development of electronic technology.[42]

The development of e-learning was actually the culmination of several preceding decades of advancements, following the introduction of the computer and Internet in the 1980s and the delivery of online courses via audio/visual technologies in the early 1990s (often termed as **distance learning**, discussed below). The early 2000s began seeing businesses using e-learning to train their employees. Then, in the early 2010s, when two Stanford University professors launched an online introductory course on artificial intelligence and more than 166,000 individuals enrolled from 190 countries, a new learning culture was spawned.[43] Suddenly online courses led to training certificates being earned and becoming highly prized; institutions of higher education began growing this culture by adding credit-earning short courses and certificates in addition to degrees. Law enforcement did not miss the opportunity to launch a number of e-learning options; soon California's police academies began merging this new culture with their curricula, implementing online training as the primary method of instruction.

Smaller police agencies—often unable to pay for travel, lodging, and per diem for training and thus seeing officers fall out of compliance with their state training standards—were also quick to get on the bandwagon. Suddenly they could train and certify their personnel without their having to leave their city or county—and remaining on the streets on patrol.[44]

Also rapidly occurring was the development of virtual reality and holographic simulations of victims, witnesses, and suspects who could interact with trainees in virtual and physical locations. This form of training delivery is ideal for problem-oriented policing, as avatars (discussed above) could be created to represent any age or ethnic group, and the issues presented could vary widely; trainees could enter these virtual simulations in dispute resolution and problem-solving situations.[45] Such training, being interactive, is also more fun for tech-savvy, younger police trainees. Furthermore, instructors have the ability to bring in a guest lecturer without having to spend much money on travel and per diem.

Some limitations and concerns come with e-learning, however. First, some subject matter involving hands-on, practical skills is difficult if not impossible to teach with online resources. Also, learners may feel a sense of isolation because online learning is a solo endeavor for the most part (although technology now allows learners to engage more actively with professors and other students).

In addition to online, web-based training, other relatively new forms of training that occur remotely have surfaced known generally as distance learning; here, training programs can be delivered in at least four ways:

1. *CD-ROM:* Trainees must have the CD and a computer, and a possible downside is that there is no good way to ask questions, provide feedback, or check progress.
2. *Home study or correspondence course:* Here, the trainee controls the study time and progress; a test is given at a designated facility at the completion of the course, and there is little interaction with the instructor.
3. *Video:* The course is recorded on a videotape or DVD, which may require the trainee's attendance at a designated meeting place for a supervised presentation; one or more officers are trained at the same time, with attendance and test scores recorded by a proctor.
4. *Webinar:* This is an Internet seminar, workshop, or lecture that may allow for live information exchange and a question-and-answer session. Using computer technology, it thus offers flexibility.[46]

For an excellent example of how a state's law enforcement agencies can receive comprehensive online training that will reduce related costs, while also partnering with government entities and private businesses to provide the most up-to-date curriculum, see the Florida Sheriffs Association, "E-learning," at http://www.flsheriffs.org/training/e-learning/.

MINIMAL CURRICULAR CONTENT FOR PROBLEM SOLVING

As we noted above, Appendix II contains a complete recommended problem-oriented policing training program developed by the federal Center for Problem-Oriented Policing. Here, however, we broadly explain the nuts-and-bolts of the training modules contained in such a program, and their rationales and objectives, which include the following.

EVOLUTION OF POLICING.   Here, we recommend emphasizing that in order to understand policing today, one must first understand its antecedents. Chapter 1 traces this evolution, through its three broad eras and including the three eras of community policing. It is important to include in this history a discussion of how our society is changing and what the police must do to confront these challenges (Chapter 2) as well as the history of the local agency where the training is being conducted. This section of training should end by providing participants with clear definitions of the separate but complementary notions of community-oriented and problem-oriented policing.

COMMUNITY ENGAGEMENT.   This subject matter is indispensable, especially given the current police–minority climate. Here, participants are introduced to the concept of community policing and its primary components. The desired outcomes for this part of the training are that they be able to:

- Define what is meant by the word "community" and the concept of "community policing" and its components.
- Identify why police must collaborate with the community to solve problems.
- Know how to develop a community profile that analyzes its problems and identifies its leaders and available resources.
- Know how to communicate and collaborate with the community (including other city or county departments, local businesses, social services agencies, and so forth) through public meetings, newsletters, and contact with leaders, groups, and organizations.
- Understand a community's cultural, ethnic, and racial diversity.
- Discuss community-oriented government, including the concepts of "total quality" and "customer service" in policing.

DIVERSITY TRAINING.   Training should include a strategy for policing in a multicultural society. As Chapter 3 described, we live in an increasingly diverse society with many new cultural mores and languages that pose new challenges for police. Policing these new communities requires understanding and new skills. Especially given our "global village" and its current state of affairs, it is important that police personnel be exposed to different cultures in order to generally make them better and more effective officers and assist in their problem-solving efforts.

PROBLEM SOLVING: BASICS AND EXERCISES.   The PBL concept was introduced earlier in this chapter. Here, we discuss this approach more specifically as it relates to community policing and problem solving. This session of training entails teaching officers the basics of conflict resolution, which is the focus of this strategy; it puts the community policing philosophy into practice, or "walks the talk" of this philosophy. The analysis of problems is the most important component of problem solving. In-depth analysis provides the information necessary for officers to develop effective responses. The SARA (for scanning, analysis, response, and assessment) problem-solving process, which was discussed in detail in Chapter 5, is presented through an interactive lecture and use of case studies. The desired outcomes for this segment include the following:

- Identifying each component and principal element of the SARA process.
- Learning the importance of in-depth analysis in the complete identification of a problem.

- Learning to identify and apply a variety of responses to a problem.
- Discussing the application of situational crime prevention and crime prevention through environmental design (CPTED) concepts on the environmental influences on crime and disorder.
- Discussing the importance of both quantitative and qualitative evaluation measures of problem-solving efforts.
- Discussing how accountability, empowerment, service orientation, and partnership fit into problem solving.

Facilitators should divide the classes into small workgroups and ask them to examine each problem, developing strategies for analyzing, responding to, and assessing the effectiveness of their problem-solving efforts. Figures and tables throughout Chapter 5 can be used to lead officers through the process. Brainstorming should be discussed and used as an appropriate tool to foster innovative and creative thinking in the workgroups.[47] The desired outcomes for this segment include the participants' ability to do the following:

- Identify problems on the officer's beat.
- Demonstrate an understanding of the problem analysis triangle.
- Identify the diversity of resources available, the variety of strategies to address the problem, and some crime prevention techniques.
- Evaluate the results using methods similar to those used in the analysis of the problem.
- Discuss the advantages and disadvantages of the methods used.

Once the problem-solving exercises are completed, each group will have the opportunity to present its problem to the entire class and explain each step of the SARA model. Through these presentations, the participants will be exposed to the problem-solving efforts of the other groups. This method of instruction not only provides officers with a practical exercise but also gives them the opportunity to work through an actual problem on their beat.

CASE STUDIES. Trainers can use case studies involving the use of the SARA model of problem solving for neighborhood crime and disorder. Case studies allow the instructor to put the theory into practice, and demonstrate the flexibility of the model as well as emphasize important steps, such as analysis. As mentioned above, it is best to localize the case studies in order to provide a real-world flavor and to help trainees gain a better understanding of the material. For this purpose, the Problem Oriented Policing (POP) Guides, utilized/cited in many chapters of this book, can be invaluable. These guides—now with more than 70 different titles—summarize knowledge about how the police can address a variety of problems.

ROLES OF LEADERSHIP AND MIDDLE MANAGERS. Executive leadership and middle managers' support are critical to implementing and maintaining the organizational changes required by problem-oriented policing (as discussed in Chapters 8 and 9). In many instances, the ultimate challenge to a police organization is to change its hierarchical, paramilitary structure. Supervisors, managers, and executives working within a flattened problem-oriented policing organization would require new skills to ensure the successful adaptation and functioning of the police organization.[48]

THE FIRST-LINE SUPERVISOR AS COACH AND MANAGER. As we pointed out in previous chapters, problem-oriented policing requires the support of the first-line supervisor in particular. Supervising in this organization means a change from being a "controller," primarily concerned with rules, to being a "facilitator" and "coach" for officers involved in problem solving. Supervisors must learn to encourage innovation and risk taking among their officers and be skilled in problem solving. Finding the time for officers to engage in problem solving and tracking their efforts are also challenges for first-line supervisors.

SUPPORT PERSONNEL. Support personnel provide officers with information that is vital to the success of this strategy. For example, it would be difficult for officers to engage in problem solving if the dispatcher, unaware of this philosophy, was concerned only with eliminating pending calls and continued to dispatch officers to low-priority calls.

COMMUNITY AND BUSINESS LEADERS. Because the community plays a vital role in this strategy, the department and officers must educate citizens about problem-oriented policing; these includes use of newsletters, public service announcements, neighborhood meetings, and citizens' police academies. It is also important that business leaders be oriented in the strategy. Business and industrial leaders can be valuable allies, maybe even providing financial support in causes they believe will help the community.

OTHER GOVERNMENT AGENCIES. Previous chapters have also discussed how problem solving necessarily involves agencies other than the police or sheriff's departments. A large percentage of calls for service (CFS) handled by the police involve noncriminal matters that can be better addressed by other city or county agencies. Furthermore, there is considerable overlap between agencies; for example, a deteriorating neighborhood might involve the health, fire, zoning, prosecutor's, street, social services, or other departments. Thus, it is imperative that key persons in those organizations be trained in the philosophy and workings of community policing and CPTED.

ELECTED OFFICIALS. As noted in other chapters, politicians must also be involved and educated early in the planning and implementation of this strategy. They often have the final word on whether new ideas or programs will be funded and implemented. The education of politicians regarding problem-oriented policing is important for understanding that this philosophy is unique.

RESOURCES ON THE WEB

The Internet provides police officers and trainers with a lower-cost means of communicating with their colleagues across the nation or abroad about policies and programs. Following are some Internet addresses where trainers can conduct research and gain information concerning virtually anything about law enforcement:

- *www.usdoj.gov*
  U.S. Department of Justice (DOJ) site provides a link to all DOJ agencies and includes information about a wide range of research, training, and grants.
- *www.officer.com*
  This directory is related to law enforcement issues.
- *www.census.gov*
  U.S. Census Bureau site provides demographic information by jurisdiction.
- *www.cops.usdoj.gov*
  The federal COPS Office site promotes policing strategies and offers a variety of grants, training, and education to state agencies and local communities nationwide.
- *www.ncjrs.gov*
  The National Criminal Justice Reference Service site functions as a clearinghouse of publications and is an online reference service for a broad range of criminal justice issues.
- *www.justnet.org/*
  The National Law Enforcement and Corrections Technology Center provides information about new equipment and technologies.
- *www.ojp.usdoj.gov/bjs*
  The Bureau of Justice Statistics site includes a variety of information about criminal justice statistics and provides links to other research Web sites.
- *www.copnet.org/directory.html* and *www.copnet.org/local/resources.html*
  COPNET site provides information about police training, job opportunities, links to other agencies, and chat rooms
- *http://www.popcenter.org/*
  The Center for Problem Oriented Policing makes readily accessible information about ways in which police can more effectively address specific crime and disorder problems. A related Web site, www.popcenter.org/conference/, provides information about the POP Center's annual POP Conference, where attendees attend workshops discussing problem solving for dozens of crime and safety problems.

26th Annual Problem-Oriented Policing Conference

Tempe Arizona, October 24-26, 2016

The Center for Problem-Oriented Policing

△ Center for Problem-Oriented Policing

Hosted by: Tempe Police Department and the Arizona State University School of Criminology and Criminal Justice

The annual Problem-Oriented Policing Conference is often described by attendees as the most substantive policing conference they've ever attended. Each year, police officers and leaders as well as crime consultants and researchers meet to discuss what they have learned about trying to reduce crime and safety problems.
Community Oriented Policing Services, U.S. Department of Justice.

- *http://www.theiacp.org/*
  The International Association of Chiefs of Police has always been a primary source of information concerning policing, but in recent years it is also leading the way in developing and commissioning research and reports on problem solving.
- *www.ncpc.org/*
  The National Crime Prevention Council, discussed in Chapter 6, seeks to help people keep themselves, their families, and their communities safe from crime, and provides tools they can use to further that goal.

Summary

This chapter has presented some of the obstacles to learning, an overview of those persons and groups needing to receive training in formal problem solving, and types and component parts of a problem-oriented policing training program.

This strategy must become a philosophy before it can become a practice. This change in thinking is the major challenge facing those involved in the training and education of police officers and the public. This challenge is enhanced because large numbers of police officers and citizens require orientation and training in this concept.

Police executives who have implemented this strategy must give due consideration to the training issue—a major aspect of police problem solving that is a *sine qua non* of this strategy: Without training, there is nothing.

Key Terms and Concepts

Adult learning
Andragogy
Bloom's taxonomy
Constitutional policing
Curriculum (for problem-solving training)

Distance learning
E-learning
Fair and impartial policing
Field training officer (FTO)
Higher education
In-service training

Knowles' andragogy
Learning organization
Mentoring
Police training officer (PTO)
Problem-based learning (PBL)

Procedural justice
Recruit academy
Roll call training

Items for Review

1. How can a problem-oriented policing training program can be structured so as to emphasize a guardian rather than a soldier mindset, constitutional policing, and fair and impartial policing?
2. Describe the basic schools of thought as per Knowles and Bloom concerning the concepts of adult- and problem-based learning, and apply them to training for problem solving.
3. Describe the characteristics of a learning organization, and why it is important for police agencies to become as such.
4. Delineate the uniqueness of training police officers in a problem-based learning method.
5. Review how knowledge is imparted at the basic recruit academy as well as with the postacademy, in-service, and roll call methods.
6. List some kinds of technologies that exist in police training, to include the use of avatars, e-learning, and distance learning.

Learn by Doing

1. You are enrolled in a criminal justice internship with the regional police academy. Knowing of your prior coursework, your academy advisor assigns you to prepare a position paper that sets forth the different approaches to teaching adults. You are to emphasize **Knowles' andragogy**—to include how Bloom's emphasis on problem-based learning can be applied to police academy students. What will you report?
2. Assuming the same scenario as in item #1 above, the academy staff see a need to implement a more solid, core community-oriented policing curriculum at the academy for recruits. You are assigned the task of drafting this model curriculum. What courses will your curriculum include? (You may wish to refer to Appendix II.)
3. Having successfully completed your internship at the regional police academy, your criminal justice professor asks you to prepare an essay on the advantages of e-learning and distance education platforms for problem-oriented policing. What will you write and emphasize?

Endnotes

1. BrainyQuote, http://www.brainyquote.com/quotes/quotes/h/helenthoma566722.html#9ULxL8hpTH2i2vi6.
2. Steve Miletich, "Police Academy 2.0: Less Military Training, more Empathy," *Seattle Times* (July 13, 2013), http://www.seattletimes.com/seattle-news/police-academy-20-less-military-training-more-empathy/.
3. Ibid.
4. Garth Kemerling, "Plato: The State and the Soul," *The Philosophy Pages*, http://www.philosophypages.com/hy/2g.htm.
5. Steve Miletich, "Police Academy 2.0: Less Military Training, more Empathy."
6. Police Executive Research Forum, *Constitutional Policing as a Cornerstone of Community Policing* (Washington, D.C.: Author, 2015), p. 11, available at: http://ric-zai-inc.com/Publications/cops-p324-pub.pdf.
7. Ibid., p. 9.
8. Ibid., pp. 9–10.
9. Ibid.
10. Adapted from a scenario in Jodie Eckleberry-Hunt and Jennifer Tucciarone, "The Challenges and Opportunities of Teaching 'Generation Y'," *Journal of Graduate Medical Education* (December 2011), pp. 458–460.
11. Ibid.
12. Ibid.
13. Ibid.
14. Harvey Sprafka and April H. Kranda, "Institutionalizing Mentoring in Police Departments," *The Police Chief* (January 2008), pp. 46–49, http://www.policechiefmagazine.org/magazine/index.cfm?fuseaction=display_arch&article_id=1375&issue_id=12008.
15. Quoted in James Uhl, "Mentoring: Nourishing the Organizational Culture," *The Police Chief* (June 2010), pp. 66–72, http://www.policechiefmagazine.org/magazine/index.cfm?fuseaction=display_arch&article_id=2115&issue_id=62010.
16. Ibid., p. 68.
17. Ibid.
18. Ibid., p. 47.
19. Adapted from "Report from the Field: Community Policing in the Academy and Beyond," *Community Policing Dispatch* 2 (11) (November 2009), http://www.cops.usdoj.gov/html/dispatch/November_2009/police_academy.htm.
20. Roger G. Dunham and Geoffrey P. Alpert, *Critical Issues in Policing* (Prospect Heights, Ill.: Waveland Press, 1989), p. 112.
21. Ibid.
22. Gerald W. Lynch, "Why Officers Need a College Education," *Higher Education and National Affairs* (September 20, 1986):11.
23. *Davis v. City of Dallas*, 777 F.2d 205 (5th Cir. 1985).
24. For a comprehensive listing of studies of higher education for police officers, see Michael G. Aamodt, *Law Enforcement Selection: Research Summaries* (Washington, D.C.: Police Executive Research Forum, 2004), pp. 1–426.
25. Ibid., p. 19.
26. Adapted from Christopher Moraff, "Can Different Training Make Police Officers Guardians, Not Warriors?" Next City, December 4, 2014, https://nextcity.org/daily/entry/change-police-training-task-force-empathy-policing.
27. Robert F. Vodde, "Organizational Paradigms for Police Training and Education," *International Police Training Journal* 2 (Interpol, February 2011), p. 17.
28. Ibid.
29. Malcolm Knowles, *Andragogy in Action* (San Francisco: Jossey-Bass, 1981).
30. Benjamin S. Bloom (ed.), *Taxonomy of Educational Objectives* (New York: David McKay Company, Inc., 1956).
31. Robert F. Vodde, "Organizational Paradigms for Police Training and Education," p. 18.

32. Ibid.

33. Howard Barrows and R. M. Tamblyn, *Problem Based Learning* (New York: Springer, 1980).

34. Peter M. Senge, *The Fifth Discipline: The Art and Practice of the Learning Organization* (London: Random House, 1990).

35. Ibid., p. 3.

36. Adapted from George Cartwright, "A Learning Organization," *Law and Order* (September 2008), pp. 71–73.

37. INTERPOL, "Overview," http://www.interpol.int/About-INTERPOL/Overview.

38. See, generally, INTERPOL's *International Police Training Journal* (Issue 2) (February 2011), which is devoted entirely to technology and simulated training, including FLETC's ABIS.

39. Valerie Atkins and William A. Norris, "Simulations and Technology for Training," in ibid., pp. 1–4.

40. Ibid.

41. Ibid.

42. Leer Believing, "e-Learning Fundamentals," http://www.leerbeleving.nl/wbts/1/history_of_elearning.html.

43. Steven Leckhart, "The Stanford Education Experiment Could Change Higher Learning Forever," *Wired* (March 20, 2012), http://www.wired.com/2012/03/ff_aiclass/.

44. Bob Harrison, "A Retrospective: Police Academy Training in 2032," *FBI Law Enforcement Bulletin* (September 9, 2014), https://leb.fbi.gov/2014/september/futures-perspective-a-retrospective-police-academy-training-in-2032.

45. Ibid.

46. Susan Reiswerg, "Distance Learning: Is It the Answer to Your Department's Training Needs," *The Police Chief* 72 (10), October 2005, http://www.policechiefmagazine.org/magazine/index.cfm?fuseaction=display_arch&article_id=726&issue_id=102005.

47. Nancy McPherson, *Problem Oriented Policing* (San Diego, Calif.: San Diego Police Department Training Outline, 1992), p. 2.

48. Province of British Columbia, Ministry of Attorney General, Police Services Branch, Community Policing Advisory Committee Report, p. 56.

Evaluating and Assessing Outcomes:
Do the Responses "Measure Up"?

LEARNING OBJECTIVES

As a result of reading this chapter, the student will understand:

- The differences between performing an assessment and an empirical impact evaluation of a problem-solving project
- The kinds of knowledge, skills, and abilities needed to perform structured evaluations and less-structured assessments
- Some of the measures and tools used for program evaluation
- How and why it is desirable to evaluate police organizations and individual officers in their problem-solving efforts
- Why it is desirable for a police agency to employ community surveys

TEST YOUR KNOWLEDGE

1. An assessment completely and accurately measures whether or not a particular problem-oriented policing initiative made a difference, while an impact evaluation of the initiative does not.
2. Understanding and accomplishing the SARA problem-solving process is sufficient for knowing whether or not police responses to crime actually worked.
3. Performing assessments and impact evaluations of police problem-solving efforts involve essentially the same approaches and personal skills and abilities.
4. Learning "what works" in crime prevention programs is critical for criminal justice as well as for policing.
5. Community surveys are a vital part of the police problem-solving strategy.

Answers can be found on page 278.

All things have two handles: beware of the wrong one.
—RALPH WALDO EMERSON

Not everything that counts can be counted; and not everything that can be counted counts.
—ALBERT EINSTEIN

INTRODUCTION

Before embarking on discussions of evaluating and assessing outcomes of problem-solving efforts, we must first be very forthright: these materials will probably represent the kinds of career ambitions possessed by only a small proportion of criminal justice students and practitioners. Furthermore, a certain set of skills is required to perform assessments and evaluations. Put another way, it would be virtually impossible to bring in a police officer from the street, bestow upon him or her the title of agency assessor or evaluator, and await feedback concerning which policing strategies in effect are working and not working.

In short, there is an esoteric body of knowledge and understanding that is necessary to this role and process—something that is "intended for or likely to be understood by only a small number of people with a specialized knowledge or interest," and requiring or exhibiting knowledge that is restricted to a small group.[1] But they nevertheless remain critical, even so that one of the major criticisms of policing efforts lies with the lack of testing to see if their problem solving responses and strategies worked.

Therefore, our limited purpose here is to provide students with a familiarization with the topics so they may understand what a full-blown assessment or evaluation entails. As we have mentioned in several previous chapters, contemporary emphases on agencies tightening the belt, being more accountable, and doing more with less combine to make it imperative that they make every attempt to allocate their resources wisely.

We begin by discussing the differences between assessments and impact evaluations. Next is a review of the kinds of knowledge, skills, and abilities that are generally required for program evaluators, as well as several available measures and tools for this purpose. After a review of how and why problem-solving police organizations and officers are evaluated, we review the use of community surveys. The chapter concludes with a summary, review questions, and several scenarios and activities that provide opportunities for you to "learn by doing." Several excellent resources for developing the ability to perform impact evaluations and assessments are provided throughout the chapter as well as in the endnotes.

ASSESSMENTS VIS-A-VIS IMPACT EVALUATIONS

As was also noted above, despite the widespread use and popularity of the community policing and problem-solving strategy, little empirical research exists concerning whether or not those initiatives are cost-efficient and successfully reduce public fear and incidence of crime and disorder. As observed in a federal report, *Understanding Community Policing: A Framework for Action*,[2] ongoing input, **evaluation**, and feedback from both inside and outside the police organization are essential to making community policing work.

A strength of the **SARA** (for scanning, analysis, response, assessment, discussed in Chapter 5) problem-solving process is that it inherently demands that police perform an **assessment** of their problem-solving efforts, such as the number of calls for service, arrests made, noise complaints addressed, shots-fired reported, and so forth, in the aftermath of launching the responses. However, an assessment does not provide a complete measure of whether or not a particular problem-oriented policing initiative made a difference. For that to be determined, an **impact evaluation** of the initiative is required.

As an example, assume that the police have recently observed a spike in evening ATM robberies located on the exterior of banks in a particular part of the city. They increase patrols so as to be more visible in the area, employ stakeouts, and add more detectives to work the cases. Within a month, reports of robberies near these ATMs plummet, and of course the police believe their efforts were responsible for the virtual elimination of the problem. But can they be certain of their reasoning? What if a private security firm offered a free month's worth of patrolling to the banks if they contracted their services, several of the affected banks installed outside cameras, and the person responsible for most of these robberies decided to change to residential burglaries as a more lucrative and less dangerous way to "earn" a living? Keep this example in mind as we discuss differences between performing an assessment and an impact evaluation below.

Assessments and evaluations are thus different from, but complementary to, one another. Assessments—which can also be termed **outcome evaluations**—occur at the final stage of SARA and ask the following kinds of baseline questions: Did the response occur as planned, and did all the response components work? Did the response result in fewer calls for service to the area? More arrests? Fewer reported gang activities?[3]

The purpose of assessing a problem-solving effort is thus to help police make better decisions by answering two specific questions:

1. Did the problem decline? Answering this question helps them to decide whether to end the problem-solving effort and focus resources on other problems.
2. If the problem did decline, did the response cause the decline? Answering this question helps to decide whether to apply the response to similar problems.[4]

Another example is as follows: after performing a careful analysis, problem-solving officers determine that in order to curb a street prostitution problem, they will heighten patrols in the area, change several streets to one-way thus creating several dead-end streets to thwart cruising "johns," and work with courts and social services so that convicted prostitutes receive probation and assistance to gain the necessary skills for legitimate employment. An assessment under SARA determines whether the crackdown occurred, and if so, how many arrests police made; whether the street patterns were altered as planned; and how many prostitutes received job skills assistance.[5]

Note, however, that an assessment does not answer the question, "What happened to the problem?" Here is where an impact evaluation would come into play for determining if the implemented initiative caused the decline. Assume that during the analysis stage of SARA, evaluation team conducted a census of prostitutes operating in the target area. They also asked the traffic engineering department to install traffic counters on the major thoroughfare and critical side streets to measure traffic flow and to determine how customers move through the area. The evaluation team made covert video recordings of the target area to document how prostitutes interact with potential customers. Then, after the response was implemented, the team repeated these measures to see if the problem declined. As a result of these measures, they discover that instead of the 23 prostitutes counted in the first census, only 8 can be found—a significant reduction. They also find that there has been a slight decline in traffic on the major thoroughfare on the weekends, but not at other times; however, there has been a statistically significant decline in side street traffic on Saturday nights. New covert video recordings show that prostitutes in the area have changed how they approach vehicles. In short, the team now has evidence that the problem has declined after response implementation.[6]

As this example shows, an impact evaluation has two parts: measuring the problem and systematically comparing changes in measures by using an evaluation design to determine whether or not the response was the primary cause of the change in the measure.

Also note that two other important aspects of impact evaluations are the following:

- Objectives must have been clearly defined and measurable (e.g., in the prostitution example above, objectives for addressing the problem included installing traffic counters to measure traffic flow and making covert video recordings of the target area).
- Confounding factors must be identified (e.g., did a rash of violent crimes against prostitutes during the time the problem-solving initiatives were put into place contribute heavily to their leaving the streets?).[7]

Exhibit 11–1 describes the nature of impact evaluation—as well as the kinds of knowledge, skills, and abilities to be possessed by program evaluators—by describing an in-depth, longitudinal, multisite evaluation of the Gang Resistance Education and Training (GREAT) program, to determine whether or not it met its goals.

Exhibit 11–1   Is GREAT Truly "Great"?

The University of Missouri-St. Louis received a grant from the National Institute of Justice to determine what effect, if any, the GREAT (Gang Resistance Education and Training) program had on students. GREAT, which is a 13-lesson prevention program taught by uniformed police officers to middle school students, has three stated goals: (1) to reduce gang membership; (2) to reduce delinquency, especially violent offending; and (3) to improve students' attitudes toward the police.

Results from an earlier national evaluation of GREAT found no differences between GREAT and non-GREAT youths in terms of gang membership and involvement in delinquent behavior. Based in part on those findings, the GREAT program underwent a critical review that resulted in substantial program modifications to prevent involvement in gang behavior and delinquency. The revised GREAT curriculum is taught in middle schools across the country as well as in other countries, taught by school resource officers and municipal police officers (all of whom must complete GREAT Officer Training and be certified). The program's three main goals are:

1. To help youths avoid gang membership.
2. To help youths avoid violence and criminal activity.
3. To help youths develop a positive relationship with law enforcement.

The evaluation consisted of observations of GREAT Officer Trainings, surveys and interviews of GREAT-trained officers and supervisors, surveys of school personnel, and "on-site," direct observations of officers delivering the GREAT program in the study sites.

To assess program effectiveness, evaluators conducted a randomized control trial involving 3,820 students nested in 195 classrooms in 31 schools in 7 cities. These students were surveyed six times over 5 years, thereby allowing assessment of both short- and long-term program effects. Approximately, half of the GREAT grade-level classrooms within each school were randomly assigned to experimental or control groups, with 102 classrooms (2,051 students) assigned to receive GREAT and 93 classrooms (1,769 students) assigned to the control condition. Results from analyses of data, 1-year postprogram delivery were quite favorable; we found statistically significant differences between the treatment (i.e., GREAT) and control students on 14 out of 33 attitudinal and behavioral outcomes.

However, the question remained whether the program had long-term impacts that persisted into high school. To address this question, evaluators continued to survey this group of students for three more years (most of the students were in 10th or 11th grade at the time of the last survey administration). The 4-year postprogram analyses revealed results similar to the 1-year postprogram effects, albeit with smaller effect sizes. Across 4 years postprogram, 10 positive program effects were found, including lower odds of gang joining and more positive attitudes to police.[8]

KNOWLEDGE AND SKILLS PROGRAM EVALUATORS SHOULD POSSESS

As might be indicated in the above scenario, program evaluators must possess robust skills in both **statistical techniques** and **research methodology**. The knowledge and use of criminological theory is also important to examining and understanding crime and disorder problems. The evaluator need not know every criminological theory in-depth, but should have a working knowledge of theories that have contributed the most to understanding the local crime and disorder problems police agencies face.[9] Furthermore, they would ideally have a fundamental understanding of SARA, police operations, and crime prevention strategies (e.g., routine activities theory, situational crime prevention, and crime prevention through environmental design). Finally, an important consideration concerns time: even if police personnel were to be well-steeped in empirical research, efforts such as these are labor-intensive and it is doubtful that sworn personnel would be able to forego their other duties in favor of engaging in such analyses.

An analogy to accomplishing program evaluations can be drawn with the world of computer science: most of us know the basics of what makes our computer function; however, when we have serious problems with our computer we must turn to a specially trained technician with the required knowledge and skills to make it work properly again.

And so it is with **empirical studies** of problem-oriented policing, where the police agency either uses special-trained in-house personnel, or obtains pro bono the assistance of someone trained in social research from a nearby college or university to set up and perform an impact evaluation. Institutions of higher education are a good source for such expertise, with many social science departments—economics, political science, sociology, psychology, and criminal justice/criminology—having faculty and graduate students who are knowledgeable in program evaluation and its related skills. Typically a person cannot be awarded a graduate degree in arts or sciences without first demonstrating (in the form of a written master's thesis or doctoral dissertation) that he or she possesses requisite skills in both research methodology and statistics.

For this reason, the evaluation of initiatives is certainly an area where police agencies may wish to develop a "town–gown" relationship, to bridge the gap between theory and practice.

MEASURES AND TOOLS

Impact evaluations require measures of the problem before and after the response. Therefore, one should decide how to measure the crime problem being addressed. This allows the information collected during the analysis to describe the problem before the response.

Next we describe two types of measures that are used for collecting information—quantitative and qualitative—and the importance of ensuring measurement validity.

Quantitative Measures

Quantitative measures involve numbers. The number of burglaries in an apartment complex is a quantitative measure. Such offenses can be counted before and after the response to see if a decrease is present. Quantitative measures thus allow one to use math to estimate the response's impact. For example, burglaries dropped 15 percent during the target period from before the response to after the response.[10]

Qualitative Measures

Qualitative measures allow comparisons, but math is typically not used with them. Although quantitative measures are more often used for evaluations, qualitative measures can be extremely useful. Assume, for example, that a police agency must address a problem of gang-related violence in a neighborhood. Analysis indicates that much of this violence stems from escalating turf disputes, and that graffiti is a useful indicator of intergang tension that leads to violence. The evaluator can count the number of reported gunshots, gun injuries, and gun fatalities in the year before and the year after the response. These are quantitative measures. Then, monthly photos can be taken of known graffiti hot spots both before and after the response. Assume that before the response gang graffiti was quite common, and nongang graffiti was rare. Further, many of the markings suggested that rival gangs were overwriting each other's graffiti. After the response, however, there is little gang graffiti, but nongang graffiti has increased. Further, there is no evidence of overwriting in the little gang graffiti is found. This qualitative information reinforces the quantitative information by indicating that the response may have reduced gang tensions, or that the gangs have declined.[11]

Graffiti is nothing new, but what has changed is policing's evolving focus on graffiti. Agencies keep in contact with graffiti technicians to evaluate the health of and quality of life in their communities.
Community Oriented Policing Services.

Measurement Validity

Evaluators must also ensure that quantitative and qualitative measures actually record the problem, and not something else. For example, numbers of drug arrests are often better measures of police activity than of changes in the drug problem. Therefore, one should use arrest data as a measure of the problem only if it is certain that police enforcement efforts and techniques have remained constant (Exhibit 11–2).[12]

Exhibit 11–2	New Tool Translates Research to Practice: The Evidence-Based Policing Matrix

The analysis of crime data to fight crime and the use of specialized prevention and policing strategies to address specific crime problems have been employed for many years. However, determining which strategies work in reducing crime and disorder can be challenging. Recently, the Center for Evidence-Based Crime Policy at George Mason University took crime fighting to a new level with the creation of the **Evidence-based policing Matrix**. Funded by the federal Bureau of Justice Assistance, the Matrix is a research-to-practice translation tool that organizes studies visually, allowing agencies to view the field of research and make more informed decisions about which crime fighting strategy for their community.[13]

The Matrix is a consistently updated, research-to-practice translation tool that categorizes and visually bins all experimental and quasi-experimental research on police and crime reduction into intersections between three common dimensions of crime prevention—the nature of the target, the extent to which the strategy is proactive or reactive, and the specificity or generality of the strategy. Its mapping and visualization of 97 police evaluation studies indicate that proactive, place-based, and specific policing approaches appear much more promising in reducing crime than individual-based, reactive, and general ones.[14]

The Matrix Key (which can be viewed at: http://cebcp.org/wp-content/evidence-based-policing/the-matrix/MatrixKey.pdf) indicates that the Matrix looks at the following types of interventions:

Individuals: Interventions which target distinct individuals or certain types of individuals such as violent youths, repeat offenders, sex offenders, or drunk drivers.

Groups: Interventions which target gangs or other co-offenders (individuals who offend in concert).

Microplaces: Interventions which target very small geographic locations such as a block, street segment, alley, intersection, specific address, or cluster of addresses.

Communities and neighborhoods: Interventions which target larger geographic units such as census tracts, police beats or sectors, "communities," or "neighborhoods."

Political jurisdictions: Interventions which target politically distinct and more local or within-state jurisdictions such as cities, counties, parishes, or townships.

States/nations interventions which target states or nations: These are politically distinct geopolitical areas whose laws and criminal justice systems often determine sentencing and corrections of offenders.[15]

EVALUATING ORGANIZATIONS' AND OFFICERS' PROBLEM-SOLVING EFFORTS

Today many police agencies use personnel evaluations, which can help managers make decisions about promotion, demotion, reward, discipline, training needs, salary, job assignment, retention, and termination. They also assist supervisors in giving feedback to subordinates about performance and promotional preparation, validate selection and screening tests and training evaluations, assess the effectiveness of disciplinary measures that have been used, and convey the mission and the values of the department.[16] Therefore, many agencies use **performance evaluation** as "early-warning" systems to identify actual and potential problems. Agencies involved in litigation due to complaints of police abuse have almost always been required to implement such a system as part of any settlement.[17]

With the evolution of community-oriented policing and problem solving, an entirely new way of viewing police performance measurement was needed. First, police departments and communities are urged to identify the goals they expect officers to accomplish. Second, these goals need to provide an accurate reflection of the work that police actually do. In other words, here, if officers are to spend a large amount of time on addressing community problems, then those functions should play some role in the list of the goals of policing. To evaluate officers only on their ability to apprehend offenders ignores the vital importance of all the other work that they do.[18]

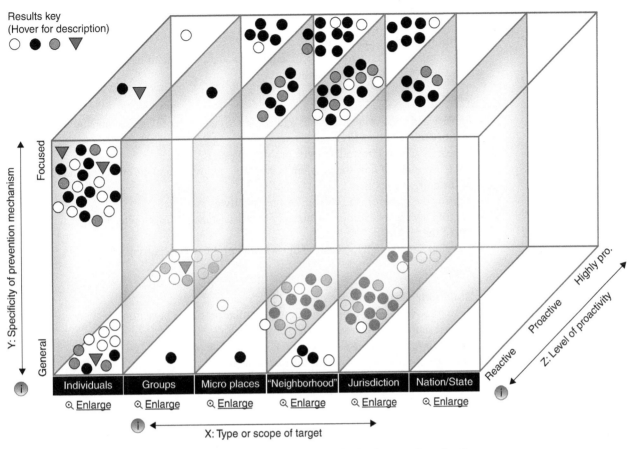

The Evidence-Based Policing Matrix is a tool that organizes evaluations of police interventions visually, allowing agencies and researchers to view the field of research in reducing crime and disorder in policing.
Courtesy Center for Evidence-Based Crime Policy, George Mason University.

Agency evaluations may be conducted on three levels: individual, organizational, and social level.[19]

The Individual Level

The process evaluation at the individual level primarily looks at the manner by which police officers spend their time during their shifts and their accomplishments in terms of problem solving. Here, evaluators might engage in ride-alongs with officers and recorded their activities and interactions with the public. In addition, the problem-solving methods that officers employed during their shifts might be noted. Individual interviews or focus groups with police officers or supervisors can also be accomplished, asking them about the amount of time that officers are engaged in problem solving and how much collaborating they have done with community members on their beats. Familiarity with their beats, community members, civic leaders, and businesses are also good indicator to use to examine the extent of problem solving engaged in by individual officers.

The Organizational Level

At the organizational level, problem solving is assessed through the agency's establishment of problem-solving processes. In this regard, departments are evaluated on their achievements of two benchmarks—SARA and CompStat.

THE SARA MODEL. The Center for Problem Oriented Policing outlined the following elements of the SARA model that the organization must, at minimum, see is accomplished:

Scanning
- Identify recurring problems of concern to the public and the police.
- Identify the consequences of the problem for the community and the police.

- Prioritize those problems.
- Develop broad goals.
- Confirm that the problems exist.
- Determine how frequently the problem occurs and how long it has been taking place.
- Select problems for closer examination.

Analysis

- Identify and understand the events and conditions that precede and accompany the problem.
- Identify relevant data to be collected.
- Research what is known about the problem type.
- Take inventory of how the problem is currently addressed and the strengths and limitations of the current response.
- Narrow the scope of the problem as specifically as possible.
- Identify a variety of resources that may be of assistance in developing a deeper understanding of the problem.
- Develop a working hypothesis about why the problem is occurring.

Response

- Brainstorm for new interventions.
- Search for what other communities with similar problems have done.
- Choose among the alternative interventions.
- Outline a response plan and identifying responsible parties.
- State the specific objectives for the response plan.
- Carry out the planned activities.

Assessment

- Determine whether the plan was implemented (a process evaluation).
- Collect pre- and postresponse qualitative and quantitative data.
- Determine whether broad goals and specific objectives were attained.
- Identify any new strategies needed to augment the original plan.
- Conduct ongoing assessment to ensure continued effectiveness.

THE COMPSTAT MODEL. As discussed in Chapter 7, CompStat involves information gathering and problem solving, with police precincts being required to solicit information from their beats and then discussing problems and solutions with community members. Beat commanders also take this information to their superiors for discussions with government officials, business leaders, community leaders, and so on. Then, from these discussions computer analyses of crime and disorder are conducted, responses are identified and implemented, and their effectiveness is evaluated. This process, coupled with SARA, has become a benchmark strategy for most police and sheriff's departments for evaluating the problem-solving efforts.[20]

The Social Level

Process evaluation at the social level involves the formation of community policing advisory groups or neighborhood meetings, so that the evaluations involve community participation. Another indicator of success is a sustained level of community participation. Several benchmarks have been established to evaluate the impact of problem solving in the community, to include:

1. Crime prevention and reduction.
2. Fear of crime.
3. Quality of life.
4. Citizen satisfaction with the police.

The premise behind problem solving is to address the root causes of crime and go beyond responding to incidents. Therefore, the reduction of the incidences of crime is a key indicator for an effective problem-solving initiative.

Another major outcome measures for police effectiveness in community policing is the fear of crime. Fear of crime is normally evaluated through a community survey (discussed more

The RAND Corporation has developed a program allowing police agencies to accurately evaluate and monitor officer performance, tracking low and high performers, and mitigating legal risk.
Community Oriented Policing Services.

below) to ascertain such indicators as fear of walking alone at night, in certain areas, and being victimized in certain ways.[21]

Quality of life involves an assessment of how the neighborhood has improved and considers social capital (discussed in Chapter 2) that is invested by community members. Although normally assessed through the use of a survey, some jurisdictions use focus groups among community leaders as means of assessing this impact. Citizen satisfaction with the police is normally assessed through community surveys and focus group discussions and normally involves such questions such as, "How satisfied are you with the police in your neighborhood?" and "How satisfied are you with the police officer who responded to your request for service?"[22]

Exhibit 11–3 describes a relatively new approach to evaluating individual officers; developed by the RAND Corporation, the Benchmark program is felt to be an accurate and fair measure of officer performance.

Exhibit 11–3   RAND's Benchmark Program

RAND Benchmark is a software application developed by the RAND Corporation for police agencies to fairly and accurately evaluate and monitor officer performance. By benchmarking each officer against a uniquely chosen set of other officers performing similar duties, it enables departments to evaluate officer performance, track low and high performers, identify outliers in particular dimensions of performance, and mitigate legal risk. By being able to rapidly identify officers who underperform or outperform their peers, agencies can address problem situations and improve overall team performance.

Whether justified or not, police agencies today are exposed to litigation and loss of public trust, which may include charges that officers are underperforming and generate a large number of complaints that officers are excessively stopping minority drivers or using excessive force. Therefore, it is imperative that agencies be proactive in early identification of problem patterns.

RAND Benchmark uses state-of-the-art techniques and selects a unique set of comparison cases to collectively match the features and conditions of an officer's activities. For example, assume that an agency wishes to evaluate some characteristic of an officer's patrol stops. To construct a proper benchmark, stops made by other officers are selected so that they collectively match the features of stops made by the officer. If 30 percent of the officer's stops occur between midnight and 1:00 a.m., so will the stops in the officer's benchmark. The chosen set of benchmark cases is different for every officer so that each officer is fairly compared with his or her peers and every performance benchmark is as accurate as possible.[23]

NOT TO BE OVERLOOKED: COMMUNITY SURVEYS

Citizen surveys are a vital part of a problem-solving strategy, and can be used for a variety of purposes: to provide information to patrol officers, evaluate program effectiveness, and prioritize crime and disorder problems. Police agencies should attempt to "feel the pulse" of their communities; so the importance of surveying community needs cannot be overstated. The mood of the public should be a vital consideration when the police make public policy decisions.[24]

Done properly, however, **surveys** are very labor-intensive and expensive; therefore, consideration should be given to the use of volunteers for the former, and budgetary limitations with the latter. Persons who are about to conduct community surveys will find a very valuable resource in a joint publication by the federal Bureau of Justice Statistics and the Office of Community Oriented Policing Services: *Conducting Community Surveys: A Practical Guide for Law Enforcement Agencies.*[25] It explains the use of surveys by police agencies and includes survey development, administration, and interpretation of results.

Following are several key issues to resolve before developing a questionnaire[26]:

- *What are the specific purposes of the survey, and what kinds of questions will be consistent with those purposes?* Without clear goals, the number of questions tends to mushroom. This increases the amount of time required to administer each survey, which is a burden on both interviewer and interviewee.
- *How will the survey be administered—by mail, by telephone, or in person?* A questionnaire can be mailed to everyone in the sample to complete and return; the sampled respondents can be interviewed by telephone or they can be interviewed in person (at home, in the office, on the bus, or wherever they are). Mail surveys can be quite expensive if a large population is to be sampled, however.[27] There are advantages and disadvantages to each type of survey that should be explored prior to determining which type is to be used.
- *How much time will it take to complete the survey, and is this a reasonable amount of time to impose on respondents?* Remember that completion of a survey is an intrusion on the time of others. About 10 to 15 minutes to complete a questionnaire is reasonable, but if examining, say, problems involving drugs and violence, 30 to 40 minutes might be reasonable. The key is to be considerate about demands on others.

Furthermore, surveys can explore residents' participation in community organization, perceptions of the police, victimization experiences, and fear of crime.[28]

Exhibit 11–4 provides a look at a foreign venue in the area of community canvassing: Sweden's use of a research and development center, a national crime prevention council, and local efforts in achieving crime prevention.

Not to be overlooked by police is the use of a community survey for determining the level of crime and disorder, quality of life, and fear of crime in neighborhoods.
James Lawler Duggan/Reuters Pictures.

Exhibit 11–4 Going Global: Sweden's Use of Crime Prevention Committees

Sweden, with a population of 8.2 million, is a relatively homogeneous country, although immigrant groups now total over 10% of the population, mostly from North Africa and the Middle East. With many years of experience in maintaining an open, compassionate society, this philosophy also helps to foster the country's approach to community policing as well as its policies on police structure and administration.

Sweden began its work in community policing in the early 1970s with the establishment of a national center for research and development, with the goal of reducing crime at its community roots. The National Council for Crime Prevention (NCCP) was created to involve all communities. However, the Council goes a step further; it performs evaluations of those communities' efforts in crime prevention techniques. After determining which crime prevention programs are successful, the Council then distributes the "best and brightest" ideas and programs among all of its local police departments. It also supplies politicians, decision-makers, the media, and the general public with information and data on crime prevention locally.

In 1992, the NCCP began forming local crime prevention committees; eventually, local committees were established in 232 communities, working closely with local police as well as with social services, youth and family services, schools, and other agencies. Police representatives sit as voting members on the councils, which affords police the opportunity to engage in a dialogue that forms their community policing efforts; the police also act as advisors and consultants for the committees' various projects.

Thus, in Sweden, crime prevention began as a theory, and then became an administrative structure, where it facilitated the introduction of community policing and provided a forum for the community as well as for the police. This has had the side benefit of ensuring that the local police are not aloof and are more user-friendly and accountable for their actions. Another result is that the police are much more effective, successful, and respected by their constituents.

Other countries, including Italy, Switzerland, Germany, France, and Denmark have also found these interagency outreach teams to be one of the most effective forms of community policing activities.[29]

Summary

This chapter began with the general proposition that the criminal justice field, today more than ever, needs to know "what works" in terms of its policies and practices. We also emphasized the fact that assessing and evaluating the impact of community-oriented policing and problem solving is critical—and, if done properly, highly challenging; as noted, it is very challenging, indeed, for one to become a skilled program evaluator. Although there is no one measurement process that will work for problem-oriented policing initiatives in all communities, this chapter offered a comprehensive view of the rationales, general guidelines, methods, and criteria for measuring social interventions. Several examples of successful empirical evaluations of problem-solving initiatives were also provided.

Key Terms and Concepts

Assessment	Measurement validity	Quantitative measures	Statistical techniques
Empirical study	Outcome (process)	RAND Benchmark Program	Surveys
Evaluation/impact evaluation	evaluation	Research methodology	
Evidence-Based Policing	Performance evaluation	SARA (problem-solving	
Matrix	Qualitative measures	process)	

Items for Review

1. Describe the major differences between assessments (as defined in the SARA problem-solving process) and an empirical impact evaluation of a problem-solving strategy.
2. Describe the kinds of knowledge, skills, and abilities that a problem-solving program evaluator must possess.
3. What measures and tools are available for program evaluation?
4. What methods exist for evaluating a police organization's or individual officer's problem-solving performance?
5. What are the benefits of using surveys for evaluative purposes?

Learn by Doing

1. Knowing that you excelled in your research methods and statistics courses at university, a local police lieutenant—now supervising its crime research and analysis unit—contacts you for assistance. It seems the department recently completed a problem-solving project involving crime and disorder at motels in a rundown part of town. The lieutenant asks you to explain how they might go about examining outcomes of their SARA efforts as well as performing a full-blown impact evaluation. What general recommendations will you make? How would you describe what a truly empirical study contains?

2. You are contacted for advice by a police supervisor. It seems her community policing team—composed of four deputies who are supposed to be dedicated to problem-solving efforts in a particular area of the county—are not getting the job done. Citizens are complaining about crime and disorder and nothing is accomplished at advisory board meetings. The deputies seem to lack overall knowledge of the area as well as any sort of plan, direction, or motivation to engage in problem-solving efforts. The supervisor is in desperate need of advice concerning criteria for evaluating the deputies' performance so as to determine whether they should be retrained or reassigned. How will you proceed, and what criteria will you recommend?

3. You are consulting with a small agency in another state that is engaged in problem-solving activities. It now wishes to survey the community concerning their fears and concerns, views toward the police, observations of crime and disorder, and so on. What information and caveats will you provide concerning the types of surveys that might be developed?

Endnotes

1. *Merriam-Webster Dictionary*, http://www.merriam-webster.com/dictionary/esoteric.
2. U.S. Department of Justice, Bureau of Justice Assistance, *Understanding Community Policing: A Framework for Action* (August 1994), p. 28, https://www.ncjrs.gov/pdffiles/commp.pdf.
3. John E. Eck, *Assessing Responses to Problems: An Introductory Guide for Police Problem-Solvers* (Washington, D.C.: U.S. Department of Justice, Office of Community Oriented Policing Services, August 2011), pp. 11–13.
4. Ibid.
5. Ibid., pp. 15–18.
6. Ibid.
7. Ibid.
8. Finn-Aage Esbensen, Wayne Osgood, Dana Peterson, Terrance J. Taylor, Dena Carson, Adrienne Freng, and Kristy Matsuda, *Process and Outcome Evaluation of the G.R.E.A.T. Program* (December 2013), https://www.ncjrs.gov/pdffiles1/nij/grants/244346.pdf.
9. Rachel Boba, *Problem Analysis in Policing*, U.S. Department of Justice, Office of Community Oriented Policing Services (March 2003), http://www.popcenter.org/library/reading/pdfs/problemanalysisinpolicing.pdf.
10. Eck, *Assessing Responses to Problems*, p. 15.
11. Ibid.
12. Ibid.
13. For an overview of the RAND Matrix, see the Bureau of Justice Assistance, BJA's Justice Today, "New Tool Translates Research to Practice," https://www.bja.gov/JusticeToday/JT_08_12.pdf.
14. Ibid.
15. See Cynthia Lum, Christopher S. Koper, and Cody W. Telep, "The Evidence-Based Policing Matrix," *Journal of Experimental Criminology* 7 (2013):3–26.
16. David Carter, *Considerations in Program Development and Evaluation of Community Policing* (Wichita, Kans.: Regional Community Policing Institute, 2000), http://webs.wichita.edu/depttools/depttoolsmemberfiles/rcpi/Policy%20Papers/CP%20Devel%20and%20Eval.pdf.
17. Ibid.
18. Edward Maguire, "Measuring the Performance of Law Enforcement Agencies—Part 1 of a 2-Part Article," Commission on Accreditation for Law Enforcement Agencies, http://www.calea.org/calea-update-magazine/issue-83/measuring-performance-law-enforcement-agencies-part-1of-2-oart-articl.
19. Melchor L. de Guzman, "Problem-Solving Initiatives: Assessment and Evaluation," in Kenneth J. Peak (ed.), *Encyclopedia of Community Policing and Problem Solving* (Thousand Oaks, Calif.: Sage, 2013), pp. 315–323.
20. Ibid.
21. Ibid.

22. Ibid.; see also Mary Ann Wycoff and Timothy N. Oettmeier, *Evaluating Patrol Officer Performance Under Community Policing: The Houston Experience* (Washington, D.C.: National Institute of Justice, 1994).

23. RAND Corporation, Center on Quality Policing, *RAND Benchmark: Accurate Police Officer Performance Benchmarking and Evaluation*, http://benchmark.rand.org/RAND_Benchmark_brochure.pdf.

24. Mervin F. White and Ben A. Menke, "A Critical Analysis on Public Opinions Toward Police Agencies," *Journal of Police Science and Administration* 6 (1978):204–218.

25. Deborah Weisel, *Conducting Community Surveys: A Practical Guide for Law Enforcement Agencies* (Washington, D.C.: U.S. Department of Justice, Bureau of Justice Statistics, Office of Community Oriented Policing Services, 1999).

26. See, for example, Ken Peak, "On Successful Criminal Justice Survey Research: A 'Personal Touch' Model for Enhancing Rates of Return," *Criminal Justice Policy Review* 4 (3) (Spring 1992):268–277; Don A. Dillman, *Mail and Telephone Surveys: The Total Design Method* (New York: John Wiley & Sons, 1978); Arlene Fink and Jacqueline Kosecoff, *How to Conduct Surveys: A Step-by-Step Guide* (Beverly Hills, Calif.: Sage, 1985); Floyd J. Fowler, *Survey Research Methods* (Newbury Park, Calif.: Sage, 1988); Abraham Nastali Oppenheim, *Questionnaire Design, Interviewing, and Attitude Measurement* (New York: St. Martin's Press, 1992); Charles H. Backstrom and Gerald Hursh-Cesar, *Survey Research* (2nd ed.) (New York: Macmillan, 1981).

27. Police Executive Research Forum, *A Police Practitioner's Guide to Surveying Citizens and Their Environment* (Washington, D.C.: U.S. Department of Justice, Bureau of Justice Assistance, 1993), https://www.ncjrs.gov/pdffiles/polc.pdf, p. 22.

28. Timothy S. Bynum, *Using Analysis for Problem-Solving: A Guide for Law Enforcement* (U.S. Department of Justice, Office of Community Oriented Policing Services, 2002), pp. 25–26, http://www.cops.usdoj.gov/pdf/e08011230.pdf.

29. Los Angeles Community Policing, "Community Policing in Europe: Structure and Best Practices in Sweden, France, Germany," http://www.lacp.org/Articles%20-%20Expert%20-%20Our%20Opinion/060908-CommunityPolicingInEurope-AJ.htm.

PART V

Addressing Today's Crime and Disorder

To this point in the book, we have examined community policing and problem solving and its component parts and requisite agency conditions from many perspectives, all of which must be viewed as parts of the whole—as well as essential for problem-oriented policing to successfully address crime and disorder. In Chapters 12 and 13, we consider very troublesome areas of crime and disorder and what appears to work in terms of problem solving. We will draw from many examples and "success stories" in discussing this broad array of problem-solving approaches.

12

Problem Solving in Practice:
"What Works" with Drugs, Youth Gangs and Violence, and Neighborhood Disorder

LEARNING OBJECTIVES

As a result of reading this chapter, the student will understand:

- How the war on drugs is changing in terms of the nature and types of problems now confronting the police, as well as strategies and legislation for combating drug abuse

- The problems of youth crime in general, as well as their involvement with gangs, gun violence, graffiti, cyberbullying, and school violence

- How neighborhood disorder can lead to serious community problems, and some of the challenges and means involved with addressing it

TEST YOUR KNOWLEDGE

1. The United States is the only country in the world where personal use of marijuana is legal in some states.

2. Experts calculate that legalizing marijuana would cost $13.7 billion per year due to the cost of enforcement and administration of oversight.

3. Good news: the juvenile arrest rate for all offenses reached its highest level about two decades ago and has been declining since.

4. Cyberbullying has surfaced as a major problem, but it still lags behind physical bullying in schools in frequency.

5. The companion problems of neighborhood disorder and abandoned buildings can, if left unchecked, lead to serious crime.

Answers can be found on page 278.

INTRODUCTION

How does community-oriented policing and problem-solving function in practice? While the preceding chapters have traced its origin, preparation, and methods, this chapter (as well as the following chapter) demonstrates how its practical application may help to succeed with a variety of crime and disorder problems. Indeed, whether or not these strategies succeed is the sole test concerning the efficacy of this strategy, and thus this chapter's sole focus will be on "what works" as police attempt to deal with these problems.

This chapter focuses on four areas that are particularly troublesome or challenging for today's society and police. First, we examine the changing war on drugs and general problem of drug offenses; included are discussions of the status of several types of drugs and how "pulling levers" and legislative enactments assist police in addressing this long-standing, widespread problem. Then we look at the broad problem of youth crimes, to include their involvement with gangs and graffiti, human trafficking, and gun violence; also included are the corollary issues of cyberbullying and school violence. Finally, we consider some strategies used to overcome neighborhood disorder, particularly problem properties and abandoned buildings. Eight exhibits as well as a number of examples and case studies disseminated throughout the chapter will help to demonstrate successful initiatives.

The chapter concludes with key terms and concepts and items for review sections as well as "Learn by Doing" scenarios, where you can experience some difficult challenges that police officers might confront.

THE (CHANGING) WAR ON DRUGS

The year 2013 will go down in history as the onset of major changes with the United States **war on drugs**. As will be seen below, states began to change their laws with respect to marijuana, a majority of Americans supported marijuana legalization, and world leaders began calling for an end to the drug war; furthermore, U.S. Attorney General Eric H. Holder, Jr., came out against racist mandatory minimum drug laws and mass incarceration, celebrities issued a letter to President Barack Obama saying "No More Drug War," and Uruguay (followed by several other foreign venues) became the first country in the world to legalize marijuana.[1] This chapter expands on several of these developments.

Marijuana

The United States now imprisons about 2.2 million persons, and the majority of those incarcerated are in prison or jail for drug violations[2] Many of those violations involve marijuana, where the social and political opinion is changing, as evidenced by state legalization and the federal government's response. Four states—Colorado, Washington, Oregon, and Alaska—and the District of Columbia have passed measures to legalize marijuana use, while an additional 17 states have decriminalized certain amounts of marijuana possession. Now half of U.S. states (25 plus in the District of Columbia) allow use of medical marijuana. Such modifications in law and attitude represent a significant "chink in the armor" of the nation's drug laws. It is no surprise, then, that marijuana is the most commonly used and abused illicit drug in the United States, with more people using marijuana than all other illicit drugs. Eighty percent of police agencies report that marijuana availability is high in their jurisdictions, due to large-scale marijuana importation from Mexico, increasing domestic indoor grows, and an increase of marijuana cultivated in states that have legalized or medical marijuana initiatives.[3]

BOX 12–1

Foreign Venues Support Marijuana Legalization

Following are recent actions taken in five selected foreign venues regarding the enforcement, legalization, and/or possession under their **marijuana laws.**

- In August 2013, Uruguay became the world's first nation to legalize marijuana; the new law allows the government to control the cultivation, trade, and sale of the crop.[8]
- In Colombia, the country's highest court ruled that minor possession of the drug was not a jailable offense.[9]
- The Czech Republic decriminalized minor possession of marijuana for private use in 2010 and enacted a law legalizing medical use (however, local growth is restricted to registered firms).[10]
- Argentina's Supreme Court deemed it unconstitutional in 2009 to punish people for private marijuana use as long as no one else was harmed, thus effectively authorizing its personal use.[11]
- In Mexico, marijuana users can possess up to 5 grams legally; two former presidents have advocated for decriminalization in order to curb cartel violence.[12]

Public support for legalizing adult use of marijuana has been increasing since the early 1990s.[4] Opponents, however, argue that marijuana legalization can serve as a stepping-stone to harder drugs, result in people driving while "stoned" and thus pose a danger, increase the chances of the drug being used by kids, cause physical damage to users, and lead to the possible legalization of harder drugs.[5]

CONFLICTING FEDERAL LAW. A glaring aspect of legalization is that such laws are wholly in violation of federal law. Specifically, since 1970 the Code of Federal Regulations, Title 21, Section 1308.11, has listed marijuana as a Schedule I controlled substance,[6] meaning that it has no medical value and that the potential for abuse is high.[7]

Support for marijuana legalization is rapidly outpacing opposition. A slim majority (53%) of Americans say the drug should be made legal, compared with 44% who want it to be illegal. Opinions have changed drastically since 1969, when Gallup first asked the question and found that just 12% favored legalizing marijuana use. Much of the change in opinion has occurred over the past few years—support rose 11 points between 2010 and 2013 (although it has remained relatively unchanged since then).[13]

A Harvard University economist estimated that legalizing marijuana would save $13.7 billion per year in government expenditures on enforcement of prohibition by eliminating arrests for trafficking and possession as well as costs for related courts and jail/prison activities.[14]

Exhibit 12–1 provides an opportunity for you to briefly consider both sides of the marijuana legalization debate, and to consider which side or argument you believe should prevail.

Exhibit 12–1   Marijuana Legalization: You Decide

It may be ironic that both sides of the marijuana controversy actually have the same goal: putting an end to the U.S. drug problem. However, each side makes arguments that should be examined prior to making public policy.

First, those who are opposed to marijuana legalization argue that punishing its users with fines and jail time will deter other people from using the drug (however, that has not been the case throughout marijuana's history). Furthermore, many if not most such users are nonviolent, petty offenders who are expensive to incarcerate and may well come out of jail or prison more dangerous and hardened than before. The relative success of drug courts (see Chapter 9) suggests these "offenders" need treatment rather than punishment.

In the other camp are those who believe marijuana is a part of our culture, has medical value, and should be legalized and its users go unpunished. Potential problems with this latter view are that legalization may well substantially increase the use of marijuana (including by motor vehicle operators), and that there is no evidence to support the notions that legalization will result in close regulation and the cessation of illegal sales.

More arguments can certainly be made on both sides, but which faction's arguments wins your support, and why?

Cocaine

Since 2007, cocaine availability levels in the United States have fluctuated slightly but continued at consistently lower levels than prior to 2007.[15] Most cocaine available in the United States continues to be produced in Colombia and smuggled across the Southwest Border and, to a lesser extent, through the Caribbean. The federal government has retreated somewhat even in its treatment of cocaine offenders. In 2010, Congress passed the Fair Sentencing Act, reducing the disparity between sentences for crack cocaine offenses versus powder cocaine offenses.

Prescription Drug Abuse: When Jails Become Rehab Clinics

A problem that is expanding and increasingly confronting our society and its criminal justice system is the abuse of prescription painkillers. An estimated 100 million Americans suffer from chronic pain. Therefore, as new painkillers have been developed and increasingly prescribed by health professionals to provide extended relief, it is no surprise that about 219 million opioid prescriptions are now written each year in the United States;[16] the longer a person is on such a drug, the better the chance that he or she will become addicted or develop a resistance to the drug's effects; indeed, about 2.1 million Americans are estimated to be addicted. Some people have addictions so severe that they dissolve their pills and inject them with a syringe as often as 20 times per day, often sharing the same needles. About 50 Americans—more than 17,000 total—die each year from prescription-opioid overdoses.[17]

Law enforcement efforts include the federal Drug Enforcement Administration (DEA) fining Walgreens $80 million for allowing opioids to be possessed by criminals, and two CVS stores had their pharmaceutical licenses revoked for lax oversight of opioids. In Scott County, Kentucky, a common means of getting rid of one's addiction is by going cold turkey in jail. The sheriff has stated that the local jail is in fact the county's rehab and counseling clinic; about 90 percent of the jail's inmates are incarcerated for prescription-drug-related crimes. The sheriff convinced the state's governor to issue an emergency order overriding the state's law against needle-sharing in order to allow syringe-swapping in the area.[18]

Figure 12.1 depicts the extent of the U.S. prescription-drug problem in terms of sales, deaths, and treatment admissions.

In November 2013, the Federal Drug Quality and Security Act (HR 3204) was signed into law. The Act establishes a system to track **prescription drugs** from the time they are manufactured until they are sold to the consumer. The Act calls for drug manufacturers, repackagers, wholesale distributors, and dispensers to maintain and to issue key information about each drug's distribution history. Within four years of the law's establishment, prescription drugs are to be serialized in a consistent way industry-wide. This will allow for efficient tracking in order to respond to recalls and notices of theft and counterfeiting.[19]

Methamphetamine

Methamphetamine (meth) availability is increasing in the United States, and availability is directly related to high levels of methamphetamine production in Mexico; the number of meth laboratories seized in Mexico has increased significantly since 2008, and seizures at the

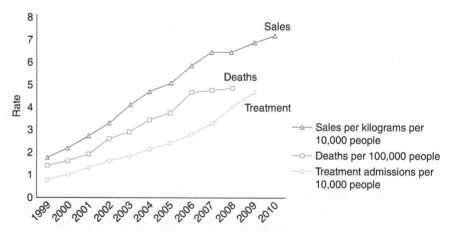

FIGURE 12–1   Rates of Prescription Painkiller Sales, Deaths, and Substance Abuse Treatment Admissions (1999–2010).

Sources: National Vital Statistics System, 1999–2008; Automation of Reports and Consolidated Orders System (ARCOS) of the Drug Enforcement Administration (DEA), 1999–2010; Treatment Episode Data Set, 1999–2009, http://www.cdc.gov/vitalsigns/painkilleroverdoses/infographic.html.

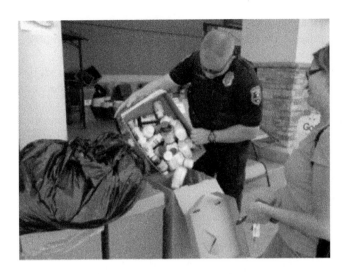

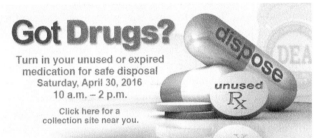

More than 2 million Americans are addicted to prescription drugs; one solution for police is a project allowing citizens to anonymously dispose of unwanted and expired medications.
Courtesy of Drug Enforcement Administration.

Southwest Border increased more than threefold over the past five years. Still, about 40 percent of police agencies report that meth is highly available and easily obtained at any time. Its abuse and availability are much higher in the Western United States, although thousands of kilograms of Mexican meth are seized along the Southwest Border annually. The vast majority of methamphetamine laboratories seized in the United States are the small capacity production laboratories, known as "one-pot" or "shake-and-bake" laboratories. These laboratories produce small amounts of methamphetamine, generally for personal use or use among a small group of people. Small lab operators use simple methods to manufacture methamphetamine, such as mixing pseudoephedrine and other household items in a plastic soda-type bottle. The mixture creates a chemical reaction, which produces methamphetamine. This method of production is highly volatile and dangerous, and is susceptible to error resulting in fires or explosions.[20]

Heroin

The threat posed by heroin in the United States is increasing in areas across the country, with about 30 percent of police agencies reporting that heroin is the greatest drug threat in their area (second only to meth, at 32 percent). Furthermore, heroin availability is increasing throughout the nation. As with meth, seizures at the Southwest Border are also rising as Mexican traffickers increase heroin production and transportation. Heroin seizures at the border more than doubled over five years, since 2009.[21] As a result, heroin overdose deaths are increasing in many U.S. cities and counties. In addition to increased enforcement actions toward heroin, following are some measures law enforcement agencies are taking to address the problem:

- The Quincy, MA Police Department (PD) was the first in the nation in October 2010 to require every officer on patrol to carry naloxone (naloxone blocks or reverses the effects of opioid medication and is used to treat a narcotic overdose in an emergency situation);[22] since that time they have administered the drug more than 200 times and have reversed more than 95 percent of those overdoses.

- Police departments in other areas are training officers to carry naloxone in response to increased opioid overdoses in those areas. All Vermont State Troopers will also be issued naloxone.
- In March 2014, the U.S. Attorney General publicly urged law enforcement agencies to train and equip their personnel to administer naloxone, noting that 17 states and Washington, DC, have amended their laws to increase access to naloxone, resulting in over 10,000 overdose reversals since 2001.
- In March 2014, Massachusetts' governor declared the growing opioid addiction a public health emergency and used his emergency powers to permit first responders to carry and administer naloxone.[23]

Synthetic "Designer" Drugs

Synthetic cannabinoids, commonly known as "synthetic marijuana," "K2," or "Spice," are often sold in legal retail outlets as "herbal incense" or "potpourri," and synthetic cathinones are often sold as "bath salts" or "jewelry cleaner." They are labeled "not for human consumption" to mask their intended purpose and avoid Food and Drug Administration (FDA) regulatory oversight of the manufacturing process. Users claim that synthetic cannabinoids mimic the primary psychoactive ingredient in marijuana.[24] The use of synthetic drugs is quite high, especially among young people. Therefore, federal, state, and local agencies have worked to enact policies and legislation to combat this threat and to educate people about the tremendous health risk posed by these substances. Legislative measures include the Synthetic Drug Abuse Prevention Act (part of the FDA Safety and Innovation Act of 2012) which permanently placed 26 types of synthetic drugs into Schedule I of the Controlled Substances Act (CSA). In 2011, DEA began to control five types of synthetic cannabinoids, and in 2012, all but one of these substances were permanently designated as Schedule I substances under the Synthetic Drug Abuse Prevention Act on April 12, 2013, DEA again used its emergency scheduling authority to schedule three more types of synthetic cannabinoids, temporarily designating them as Schedule I substances. Finally, at least 43 states have taken action to control one or more synthetic cannabinoids.[25]

What Works: "Pulling Levers," Legislation, HIDTA

Although it is highly doubtful that the police can completely eradicate the sale (supply) and abuse (demand) of illicit and prescription drugs, they have achieved considerable success through

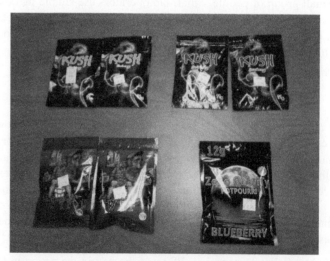

The use of synthetic drugs is quite high, especially among young people. Therefore, federal, state, and local agencies have worked to enact policies and legislation to combat this threat.
Courtesy of Drug Enforcement Administration.

the use of problem-solving strategies and the assistance of legislative enactments. It should be noted, however, that the use of police crackdowns alone—"abrupt escalations in law enforcement activities" to address certain offenses—tend to have minimal, short-term effects on drug problems. Similarly, police foot and bike patrols typically show only small reductions in drug-related arrests.

Generally, problem-solving initiatives can have extremely positive results. One such approach in use by a number of police agencies is known as "**pulling levers**" or focused deterrence. This approach uses creative methods such as directly communicating incentives and disincentives to targeted offenders (such as the promise of swift and sure prosecution if their criminal acts do not cease). Using an inter-agency working group of law enforcement, prosecution, other justice agency officials, local government, social services and community-based practitioners, police use a menu of sanctions to stop offenders from continuing their violent behavior and make them understand that they will be receiving special attention. These new strategic approaches have shown promising results in the reduction of crime (an example is provided in Exhibit 12–2).[26]

Exhibit 12–2   "Pulling Levers" for Drug Enforcement and Reduction

One successful problem-solving initiative for addressing drug abuse is the Rockford, Illinois, "Pulling Levers Drug Market Intervention." This strategy used by the Rockford Police Department (RPD) combats open-air drug markets and related offending in a high-crime neighborhood. The ultimate goal of the intervention is to reduce criminal offending, interrupt open-air drug markets, and make the high-crime community more inhabitable. The RPD uses a focused-deterrence strategy, sometimes referred to as a "pulling levers" approach.

Pulling levers consists of several steps:

▶ Diagnosing a specific crime problem.
▶ Organizing an interagency working group of criminal justice personnel.
▶ Identifying the crime patterns of chronic offenders and their criminal networks.
▶ Responding to law violators with a variety of sanctions.
▶ Providing targeted offenders with social services and community resources.
▶ Continuously communicating with offenders so they know they are receiving special attention.

Deterrence theory serves as the foundation for the Rockford Pulling Levers Drug Market Intervention. Deterrence theory holds that humans are rational beings who consider the consequences of their actions and are deterred from engaging in continual patterns of offending as a result of the certainty, severity, and celerity of punishment. In pulling levers initiatives, police officers target high-risk offenders, using specific sanctions as leverage to obtain compliance and reduce the risk of future offending. It is believed that these deterrence-based policing approaches, coupled with proactive policing, have the potential to reduce violence and other disruptive behaviors in an urban environment.[27]

High Intensity Drug Trafficking Areas Program

The High Intensity Drug Trafficking Areas (**HIDTA**) program, created by Congress with the Anti-Drug Abuse Act of 1988, provides assistance to federal, state, local, and tribal law enforcement agencies operating in areas determined to be critical drug-trafficking regions of the United States. HIDTA principally supports drug supply reduction, but law enforcement agencies have substantial experience in implementing problem-oriented policing strategies and promote and participate in community-based drug prevention and treatment programs. To accomplish this, the Administration is proposing in the budget to remove the program cap on prevention spending and to modify the restrictions currently in place for drug treatment programs. This change will enable HIDTAs to place more emphasis on expanding prevention efforts and to support initiatives that provide access to treatment for substance use disorders as part of a diversion or other alternative sentencing or community reentry program. HIDTA's budget is about $250 million per year.[28]

YOUTH AND CRIME: GANGS, GUNS, AND GRAFFITI

An old criminal-justice adage states that crime is a "young person's game." Indeed, that would appear to be the case given that 36 percent of all arrests, and 37 percent of arrests for violent crimes, are of persons under 25 years of age.[29] As you read this section, consider the generally nonpunitive, rehabilitative goals of the juvenile justice system, as well as what point juveniles who commit particularly heinous crimes should lose the juvenile court's protective shroud and be transferred to the adult courts for processing.

Juvenile Offending Today

There is good news in terms of numbers of juveniles who are arrested for all offenses in the United States: the juvenile arrest rate for all offenses climbed to and reached its highest level about two decades ago (in 1996), and has been declining since. However, there is still ample room for concern with juvenile crime. According to arrest data by the Federal Bureau of Investigation, juveniles (under age 18) commit about 11 percent of all violent crimes, and about 16 percent of all property crimes in the United States.[30]

Although many theories have been offered by experts to explain juvenile crime, no single theory has been universally accepted. Experts agree, however, that there is a correlation between juvenile crime and family dysfunction (one of the most potent influences on juvenile development), drug use and deviance (alcohol and tobacco are the drugs of choice for many juveniles), socioeconomic class (children from poor and working-class backgrounds are much more likely to engage in delinquent behavior), and educational experiences (academic achievement is considered to be one of the principal stepping-stones toward success in American society).[31]

Exhibit 12–3 provides a global perspective of juvenile treatment—specifically, the inhumane treatment of juveniles in detention in Panamanian detention centers.

Exhibit 12–3	Global Perspective: Panama's "Cruel, Inhuman" Juvenile Detention

Recently a team of researchers from the International Human Rights Clinic at Harvard Law School visited four juvenile detention centers in Panama which housed 268 juvenile detainees, or approximately 82 percent of the total population of the juvenile detention system. The team learned that Panamanian authorities routinely subjected juveniles in these centers to cruel, inhuman and degrading treatment, occasionally rising to the level of torture. In one such incident, police stood by while juveniles locked in a cell slowly burned to death. The police officers were filmed laughing while the boys screamed and begged for help; one officer told the boys to die. Authorities were also found to have routinely beaten and used tear gas on detainees, and that guards and police shot them with rubber bullets and threatened them with rifles. One director reported that in the past, it was a standard policy to inflict physical punishment for infractions such as fighting; the policy involved guards hitting detainees on the buttocks with a paddle and then sending them to the punishment cell.

One detainee was beaten for turning up the volume on a communal television set. Several others were beaten for pleading with the guards to give them water. The guards shouted obscenities at the detainees and refused to bring them water. When one juvenile threw a container of urine at a guard, as many as five guards entered the cell and beat him, continuing to do so even after they had him handcuffed.

Detainees described incidents in which guards beat, shot (with rubber bullets), punched, and kicked one juvenile for attempting to escape. The team confirmed that detention center authorities also send detainees who commit infractions to maximum security cells, where conditions also constitute cruel, inhuman, and degrading treatment. All such treatment is in violation of the United Nations' Convention on the Rights of the Child.[32]

Youth Gangs: An Overview

Certainly one of the most troubling criminal activities of our nation's youth involves their membership in **gangs**—generally defined as a group or association of peers sharing a gang name, recognizable symbols, identifiable leadership, having an identified geographic territory, holding regular meetings, and being collectively engaged in illegal activities.[33]

The latest National Youth Gang Survey estimates that there are approximately 30,000 gangs and 850,000 gang members across the United States; since about 2000, the estimated number of gangs has increased 8 percent, and the number of gang members has increased 11 percent during the past five years; however, studies have repeatedly found that most youth who join a gang do not remain in it for an extended period of time. Most youth who join a gang only remain active members for about one to two years.[34]

What Works with Youth Gangs?

Targeted patrols or a dedicated gang unit (or officer) appear to be the most frequently used measures used to combat gangs, followed by participation in a multiagency gang task force and coordinated probation searches. Less frequently reported measures are civil gang ordinances or injunctions (a court order issued in a civil case against a criminal street gang and its members to prohibit certain behavior within a defined Safety Zone—which may include associating together in public, and violating trespass and curfew laws).[35]

Finally, it should be noted that, as with other crime and disorder problems, arrests alone do not solve problems in the long term. In order to address gang problems, there must be a comprehensive, multifaceted approach to the gang problem, to include: fundamental changes in the way schools operate (acting as community centers involved in teaching, providing services, and serving as locations for activities before and after the school day); job skills development; a range of services provided to families (parental training, child care, health care, and crisis intervention); changes in the way the criminal justice system—particularly policing—responds generally to problems by increasing their understanding of the communities they serve and to solving problems; and intervention and control of known gang members—either by diverting peripheral members from gang involvement and criminal activity, or by arresting and incapacitating hard-core gang members, thus sending a message that the community will not tolerate intimidating, violent, and/or criminal gang activity.[36]

The Mara Salvatrucha (MS-13) gang is so violent that the FBI maintains an MS-13 National Gang Task Force.
Courtesy FBI.

FOCUS ON: Homeboy Industries

Alison lass Camacho Global Homeboy Network & Media Relations.

In the 1980s, Father Greg Boyle realized that a need existed to provide jobs and education as alternatives to the gangs and the senseless violence they created. So, he began a mission in 1988, which became Homeboy Industries in 2001. The program has since grown to become one of the largest, most comprehensive and successful gang intervention, rehabilitation, and re-entry programs in the country. Since the beginning, it has sought alternatives to violence, given second chances, and provided jobs and education. It is a therapeutic community, a place of healing, and a place to discover resilience. Since moving to its current location in Downtown Los Angeles, it has grown exponentially. Now, each month: more than 1000 people walk through its doors seeking job placement, free services, and referrals; there are about 800 tattoo removal sessions; and more than 400 students are tutored and mentored, and nearly 400 people receive legal and mental health counseling.

- Case Management multidisciplinary method of monitoring a trainee's 18-month plan of action as they establish and attain personal, educational, and vocational goals.
- Tattoo Removal.
- Employment Services—job preparation and placement.
- Mental Health Services—individual therapy, substance abuse counseling, and group classes.
- Legal Services.
- Curriculum and Education—including a GED program, Charter High School, life skills and enrichment classes.[37]

The federal Office of Juvenile Justice and Delinquency Prevention (OJJDP) also argues that a comprehensive, coordinated response to America's gang problem is required that coordinates prevention, intervention, enforcement, and re-entry strategies. Certainly, the Gang Resistance Education and Training (GREAT) Program, (discussed in Chapter 11) a school-based, law enforcement officer-instructed, classroom curriculum administered by OJJDP, serves to combat risk factors and helps youth develop positive life skills that will help them avoid gang involvement and violent behavior. Another program, the Blueprints for Violence Prevention project, has identified activities that have been shown to reduce violence, delinquency, and drug use with gang members or youth at risk for gang membership.[38]

Gangs are known to be involved in human trafficking, is essentially modern-day slavery and is the forced recruitment, harboring, transportation, provision, or obtaining of a person for labor or services. *Otnaydur/Shutterstock.*

Gang Involvement with Human Trafficking

Sex trafficking has traditionally been propagated by small-time local opportunists looking to make a large profit with little work. Today, however, sex trafficking rings run by gangs and other large criminal enterprises are increasingly becoming the norm. Indeed, **human trafficking** is now the world's fastest growing criminal enterprise, second only to drug trafficking and as profitable as the illegal arms trade. One can sell a person for sex many times as compared to drugs or guns which can only be sold once.

Global Centurion has identified over 200 cases of human trafficking in the United States in which gang members have been involved. The Federal Bureau of Investigation (FBI) reports that The Bloods, MS-13, Sureños, and Somali gangs are involved in human trafficking. Due to available technology and social media, street gangs are able to meet the high demand for sex with young girls and women, both luring young girls into commercial sexual exploitation as well as customers. While federal and local law enforcement agencies are aware and monitor these Web sites, it is not sufficient to stop the growing demand and ease of access for sex with young women.[39]

Gun Violence, Generally: Problem-Solving Approaches

More than two decades of gun research and intervention programs have identified strategies that—if implemented properly—can reduce **gun violence** within a given community. Not surprisingly, they follow the SARA problem-solving process. After scanning the problem, gun violence prevention and intervention initiatives involve an analysis for:

- Identifying concentrations of crime or criminal activity.
- Determining what causes these concentrations.

Then, responses are formulated to reduce these concentrations.[40]

Youth and Guns

A teenager in 2015 is more likely to die of a gunshot wound than of all other diseases combined. Youth are not only "invincible," but they often engage in risky behavior that stems from two primary factors: their search for a sense of belonging and identity, and a lack of foresight and understanding of consequences. Youth are also disproportionately represented in the perpetration of violent gun crime. People under age 30 account for 65 percent of weapons arrests, while as many as 10 percent of high school youth have reported carrying weapons.[41]

With guns in easy reach, and a young person dead every one to two hours from gun violence, it is unlikely that the perfect solution to gun violence by youth is easily attainable. So what can police and society do? What works? One strategy may lie in the fact that youth violence follows some very predictable patterns. The prime time for youth violence tends to be between 3 and 8 p.m., when there is significant idle time to be filled with solitary activities or high-risk activities like drug use, gang membership, sexual activity, and violence. The isolation afforded by texting and social media might also carry over to the realm of violence. Latchkey kids, while once a rare phenomenon, are now commonplace, with children living in homes that have been, at the very least, disrupted by single-parent dynamics and economic stress. Getting teens into programs that don't offer unstructured free time, where they can be active with adult supervision and exposed to positive adult role models, may help mind the gap during the high-risk time of day. Funding for neighborhood recreations centers, boys and girls clubs, and other such programs may be a means to impact the violence. As an old saying holds, it is easier and less expensive to build a child than to rebuild a teen who has strayed into high-risk and violent behavior. Youth should not be ending up in graves or prison cells.[42]

Some jurisdictions have also been experimenting with new problem-oriented policing approaches for preventing youth gun violence, using a "pulling levers" strategy (discussed above) and focused deterrence. This approach makes would-be offenders believe that severe consequences would follow gun violence; a key element of the strategy is the delivery of rapid follow-up prosecution when such activities persist. Evaluation research has shown this strategy to be effective in reducing gun violence among serious young offenders.[43]

Exhibit 12–4 describes a pulling-levers effort with youth gang violence in Stockton, California; Exhibit 12–5 explains a national strategy for preventing illegally obtained guns from getting into the hands of urban youth.

Graffiti: What Works

A problem that is related to, and arises from gangs involves **graffiti**—another social harm that is not only unsightly but also depreciates property values, adds to the deterioration of neighborhoods,

---

Exhibit 12–4   Operation Peacekeeper, a Problem-Solving Response in Stockton[44]

Operation Peacekeeper is a problem-oriented policing program that was implemented in 1997 to address gun violence among youth gang members in Stockton, California. The program's goal is to reduce gang involvement among urban youth aged 10 to 18 and decrease gun-related violence among gang-involved youths. It uses detailed information about gang activity to identify problem areas and reduce gang-related violence in the Boston metropolitan area.

To convey a credible, clear message about the consequences of gang violence to youths already involved in or at risk of being involved in gangs, Operation Peacekeeper relies on Youth Outreach Workers to communicate to youths that they have better options for their lives. Youth Outreach Workers are streetwise young men and women trained in community organizing, mentoring, mediation, conflict resolution, and case management. Working in neighborhood settings wherever young people at risk of violence are found—including schools, parks, street corners, and apartment complexes—the Youth Outreach Workers serve as mentors and positive role models for youth. Their role is to make sure youths understand the consequences of violence and that there are positive alternatives to gang membership.

The program uses a community policing and problem-solving paradigm to address specific problem areas and offenders. In particular, it uses the "pulling levers" deterrence strategy, which tackles a specific problematic criminal activity by implementing specialized prevention or intervention techniques. In Stockton, this strategy focused on the issue of gun violence among youth gang members.

Operation Peacekeeper uses outreach workers in collaboration with government and community-based organizations to provide resources for youths to escape a gang lifestyle. The program also depends on the involvement of the community to help influence criminal justice agencies to construct customized solutions.

Exhibit 12-5	Removing Guns from Urban Youth

Faced with a national epidemic of gun violence from the 1980s and continuing throughout most of the 1990s, the federal government launched a new effort called Project Safe Neighborhoods (PSN) to help local authorities address gun crime and get illegally obtained guns off the streets and out of the hands of urban youth. Initially, such projects focused on either reducing the demand for illegally obtained guns or reducing the supply; experience has shown, however, that a single approach is not likely to work. Rather, a sustained program is needed that addresses both demand and supply and includes federal-state-local law enforcement collaboration, community involvement, targeted intervention tactics, and continuous program evaluation.

A variety of strategies were employed in PSN, including: increased federal prosecution; joint federal-local prosecution case screening; directed police patrol; chronic violent offender programs; street level firearms enforcement teams; offender notification meetings; re-entry programs; and firearms supply side interventions. The most common prevention strategies included neighborhood development; education; and school-based prevention programs. Pulling levers strategies were used and involved the promise of federal prosecution, offender notification meetings, warrant service, and street level enforcement.

An evaluation of the effectiveness of this major multiyear, multiagency crime prevention initiative found:

▶ Reduced violent crime overall in PSN cities; reductions were greater in cities with a high-level of federal prosecution.

▶ A decline in gun-related violence in nine PSN cities that were evaluated.[45]

and contributes to economic and urban blight. However, making use of community policing partnerships, the police can have success in abating graffiti, while thus contributing to the economic health of their communities.

Most cities fight graffiti with their paintbrushes by quickly dispatching work crews to put on a fresh coat of paint over tagger or gang scribblings. Some experts, however, advocate photographing and filing graffiti markings because they represent actual communication and can be a valuable source of intelligence. Some cities have enacted ordinances that require property owners to remove graffiti within a specified period of time. Exhibit 12–6 shows an example of an antigraffiti ordinance.

Exhibit 12-6	Example of a Municipal Antigraffiti Ordinance

WHEREAS, property defaced by gang members is an act of vandalism and is against the law; and

WHEREAS, gang graffiti constitutes a public nuisance that causes depreciation of the value of the defaced property and the surrounding property and contributes to the deterioration of the neighborhood and the City in general; and

WHEREAS, depreciation of property values and deterioration of neighborhoods lead to economic blight and an increase in criminal activity and are injurious to the public health, safety, morals, and general welfare,

NOW, THEREFORE, BE IT ORDAINED BY THE CITY COUNCIL OF THE CITY OF LAKEWOOD, COLORADO, THAT:

9.85.060 NOTIFICATION OF NUISANCE. (a) The owner of any property defaced by gang graffiti shall be given written notice to abate the public nuisance on his property by removal within five (5) days after service of the notice. Such notice shall be by personal service to the owner or by posting the notice on the defaced property together with written notice mailed to the owner by first-class mail. The notice to the property owner shall contain:

1. The location of and a description of the violation;
2. A demand that the owner remove or eradicate the gang graffiti from the property within five (5) days after service of the notice;

3. A statement that the owner's failure or refusal to remove or eradicate the gang graffiti may result in abatement by the City;

4. A statement that if the costs of abatement plus the $75 fee for inspection and incidental costs are not paid to the City within 30 days after notice, an additional $75 will be assessed for administrative and other incidental costs.

Source: Adapted from the Antigraffiti Ordinance of Lakewood, Colorado, 0-91-29, Title 9, Article 85, Chapter 9.85.

Police must endeavor to eradicate the graffiti problem in order to diminish the gangs' sense of territory, improve the appearance of neighborhoods, and make a community statement that gang-type activities will not be tolerated. Following are some means for doing so:

- Detect graffiti rapidly and routinely (by monitoring graffiti-prone locations and increasing reporting).
- Remove graffiti rapidly.
- Increase natural observation of graffiti-prone locations through use of police, security personnel, and citizens.
- Conduct publicity campaigns combined with beautification efforts and cleanup days.
- Control access to (and vandal-proof) prone locations, using dark or textured surfaces and special products that are resistant to graffiti and are easy to clean.
- Focus on chronic offenders.[46]

Cyberbullying

Bullying among youth has become a major concern—particularly online or **cyberbullying**, which is at an all-time high and does not appear to be declining.[47] Many people wonder why bullying has become such a problem. One reason that is offered is that the world has simply gotten meaner in general. Certainly, the world in which today's youth live is much meaner and "brutish" than it was a generation ago. There are more school shootings, fights, violence, terroristic threats, and other forms of violence in the world. In fact, it is known that some kids who are bullied often become school shooters. It is also known that the bullies are often habitual, repeat offenders in the criminal justice system after leaving school if they have been on record as bullies in the school system. Another reason is that cyberbullying offers some anonymity and safety in distance. Finally, certain social media apps have allowed youths in high school and middle school to target specific kids and groups they do not like.[48]

While physical bullying remains a major concern (about 1 in 3 students report being bullied during the school year), over half (52 percent) of young people report being cyberbullied. Certain people are more prone to being bullied than others, including people who have weight problems or disabilities, belong to racial or religious minorities, and are LGBTQ or perceived as LGBTQ.[49]

Cyberbullying is generally not a law enforcement issue, typically falling short of the local or state cyberstalking and harassment statutes. However, when it involves a credible threat, repeated communications, or such activities as posting contact information of the victim in a pedophile chat room to provoke sexual attacks on the victim, police must become involved.[50]

What Can Police Do?

When they are contacted about bullying, police must be able to determine quickly if they need to get involved. Stopcyberbullying.org has prepared "A Guide for Law Enforcement,"[51] which serves as a checklist to help in making this decision. Generally, the police must consider the kind of threat (threatening the victim with bodily harm, the frequency of the threats (the communications are increasing or third-parties are joining in), and the nature of the threats (following the victim online, into chat rooms, favorite Web sites, signing the victim up for porn sites and e-mailing lists, breaking in to their accounts online, and posting images of the victim online).

As a rule of thumb, the more repeated the communications are, the greater the threats (or enlarging this to include third-parties); furthermore, the more dangerous the methods, the more likely the legal process needs to be used.

Police should also establish relationships with the major Internet service providers (ISPs) in advance of needing them (because time is critical in many of these cases). Police also need to learn how to track an IP address, preserve evidence, request in a timely manner that ISPs preserve the records (pending a formal subpoena).[52]

School Violence

Our K-12 and postsecondary campuses are no longer bucolic, safe havens for our nation's students. Indeed, since the 1999 school shooting in Columbine, Colorado (where two senior students murdered 12 students and one teacher, and injured 21), there have been at least 262 additional school shootings.[53] Although some groups and politicians claim there has been a school shooting, on average, every week, that would require a broad definition of school shootings that includes shootings inside school buildings or on campus grounds involving attempted or actual suicides, self-defense, accidental discharges, armed robberies, gang fights, shootings resulting from altercations, in addition to actual shooting rampages.[54] No matter how they are counted, school shootings witnessed by teachers, students, and staff members will be very traumatic; they can experience post-traumatic stress disorder, or PTSD, pain, confusion, guilt, shame, a questioning of self-worth, fear, anger, depression, and, sometimes, acute anxiety. They struggle to find a sense of safety.[55]

What Can Police Do?

First, it might be wise to discuss what police should *not* do during school shootings. Given that police presence in schools exploded following the 1999 shooting in Columbine, studies have found that school resource officers who eschew pepper spray and handcuffs, and instead built relationships with students that allowed them to proactively identify and diffuse potentially violent situations, are far more effective at keeping the peace than those officers who always arrested students after an alleged incident. Schools are also recognizing that avoiding overly punitive and police centric school discipline policies will help improve academic achievement and reform the racial disparities that still exist in our public schools.[56]

First, each school should have a safety plan, developed and implemented with police assistance and outlining prevention programs, the role of school police within the school community, and bullying prevention programs. Then, when an act of violence at school appears possible or imminent, police should first perform a threat assessment with school officials to determine risk.[28] Warning signs should include evaluating the student's family dynamics (e.g., the thinking, traditions, beliefs, and behavior patterns within the home), school dynamics (the customs, beliefs, and patterns of behavior that comprise the campus culture), social dynamics (the student's beliefs and attitudes toward drugs, friends, weapons, entertainment, violent video games, and so on), and characteristics/personality (depression, verbal expressions, bizarre actions, thoughts/obsessions, and physical behaviors).[57]

As a final note, much has changed in terms of police response since the school shooting at Columbine High, where on-scene officers followed a "contain and wait" approach, waiting 45 minutes for an elite SWAT team to arrive. Now, in active-shooter situations, police are trained to react swiftly to such situations, to rush toward gunfire and—if necessary—even step over bodies and bleeding victims in order to stop the active shooter before more lives are lost. Such training is grounded on the assumption that a gunman in a mass shooting kills a person every 15 seconds. Since Columbine, police also typically employ what are termed contact teams, where officers from any jurisdiction quickly band together to enter a building in formation and confront the shooter(s), thus shifting the shooters' focus to the officers and away from the indiscriminate killing of innocent persons in the area. Then, special-weapons teams enter to search for any remaining shooters and to rescue any hostages. Another change wrought by Columbine is that special-weapons teams now typically have armed medics and rescue teams trained to remove wounded persons under fire.[58]

NEIGHBORHOOD DISORDER

Definitions, Problems, and Responses

Certainly social and physical disorder in urban neighborhoods can, if left unchecked, lead to serious crime. This is at the heart of the now-famous "broken windows theory," which argues that even minor public incivilities such as drinking in the street, spray-painting graffiti, and breaking windows can result in predatory crime when would-be offenders assume that area residents are indifferent to what happens in their neighborhood. Certainly, visual signs of decay silently but forcefully convey messages about affected neighborhoods. Disorder also changes the calculus of prospective homebuyers, real estate agents, insurance agents, and investors.[59] Obviously the police have a strong interest in using problem-solving tactics to overcome **neighborhood disorder**.

The two examples in Exhibit 12–7 represent how police can effectively monitor problem properties with the goal of preserving quality of life for their citizens. While the two cities' goals were different, both attacked their problem through frequent collaboration with other stakeholders, engaging in problem-solving policing, and building trust with the community.

Exhibit 12–8 shows how another city, Green Bay, Wisconsin, formerly addressed neighborhood disorder on a city-wide scale.

Finally, a recent effort by Reno, Nevada, police should be mentioned. After a neighborhood became a hot spot of crime and violence (including three shootings in one month), a handful

---

Exhibit 12–7   Addressing Problem Properties: Efforts in Two Cities[60]

Problem properties are not only an eyesore; they also drain police resources, create hazardous environments, and lessen the quality of life for neighbors and community residents. Two communities have implemented innovative problem-oriented policing responses to break the cycle of repeated calls for service associated with these properties.

▶ **Drug houses:** Milwaukee used its Community Prosecution Unit (composed of law enforcement officers, city and district attorneys, probation and parole officers, a domestic violence advocate, and nuisance abatement staff) to proactively tackle the problem of drug-related properties rather than simply arresting offenders and prosecuting cases after a crime has been committed. Their mission was to reduce crime, fear, and disorder by using public–private collaborations to target nuisance activities. Police officers are empowered to discover, develop, plan, coordinate, and execute innovate ideas of their own design. One such innovative idea involved officers meeting with a local utility company to shut off an illegal electrical hookup as one tactic to gain access to other drug- and gang-related properties. After developing a strong partnership with the utility company and other municipal agencies, the members of the Community Prosecution Unit have been able to increase greatly the number of nuisance properties they have shut down.

▶ **Fighting foreclosure problems:** Manhattan, Illinois, faced a different type of problem property: the foreclosed home. With larger, nearby towns facing serious foreclosure problems, Manhattan's police department and village administrators decided to take preventive action before their problem grew too large to control. The village created a database, updated weekly, of all properties in the various stages of foreclosure. Using the database as a guide, the Police Department, Code Compliance, Public Works, and Finance developed a four-point approach to tracking and securing foreclosed structures: monitoring and securing the buildings; enforcing city codes; shutting off water service; and placing liens, if necessary, on delinquent accounts. Police officers regularly monitored the vacant houses, checked for signs of vandalism, and conducted outreach to neighbors in adjacent properties through a Neighborhood Watch program. After checking all vacant structures, Manhattan Police found that 27 percent of the area's vacant houses were not locked. They secured the houses and, using their monitoring system, identified additional potential problem properties.

| **Exhibit 12–8** | Green Bay Police Addresses Crime and Disorder[61] |

Green Bay, Wisconsin, is unique in that its police department has a team of officers dedicated specifically to neighborhoods and crime prevention. The city is divided into 10 community policing districts, each with one or two officers assigned to them. Rather than being dispatched to routine calls for service, community officers work on long-term problems in long-term assigned beats (which gives the officers an opportunity to gain familiarity, ownership, and establish relationships with citizens in their neighborhoods). Community officers employ problem-oriented policing strategies, including crime analysis, to identify trends and better understand the patterns and underlying causes of disorder, and then develop responses to solve problems. Some of those responses are described below.

Green Bay PD uses a *nuisance abatement program* to abate problems involving illegal drugs and other nuisance activity that negatively impacts neighborhoods. Given that research shows that many crimes and social disorder are in some way linked to illegal drug activity, community officers work directly with landlords to notify them when drug problems erupt and use city ordinances to cite and evict problem tenants for maintaining a public nuisance. If a landlord is uncooperative, he or she is billed for police services once certain criteria are met.

Where citizens report a rash of *graffiti*, a community officer works to identify and arrest those individuals responsible by working with members of the community.

Working with the city attorney, *criminal gang residences* that house a number of violent gang members committing robberies and home invasions were ordered vacated by a judge. This action involved a partnership of patrol officers, the Gang Task Force, and neighborhood residents to gather the information needed to shut down the problem residence.

Green Bay police also partnered with citizens in a downtown neighborhood to improve their quality of life through a project called "Clean Sweep." This project entailed a systematic approach in dealing with *neighborhood drug houses* that went beyond traditional methods of policing. It focused not only on the underlying causes of social disorder but also included a new strategy of community engagement which kept residents informed, generated citizen tips, and restored peace and order (officers received a crime prevention award for this effort).

Synthetic (K2 or "spice") drugs had become popular and were finding their way into the schools. The city enacted an ordinance banning the substance, and officers soon seized of over $65,000 of K2, which served to greatly reduce the drug's availability to our youth.

GBPD launched a *prescription drug collection program*. Controlled substances such as OxyContin and Hydrocodone are commonly abused and may fall into the wrong hands. Since its inception, GBPD recovered more than 2,000 pounds of such medications, which were then properly destroyed in an environmentally sound manner.

---

of officers composing a Neighborhood Contact Team visited about 45 homes in the area, giving youths high-fives, hugging residents, and providing them information about community resources for combating poverty and crime and learning what residents would like to see more in their area. Residents were informed of the new "my RPDApp," which allows them to report a crime, concern, problem, or complaint; submit feedback; review crime prevention tips, and navigate to police stations, hospitals, and community resources. To be sure, the officers wanted to reassure residents that they can feel safe in their homes, but they also, as one officer put it, "humanized the badge."[62]

Responding to Problems of Abandoned Buildings

At the root of problem solving lays the creation of a safe, attractive environment where criminals know they will be observed and possibly arrested. And while the term "**abandoned buildings**" does not necessarily connote an image of something at the core of neighborhood disorder, problem-solving experience has shown that unoccupied buildings that are in grave disrepair—perhaps boarded up, strewn with trash, and scrawled with graffiti—will quickly lead to crime and disorder (another concept at the heart of the "broken windows" theory).[63]

The first challenge for police is to seek to legally define "abandoned building" as there is no universal definition. Yet, how a city or county defines terms such as "property," "vacant," "building," "abandoned," and "temporarily vacant" will dictate the legal remedies available for abating the problem. Generally, in order to be classified as abandoned, a building must typically be a hazard to the health and welfare of the community; the owner must relinquish his or her rights to the property; and the property must be vacant for a period of time. The time element of the definition is important because property laws also grant owners sufficient time to make needed repairs or to dispose of the property. Simply because someone is not living in the house at the moment does not render it abandoned even if it needs repairs.

Abandoned properties become police problems when they attract crime and disorder. They provide cover, concealment, and opportunities for motivated criminals. As its reputation for being a suitable criminal environment becomes known, the property is used by offenders more frequently, which increases crime and disorder conditions. And, because no one is present to guard it or to regulate behavior, crime and disorderly conduct may escalate.

Abandoned properties thus contribute to a self-perpetuating cycle of blight: tenants and building owners will not rehabilitate the property when fear and crime exist, and the government cannot reduce fear and crime when the neighborhood is beset by abandoned properties. Fear of victimization in areas rife with abandoned buildings leads residents to exercise outdoors less frequently; also, the elderly are particularly fearful when their environment contains vacant buildings. Fires may be set deliberately by property owners facing mortgage problems, youth engaging in mischief, or accidentally by squatters, drug users, homeless who are cooking or keeping warm, or curious unsupervised children playing in the building.[64]

Therefore, for all of the above reasons, it is imperative that police analyze the local problem of abandoned buildings to better understand the factors contributing to them. Once analyzed, possible responses can be considered for addressing the problem and a plan laid out for assessment. Generally, police will want to use three strategies for abandoned properties. First, prevention strategies are aimed at motivating the current owner to maintain the property and remain in the house. Second, management strategies involve appropriate enforcement action: seizing the property, or conveying it to a new owner who can manage it according to the law while working to restore it as a productive tax-generating parcel. Finally, reuse strategies attempt to restore the property by creating a market for it and collecting property taxes.

Summary

This chapter has applied problem-oriented policing to the street, demonstrating how it works with several specific crimes and problems of disorder: drug violations and **youth crimes** (including gangs and graffiti, gun violence, bullying, and **school violence**). Eight exhibits and other examples demonstrated the kinds of methods that the police are adopting to address these problems.

The efficacy of the problem-solving strategy in dealing with these problems was convincingly demonstrated. The police agencies described in this chapter and their peers across the United States are realizing many successes, breaking with tradition and attacking the contributing or underlying problems while empowering neighborhoods to defend themselves against crime and deterioration.

We also emphasized that for each of the problem areas discussed, the success of problem-oriented policing strategies was highly dependent on the police having laid the groundwork—doing the kinds of preparatory work described in earlier chapters and understanding and properly applying the SARA process discussed in Chapter 5.

Key Terms and Concepts

Abandoned buildings	Gun violence	Methamphetamine initiative	School violence
Cyberbullying	HIDTA	Neighborhood disorder	War on drugs
Gang	Human trafficking	Prescription drug use	Youth crime
Graffiti	Marijuana laws	"Pulling levers"	

Items for Review

1. Describe how the nation's war on drugs is changing, particularly with regard to personal and medical marijuana use.
2. Review the kinds of problem-solving strategies that may be employed to address drug problems.
3. Provide an overview of the problems surrounding prescription and synthetic drugs.
4. Explain the general meaning of focused deterrence and "pulling levers" for problem solving.
5. Describe how problem-oriented policing efforts can be directed toward youth crimes, particularly gangs, graffiti, and gun violence.
6. Review the extent and nature of cyberbullying and ways in which the problem may be addressed.
7. Describe the problem of school violence—specifically school shootings—and the kinds of strategies and tactics in use for dealing with them.
8. Explain the definition and problem of neighborhood disorder, to include abandoned buildings, and what the police can do to overcome it.

Learn by Doing

1. You are a deputy chief of police and have been invited to appear at a luncheon meeting of a local civic group concerning how the drug problem appears to be changing nationally. Explain how you would respond. Assume someone in the group asks about the kinds of legal, technical, and policy issues that are at the heart of the marijuana-legalization question. How will you answer?
2. During the same presentation (in scenario #1 above), you are asked to comment on what plans and tactics a police agency should have in place for dealing with a school shooting. How will you reply?
3. Also during your luncheon speech, a guest brings up the fact that youth gun violence appears to be increasing locally and nationally; she wants to know what kinds of initiatives the police can undertake to deal with the problem. How will you respond?

Endnotes

1. Tony Newman, "10 Ways the War on Drugs Changed Forever in 2013," *Salon* (December 17, 2013), http://www.salon.com/2013/12/17/10_ways_the_war_on_drugs_changed_forever_in_2013_partner/.
2. "The Drug War, Mass Incarceration and Race," *Drug Policy Alliance Fact Sheet* (January 2015), http://www.drugpolicy.org/sites/default/files/DPA_Fact_Sheet_Drug_War_Mass_Incarceration_and_Race_Jan2015.pdf.
3. U.S. Department of Justice, Drug Enforcement Administration, *National Drug Threat Assessment Summary 2014* (Washington, D.C.: Author, November 2014), p. 25.
4. Micah Cohen, "Marijuana Legalization and States Rights," *New York Times* (December 8, 2012), http://fivethirtyeight.blogs.nytimes.com/2012/12/08/marijuana-legalization-and-states-rights/?pagewanted=print.
5. BalancedPolitics.org, "Should Marijuana Be Legalized Under Any Circumstances?" (August 6, 2011), http://www.balanced-politics.org/marijuana_legalization.htm.
6. See Drug Enforcement Administration, "Title 21 CFR, Part 1300–1399," http://www.deadiversion.usdoj.gov/21cfr/cfr/index.html.
7. "Medical Marijuana: Research, Not Fear," *Los Angeles Times* (July 13, 2011), http://articles.latimes.com/2011/jul/13/opinion/la-ed-marijuana-20110713.
8. Lizette Borelli, "Uruguay to Legalize Marijuana for Entire Country: Will the Bill Save Money and Lives?" *Medical Daily* (August 13, 2013), http://www.medicaldaily.com/uruguay-legalize-marijuana-entire-country-will-bill-save-money-and-lives-248250.
9. Natalie Dalton, "Marijuana Should Be Legalized Worldwide: Santos," *Colombia Reports* (October 25, 2011), http://colombiareports.com/marijuana-should-be-globally-legalized-santos/.
10. "Czech Republic Legalizes Medical Marijuana Use," *The Huffington Post* (February 15, 2013), http://www.huffingtonpost.com/2013/02/15/czech-republic-medical-marijuana_n_2693657.html.
11. Arthur Brice, "Argentina Court Ruling Would Allow Personal Use of Pot," *CNN.com/World* (August 25, 2009), http://www.cnn.com/2009/WORLD/americas/08/25/argentina.drug.decriminalization/.
12. *Washington Post*, "Time to Legalize Marijuana in Mexico City" (editorial appearing in TicoTimes.net, July 27, 2013), http://www.ticotimes.net/More-news/News-Briefs/Time-to-legalize-marijuana-in-Mexico-City_Sunday-July-28-2013.
13. Pew Research Center, "6 Facts about Marijuana" (April 14, 2015), http://www.pewresearch.org/fact-tank/2015/04/14/6-facts-about-marijuana/.
14. Rob Reuteman, "The Cost-and-Benefit Arguments Around Enforcement," *CNBC* (April 20, 2010), http://www.cnbc.com/id/36600923.
15. Drug Enforcement Administration, *National Drug Threat Assessment Summary 2014*, p. 23.
16. Massimo Calabresi, "The Price of Relief," *Time* (June 15, 2015), pp. 25–33.
17. Drug Enforcement Administration, *National Drug Threat Assessment Summary 2014*, p. 4.
18. Calabresi, "The Price of Relief," p. 33.
19. Drug Enforcement Administration, *National Drug Threat Assessment Summary 2014*, p. 7.
20. Ibid., p. 19.
21. Ibid., p. 16.
22. Drugs.com, "Naloxone," http://www.drugs.com/naloxone.html.

23. Drug Enforcement Administration, *National Drug Threat Assessment Summary 2014*, p. 17.

24. Office of National Drug Control Policy, "Synthetic Drugs," https://www.whitehouse.gov/ondcp/ondcp-fact-sheets/synthetic-drugs-k2-spice-bath-salts.

25. Ibid.

26. Bureau of Justice Assistance, Smart Policing Initiative, "The Effects of 'Pulling Levers' Strategies on Crime," http://www.smartpolicinginitiative.com/library-and-multimedia-resources/crime/effects-pulling-levers-strategies-crime.

27. Adapted from National Institute of Justice, CrimeSOLUTIONS.GOV, "Rockford Pulling Levers Drug Market Intervention," http://www.crimesolutions.gov/ProgramDetails.aspx?ID=400.

28. Drug Enforcement Administration, "High Intensity Drug Trafficking Areas (HIDTA)," http://www.dea.gov/ops/hidta.shtml.

29. Federal Bureau of Investigation, Uniform Crime Reports, *Crime in the United States 2014*, "Arrests," Table 41, https://www.fbi.gov/about-us/cjis/ucr/crime-in-the-u.s/2014/crime-in-the-u.s.-2014/tables/table-41.

30. Office of Juvenile Justice and Delinquency Prevention, *Statistical Briefing Book* (December 9, 2014), http://www.ojjdp.gov/ojstatbb/crime/JAR_Display.asp?ID=qa05200.

31. David W. Roush, *A Desktop Guide to Good Juvenile Detention Practice* (Washington, D.C.: Office of Juvenile Justice and Delinquency Prevention, 1996), pp. 26–27.

32. For a full description of the standards of treatment for juveniles under the Convention on the Rights of the Child, see United Nations, http://www.ohchr.org/en/professionalinterest/pages/crc.aspx.

33. U.S. Department of Justice, Office of Juvenile Justice and Delinquency Prevention, *Youth Gangs* (December 1997), p. 1, https://www.ncjrs.gov/pdffiles/fs-9772.pdf.

34. National Gang Center, "Frequently Asked Questions About Gangs," http://www.nationalgangcenter.gov/About/FAQ#q1.

35. See U.S. Department of Justice, Office of Juvenile Justice and Delinquency Prevention, *NGC Newsletter* (Winter 2013), p. 1, https://www.nationalgangcenter.gov/Content/Newsletters/NGC-Newsletter-2013-Winter.pdf.

36. Catherine H. Conly, Patricia Kelly, Paul Mahanna, and Lynn Warner, Lynn, *Street Gangs: Current Knowledge and Strategies* (Washington, D.C.: U.S. Department of Justice, National Institute of Justice, 1993).

37. See Homeboy Industries, http://www.homeboyindustries.org/; also see Homeboy Industries, http://www.homeboyindustries.org/what-we-do/.

38. Office of Juvenile Justice and Delinquency Prevention, *Statistical Briefing Book*.

39. Michelle Lillie, "Gang Involvement with Human Trafficking" (November 18, 2013), http://humantraffickingsearch.net/wp/gang-involvement-with-human-trafficking/.

40. National Institute of Justice, "Problem Solving to Reduce Gun Violence," http://www.nij.gov/topics/crime/gun-violence/prevention/pages/problem-solving.aspx.

41. Elaine Cox, "Ending the Epidemic of Youth Gun Violence,", U.S. News & World Report, (October 19, 2015), http://health.usnews.com/health-news/patient-advice/articles/2015/10/19/ending-the-epidemic-of-youth-gun-violence.

42. Ibid.

43. Anthony Braga, "Responses to the Problem of Gun Violence Among Serious Young Offenders," Center for Problem-Oriented Policing, 2012, http://www.popcenter.org/problems/gun_violence/3.

44. Adapted from National Institute of Justice, CrimeSOLUTIONS.GOV, http://www.crimesolutions.gov/ProgramDetails.aspx?ID=51

45. National Institute of Justice, "Project Safe Neighborhoods: Gun Violence Programs: Project Safe Neighborhoods," http://www.nij.gov/topics/crime/gun-violence/prevention/pages/project-safe-neighborhoods.aspx; also see David Sheppard, Heath Grant, Wendy Rowe, and Nancy Jacobs, Fighting Juvenile Gun Violence (Washington, D.C.: U.S. Department of Justice, Office of Juvenile Justice and Delinquency Prevention, September 2000), pp. 10–11, https://www.ncjrs.gov/pdffiles1/ojjdp/182679.pdf.

46. Deborah Lamm Weisel, *Graffiti* (Washington, D.C.: U.S. Department of Justice, Office of Community Oriented Policing Services, 2002).

47. Nobullying.com, "Why Is Cyber Bullying a Problem?" (August 27, 2014), http://nobullying.com/why-is-cyber-bullying-a-problem-and-how-to-stop-it/.

48. Nobullying.com, "The Complicated Web of Teen Lives: 2015 Bullying Report" (September 10, 2015), http://nobullying.com/the-complicated-web-of-teen-lives-2015-bullying-report/#_Toc412550278.

49. National Bullying Protection Center, "Bullying Statistics," http://www.pacer.org/bullying/about/media-kit/stats.asp.

50. Stop cyberbullying, "What's Law Enforcement Supposed to Do?" http://stopcyberbullying.org/whats_the_law/law_enforcement_purpose.html.

51. Stopcyberbullying.org, "A Guide for Law Enforcement," http://www.stopcyberbullying.org/lawenforcement/telling_the_difference.html.

52. Ibid.

53. Michael Roberts, "Columbine to Oregon's Umpqua College: Tragic List of School Shootings Since '99," *Westword* (October 6, 2015), http://www.westword.com/news/columbine-to-oregons-umpqua-college-tragic-list-of-school-shootings-since-99-5844141.

54. Michelle Yee He Lee, "Has There Been One School Shooting per Week since Sandy Hook?" *The Washington Post* (June 29, 2015), https://www.washingtonpost.com/news/fact-checker/wp/2015/06/29/has-there-been-one-school-shooting-per-week-since-sandy-hook/.

55. Edward Mooney, Jr., "After School Violence, Traumatized Teachers Need Help," *CNN* (November 22, 2013), http://www.cnn.com/2013/10/23/opinion/mooney-teacher-shooting/.

56. Sheila A. Bedi, "We Can't Arrest Our Way to Safer Schools," *U.S. News & World Report* (December 14, 2013), http://www.usnews.com/opinion/articles/2013/12/14/one-year-after-newtown-adding-more-cops-doesnt-prevent-school-shootings.

57. Brandi Booth, Vincent B. Van Hasselt, and Gregory M. Vecchi, "Addressing School Violence," *FBI Law Enforcement Bulletin* (May 2011), https://leb.fbi.gov/2011/may/addressing-school-violence.

58. "Shoot First: Columbine Tragedy Transformed Police Tactics," *USA Today* (April 19, 2009), http://usatoday30.

usatoday.com/news/nation/2009-04-19-columbine-police-tactics_N.htm.

59. U.S. Department of Justice, National Institute of Justice, *Disorder in Urban Neighborhoods* (February 2001), p. 40.

60. Adapted from Zoe Mentel, "Shutting the Door on Foreclosure and Drug-Related Problem Properties: Two Communities Respond to Neighborhood Disorder," *Community Policing Dispatch* 2(7) (July 2009), http://cops.usdoj.gov/html/dispatch/July_2009/communities_respond.htm.

61. Adapted from Green Bay Police Department, "Neighborhood Policing," http://www.gbpolice.org/?page_id=93.

62. Jenny Kane, "Shootings Prompt Friendly House Visits from Police," *Reno Gazette Journal* (January 1, 2016), p. 1A.

63. Jon M. Shane, *Abandoned Buildings and Lots* (Washington, D.C.: Office of Community Oriented Policing Services, July 2012), pp. 6–8.

64. Ibid., pp. 8–12.

Addressing Offenders and Victims:
Mental Illness, Domestic Violence, Cyber Criminals, and Human Trafficking

LEARNING OBJECTIVES

As a result of reading this chapter, the student will understand:

- The definition of, and problems relating to, mental illness, and the kinds of approaches police can take to deal with them

- The problem of domestic violence, and various methods for addressing it

- The nature of cybercrime/identity theft, and what police can attempt to do to diminish related victimization

- The nature and extent of human trafficking, and the kinds of responses and legislation that have evolved to help to combat it and to assist victims

TEST YOUR KNOWLEDGE

1. Because of the myriad of care facilities provided for them, police officers rarely encounter mentally ill persons on the street.

2. Two long-standing policies for officers responding to domestic violence calls include sending at least two officers to the scene and separating the parties so each can speak candidly.

3. About half of American adults have their personal information stolen by hackers each year, primarily through data breaches at large companies.

4. Nearly all (about 90 percent) of identity theft victims report the incident to police.

5. Of the estimated 2.4 million people in the world who are victims of human trafficking, very few of them are exploited as sexual slaves; most are in forced-labor situations.

Answers can be found on page 278.

> *The human story does not always unfold like a mathematical calculation on the principle that two and two make four. Sometimes in life they make five or minus three; and sometimes the blackboard topples down in the middle of the sum and leaves the class in disorder.*
> —WINSTON CHURCHILL

INTRODUCTION

The four major crime problems that were addressed in Chapter 12 in relation to community-oriented policing and problem solving—those involving drugs, gangs, youth crimes, and **neighborhood disorder**—can and do plague many Americans in their communities. However, millions of Americans are also affected each year by the issues and problems that are discussed in this chapter. In that sense, these are in no way lesser problems for those persons who are personally involved with or are being victimized by these situations.

We consider the following crimes and social problems: mental illness, domestic violence, cybercrime, and human trafficking. As in Chapter 12, emphasis will be placed on the kinds of problem-solving responses that have been developed by police for dealing with them. Examples of such responses are provided in seven exhibits, disseminated throughout the chapter. The chapter concludes with key terms and concepts as well as review items sections, and some "Learn by Doing" scenarios where you can apply your knowledge to chapter materials.

COPING WITH THE MENTALLY ILL POPULATION

When the Problem Becomes Lethal

- Aaron Alexis entered Building 197 of the Washington Navy Yard in September 2013, carrying a backpack containing a disassembled shotgun and ammunition and a plan to kill multiple people. In less than 90 minutes, Alexis had shot and killed twelve and injured three. A disturbing question entered the nation's collective mind—was Alexis mentally ill and could police or medical professionals have stopped him? During Alexis' four years in the U.S. Navy, he was cited eight times for misconduct and arrested three times for mischief and disorderly conduct, with two of his arrests stemming from shooting-related incidents. Later, Alexis reported hearing voices and believed low frequency electromagnetic waves were controlling him. He twice sought help at hospital emergency rooms for insomnia and after reporting to health professionals that he was not in danger of harming anyone, he was prescribed antidepressants. To most mental health and law enforcement professionals, these symptoms—voices, delusions, and attention-seeking behaviors—are all hallmarks of potentially serious **mental illness**, such as schizophrenia, paranoia, or schizoaffective disorder.[1]
- In September of 2012, when Mohamad Bah's mother became concerned about his erratic behavior as he holed up in his apartment, she called 911 and asked for help for her mentally ill son. New to the country, she expected medical professionals to arrive, but instead New York Police Department officers responded. When Bah opened the door to officers, he was naked and holding a knife. Officers pulled the door shut and called for an emergency services unit (ESU) because Bah was apparently "emotionally disturbed." When Bah refused to open the door to ESU officers, the team forced its way in and Bah lunged at them with the knife. Officers deployed an electronic control device and shot him with a rubber bullet, but Bah continued to come at them, eventually stabbing

America's jails and prisons have been termed the "new asylums" because they house more mentally ill persons than any psychiatric hospital in the country.
Photographee.eu/Shutterstock.

two officers. Police then fatally shot Bah—and later unleashed considerable criticism against the NYPD for not having an effective training program for officers to deal with the mentally ill.[2]

And so begins the criminal justice system's role as the primary mental health system in this country. These brain diseases bring the mentally ill into increasing contact with the police and the criminal justice system, which has become the nation's de facto mental health system. But being mentally ill is not a crime, and the rule of law and due process means that we cannot prosecute persons for mere status or for behaving oddly unless they are indeed breaking the criminal law.

Consider these questions: at what point should police officers and other criminal justice professionals see trouble brewing, and what legal tools are available to them to help the mentally ill? Why was someone like Alexis able to buy the gun he used to commit this mass shooting? And what happens to mentally ill offenders if they are processed in the system?

Front-End, Back-End Issues

At the front end of the problem, an estimated 20 to 40 percent of police calls for service involve a mentally ill person,[3] while an estimated 7 percent of police contacts in jurisdictions with 100,000 or more people involve the mentally ill. One survey found that about 9 in 10 (92 percent) of patrol officers have at least one encounter with a mentally ill person in crisis each month, and officers average about six such encounters per month.[4] On the back end, America's jails and prisons have been termed by the Treatment Advocacy Center[5] as the "new asylums" because they house more mentally ill persons than any psychiatric hospital in the country. Researchers have found that more than half the inmates in jails and state prisons are mentally ill, particularly with depressive disorder, schizophrenia, and bipolar disorder.[6]

What Can Police Do? The Success of CIT

The deinstitutionalization of mental health centers began to occur in the latter half of the 20th century—what has been termed a "psychiatric Titanic"[7]—and left police officers with few options or resources when dealing with individuals struggling with mental disorders. [This movement was justified for the most part, however; previously, when dispatched to homes to deal with mentally ill individuals, officers could in effect unilaterally elect to remove them from their homes and put them in jail, from which they might be committed to a mental health facility.] Many of these persons who were prevented from entering the nation's public psychiatric hospitals were severely mentally ill and found themselves living on the streets or in shelters. Fewer locations existed where law enforcement personnel could take these persons for treatment, and, due to funding restrictions, the individuals were expected to pay for their own mental health care. Often, they could not afford or simply did not have medical insurance. Police officers thus became first responders and the criminal justice system became America's mental health system.[8]

However, there are solutions and responses available to the police. Perhaps the best-known response is a result of a Memphis, Tennessee, police officer's response to a call in 1988 involving a man wielding a knife.[9] The man would not comply with the officer's demands to disarm, and the officer had to resort to deadly force. The man suffered from schizophrenia and likely could not separate fact from fiction when dealing with the officer. This incident led to reforms and what is now known as the "Memphis Model"—a program to train officers to deal with mentally ill individuals.

Another result was the creation of **Crisis Intervention Training/Teams** (CIT), where officers learn to approach mentally ill suspects differently, using body language and voice commands to de-escalate situations and to ease emotionally disturbed persons into compliance and safety. Officers are also trained to know the various diversionary options in their jurisdiction—where to admit such people into mental health/medical facilities rather than taking them to jail. CIT training is critical for the modern officer. But to date, only about 2,700 agencies nationwide use the program, although advocates call for such programs to be standard police training everywhere (see Exhibit 13–1).[10]

Group therapy cages for inmates at Mule Creek State Prison in Ione, California.
U.S. District Court.

Exhibit 13–1   A CIT Example in Virginia

The Roanoke, Virginia, County Police Department, one of the first to implement CIT training in Southwestern Virginia, provides an example of how a CIT program may be structured. First, roughly half of their 140 police officers are certified in CIT methods. There always is at least one CIT-trained officer available during each shift. Police recruits receive various CIT training blocks throughout their academy instruction, although this training does not meet all standards necessary for certification. The department also participates in an annual, weeklong CIT training course, hearing from speakers and professionals from mental health arenas who offer seminars to police officers. The training also includes on-site visits to local rehabilitation centers and hospitals. Officers participate in role-playing scenarios and other hands-on training.

When working with persons having mental disorders, the department uses a three-prong test to ascertain (1) whether individuals pose a danger to themselves, (2) if a person endangers others, or (3) whether individuals cannot care for themselves. If a person meets any of these criteria, the officer will take the individual into emergency custody as provided in state statute. The person then will be transported to an emergency medical facility where an emergency outreach service worker further evaluates the individual. After the evaluation, if the EOS worker deems the individual to be at risk or a threat, a temporary detention order may be placed on the person, and the individual will be held in a mental health facility pending further evaluation.[11]

Note: The Seattle, Washington, Police Department Web site provides a short video of police partnering with mental health experts at http://www.seattle.gov/police/work/cit.htm.

Some researchers believe that programs like CIT are difficult for organizations to fully adopt because they involve making large scale changes to almost every facet of police operations—from training and scheduling to dispatch and patrol as well as forging partnerships with the mental health community. In the current landscape of CIT, one organization can make changes to their training requirements while another can make systemic changes to all standard operating procedures and both agencies can purport to practice the program. These differences make it difficult to measure the effectiveness of CIT as whole.[12]

Following are several strategies for police that are essential for providing a foundation for problem reduction:

- *Work with the mental health community.* Mental health professionals can be viable partners with the police. They can provide training and direct assistance during

Exhibit 13–2	Repeat Calls in North Carolina

In Charlotte, North Carolina, police were called to a single residential address over 100 times in regard to trash, property in disrepair, and threats to neighbors. An unmarried couple lived at the residence, and when police targeted the situation, they learned that the woman suffered from mental illness and that she had completely intimidated her common-law husband while also terrorizing the neighborhood. Police identified relatives of the man and gained their assistance once a long-term involuntary commitment for the woman was obtained. The house and property were then completely cleaned up. The man chose to remain at the residence. Once the woman was released from inpatient care, she moved to a different residence and started working. During the follow-up period, both people were reported as doing well, and the police department received no further calls.[14]

emergencies as well as inpatient and outpatient services for people with mental illness and operate emergency facilities.

- *Work with emergency hospitals.* Emergency hospitals (whether general hospitals or specialized psychiatric hospitals) to which police may take people in crisis are important elements of the mental health system. Police agencies should meet with hospital staff periodically to clarify expectations, develop workable protocols, and address problems and issues.
- *Appoint police liaison officers.* Officers can liaise with the entire mental health community, including sitting on appropriate boards and committees. In addition, departments can appoint liaison officers for each mental health facility (hospital, shelter, group home, etc.) in the jurisdiction for problem-solving location-specific issues to reduce and prevent crimes, disorder, and calls for service at current and potential hot spots.
- *Train generalist police officers.* Officers must know how to handle incidents involving people with mental illness. Proper training typically integrates lecture, discussion, tours of mental health facilities, and role-playing. Several recent studies have found improvements in both attitudes and knowledge about mental illness as well as improvements in officers' confidence in identifying and responding to persons with mental illness. Thus, evidence to date suggests that CIT training improves officer knowledge, attitudes, and confidence, at least in the short term.
- *Use less-lethal weapons.* Maintaining a calm demeanor, using good oral and nonverbal communication, and using proper tactics are far better alternatives, when possible, than deadly force.
- *Target repeat criminals, locations, and hotspots.* It is widely recognized that a relatively small proportion of offenders and locations are responsible for a relatively large proportion of offenses, so attention should be focused on them (Exhibit 13–2 describes such a situation in Charlotte, North Carolina).[13]

DOMESTIC VIOLENCE

Dangers and Approaches

As with their dealings with mentally ill persons, police responses to **domestic violence** has undergone fundamental changes over the last 30 years. In the past, a police officer had virtually limitless authority to arrest one, both, or neither of the parties involved in domestic violence (even when one or both of them has been severely injured). Still, much work remains to be done, because domestic violence too often remains the "hidden crime," committed behind closed doors, and thus does not receive the same level of focus as crimes that are committed in public. It can also become a violent incident; a survey of police agencies by the Police Executive Research Forum (PERF) found that 14 percent of all homicides involve domestic violence, and about one-fourth of all aggravated assaults involved domestic violence.[15]

Nearly all (95 percent) of the agencies surveyed had a specific policy regarding officers' response to incidents of domestic violence. Common practices discussed in the policies include:

- *Approach carefully:* First responders are to observe and listen before announcing their presence, in order to protect themselves and gather information. Many agencies also require that at least two officers be sent to any domestic violence call.

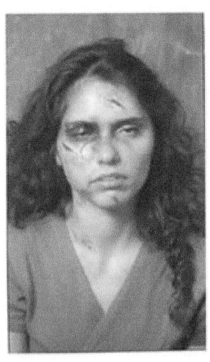

He says it won't happen again

Domestic violence is not rare; furthermore, it occurs at all social, economic, and cultural levels of society.
Knox County Sherffi's Office.

- *Separate the parties:* Many agencies have officers separate the parties at domestic dispute calls and interview them separately, so each can speak candidly without being overheard.
- Some departments require that photographs of the victim be taken.
- *Collect evidence:* Photographs of victims' injuries, the crime scene, weapons recovered, witness statements, medical records, and/or audio/video recordings of statements.
- *Obtain protection orders:* Most agencies assist victims who desire emergency orders of protection; about 9 in 10 agencies provide victims with information on how to obtain an order; 44 percent assist victims in filling out paperwork for an order; and 29 percent accompany victims to court to obtain an order.
- *Perform lethality assessments:* Forty-two percent of agencies use lethality assessments to determine the level of danger to the victim. These tools consist of questions to indicate whether the victim is at high risk, such as whether the offender's violence has increased in frequency or severity, has a criminal record or a history of drug or alcohol abuse, has violated a restraining order, has made threats of homicide or suicide, has access to firearms, and so on.
- *Do domestic violence crime analysis:* High percentages of agencies document domestic violence incidents by location and by perpetrator.
- *Have protocols for protecting children:* About half of police agencies have special follow-up protocols for cases in which children are present. Many such agencies require that local child protective services agency be contacted, and some can file child abuse charges or increase the penalties for domestic abuse if a child witnesses domestic violence.[16]

Exhibit 13–3 describes a legal conundrum that arose out of a domestic violence case in Colorado. After reading the facts, respond to the questions posed.

Exhibit 13–3 | Legal Aspects of DV

What, if any, legal obligation is held by the police to protect someone from their estranged spouse who has been served with a legal restraining order? That question was at the crux of a lawsuit from Castle Rock, Colorado, which was ultimately heard by the United States Supreme Court. Jessica Gonzales' restraining order required her husband to remain at least 100 yards from her and their three daughters except during specified visitation times. One evening the husband took possession of the three children in violation of the order; Mrs. Gonzalez repeatedly urged the police to search for and arrest her husband, but they took no immediate action (due to Jessica's allowing her husband to take the children at various hours). At approximately 3:20 AM, the husband appeared at the city police station and instigated a shoot-out with the police (he died). A search of his vehicle revealed the corpses of the three daughters, whom the husband had killed. U.S. cities are generally immune from lawsuits, so in this case the Supreme Court was asked to decide whether Jessica Gonzales could sue the city because of inaction by its police officers.

1. Were the police *morally* responsible for the deaths of the three girls?
2. Were the police *legally* responsible for their deaths?
3. If you believe Jessica should be allowed to sue the city, and the police were liable, how much financial compensation should Jessica receive?

See the corresponding note at chapter's end for the outcome and whether or not the city was deemed to be liable for its police department's actions.[17]

The Family Justice Center Concept

The San Diego Family Justice Center (SDFJC) was created in 2002, and by 2003 had become a national model; in fact, that same year President George W. Bush created the President's Family Justice Center Initiative with the goal of instituting Family Justice Centers across the nation. All necessary services are located at the SDFJC, which is staffed with eight detectives, 12 attorneys, 23 sheriff's deputies, and 8 victim advocates who collaborate and share information. Exhibit 13–4 discusses SDFJC in more detail.

Exhibit 13–4	The San Diego Family Justice Center

The San Diego Family Justice Center (SDFJC) provides help and hope to victims of family violence and their children.
San Diego Family Justice Center.

SDFJC was the first of its kind in the United States and provides help and hope to victims of family violence and their children. Every day, those impacted by family violence, child abuse, and elder abuse, find safety, protection from their abuser, legal help, counseling, food, clothing, spiritual support, medical assistance, and so many other free services from the Center's professionals and volunteers. Its mission is to stop family violence, make victims safer, hold batterers accountable, and provide long-term support for victims and children through collaboration and coordinated services.

The SDFJS is a "one-stop" help center that provides the majority of services needed by victims of family violence. Under one roof, 25 agencies have come together to provide medical, legal, and social services to victims of domestic violence, elder abuse, and child abuse. Since opening, the SDFJS has effectively engaged law enforcement, prosecutors, medical professionals, clergy, social service workers, volunteers, hospitals, and shelters to provide comprehensive services to approximately 23,000 victims of family violence and their children.[18]

According to INTERPOL, cybercrime is one of the fastest growing areas of crime and includes attacks against computer hardware and software, financial crimes and corruption, and abuse.
Shutterstock.

CYBERCRIME

Not Only in Film: Extent of Victimization

Cybercrime is not something that is only found in fiction—such as the movies "Hackers," "War Games," "The Net," "Firewall," and "Untraceable". There are an estimated 1.5 million annual cyberattacks (4,000 per day, 170 per hour); so online crime is a real threat to anyone on the Internet. It is also estimated that businesses are attacked an average of about 17,000 times per year.[19] Of course, governments make tempting targets for cyber criminals as well.

About half of American adults have their personal information stolen by hackers each year, primarily through data breaches at large companies. That amounts to about $18 billion in credit card fraud for the year.[20] And although it is difficult to measure the financial costs of cybercrime, one antivirus protection firm estimates that the annual global cost of such crime could be over $400 billion.[21]

Types, Tactics, and Training

Cybercrime occurs in many forms—online identity theft, financial fraud, stalking, bullying, hacking, e-mail spoofing, information piracy and forgery, intellectual property crime, and even romantic enticements (see Exhibit 13–5). In this section, we will focus on some examples of cybercrime and police training for responding to it, and discuss in more detail the problem of identity theft (Exhibit 13–5).

Exhibit 13–5	A Cautionary Tale: The Cyber Criminal at Work

A 29-year-old Michigan man was sentenced to five years in federal prison for interstate stalking in a case of online romance. Brian Hile traveled to San Diego from Michigan intending to kill a woman and her boyfriend after the pair had unwittingly gotten caught up in Hile's virtual love affair. Hile had been ensnared in a "catfishing" scheme, where a person uses social media to pretend to be someone they are not, typically to engage in misleading online romances. During one Internet-only relationship lasting two years, Hile exchanged explicit photos and romantic communications with someone he believed to be a woman. When he learned that "she" was actually a man living in South Africa, Hile became enraged and vowed to find the man who deceived him as well as the woman whose images played a role in the deception.[22]

Hile's primary target for revenge was the man who duped him, but South Africa was too far away so instead he went after the woman. Even though he knew she had nothing to do with the actual romance scam, he assumed that because her photos were used, she was somehow responsible for what had happened to him. Determined to learn the woman's identity,

Hile conducted an extensive online search and used hacking tools. Eventually, he was able to hack into her e-mail account and compile detailed personal information about her and her live-in boyfriend as well as their extended family and friends. Armed with her address, Hile traveled from Michigan to San Diego to exact his revenge. Fortunately, his family sensed that he was planning something and alerted police, which led to his detention in San Diego. At the time of his arrest, he was in possession of the woman's address, telephone numbers, and even information concerning favorite restaurants. He also had duct tape, zip ties, and a to-do list that included obtaining a knife and chloroform. Had he gotten to her residence, he would likely have hurt or killed the woman. Hile was convicted in August 2013.[23]

Parlez-Vous Cyber-Speak?

How well do you know the language of e-crime? Try matching the terms on the left with the definitions on the right, then check the answers to see how well you did.

From Parlez-vous Cyber-speak?" *TechBeat* (National Institute of Justice), Winter 2004, p. 2, https://www.justnet. org/pdf/CyberCopsWint04.pdf.

Terms	Definitions
1. Steganography	a. A unique string of numbers that identifies a computer or device on the Internet.
2. Firewall	b. A malicious program that masquerades as a benevolent one.
3. Trojan Horse	c. A type of network in which individual users connect to each other directly, without a centralized server. Can be used to share files (legal or illegal) easily among individuals.
4. IDS (Intrusion Detection System)	
5. Network Sensor	d. The art of hiding data or pictures within a file or files.
6. Peer-to-Peer (P2P) Network	e. The act of capturing packets of data flowing across a computer network.
7. Information Assurance	f. An attack that seeks to slow or disable a network by overwhelming it with useless traffic.
8. Cybersecurity	g. The protection of data and systems in networks connected to the World Wide Web.
9. IP Address	h. A system that scans areas within a computer or network for possible security breaches.
10. E-mail Spoofing	i. The act of deceiving people into divulging information that allows access to computers and network infrastructure.
11. Denial of Service (DoS)	j. The protection of information systems to ensure their integrity.
12. Social Engineering	k. A set of related programs that protect a private network from users based outside the network.
13. Packet Sniffing	l. A program that monitors or "sniffs" a system for problems.
	m. The act of forging the header information on an e-mail so that it appears to have originated from somewhere other than its true source.

Answers: 1. d; 2. k; 3. b; 4. h; 5. l; 6. c; 7. j; 8. g; 9. a; 10. m; 11. f; 12. i; 13. e.

A number of major initiatives have been launched for combating cybercrime. One of the most ambitious is the New York **Electronic Crimes Task Force** (NYECTF), which is actually a partnership between the U.S. Secret Service and a host of other public safety agencies and private corporations to fight electronic crime. NYECTF was formed in January 1995, originally as a small squad of Secret Service agents primarily involved with telecommunications fraud. But as technologies improved and criminals found more sophisticated ways to abuse those technologies, it became necessary for law enforcement to do likewise.[24]

Today Electronic Crimes Task Forces (ECTFs) exist in 28 states, in the District of Columbia, and in London and Rome; they work with INTERPOL and private concerns such as Verizon in its data breach investigations, and share a common purpose: the prevention, detection, mitigation, and aggressive investigation of attacks on the nation's financial and critical infrastructures. Specifically, they investigate information technology-related crimes, including credit card theft, attacks on the banking and finance infrastructure, and identity fraud. They provide support and resources for field investigators who are engaged in criminal enterprises that have significant economic or community impact; involve organized criminal groups, multiple districts, or transnational organizations; and use new schemes or technology.[25]

Some criminal statutes fall under Secret Service jurisdiction, for example Title 18 U.S. Code, Sections 1028–1030, were written specifically to address crimes involving information technology. Title 18 U.S. Codes 1028, 1029, and 1030 cover identity fraud, device access fraud, and computer fraud. The mission has evolved to keep pace with the way society has changed and the way it uses technology. In a given year, the Secret Service will arrest more than 1,000 individuals for cybercrime violations that, in total, are responsible for nearly $250 million in fraud losses. Since 2010, the service has arrested more than 4,900 cybercriminals. Recent cases include the recent Target department store database breach and theft of about 40 million credit and debit card records and 70 million additional records with customer information, including addresses and telephone numbers.[26]

Since the information technology revolution began, law enforcement has faced the growing problem of cybercrime. But a lack of resources and trained personnel has found many agencies unable to keep abreast of investigative techniques and technologies required to combat cybercrime. Along with trained personnel to investigate such traditional crimes as murder, arson, theft, and assault, law enforcement needs "cyber cops" to fight electronic crime. To meet this growing need, the CyberScience Laboratory (CSL) at the National Institute of Justice's National Law Enforcement and Corrections Technology Center and its e-Crime Intern Program in Rome, New York, provide college and high school students with a unique opportunity to gain knowledge and hands-on experience in the field of cyberscience in the law enforcement community. This program is a joint venture between academia and both the public and private sectors in an effort to train students in cyberscience developments.[27]

DHS Involvement

In addition to the U.S. Secret Service, the Department of Homeland Security (DHS) also works with U.S. Immigration and Customs Enforcement (ICE) Homeland Security Investigations Cyber Crimes Center, which delivers computer-based technical services to support domestic and international investigations into cross-border crime. Also within DHS is the Law Enforcement Cyber Incident Reporting resource, which provides information for state, local, tribal, and territorial law enforcement on when, what, and how to report a cyber incident to a federal entity.[28]

Identify Theft: Nature and Victim/Police Responses

Identity (ID) theft is a crime where a thief steals one's personal information, such as his or her full name or social security number, to commit fraud. The ID thief can use this information to fraudulently apply for credit, file taxes, or get medical services. These acts can damage one's credit status and cost considerable amounts of time and money to restore their good name. Worse yet, one may not know that he or she is a victim of **identity theft** until encountering mystery bills, credit collections, denied loans, and so on.[29]

It is estimated that 17.6 million persons ages 16 or older are victims of at least one incident of ID theft each year. Most such victims discover the incident only when a financial institution contacts them about suspicious activity or they notice fraudulent charges on an account. The majority of ID theft victims have no idea how the offender obtained their personal information, and 9 in 10 cases, ID theft victims did not know anything about the offender. Two-thirds of identity theft victims suffer financial losses, and victims whose personal information was used to open new account in their name experienced greater out-of-pocket financial losses. About half of these victims suffer losses of $99 or less, while about one in seven lose $1,000 or more.[30]

Most (52 percent) victims are able to resolve their problems in a day or less, but about one in ten spends more than a month trying to clear their name and financial problems. The latter victims are more likely to experience work and personal problems than those who resolve their

victimization relatively quickly. Some victims must spend six months or more resolving financial and credit problems; in these cases, about 29 percent experience severe emotional distress.

Very few (about 10 percent) identity theft victims report the incident to police. The majority (87 percent) of these victims do, however, contact a credit card company or bank to report misuse or attempted misuse of an account or personal information.[31]

The response strategies provided below provide some essential actions for combating ID theft. As always, it is critical that officers tailor responses to the offense circumstances and can justify each response based on a reliable analysis. In most cases, an effective strategy will involve implementing several different responses.

General Considerations for an Effective Response Strategy

As we have seen, ID theft is a complex crime, composed of many subcrimes and related to many other problems. Thus, this offense falls under the authority of many different agencies, including the local police, Secret Service, Postal Inspection Service, FBI, Homeland Security, local government offices, and motor vehicle departments, to name just a few. Regional and state law enforcement agencies may have established multiagency task forces to combat identity fraud. For example, the Financial Crimes Task Force of Southwestern Pennsylvania consists of local law enforcement, Secret Service agents, and postal inspectors (see Exhibit 13–6).

Exhibit 13–6   A Financial Crimes Task Force in Pennsylvania

United States Department of Justice.

Established in 1995, the Financial Crimes Task Force of Southwestern Pennsylvania has been investigating, arresting, and prosecuting criminals involved with financial crimes including mail theft and identity theft. The Financial Crimes Task Force was formed to develop a cooperative effort with various federal, state, and local law enforcement agencies, to address the problems of financial crimes and identity theft.

The Task Force investigates and prosecutes criminal offenses involving split-deposit schemes, counterfeit checks and money orders, mail theft, wire and Internet fraud, stolen government checks, identity theft, and identity take-overs within Southwestern Pennsylvania, placing an emphasis on organized activity. The task force aggressively investigates and prosecutes offenders in state and federal courts.

This Web site is designed to assist and educate in dealing with the complexity of financial crimes. Information is provided in dealing with the prevention of financial crime and the necessary steps to take if you become a victim. This Web site has a comprehensive section dealing with the most common scams and a listing of agencies and organizations who can provide you with additional information.[32]

However, because of the complexity—and expense—of developing multiagency task forces, initial efforts should focus on local factors that will help reduce or prevent identity theft and mitigate the harm done to victims. Thus, responses should involve a two-pronged approach:

- *Prevention:* What to do to prevent identity theft from occurring.
- *Victim assistance:* How to respond to victims who need help.[33]

These two stages are closely related, so collecting information in one stage helps in addressing the other. Following are recommended measures that police adopt for responding to identity theft:

1. *Encourage businesses' awareness of their responsibility to protect employee and client records.* Having a privacy policy, training employees, and limiting data collection and access to information needed and data disclosure are some approaches.
2. *Educate people about protecting their personal information.* Police can inform people that the Internet has an enormous amount of information about how to avoid becoming an identity theft victim, and they can tell people that the Federal Trade Commission's publications are excellent.
3. *Collaborate with government and other service organizations to protect private information.* It is important that the police work with agencies and businesses to keep Social Security numbers, birth certificates, and other such information out of general circulation; prohibit their sale; restrict access to such information; investigate identity theft cases; and help victims resolve problems.
4. *Work with local banks to encourage credit card issuers to adopt improved security practices.* Although major credit card companies have national reach, the police can work with local banks to establish procedures for local identity theft victims to repair the damage done and to get their accounts operating again. Credit card companies can also be pressured to put policies in place that include better identity verification for credit card usage, photographs on credit cards, identity verification, and passwords on credit accounts.
5. *Track delivery.* Much of identity theft involves the delivery of documents and products, and stolen merchandise is often delivered to vacant houses and mailboxes. Maintaining close relationships with local postal inspectors and delivery companies may help to track items back to the thieves.[34]

HUMAN TRAFFICKING

By Presidential decree in December 2012, each January is designated as National Slavery and Human Trafficking Prevention Month, which, according to the Department of Homeland Security (DHS), is to remind Americans more than 150 years since the Emancipation Proclamation that we need to "rededicate ourselves to bringing an end to slavery and **human trafficking**."

In Chapter 12 we discussed human trafficking activities by gangs. Here we discuss this international problem in terms of its nature, extent, and what police can do address this growing crime problem.

"Modern Day Slavery" for Victims

Human trafficking is essentially modern-day slavery and affects thousands of people in the United States. Under the Trafficking Victims Protection Act of 2000 (TVPA), human trafficking is the recruitment, harboring, transportation, provision, or obtaining of a person for labor or services, through the use of force, fraud, or coercion, for the purpose of subjection to involuntary servitude, peonage, debt bondage, or slavery. It includes sex trafficking, in which a commercial sex act is induced by force, fraud, or coercion, or in which the victim is under 18 years of age.

Men, women, and children are victimized by human trafficking and often recruited due to preexisting problems such as mental illness, drug abuse, and/or family dysfunction. Trafficked persons originate from countries around the world but can also be U.S. citizens. They are often forced to work in the sex industry; indeed, the United Nations estimates that of the 2.4 million people in the world who are victims of human trafficking at any one time, about 80 percent of them are being exploited as sexual slaves.[35] However, many are in forced-labor situations such as domestic servitude, manufacturing, construction, or migrant agricultural work.[36]

What Works? Collaboration Is Key

No one agency can prevent human trafficking, protect victims of human trafficking, and prosecute traffickers; therefore, first and foremost, relationships must be developed between law enforcement and social services agencies before human trafficking can be addressed and victims assisted. Both parties, in order to delegate tasks and to clearly define each agency's role, relationships should be fostered before the two agencies ever work together to serve a victim of trafficking.

Human trafficking typically occurs behind the closed doors of private homes or under the radar of legitimate businesses; crime rings have also become quite astute in the methods of smuggling persons across borders and hiding victims of trafficking as they move them between cities. Victims believe the promise of traffickers of a better life in the United States, only to find they have been lied to, forced into servitude, or otherwise victimized. These victims need assistance and benefits, the TVPA granted Congress the ability to appropriate funding for human trafficking prevention and prosecution.

The T Visa

Several immigration laws were created to protect victims of trafficking. For example, the "T" visa was created in 2000 and allows some victims of human trafficking and immediate family members to remain and work temporarily in the United States if they agree to assist law enforcement in testifying against the perpetrators. Such legislation was necessary because victims of

Human trafficking is essentially modern-day slavery and is the forced recruitment, harboring, transportation, provision or obtaining of a person for labor or services.
Arto/Fotolia.

human trafficking are usually undocumented in the United States and subject to deportation; therefore, while a criminal case is developing against the victim's trafficker or traffickers, the victim may now be granted continued presence in order to legally remain here to assist with the legal prosecution. The **T visa** also thus protects the victim from being forced to return to his or her country of origin and be vulnerable to threats and abuse by the traffickers. Furthermore, three years after obtaining a T visa, one may apply for permanent resident status here and even file for immediate family members to join them legally in the United States.[37]

In addition, the U.S. Department of Health and Human Services (HHS) has a certification process for victims of human trafficking allowing them to apply for federal and state benefits and programs; they may receive food stamps, Medicaid, and cash assistance, and may be deemed eligible for early employment and cash assistance programs. Such benefits offer victims a fresh start and the opportunity to obtain legal employment and appropriate and safe housing.[38]

The Office of Victims of Crime

The Department of Justice Office for Victims of Crime (OVC) also offers funding for anti-trafficking programs to serve precertified victims of trafficking; this program also supports the TVPA's goals of preventing and prosecuting human trafficking; it also offers victims case management, legal assistance, clinical intervention, housing, and medical care. Victims may also obtain transportation, emergency financial assistance, literacy classes, English as second language classes, and employment services.[39]

Additional Law Enforcement Efforts: The Diagnostic Center

Effectively addressing human trafficking can be extremely challenging for communities that do not possess established practices for identifying and protecting human trafficking victims and investigating and prosecuting cases. Now, however, the U.S. Department of Justice (DOJ), Office of Justice Programs, provides assistance in what is termed a Diagnostic Center. Established in 2012, Diagnostic Centers employ data-driven strategies for combating human trafficking. As shown in Exhibit 13–7 with the situation in Albert Lea, Minnesota, the Center has programs and initiatives that can address problems of human trafficking.

Exhibit 13–7	The Diagnostic Center Approach in Minnesota

The city of Albert Lea, Minnesota, became involved with the federal Diagnostic Center to assess the impact of human trafficking, particularly sex trafficking, and to identify best practices to address these crimes. With a population about 20,000 and a geographical area less than 15 square miles, Albert Lea would not otherwise have had the ability to address a case of human trafficking that surfaced because of a detective's encountering several exotic dancers who were victims.

Seeking to be proactive, the Albert Lea Police Department (ALPD) asked the Diagnostic Center for help. Specifically, it requested assistance with: (1) identifying the extent of human trafficking for sexual purposes by collecting and analyzing data; (2) improving law enforcement training in human trafficking; and (3) raising community awareness to combat the problem.

The center analyzed: the locations of offenses; arrest data for sex trafficking and prostitution and for those soliciting sex; data on juvenile offenses such as runaways; a case review of charges of child abuse and drug trafficking; referrals for prosecution for any of these offenses; and victim and offender demographic information. In addition, interviews were conducted with police officers and others in criminal justice agencies, victim service providers, community leaders, health care providers, school administrators, and other key stakeholders.[40]

Following the steps, in about three weeks, four men were arrested for solicitation. Although the diagnostic analysis did not identify a specific sex trafficking ring, it did find the presence of sex trafficking indicators in the community, including a related high volume of vehicles passing through, hotel occupancy rates, and Albert Lea's proximity to communities with known human trafficking. The Diagnostic Center spurred community efforts to recognize these crimes and the creation of a support network for victims to help them escape their perpetrators. These developments also led to intense training of ALPD officers to recognize human trafficking more proactively.[41]

Summary

Like Chapter 12, this chapter has applied problem-oriented policing initiatives to issues and problems that warrant special kinds of attention. Seven exhibits were provided, each showing the efficacy of problem solving in addressing a particular problem.

Although we stated it in Chapter 12, it bears repeating that for each of the issues and problems discussed, the success of problem-oriented policing strategies is highly dependent on the police having laid the groundwork—doing the kinds of preparatory work described in earlier chapters as well as having a firm grasp of and properly applying the SARA process (discussed in Chapter 5).

Key Terms and Concepts

Crisis Intervention Team (for addressing mental illness)	Diagnostic Center approach	Family Justice Center concept	Mental illness
Cybercrime	Domestic violence	Human trafficking	Neighborhood disorder
	Electronic Crimes Task Forces	Identity theft	T visa

Items for Review

1. Describe some of the front-end and back-end issues involved in dealing with mentally ill persons.
2. List several strategies for police that are essential for providing a foundation for problem reduction among the mentally ill population.
3. Review what police agencies can do to address mental illness using the Crisis Intervention Team concept.
4. Explain in brief how police treatment of domestic violence has changed over the past three decades.
5. What are some common practices contained in police policies regarding officers' response to incidents of domestic violence?
6. Describe the types of cybercrime that exist today, and some police tactics for dealing with it; include initiatives of the Electronic Crimes Task Force in New York and the U.S. Secret Service in your response.
7. Define what is meant by identity theft, and the extent/nature of victimization in the United States each year.
8. Explain what law enforcement measures can be taken to combat identity theft and other financial crimes; include the task force in Pennsylvania in your response.
9. Define human trafficking, its extent, the nature of most victimization, and how law enforcement can work to address it; include the diagnostic center approach in Minnesota in your response.

Learn by Doing

1. The editorial board for a local newspaper has contacted your criminal justice professor seeking a "Guest Editorial" describing how the CIT concept works to address mental illness. She asks you, as her independent-study student, to prepare an outline explaining this concept. What will your outline contain?
2. A state legislator has become very concerned with reports that incidents of domestic violence have been increasing, and contacts your police chief to see what is being done about it locally. As the chief's crime analyst, what will you say can be done to cope with this problem?
3. The chairperson of your county commission recently became an ID theft victim and asks the sheriff what she can do to clear up the matter and restore her good name. As the sheriff's research analyst, you are asked for input. What will you say?
4. You are assigned an essay question to describe the measures police are taking to combat human trafficking as well as approaches such as the T visa for assisting victims. How will you respond?

Endnotes

1. "In-Depth: The Washington Navy Yard Shooting," *CBS News* (2013), http://www.cbsnews.com/feature/washington-navy-yard-shooting/.
2. Agnes Radomski, "It's Time for The NYPD to Stop Treating Mentally Ill New Yorkers Like Criminals," *The Nation* (October 9, 2014), http://www.thenation.com/article/181926/its-time-nypd-stop-treating-mentally-ill-new-yorkers-criminals#.
3. Kevin Johnson, "Memphis Program Offers Example for Police and Mentally Ill," *USA Today* (October 2, 2013), http://www.usatoday.com/story/news/nation/2013/10/02/police-navy-yard-mental-illness-alexis-shooting/2910763/.
4. Gary Cordner, "People with Mental Illness," Center for Problem-Oriented Policing (2006), http://www.popcenter.org/problems/mental_illness/print/.

5. Treatment Advocacy Center, *The Treatment of Persons with Mental Illness in Prisons and Jails: A State Survey (Abridged)* (April 8, 2014), p. 4, http://tacreports.org/treatment-behind-bars/executive-summary.

6. Sam P.K. Collins, "Introducing Mental Health Courts," *Think-Progress* (April 10, 2015), http://thinkprogress.org/health/2015/04/10/3645289/mental-health-prison-report/. *Note*: "Mental illness" refers generally to diagnosable diseases of the brain recognized in the American Psychiatric Association's Diagnostic and Statistical Manual, such as schizophrenia, psychosis, bipolar disorder, and schizoaffective disorder, for example.

7. "Deinstitutionalization: A Psychiatric Titanic," *Frontline* (May 10, 2005), http://www.pbs.org/wgbh/pages/frontline/shows/asylums/special/excerpt.html.

8. Rick Jervis, "Mental Disorders Keep Thousands of Homeless on Streets," *USA Today* (August 27, 2014), http://www.usatoday.com/story/news/nation/2014/08/27/mental-health-homeless-series/14255283/.

9. Kevin Johnson, "Memphis Program Offers Example for Police and Mentally Ill."

10. Ibid.

11. Adapted from Christian Mason, Tod W. Burke, and Stephen S. Owen, "Responding to Persons with Mental Illness: Can Screening Checklists Aid Law Enforcement?" *FBI Law Enforcement Bulletin* (February 2014), https://leb.fbi.gov/2014/february/responding-to-persons-with-mental-illness-can-screening-checklists-aid-law-enforcement.

12. For more information, see Amy C. Watson, Melissa Schaefer Morabito, Jeffrey Draine, and Victor Ottati, "Improving Police Response to Persons with Mental Illness: A Multi-Level Conceptualization of CIT," *International Journal of Law and Psychiatry* 31 (2008):359–368.

13. Adapted from Gary Cordner, "People with Mental Illness," p. 2.

14. Ibid.

15. Police Executive Research Forum, "Police Improve Response to Domestic Violence, But Abuse Often Remains the 'Hidden Crime'," *Subject to Debate* 29 (1) (January/February 2015):1–7. http://www.policeforum.org/assets/docs/Subject_to_Debate/Debate2015/debate_2015_janfeb.pdf.

16. Ibid.

17. The U.S. Supreme Court said, in a 7-2 decision, that Gonzales could not sue the city and claim the police had violated her rights to due process. Furthermore, it held she had no constitutionally protected interest in the enforcement of the restraining order. The opinion also established that the holder of a restraining order is not entitled to any specific mandatory action by the police; rather, restraining orders only provide grounds for arresting the person restrained by order. See: *Castle Rock v. Gonzales*, 545 U.S. 748 (2005).

18. Adapted from California Evidence-Based Clearinghouse for Child Welfare, "Welcome to the San Diego Family Justice Center!" http://www.sandiego.gov/sandiegofamilyjusticecenter/; also see ibid., http://www.cebc4cw.org/program/san-diego-family-justice-center/detailed.

19. "These Cybercrime Statistics Will Make You Think Twice About Your Password: Where's the CSI Cyber Team When You Need Them?" *CBS* (March 4, 2015), http://www.cbs.com/shows/csi-cyber/news/1003888/these-cybercrime-statistics-will-make-you-think-twice-about-your-password-where-s-the-csi-cyber-team-when-you-need-them-/.

20. Ibid.

21. McAfee, "Net Losses: Estimating the Global Cost of Cybercrime" (June 2014), http://www.mcafee.com/us/resources/reports/rp-economic-impact-cybercrime2.pdf.

22. Adapted from Federal Bureau of Investigation, "Cyber Stalker: A Cautionary Tale About Online Romance and Revenge" (December 23, 2013), https://www.fbi.gov/news/stories/cautionary-tale-of-online-romance-and-revenge1.

23. Ibid.

24. National Institute of Justice, "Tech Beat: Catching the Cyber Crook," *Summer* (2000), https://www.justnet.org/pdf/CyberCrookSum2000.pdf.

25. George I. Seffers "Ramping Up the Cyber Criminal Hunt," *Signal* (March 1, 2014), http://www.afcea.org/content/?q=ramping-cyber-criminal-hunt.

26. Ibid.

27. National Institute of Justice, "Tech Beat: Cyber Cops in Training," https://www.justnet.org/pdf/CyberCopsWint04.pdf.

28. Department of Homeland Security, "Combating Cybercrime," http://www.dhs.gov/topic/combating-cyber-crime.

29. Graeme R. Newman, "Identity Theft," 2004, http://www.popcenter.org/problems/identity_theft/; also see USA.gov, "Identity Theft," at https://www.usa.gov/identity-theft.

30. Ibid.

31. Ibid.

32. Adapted from Financial Crimes Task Force of Southwestern Pennsylvania, http://www.financialcrimestaskforce.com/.

33. Ibid., pp. 32–41.

34. Ibid.

35. "U.N.: 2.4 Million Human Trafficking Victims," *USA Today* (March 4, 2012), http://usatoday30.usatoday.com/news/world/story/2012-04-03/human-trafficking-sex-UN/53982026/1.

36. Joy M. Braun, "Collaborations: The Key to Combating Human Trafficking," *The Police Chief* 70 (December 2003), http://www.policechiefmagazine.org/magazine/index.cfm?fuseaction=display_arch&article_id=173&issue_id=12200368–74.

37. U.S. Citizenship and Immigration Services, "Victims of Human Trafficking: T Nonimmigrant Status," http://www.uscis.gov/humanitarian/victims-human-trafficking-other-crimes/victims-human-trafficking-t-nonimmigrant-status.

38. U.S. Department of Health & Human Services, Office of Refugee Resettlement, "Fact Sheet: Certification for Adult Victims of Trafficking," http://www.acf.hhs.gov/programs/orr/resource/fact-sheet-certification-for-adult-victims-of-trafficking.

39. Office for Victims of Crime, "Human Trafficking Task Force e-Guide," http://ovc.ncjrs.gov/humantrafficking/; Also see Office of Justice Programs, *Executive Reference Guide: Human Trafficking* (August 2013), https://www.ojpdiagnosticcenter.org/sites/default/files/spotlight/download/Manassas_ERG_090513_508%5B1%5D.pdf.

40. Adapted from Katherine Darke Schmitt, "The Justice Department's Diagnostic Center Provides Technical Assistance to Address Human Trafficking," *The Police Chief* 81 (July 2014), http://www.policechiefmagazine.org/magazine/index.cfm?fuseaction=display_arch&article_id=3395&issue_id=72014.

41. Office of Justice Programs, "Diagnostic Center Presents Analysis of Sex Trafficking in Albert Lea, MN," n.d., https://www.ojpdiagnosticcenter.org/content/diagnostic-center-presents-analysis-sex-trafficking-albert-lea-mn.

PART VI

Challenges Ahead

Future Opportunities and Obstacles

LEARNING OBJECTIVES

As a result of reading this chapter, the student will:

- Understand concerns with policing's tendency to use, and to be criticized for applying labels and creating new "eras"
- Know of the drivers and factors that will influence policing in the future
- Have fundamental knowledge of the ways in which technologies will shape policing in the future
- Comprehend the need for today's police executives to provide strong leadership in the future, particularly in the areas of militarization, public trust, succession planning, civilianization, and maintaining the role and functions of community policing

TEST YOUR KNOWLEDGE

1. Policing can now be honestly said to have entered a new era, termed "Information Application."
2. In the future, there will be continuing pressure to reduce the costs of policing, to include salaries and pension benefits.
3. Most experts agree that technologies in policing have advanced to about the extent that is possible.
4. The SARA problem-solving process can be of value in addressing terrorism and cybercrime.
5. Science, particularly social science, has yet to be realized and applied in any central or meaningful way to police functions.

Answers can be found on page 278.

INTRODUCTION

In previous chapters, we examined several of the challenges facing today's police, emphasizing the combined strategies of community policing, problem-oriented policing and how those strategies can assist in addressing crime and disorder, including transparency and connecting with the community, police accountability, policing minority groups, protecting the homeland, preventing crime, tools for problem solving, changing agency culture, training for problem solving, and the effects of the Great Recession. This chapter expands and adds to those discussions in the context of future considerations.

Perhaps more than anything else, this book has demonstrated that today the only permanent aspect of policing is change. The historically tradition-bound domain of policing is now highly dynamic and will continue to be so, as will be seen in this chapter. But much work and change remains to be done. The question "What will the future bring?" remains at the forefront of policing and becomes even more poignant and ominous when we consider the world's present state of affairs.

The chapter begins by considering the language used by people in policing, specifically the apparent tendency of some leaders to use labels and create new "eras" of policing whenever a new strategy or tactic surfaces; here we call for greater resistance to this trend. Next is a look at several **drivers** and factors that will influence the future of policing, and then review the role of technologies in the future of policing as well as that of local police and problem-oriented policing in addressing terrorism and cybercrime. Then we discuss next the need for today's police executives to provide strong leadership in several areas, to include what is perceived by some to be excessive **militarization** of police, the need for transparency and to engage in succession planning (grooming future leaders), the anticipated reliance on civilian employees, and the need to keep the focus on community policing and related training. We conclude the chapter with a summary, a listing of the chapter's key terms and concepts, review questions, and several "Learn by Doing" scenarios, where you can apply your knowledge of the future to hypothetical situations.

FIRST THINGS FIRST: JETTISON THE JARGON

It is always interesting to read professional magazine and journal articles where the authors make bold predictions about policing's future based on a single program or strategy. Some of the predictions are tantamount to putting a powerful new engine and other upgrades into a 1960s vintage Ford Mustang and then renaming the vehicle. Do the modifications or new technologies improve the car's performance? Without question they do. But these changes do not alter what the car is at its root—a vintage Mustang.[1]

Similarly, some people view the current era of policing as being intelligence-led or predictive policing. Still others say we are in an information era or that "we're not doing community policing now, we're doing CompStat." We believe that the general use—and at times misuse—of words such as "era" and police use of language and clichés are problematic and create more harm and confusion than they help.

Policing is indeed in an information "age" but not in an information "era." The three primary eras of policing (discussed in Chapter 1) have not changed; therefore, the time has come to seriously question this use of clichés and tendency to label things anew.

This is not a minor issue for the field. Indeed, one of the long-standing, major criticisms of policing has been its tendency to quickly and, to some, blithely put new labels on different strategies and tactics (which have sometimes been caustically termed as policing's "flavor of the month") and to use labels that are not altogether accurate. This criticism has certainly been lodged against community policing, owing largely to the fact that in the past some agencies failed to properly articulate, grasp, train for, and implement the strategy, and too often merely creating a peripheral "unit" or, say, assigning an officer to bicycle or foot patrol and then anointing theirs a community policing organization.[2]

As an example of this drift into "era-speak," a ranking member of the Los Angeles Police Department once described predictive policing as follows:

> The LAPD has assumed a leadership role in translating these successes into the next era of policing: predictive policing. By developing, refining, and successfully executing on the predictive-policing model, the LAPD is leveraging the promise of advanced analytics in the prevention of and response to crime.[3]

With what we believe is a high degree of irony, a mere two months before the aforementioned comments were published, an assistant U.S. Attorney General stated at a predictive-policing conference:

> I think our first order of business is to define what we mean by "predictive policing." We've become so accustomed to labels in law enforcement. Is predictive policing just another label for another policing model? Or is it a larger concept—something that incorporates many policing paradigms?[4]

These differing points of view concerning the work of policing is obviously confusing— and such blithe movement from one description to another of policing strategies can only serve

Policing tends to devise a lot of new jargon, acronyms, and "eras." But regardless of all its language, complexities, and technologies, good police work fundamentally involves helping people with problems involving crime and disorder.
Yuri_Arcurs/Getty Images.

to undercut the good work that police do. As indicated above, the police have long suffered under the yoke of the "flavor-of-the-month" criticism, and it is time to be much more wary in terms of describing its role and functions.

In sum, we believe that community policing, problem solving, intelligence-led policing, smart policing, and predictive policing are not separate and distinct entities and strategies. Rather, they are all management tools for *analyzing crime* (under the SARA model) and will advance the evolution of problem-oriented policing to better address 21st century challenges of crime and disorder.[5] As stated by one police chief, "When I came to my department, I tried to stay away from buzz words. I put it simply—the focus is on good police work."[6] And as an academic described it, "By 2022 chiefs may be able to answer accurately the all-important question, 'What business are you in?'"[7]

DRIVERS AND FACTORS INFLUENCING THE FUTURE OF POLICING

The very foundations of today's policing organizations were shook by the recent Great Recession and a series of economic and societal forces. What was demonstrated was that, today and in the future, police must anticipate and adapt to these forces. In this section, we briefly consider several factors that will "drive" the future of policing in general, to include community policing, in the foreseeable future.[8] Of course, terrorist attacks, changes in technologies, and other such dynamics discussed later in the chapter should also be included in this discussion.

Economic Impacts

The combination of tight budgets and rising personnel costs has made it difficult for police departments across the country to continue providing the same level and quality of services. Even if police were to receive higher levels of funding due to an improved economy, the rising costs of policing (through labor contracts, higher equipment and technology costs, unforeseen increases in costs of commodities such as gasoline, and so on) might still be seen as an opportunity to reexamine the structure and function of police departments and the broad array of services they provide.

Looking ahead, there will be continued pressure to consider reductions of pension and other benefits (discussed below), which could in turn impact recruitment. As part of this process, there will be greater numbers of discussions concerning consolidation of agencies, formation of contract cities, merger of city agencies such as police and fire services (generally termed public safety departments), and partnerships with private companies for services.

Demographic Shifts

Migration and other demographic shifts have, and will continue to influence the types of crimes that police departments respond to. Law enforcement will need to consider ways to deal with immigrant criminal gangs, closed and distrustful communities, ethnic rivalries and feuds, types of crime common to some groups (e.g., human trafficking), and a lack of understanding of U.S. laws and customs. Law enforcement may need to make aggressive efforts to increase its number of bilingual officers.[9] While the overwhelming majority of immigrants will be law abiding citizens, there will be obvious challenges for the police.

Another demographic change long in coming is the overall aging of the nation. Greater numbers of senior citizens pose new concerns and challenges for police organizations. For example, police will receive more calls for help regarding crime that is both real and perceived—e.g., items merely mislaid but perceived as stolen. And those calls will more and more often concern victimizations employing technology with which the elderly victims are unfamiliar.[10] Another resulting change is the influx of Generation X and Millennials into the workforce (discussed in Chapter 8). Their focus on work/life balance, and need for their work to be meaningful, educational, and challenging will increase the amount of organizational turnover and likely require more frequent testing processes. As that occurs, it might behoove agencies in a geographic area to pool resources and conduct regional testing.[11]

The budget and changes in the economy will also be the primary factor in determining staffing levels in law enforcement agencies in the foreseeable future. Today, the deployment of patrol resources is often determined by software relying on data such as calls for service, arrests, response time, and so on. In the future, however, it is likely that staffing deployment software will provide information that will better deploy those resources more efficiently; and if crime rates continue to decline, surely there will be greater calls for community policing strategies.[12]

As indicated above, the consolidating of some service agencies (e.g., several smaller police agencies into one large agency, or police and fire), **civilianization**, and volunteer programs will eliminate duplication of certain services.[13]

The public has also become much more sensitive to public employee salaries and benefits—particularly those persons struggling at their low salaries or have been laid off from their jobs. The recent decision in dozens of states to remove nearly all collective bargaining from public employees will likely foment more public resentment toward those in law enforcement and fire service. Another factor to consider is the impact of right-to-work statutes on labor agreements and negotiations. Currently, about two dozen states have right-to-work laws which guarantee that no person can be forced to join a labor union and pay union dues as a condition of employment. Other states allow the creation of the union shop which effectively requires union participation or the payment of dues. With states having differing laws governing employee–employer relations, the unionized police organization of the future will be challenged to create a work environment where the union does not have overly broad power and influence.[14]

TECHNOLOGY

New and emerging technology is changing the way police function. However, while those same **technologies** improve efficiency and transparency, they also raise privacy concerns—and are very costly. Body-worn cameras, less-lethal technologies, communications equipment, and social media all require an informed and legal review of policies, practices, and procedures, which should be developed with input from the community and constitutional scholars.[15] And while a greater proportion of crimes may be solved with the aid of modern technology, conversely, more crimes (and a greater variety of them) may be committed by use of technology. Therefore, it is important to consider both the potential benefits and repercussions of increased technology in the police organization of the future. The cost of these technology systems can be significant at the same time that the available funding for such systems has been reduced in many agencies.[16]

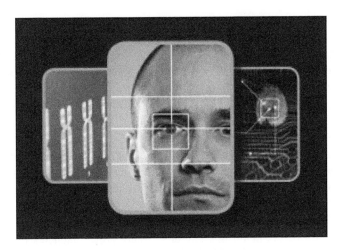

Biometrics has been used to authenticate individual identities and determine who someone is. In the future, however, the FBI's Biometric Center of Excellence hopes to harness more benefits of this technology.
Courtesy FBI.

A Glimpse of What's Here, What's on the Horizon

When asked what their police forces will look like in 20 years, police chiefs probably say "much like now."[17] This should not be their response, at least with respect to ongoing advances in technology. Therefore, just as officers are taught to operate video and laser radar for traffic control and an array of less-lethal weapons of defense, they must learn how to use (and, often, be certified in) an array of technologies. An example of what is coming (or is already here) will make the point.

Assume that two police officers are sent to the scene of a domestic violence incident. While enroute, the officer has been given by dispatch all relevant details on any previous domestic violence at the address, profiles of the couple, whether any weapons have been used, whether weapons are registered at the address, and so on. When officers arrive, they secure the scene and begin separate interviews of the husband and wife. The wife says something in a language the officer cannot understand, so the officer pulls up a language detection program on her iPhone and has the wife repeat what she said. The software recognizes the language as Indonesian and begins to translate the wife's words into English automatically, allowing the officer to understand the events, a transcript of which is recorded in real time. The officer takes high-resolution photos of the wife's injuries with her phone. Meanwhile, her partner gets biometric data from the husband—pictures of his eyes for iris configuration analysis, as well as his whole face for creating a template for facial recognition analysis. The biometric data are sent remotely to the police department's secure computing cloud. Meanwhile, as the other officer interviews the husband with a same two-way translator, a geometric configuration of the man's face and irises is calculated and run through databases to see if he is or has been involved in other criminal activities. The statements of both parties are sent remotely to the department's case management system, along with accompanying pictures and the results of the background checks on each of them.[18]

This scenario is not fictional, as most of these technologies are already in use. New York and Los Angeles now have "real-time crime centers" (discussed in Chapter 7) involving many such tools. While language translators are not currently powerful enough to provide real-time translation, they are rapidly approaching this level. Megapixels and cloud computing are becoming increasingly cheap, allowing for the near-instant transfer of precise, unadulterated information from scene to station. Biometric data for identification is expanding in society and may one day become the norm, making the collection of alternative forms of biometric data important for police organizations. Miniature biometric data-collection apparatuses are becoming increasingly cost efficient. Blood samples, iris scans, and DNA typing may, at some point in the future, replace fingerprinting as cheaper and more precise ways of identifying criminals.[19]

Looking for Patterns, Making Predictions

The ability of predictive analytics to recognize behavioral patterns is growing rapidly; already these methods can be used to determine patterns in crime data and behavior. Using video surveillance to isolate abnormal behavior in a spatial area, cameras can also be programmed to "learn" normal human behavior in order to detect unusual or suspicious behavior. Examples would include people standing too close to one another, or two people standing at an ATM at the same time, which could indicate that a robbery is taking place. Cameras can also be programmed to constantly and quietly monitor activity and then to alert authorities when there is something suspicious that needs to be addressed. Police departments can then focus their resources in areas most likely to be affected by crime.[20]

POLICE–PRIVATE PARTNERSHIPS.   The potential for police partnerships with private parties is increasing exponentially due to the improved data collection ability of private organizations. Police now partner with private security firms and retail services to improve their ability to respond to incidents and emergencies. In fact, in some cases, private firms are collecting more and better information on the people with whom they interact than do police organizations; police can leverage this information to aid in criminal investigations.[21]

POLICE–COMMUNITY PARTNERSHIPS.   As noted in Chapter 4, many police agencies use social media to alert citizens to activities of interest and keep them informed of goings-on in the city; agencies are also utilizing online applications to improve citizens' access to police services, such as filing reports or complaints. Most laptops are now sold with a built-in webcam, and users can access their laptops remotely. Police may also be able to promote workshops and community programs to inform people of ways that they can help protect themselves or better help the police when a crime does occur.[22]

New Tech Challenges Await

Certainly all of these "gee whiz" technologies bode well for policing's future. However, many legal issues are lurking nearby that also promise to slow their adoption or perhaps elevate their cost. For example, how will law enforcement deal with the emerging issues connected with unmanned aerial vehicles (drones) and nanotechnology vis-á-vis right to privacy? Legal questions have already been confronted regarding arrestees' cell phones and are surrounding the searches of suspects' computers. The personal information of interest about the suspect will be somewhere, but it may be in the cloud (or even stored for convenience by the service provider on someone else's computer). Whatever technologies emerge in the future, the police will also need to be aware of the criminal element's affinity for and uses of those same technologies, while also developing protocols for dealing with technological evidence. In the future, the police must keep abreast of those technological changes and prepare for likely changes before

A sign of the future? The TruPoint 300 is a small, lightweight, and compact laser measurement tool that can assist police in crash and crime scene investigations. It offers an alternative to traditional (human measurement with wheel and tape) as well as bulky and very expensive survey equipment.
Courtesy Laser Technology, Inc.

they happen. Being reactive will not work; rather, assuming a proactive stance will allow police to anticipate how those technologies will affect new and more sophisticated crimes.[23]

Everyone is aware of Newton's Third Law of Motion: for every action, there is an equal and opposite reaction. If problem-solving officers respond to crimes in Beat A, then crime may well increase and become more profitable in Beat B. A good example is the tighter restrictions placed on sales of pseudoephedrine—the drug in decongestants used to produce illegal methamphetamines—being largely responsible for the production of methamphetamines relocating to Mexico.[24]

Four Considerations When Deploying New Technologies

Paul Rosenzweig, who previously served as Deputy Assistant Secretary for Policy at the U.S. Department of Homeland Security, maintains that there are at least four factors that need to be addressed when police executives consider deploying new technologies:[25]

1. *Cost:* This should be the first consideration when deploying technology. As we noted in Chapter 7, body-worn cameras are now being used more widely in policing. While their initial purchase cost may be rather modest, consideration must be given to operation and maintenance costs of the new system (i.e., data storage, training of users, maintenance, and preparation for court). Unmanned aerial vehicles (drones) carry similar demands on resources.
2. *Determining and managing expectations:* When they reach a point where they are collecting massive volumes of data, officers will face a nearly impossible dilemma: on one hand, police will be expected to have near-perfect knowledge of past events, captured by a variety of sensor devices. On the other hand, officers will be accused by

Police can avail themselves of a variety of new technologies, such as this automated license-plate reader mounted on the front of the vehicle that is connected to the in-car computer and can read thousands of license plates in searching for wanted vehicles.

Mikael Karlsson/Alamy Stock Photo.

some of collecting impermissibly large amounts of data on innocent citizens and retaining the data for retrospective analysis. Concerns about the Big Brother syndrome will become the reality.

3. ***Planning for privacy:*** New data-collection systems pose realistic concerns for the privacy of those citizens who are subject to scrutiny. For example, with body-worn cameras, what should be the rules around retention and disclosure of the video they produce? What about video of victims of spousal abuse? Child victims of sexual offenses? The privacy rights of innocent third-parties whose pictures are collaterally captured? Even the privacy of police officers themselves would be jeopardized.

4. ***Security implications:*** Police leaders must consider the security requirements for the data they are collecting—which often includes the most sensitive personal data. For this reason, the FBI and other organizations have developed guidelines for the cloud-based storage of criminal justice information. Inevitably, police agencies will need to deploy cloud-based storage systems; when that occurs they will need to consider whether or not all of their data are being maintained at the highest security level.

Exhibit 14–1 provides an example of how several of these considerations can be brought together in discussing a United Nations crime-prevention initiative.

| Exhibit 14–1 | Going Global: The United Nations Vision of "Green" Crime Prevention |

Working with the Massachusetts's Institute of Technology, the United Nations Interregional Crime and Justice Research Institute (UNICRI) has developed a research project to design and implement crime prevention based on sustainable urban design. UNICRI/MIT offers a new vision for a third generation of crime prevention through environmental design (CPTED), through sustainable, environmental design strategies that use green technologies. The proposed third-generation CPTED is also focused on reducing the fear of crime and enhancing the perception of security.

Following are four elements necessarily comprising their third-generation CPTED: places, people, technology, and networks:

▶ ***Places:*** Places that provide safe homes, secure employment, and well-maintained and cared for civic environments create a positive image of urban living that contributes to both the urbanites' standard of living and their image of their city as a desirable, safe, and secure environment in which to live and work.

▶ ***People:*** Social structures provide opportunities for people to have a voice to communicate their needs, concerns, desires, and ideas; also, government staff members can communicate with the public, creating mutual trust between citizens and city officials. Each citizen then feels responsible for the well-being of the greater community, to create an environment that holds citizens responsible for effective city performance.

▶ ***Technology:*** Technology helps citizens and government to become transparent, aware, intelligent, and energy-efficient in an environment capable of effectively responding to emergent conditions. A transparent city is a safe and secure city because no corner is hidden and no fact about it is unknown.

▶ ***Networks:*** The network is the glue that holds these four elements together as it connects places and provides efficient distribution of human and material resources. Networks also provide the mechanisms that collect, store, and manage urban-related information, as well as for delivering real-time information to the citizens, particularly for wireless services and using personal handheld devices for accessing this information.[26]

TERRORISM AND HOMELAND SECURITY

What Role for Local Police in Homeland Security?

In the view of many police administrators, the recent emphasis on homeland security often resulted in reduced community policing funding and efforts. Some observers believe that soon after 9/11, community policing was in effect kicked to the curb, as all budgets went to homeland security efforts. Still, the proactive principles of community policing and problem solving, and its emphasis on developing good relationships with the community, have not been lost on homeland security. Therefore, many police experts agree that community policing and homeland security are complementary, not mutually exclusive—that it does not have to be an either/or proposition.

Using Community Policing with Terrorism

Certain elements of community policing are compatible and, perhaps, should coexist, with antiterrorism efforts. The first among these elements is the strategic requirement for geographic focus. Community policing requires for police officers to have a permanent beat to be familiar with the community members, identify problems, and find solutions to these problems. Antiterrorism activities also require familiarity with the territory. This will enable police officers to detect suspicious movements of goods and people. Hence, geographic assignment may still be a valuable component for both community policing and antiterrorism policing. In fact, geographic focus is considered necessary to develop the other components of community policing and antiterrorism policing, that is, community partnerships.[27]

The second main component of community policing that may be compatible with antiterrorism is problem solving. Several **terrorism** scholars have pointed out that the underlying causes of terrorism should be addressed. The skills that are developed under a community policing model such as problem solving could be useful for antiterrorism policing. For instance, the SARA problem solving process could still be used to analyze the events surrounding terrorism occurrences. Ordinary events or crime could be analyzed to unravel these events' connections to the preparations for terrorist attack or planning. In particular, skills in crime analysis, crime mapping, crime prevention through environmental design, and other crime prevention strategies that have been learned in community policing could become the intervention and analytical models for antiterrorism policing.

One of the problem-solving infrastructures that emerged with antiterrorism policing is the use of Intelligence Centers or Fusion Centers. Through the collaborative efforts of local, state, and federal agents, these centers gather, analyze, and share intelligence information for the prevention and control of terrorism and other crimes. Evidence show that problem solving seems to be embraced in both the community policing and the homeland security policing eras. The third component of community policing that may be compatible with antiterrorism policing is community participation. Policing could take advantage of the community members' inputs to intelligence information. Such participation could only emerge when trust between the community and the police exists. Community information is important in gathering information about terrorist plots and detecting terrorists.[28]

CYBERCRIME AND COMMUNITY POLICING

Cybercrime involves an array of electronic devices, and is generally the electronic manipulation of data through addition or deletion of files and/or a theft of information. Specific offenses include identity theft, cyber stalking via social network sites or e-mail, child pornography, cyber bullying, embezzlement, theft, and various forms of fraud.

Cybercrime is the fastest-growing type of criminal activity in the world. Indeed, the likelihood of suffering from a violent, person-to-person crime in the physical world is now lower than that of being the victim of a virtual crime. Why face a bevy of bank cameras and security officers at a robbery, when cybercrimes are much more profitable and less risky?

Cybercriminals are no longer amateurs who play with computers just to see "what happens." Expert hackers 99 have become suppliers of sensitive information, computer programs and packages, and other tools that end users need to carry out criminal enterprises. Online criminals even shop for batches of stolen credit card numbers and other identifying information, bank account numbers and passcodes, and skimming devices.[29]

Problem-oriented policing must address cybercrime differently, as the problem often exists in both electronic and physical communities. However, the SARA problem-solving process can be used to address this type of crime. First, police scan and determine the local problems, using crime report data, citizen interviews, and personal observations. Next, they conduct an analysis, determining the causes of cybercrime, what other crimes have derived from cybercrime victimization, the most basic forms of victimization, and the available resources for addressing cybercrime. Then, police develop a variety of responses, considering what other communities have done to remedy the cybercrime problem, the kinds of interventions that might work, and the sources of data that will be gathered. Finally, they assess their responses: was the intervention plan implemented correctly? Were the listed goals obtained? Have new challenges arisen and, if so, how can they be addressed?[30]

Police should also request the assistance from community agencies to help them address the problem of cybercrime; for example, are local banks informing their customers of the risks related to online banking? Are computer repair stores offering customer vulnerability assessments to determine if an individual's computer is infected or at risk?[31]

APPLYING SCIENCE TO POLICING

The police have accomplished much in the last few decades, to include developing new strategies of crime control and prevention, introducing problem-oriented policing, hot spot policing, CompStat, Smart Policing, predictive policing, crime mapping, and other strategic innovations. New technologies have included major advancements in automatic fingerprinting systems and DNA testing. The police have begun to break down the walls separating them from academia, often enlisting the help of researchers.

Given that, however, policing experts such as David Weisburd and Peter Neyroud[32] believe there is still a fundamental disconnect between **science** and policing. By "science" they mean the broad array of methods and technologies, to include advances not only as mentioned above in forensics, but also in social science, which often has been neglected by the police. In short, there needs to be greater use of scientific models of inquiry such as problem-oriented policing. They argue that despite these advances, science has yet to move to center stage.

For example, most police practices are not systematically evaluated, and we still know too little about what works and under what conditions in policing, due to lack of impact evaluation (discussed in Chapter 11). Often, the introduction of research leaps from a "bright idea" of police practitioners or researchers rather than through systematic development of knowledge about practice. Then, police leaders try to diffuse the idea more widely in their agencies, and across agencies, without adequately having researched what the real effect was. In turn, police science is often ignored even when the evidence is unambiguous. Take for example the continued application of programs like Drug Abuse Resistance Education (DARE) and other programs that have been shown to be ineffective but continue to be supported and implemented by police agencies.[33]

How can policing be moved to include science to a central place? First, science must become a natural and organic part of the police mission, both because it can help them to define practices and programs that have promise, and because it can allow them to assess such innovations in terms of how well they work, and at what cost.[34]

NEED FOR STRONG POLICE LEADERSHIP

As Joseph A. Schafer et al. stated, "The most important job of any leader is to create the conditions for his or her subordinates to be able to perform their jobs to the best of their abilities."[35] In this section, we discuss several areas in which police leaders must be extremely sensitive to the image they project to the public they serve as well as some areas in which they must demonstrate that their agency has the proper "conditions" to perform their functions.

Militarization of the Police

In Chapter 3, we discussed the vast amount of controversy generated concerning the use of the state's national guard and military equipment and tactics in Ferguson, Missouri, and across the nation. We noted that many people are upset about the millions of pieces of surplus military equipment that have been given to local police departments across the country, including helicopters and airplanes. In Chapter 8 we mentioned the "optics" of such a police response—the image that is created when police bring heavy equipment to the scene of a demonstration or wearing protective riot gear if there is no indication that a demonstration will be violent.

Furthermore, many people express concerns about whether, and the extent to which, the residual effects of 9/11 have affected or overshadowed the development and function of community policing in many agencies. Specifically, they wonder whether this nation has recently experienced too great a shift in emphasis and resources by federal and local governments from community policing, in favor of one that is now "militarized," "federalized," and antiterrorism in its orientation and funding. The question becomes whether or not there can be a dual role for the police—one that is both community-policing as well as militaristic in its orientation. On the one hand, certainly the public appreciates having a public servant and guardian who can mobilize the community and develop problem-solving strategies toward protecting their neighborhoods against gang members, drug dealers, and general crime and disorder. Conversely, however, whenever citizens experience a serious problem, danger, or victimization, they certainly appear to want their police officers to forcefully and swiftly enforce the law, bringing to bear whatever tools and resources are required to do the job.

It should be noted, of course, that not all police personnel in the United States, nor its civilian population, perceive a problem or a threat of harm posed by increased collaboration between the police and the military. And, for their part, the police will no doubt welcome military assistance rendered during such crises as hurricanes or terrorist attacks. State national guard units have a nearly 400-year history in the United States, back to when the colonists organized able-bodied male citizens for protection. Indeed, it is not only acceptable but even comforting for many people to see military forces standing vigilant against terrorists in domestic venues. Others, however, may hold an image of U.S. soldiers patrolling the streets or knocking on doors in the middle of the night as frightening and opposed to the American way of life.

Transparency and Public Trust

The public today is more informed about what is occurring in the community and more police incidents are being captured on video. With this level of exposure, officer conduct and professionalism will likely continue in the future to be an issue and involve constant scrutiny by the public, which expects and deserves officers to act professional at all times. This constant scrutiny will require more interaction with the public on commonly accepted police best practices and behavior and may lead to greater civilian oversight to provide a more open and transparent look at police conduct and policies.

Another aspect of transparency and trust is that online media outlets (such as blogs and social media) have gained more acceptance and credibility among the general public, particularly among the younger generation. As more second and third tier "media" become more mainstream, law enforcement will find itself having to modify its media relationships and even craft different messages depending upon the outlet. While many police agencies already use online blogs or other electronic mediums, police agencies may have to monitor information outlets never considered before to stay on top of what is being reported about law enforcement in their community. Agencies will also have to make their communication products interesting and relevant so that the public is more inclined to turn to police agencies directly as a source rather than some other outlet. This is easier said than done since many agencies do not consider maintaining and updating their Web site as a primary duty.[36]

Succession Planning

Succession planning is a process whereby police organizations take affirmative steps to plan for filling vacancies they know will exist in key positions. Studied extensively by scholars of various stripes, effective succession planning involves identifying the right people for the job and developing them in ways that will allow them to assume the mantle of leadership if and when the time comes.

Through attention to the essential underpinnings of succession planning and by undertaking specific implementation steps, police organizations should be able to ensure the leadership vitality of the agencies and nurture and develop organizational culture in the desired direction.

Succession planning has been the focus of scholarly attention for some time. Effective succession planning requires active and intentional management of the flow of persons into (and out of) the organization as well as the identification and development of persons who will occupy those key roles in the future. To borrow Jim Collins's metaphor used in his description of how to make "good" organizations "great," effective succession planning will require organizations to: (a) get the right people on the bus, (b) get the wrong people off the bus, and (c) get the right people in the right seats.[37]

Losing our police leaders is a problem, but not one that we must passively accept. Consistent with the community policing philosophy, we can anticipate the problem and implement solutions in the form of succession planning.[38]

The department should also take advantage of training opportunities not only to improve specific skills of their officers and civilian personnel, but also to increase their leadership abilities. Leadership development for midlevel managers (e.g., sergeants and lieutenants) is important, although harder to come by. The policing profession must continue to develop and support professional development through leadership training, networking opportunities, and other pursuits that encourage cross-fertilization of ideas and ongoing education.[39]

Civilianization

Use of civilian employees in police organizations is another growing trend and may likely continue in the future. Such employees are now being trained for many duties that sworn officers historically performed; this carries tremendous potential cost savings—which in turn may allow agencies to spend more money on needed technology or infrastructure. Furthermore, civilian employees typically have less union representation than sworn staff, which could affect the hiring and firing of civilian employees as well as the job protection of sworn staff.

But there should be clearly defined roles for both civilian and sworn staff. Greater use of civilians could lead to more civilian injuries given the potential for seemingly innocuous encounters to instantly turn violent. In general, therefore, the potential benefits and repercussions from greater use of civilians as well as the impacts on the structure of police organizations should be considered carefully.[40]

Keeping the Focus on Community Policing

Community policing is felt to be quality police service. Still, some police officers resist—and may well continue to oppose—the transition to community policing and problem solving if they view it as "soft" on crime or not "real" policing.

The focus of many agencies and their government leaders—and some police academies'—has been placed much more heavily on tactics and equipment in recent years. As noted by Chief Betsy Hard of the Bloomfield, Connecticut Police Department, "Academies are emphasizing the edicts the profession is receiving—homeland security and intelligence— not problem solving or community policing." Similarly, Chief Theron Bowman of the Arlington, Texas Police Department, stated that "One of my greatest challenges is ensuring that community policing moves forward. It is who we are and what we do. It isn't who other departments are yet. As police officers and experts on the community policing philosophy, we need to take a leadership role and show other departments what the community orientation is all about."[41]

Obviously, consistent, progressive leadership will be necessary in the future to advance and spread community policing. All agency leaders must communicate to employees that community policing is not a short-lived program or an appendage to the agency, but rather a philosophical approach to delivering police services in a democracy. Furthermore, given that patrol officers work directly with the public, agencies must stress to new officers—throughout recruitment, academy training, and in their daily service—that the agency adheres to the community policing philosophy. Even during the recruitment process, agency personnel should seek to adopt screening processes that select persons who have a service orientation and will be committed to community policing. Agency leaders must also ensure that policies and procedures are congruent with the community policing philosophy, officers are evaluated in a community policing context and receive commendations for their successes, and promote and reward officers who serve as role models and leaders to others in the agency.

Training

In Chapter 10 we briefly examined some of the training methods (including "gamification") and curricula that are required for today's problem-solving police officer. Certainly, the curricula and methods of **training** of police officers will continue to evolve and become more technological and sophisticated in the future. Indeed, today's challenges with terrorism, cybercrime, financial crimes in particular—will continue to pose tremendous demands on the police and require that they remain abreast of new and sophisticated criminal methods.

Fortunately, the future promises to be very exciting in this regard; with the assistance of computers, the nature and breadth of problem-oriented policing training sessions to be offered are limited only by agency budgets and imagination. Virtual reality and holographic simulations of victims, witnesses, and suspects will continue to expand in use, with avatars used to represent any age, ethnic group, and scenario. It is also anticipated that by 2025 regional training facilities will replace the community college academy system, where hands-on role-play instruction as well as driving tracks, indoor and outdoor firearms ranges, and life-size cityscapes will simulate call response. Lists of available online courses will continue to expand in nature, as will opportunities for online distance learning. Refresher modules will become more available for personnel seeking or being mandated to strengthen their skills. Greater emphases will be placed on training officers to remain physically fit, enhance their communication skills (through virtual reality simulations), and to enter almost any environment and engage in a variety of police contacts.[42]

Peace Officers Standards and Training (POST) organizations in all states should continually monitor training requirements to better meet the needs and demands of tomorrow's recruit; further, methods of training delivery should be continually scrutinized to ensure they effectively and efficiently impart knowledge and skills in a manner best suited to adult learners.[43]

Summary

Is the cup half full, or is the cup half empty? Should we be optimistic or pessimistic about the nation's and policing's future? The answers are unclear. One thing that is for certain is that our society is changing.

This chapter has examined the future, including the need for police to plan for it as well as some prognostications for the problem-oriented policing strategy. What is clear is that this is a very exciting and challenging time to be serving in police agencies.

The years ahead are not going to be tranquil, either inside or outside of police agencies. Many dangers and issues now exist that increasingly compel us to "read the tea leaves" with greater trepidation. Therefore, today's police leaders must not wait for someone else to set the pace. Bold leadership is essential today to prepare for the future and implement necessary reforms. More than ever, police leaders must ensure that the best and brightest individuals are recruited, trained, and become the best officers they can be. Challenges have always existed for the men and women who wear a badge, but certainly they will be challenged in their ability to successfully confront what the future will bring.

Key Terms and Concepts

Civilianization
Cybercrime
Drivers

Militarization
  (of police)
Science (in policing)

Succession
  planning
Technologies

Terrorism
Training

Items for Review

1. Explain the authors' concerns with the language of policing in general, and particularly the tendency to use new labels and to create new eras of policing.
2. Review the drivers and factors that will influence policing in the future.
3. In what ways will technologies will assist and shape policing in the future?

4. How can problem-oriented policing help to address terrorism? Cybercrime? Focus on use of the SARA model.
5. Explain how today's police executives can provide strong leadership in the future, particularly in the areas of militarization, public trust, succession planning, civilianization, and maintaining the role and functions of community policing.

Learn by Doing

1. As the head of your agency's planning and research division, you have been assigned by your police chief to attend a "Future Leaders Conference" sponsored by your area Chamber of Commerce. You are to present your agency's vision of the kinds of challenges that will be facing police leaders in the year 2025, particularly with regard to technologies and terrorism. What will be your responses?
2. Your police department has a history of promoting from within, and the popular chief has just announced that he will retire in one year. While guest lecturing to your agency's Citizens' Police

Academy, one of the attendees is extremely concerned about what your agency has been doing in the area of succession planning to ensure that a highly qualified individual will become the next chief. Assuming police leadership has been very active and innovative in doing so, what will be your response?

3. You have been invited to attend a conference with your criminal justice professor and to co-author a scholarly paper setting forth how problem-oriented policing can provide assistance in support of homeland security in the future. What will be your basic position?

Endnotes

1. Ronald W. Glensor and Kenneth J. Peak, "New Police Management Practices and Predictive Software: A New Era They Do Not Make," in Debra R. Cohen McCullough and Deborah L. Spence (eds.), *American Policing in 2022: Essays on the Future of a Profession* (Washington, D.C.: U.S. Department of Justice Office of Community Oriented Policing Services, 2012), pp. 11–15.
2. Ibid.
3. Charlie Beck, "Predictive Policing: What Can We Learn from Wal-Mart and Amazon about Fighting Crime in a Recession?" *The Police Chief* 76(11) (November 2009):18–24.
4. Laurie Robinson, "Predictive Policing Symposium: Opening Remarks" (speech given at the Predictive Policing Symposium in Los Angeles, California, November 18, 2009), www.nij .gov/topics/law-enforcement/strategies/predictive-policing/ symposium/opening-robinson.htm.
5. Glensor and Peak, "New Police Management Practices and Predictive Software: A New Era They Do Not Make," p. 15.
6. Sidney Fuller, quoted in Drew Diamond and Deirdre Mead Weiss, *Community Policing: Looking to Tomorrow* (Washington, D.C.: U.S. Department of Justice, Office of Community Oriented Policing Services, May 2009), p. 19.
7. Louis Mayo, quoted in Debra R. Cohen McCullough and Deborah L. Spence (eds.), *American Policing in 2022: Essays on the Future of a Profession* (Washington, D.C.: U.S. Department of Justice Office of Community Oriented Policing Services, 2012), p. 35.
8. Bureau of Justice Assistance, *The BJA Executive Session on Police Leadership: Organization of the Future Report* (Washington, D.C.: U.S. Department of Justice, Bureau of Justice Assistance, 2011), pp. 6–10.

9. Gregory F. Treverton, Matt Wollman, Elizabeth Wilke, Deborah Lai, *Moving Toward the Future of Policing* (Santa Monica, Calif.: Rand Corporation, 2011).
10. Ibid.
11. Bureau of Justice Assistance, *Organization of the Future Report*, p. 8.
12. Ibid., pp. 6–10.
13. Ibid.
14. Ibid.
15. *President's Task Force on 21st Century Policing Implementation Guide* (Washington, DC: Office of Community Oriented Policing Services, 2015), pp. 2–3.
16. Bureau of Justice Assistance, *Organization of the Future Report*, p. 8.
17. Treverton et al., *Moving Toward the Future of Policing*, p. 1.
18. Adapted from ibid.
19. Ibid.
20. Ibid., p. 80.
21. Ibid., p. 83.
22. Ibid.
23. Ibid.
24. Ibid.
25. Paul Rosenzweig, "Future of Policing: 4 Factors to Consider When Deploying New Technologies, *Government Technology* (December 4, 2015), http://www.govtech.com/opinion/Future-of-Policing-4-Factors-to-Consider-When-Deploying-New-Technologies.html?utm_medium=email&utm_source= Act-On+Software&utm_content=email&utm_campaign=4%20 Factors%20to%20Consider%20When%20Deploying%20 New%20Police%20Technologies%2C%20New

%20York%27s%20Community-Aggregating%20Power%20
Pilot%20Passes%20Milestone&utm_term=Future%20of
%20Policing%3A%204%20Factors%20to%20Consider%20
When%20Deploying%20New%20Technologies.

26. United Nations Interregional Crime and Justice Research Institute (UNICRI), *Improving Urban Security through Green Environmental Design: New Energy for Urban Security*, p. 22, http://www.unicri.it/news/2011/1104-2_urban_security/110414_CRA_Urban_Security_sm.pdf.

27. Melchor C. de Guzman, "Future Impact of Community Policing on Terrorism," in Kenneth J. Peak (ed.), *Encyclopedia of Community Policing and Problem Solving* (Thousand Oaks, Calif.: Sage, 2013), pp. 403–405.

28. Ibid.

29. Treverton et al., *Moving Toward the Future of Policing*, p. 98.

30. Aaron A. Harnish, "Cybercrime and Community Policing," in Kenneth J. Peak (ed.), *Encyclopedia of Community Policing and Problem Solving* (Thousand Oaks, Calif.: Sage, 2013), pp. 111–113.

31. Ibid.

32. David Weisburd and Peter Neyroud, *Police Science: Toward a New Paradigm* (Washington, D.C.: National Institute of Justice, and Harvard Kennedy School, January 2011), pp. 2–3.

33. Ibid., p. 4.

34. Ibid., pp. 11–12.

35. Quoted in Joseph A. Schafer, Michael E. Buerger, Richard W. Myers, Carl J. Jensen, and Bernard H. Levin, *The Future of Policing: A Practical Guide for Police Managers and Leaders* (Boca Raton, Fla.: CRC Press, 2012), p. 235.

36. Bureau of Justice Assistance, *Organization of the Future Report*, p. 9.

37. For an overview of Collins' thoughts and quotes, see Kimberly Weisul, "Jim Collins: Good to Great in 10 Steps" (May 7, 2012), http://www.inc.com/kimberly-weisul/jim-collins-good-to-great-in-ten-steps.html.

38. Phillip M. Lyons, Jr., "Succession Planning," in Kenneth J. Peak (ed.), *Encyclopedia of Community Policing and Problem Solving* (Thousand Oaks, Calif.: Sage, 2013), pp. 397–400.

39. Treverton et al., *Moving Toward the Future of Policing*, pp. 26–27.

40. Bureau of Justice Assistance, *Organization of the Future Report*, p. 6.

41. Quoted in Diamond and Mead Weiss, *Community Policing: Looking to Tomorrow*, p. 20.

42. Bob Harrison, "A Retrospective: Police Academy Training in 2032," *FBI Law Enforcement Bulletin* (September 2014), https://leb.fbi.gov/2014/september/futures-perspective-a-retrospective-police-academy-training-in-2032.

43. Treverton et al., *Moving Toward the Future of Policing*, pp. 26–27.

ANSWERS

CHAPTER 1
1. f
2. f
3. t
4. f
5. t
6. f
7. F

CHAPTER 2
1. f
2. t
3. f
4. f
5. t
6. t

CHAPTER 3
1. f
2. t
3. f
4. F

CHAPTER 4
1. f
2. f
3. f
4. t
5. t
6. t
7. f
8. F

CHAPTER 5
1. f
2. t
3. f
4. t
5. F

CHAPTER 6
1. f
2. f
3. t
4. t
5. T

CHAPTER 7
1. f
2. t
3. t

4. f
5. F

CHAPTER 8
1. f
2. f
3. t
4. t
5. T

CHAPTER 9
1. f
2. f
3. t
4. f
5. T

CHAPTER 10
1. f
2. f
3. t
4. f
5. F

CHAPTER 11
1. f
2. f
3. f
4. t
5. T

CHAPTER 12
1. f
2. f
3. t
4. f
5. t

CHAPTER 13
1. f
2. t
3. t
4. f
5. f

CHAPTER 14
1. f
2. t
3. f
4. t
5. t

APPENDIX I

Award-Winning Problem-Solving Case Studies

Although many examples of successful problem-solving initiatives are dispersed throughout the text, here we briefly provide three case studies that specifically concern police application of problem-solving techniques. They are taken from *Problem-Solving Tips: A Guide to Reducing Crime and Disorder Through Problem-Solving Partnerships* (2d ed.) (Washington, D.C.: Office of Community Oriented Policing Services, July 2011), pp. 31–37.

These examples illustrate the use of the SARA model and feature responses that are linked to comprehensive problem analyses. The COPS Office is not promoting a particular set of responses to problems and acknowledges that there is room for disagreement regarding the responses selected and their relative impact.

PLANO, TEXAS, ADDRESSES TRAFFIC CONGESTION NEAR SCHOOLS

Scanning

Residents of a neighborhood near Barron Elementary School complained to their neighborhood officer about seemingly intractable traffic problems, including congestion, speeding, red light running, illegal parking, and crashes. Traditional law enforcement efforts, including surveillance and citation, had been intermittently attempted over multiple years but did not result in sustained improvement.

Analysis

The neighborhood officer undertook a thorough analysis of empirical data, environmental factors, and behavioral patterns. Barron is located at the corner of a major four-lane thoroughfare and a narrow residential street. The school specializes in preschool-aged children with disabilities, resulting in a majority of parents choosing to drive their children to and from school. The only means of dropping off or picking up a student was to enter and exit the residential neighborhood, and parents reported that instead of attempting to use the inadequate carpool lane, they routinely stopped in the middle of the street and encouraged their children to run across the street.

While traffic-related calls for police service were not unusually high when compared to other neighborhoods with schools, crashes were much more common in the Barron neighborhood. After reviewing the circumstances of each crash in the neighborhood, the officer determined that each was the result of a traffic violation committed in an attempt to circumvent the traffic plan within the neighborhood. Peak times for congestion came in 15-minute increments and occurred during morning and afternoon drop-off and pick-up, amounting to only 1 hour per weekday: 7:45–8:00 AM, 10:45–11:00 AM, 11:15–11:30 AM, and 2:45–3:00 PM. Residents had repeatedly complained to the city traffic engineering department, resulting in temporary changes to traffic signal timing. The officer determined that education and enforcement, combined with permanent traffic design and control changes, were required to address these chronic problems.

Response

The officer developed strategies within three realms: education, enforcement, and traffic management. She changed her work hours to coincide with the peak problem periods. Working with school staff, parents, and residents, she created and distributed maps of alternative egress routes from the neighborhood. She also created and distributed flyers—translated into Spanish by school staff—to educate parents and explain changes to the traffic plan. School-provided traffic signs were replaced with city-made signs to authorize police enforcement. Once the education period had elapsed, the officer began stopping every observed violation during the peak periods. This occasionally meant stopping as many as seven vehicles at one time. Working with the traffic engineering department, a new traffic plan was developed, including a new carpool lane that dispersed vehicles away from the residential neighborhoods and the most congested intersection.

Visual obstructions to signage—like tree limbs—were removed and traffic control devices were installed to re-route traffic. Parking was restricted and enhanced signage was installed. Four marked crosswalks were created for pedestrian access and school-zone lights were synchronized with dismissal times. Traffic signal cycles were precisely programmed to coincide with peak use times to ease ingress and egress without unnecessarily disrupting the area's traffic flow during nonpeak times. Last, after years of discussion between the city and the area's resident association, a park access road was constructed, facilitating easier access to the neighborhood for residents without inviting school traffic back onto the residential streets.

Assessment

Comparing pre- and post-response survey results showed that resident and parent frustrations were reduced, and a majority of respondents believed that improvements had been realized in terms of both traffic congestion and safety concerns. The neighborhood officer reported that traffic flowed at a reasonable rate during both peak and nonpeak hours and that the historic blockage of residential streets had been virtually eliminated. The purposeful displacement of traffic was carefully planned and was deemed by all parties to have effectively distributed vehicles. Crashes were reduced by 90 percent (from 10 to 1) in just two years.

CHULA VISTA, CALIFORNIA, PROBLEMS AT HOTELS AND MOTELS

Scanning

The city's approximately two dozen hotels and motels continued to generate unacceptable levels of calls for police service and reported crime despite a variety of efforts by stakeholders, including police, other city agencies, and local business groups. Earlier attempts to curb the crime and disorder, which included enhanced police enforcement and adoption of city ordinances prohibiting hourly room rentals and requiring guests to show identification at check-in, proved unsuccessful.

Analysis

The Chula Vista Police Department undertook an analysis of calls for service and crime and disorder data, discovering that motels were routinely the most common location for drug arrests in the city. Furthermore, most calls-for-service originated in motel rooms as opposed to the common areas or parking lots. During interviews of motel customers, the police learned that 75 percent of them were San Diego County residents, many who reported being homeless or nearly homeless. The Center for Criminal Justice Research from California State University, San Bernardino, was brought in to create and implement both a motel management survey and an environmental analysis instrument. The survey identified poor management practices that correlated to high levels of calls-for-service. These motel management practices included catering to local clientele and renting rooms to long-term guests. The environmental analyses reviewed security measures, access control, and visible signs of disorder on the property. Many of the motel rooms throughout Chula Vista lacked basic, industry-accepted security measures like deadbolts, peepholes, and chains or swing-bars on external doors. The police department calculated a calls-for-service per room ratio for each hotel and motel in the city. The initial ratios ranged from 2.77 to 0.11 calls-for-service per room. Plotting these motel-room call-for-service ratios on a map revealed that the size or location of a motel property had little to do with its likelihood for generating calls-for-service and disorder. Analysis of the variation in motel-room prices suggested that, contrary to longstanding local belief, low prices alone did not seem to cause calls-for-service. Ultimately, the stakeholder group developed an array of responses based on the principle that the managers and owners of the hotels and motels were in the best position to control crime and disorder through sound management practices.

Response

Beginning in 2003, the first phase of responses was initiated. A meeting was held with motel owners, police, code enforcement, and the Chamber of Commerce. Property-specific calls-for-service data were provided to owners and were sent on a regular basis. A checklist of best practices designed to reduce problems was distributed to each property owner. Code enforcement officers began an annual inspection program to ensure compliance with state and local codes. During one five-year period, a 7 percent reduction in calls-for-service to motels was realized, but motels still remained the top drug-arrest location in Chula Vista. The second phase of responses was launched. The City Attorney's office and other City agencies were brought in to assist in drafting a motel-management ordinance modeled after several similar laws throughout the country. Under the new law, all motels are required to apply for and obtain an annual operating permit from the City. The granting of the permit was to be based on the condition of the hotel, the use of standard security features for rooms, and the maintenance of an acceptable call-for-service ratio. The standard acceptable ratio was determined to be the 2005 median ratio for all motels in the city. Property owners were required to take preventive measures and develop and implement specific responses to problems at their motels. The City committed to assist motel owners in mitigating their problems but would not mandate specific remedial actions. The ordinance was endorsed by area business groups, including the Chamber of Commerce, and passed the City Council unanimously.

Assessment

All motels wishing to continue operations came into compliance with the new ordinance within the second year of the law's enactment. Calls-for-service to Chula Vista motels were reduced by 49 percent. Drug arrests at motels decreased 66 percent. All reported crimes decreased 70 percent, with violent crimes and crimes against persons dropping 49 percent. Officers spent 52 percent less time at motels throughout the city, freeing up 1,240 patrol hours during the first year of the ordinance's enactment. Motels' quality, appearance, and management practices improved; several hotels were sold to new owners; and the number of substandard units in the city (i.e., those without deadbolts, peepholes, and door chains or security bars) dropped from 378 to 0. The City reported an increase in the transient occupancy tax (room tax) receipts. No displacement of crime or disorder was reported either at nearby apartment complexes or at motels in neighboring jurisdictions during the first two years of the ordinance's enactment.

CHARLOTTE-MECKLENBURG, NORTH CAROLINA, BURGLARIES FROM STORAGE FACILITIES

Scanning

During one year, the Charlotte-Mecklenburg Police Department saw a 28 percent increase in commercial burglaries, 7 percent of which occurred at mini-warehouse or storage facilities. Most of the incidents involved multiple units within one facility, with an average of 3.5 victims per incident. A sergeant and two detectives were assigned to initiate a problem-solving effort to address the storage-facility burglaries.

Analysis

The detectives began their analysis by reading each of the 99 storage-facility burglary reports. Of the 99 reports, 71 occurred at one of 28 facilities and accounted for 291 individual victims. The detectives identified a total of 75 storage facilities in the jurisdiction and realized that most facilities did not have significant burglary problems. When the facility locations were mapped in relation to crime data, no correlation was found between the location of a facility, the occurrence of burglary at the facility, and the level of crime in the surrounding neighborhood. Reports were analyzed to determine whether there were any particular kinds of property being targeted, but the detectives found no reliable patterns. In an effort to identify variances in design, policy, and practice that might account for different levels of victimization, the detectives visited each of the 75 facilities. One key finding from these visits was that the use of disc-style locks seemed to be the most effective measure for securing individual storage units. The one facility requiring customers to use disc locks on its units had not suffered a single burglary incident.

Response

In order to test their hypothesis that the use of disc locks would substantially reduce the occurrence of burglary, the police department designed a study involving three locations: two storage facilities that would suggest, but not require, that their customers use the disc locks, and the one facility already requiring the use of the locks. The police department purchased the disc locks for use in the study and launched the initiative. Once the test was underway, the detectives collaborated with the mini-storage industry and area owners to develop a "best practices" guide. The recommendations in the guide relate to performing background checks on customers, educating renters on burglary prevention, restricting customer access to the units in times when on-site managers were present, encouraging the use of disc locks, improving lighting, using surveillance cameras, and providing the police the access codes to enter the facilities.

Assessment

Compared to the year prior to the study, the facilities involved in the study realized a 58 percent reduction in the number of reported burglary incidents and a 69 percent reduction in the number of individual burglarized units during the one-year test. Highlighting the utility of the disc locks is the fact that one incident at one of the test facilities involved entry into 26 separate storage units, none of which was secured by a disc lock. This single burglary incident accounted for 79 percent of that facility's burglaries during the test period. Also during the test period, there was a 39 percent increase in the number of reported burglary incidents and a 45 percent increase in the number of individual burglarized units at facilities not involved in the study.

APPENDIX II

Model Academic Curriculum for Problem-Oriented Policing

Developed in 2006 by the U.S. Department of Justice, Office of Community Oriented Policing Services, Center for Problem-Oriented Policing; available at http://www.popcenter.org/learning/model_curriculum/files/Model_Academic_Curriculum_Syllabus.pdf.

INTRODUCTION

This curriculum has been designed for undergraduate education, but with minor modifications it can be used for graduate-level education, preservice police training, in-service police training, and/or community-based training. It is recommended that students complete an undergraduate policing course as a prerequisite to this course.

PROBLEM ORIENTED POLICING AND PROBLEM SOLVING

Module 1—The Evolution of Policing

Topics

- Fundamental Objectives of Policing and the Primary Police Functions
- A Brief History of Policing
- Policing Styles and Strategies
  - Types of Patrol
  - Broken Windows Theory
  - One Traditional Police Response—The Benefits and Consequences of Police Crackdowns

Module 2—Community Policing

Topics

- The Early History of Community Policing
- Community Policing—An Overview
- Community Oriented Policing versus Problem Oriented Policing (COP and POP)

Module 3—Introduction to Problem Oriented Policing

Topics

- POP and the History of POP
- Defining a Problem
- Key Elements of POP
- Why Use POP Today?

Module 4—The SARA Model

Topic

- The SARA Process

CRIME THEORIES AND SITUATIONAL CRIME PREVENTION

Module 5—Crime Theories and Crime Opportunity

Topics

- The Problem Analysis Triangle
- Routine Activities Theory
- Crime Pattern Theory
- Rational Choice Theory
- 10 Principles of Crime Opportunity

Module 6—Situational Crime Prevention

Topics

- An Overview of Situational Crime Prevention
- Problem Oriented Policing and Situational Crime Prevention

RESEARCHING/SCANNING AND ANALYZING PROBLEMS

Module 7—Identifying and Researching Problems

Topics

- Identifying and Researching a Problem
- Using Available Research Tools

Module 8—Problem-Solving Resources

Topic

- Problem Specific Guides for Police

Module 9—Crime Analysis for Problem Solvers in 60 Small Steps

Topic

- Crime Analysis for Problem Solvers in 60 Small Steps

RETURNING TO THE CRIME TRIANGLE—RESPONDING TO PLACES, OFFENDERS, AND TARGETS/VICTIMS

Module 10—Responding to Crime Places

Topics

- Hot Spots
- Risky Facilities
- Crime Prevention Through Environmental Design
- Displacement and Displacement Theory
- Closing Streets and Alleys to Reduce Crime

Module 11—Responding to Offenders

Topics

- Thinking and Acting Like an Offender
- Using Offender Interviews to Inform Police Problem Solving
- An Example of an Offender-Based Response—The Boston Gun Project: Operation Cease Fire

Module 12—Responding to Targets/Victims

Topics

- Analyzing Repeat Victimization
- Responding to Repeat Victimization

ASSESSING YOUR PROBLEM-SOLVING STRATEGY AND OTHER CHALLENGES TO IMPLEMENTING POP PROJECTS

Module 13—Assessing and Evaluating Responses

Topics

- Assessment and Evaluation—Assessing Responses to Problems
- Conducting Community Surveys

Module 14—Challenges and Future Considerations for Implementing Successful POP Projects

Topics

- Time—The 4th (missing) Dimension of the Problem Analysis Triangle
- Barriers to Implementation
- Shifting and Sharing Responsibility for Public Safety

CREDITS

Chapter 1

Excerpt on p. 4: Quote by Hon. David A. Hardy; **Excerpt** on p. 4: Quote by Oliver Wendell Holmes; **Box** 1–1 on p. 5: From "The New Police" in Chapter 12, *A History of Police in England,* by William Lauriston Melville Lee. Published by Methuen and Company; **Excerpt** on p. 13: From *The Police and the Community,* by Louis A. Radelet. Published by Macmillan, © 1986; **Excerpt** on p. 15: Goldstein, Policing a Free Society, pp. 22–24; **Excerpt** on p. 18: From Community Policing Defined, US Department of Justice; **Box** 1–2 on p. 18: Based on Gayle Fisher-Stewart, Community Policing Explained: A Guide for Local Governments (Washington, D.C.: U.S. Department of Justice, Office of Community Oriented Policing Services, and the International City/ County Management Association, July 2007); **Excerpt** on p. 19: Willard M. Oliver, "The Third Generation of Community Policing: Moving Through Innovation, Diffusion, and Institutionalization," Police Quarterly 3 (December 2000):367–388; **Table** 1–1 on p. 21: Based on George L. Kelling and Mark H.Moore, The Evolving Strategies of Policing (Washington, D.C.: U.S. Department of Justice, National Institute of Justice Perspectives on Policing, November 1988); **Excerpt** on p. 22: U.S. Department of Justice, Office of Community Oriented Policing Services, "Community Partnerships: A Key Ingredient in an Effective Homeland Security Approach," Community Policing Dispatch 1(2) (February 2008), p. 2; **Exhibit** 1–1 on p. 23: Simon Robins, "Addressing the Challenges of Law Enforcement in Africa: Policing in Sierra Leone, Tanzania, and Zambia," Institute for Security Studies, Policy Brief No. 16, October 2009, http://dspace. africaportal.org/jspui/bitstream/123456789/30885/1/NO16OCT09. pdf?1

Chapter 2

Figure 2–1 on p. 28: From Community Policing Defined, U.S. Department of Justice; **Exhibit** 2–1 on p. 30: Based on Kevin Johnson, "Providence one of many U.S. police forces feeling Ferguson aftershocks" USA Today, January 1, 2016; **Exhibit** 2–2 on p. 32: Based on Jenny Kane, "Shootings prompt friendly house visits from police," Reno Gazette Journal, January 1, 2016, pp. 1A, 6A; **Exhibit** 2–3 on p. 33: Based on Volunteers in Police Service, "VIPS Focus," pp. 1–3, http://www.policevolunteers.org/pdf/2007%20 Award.pdf; **Excerpt** on p. 36: Tom Casady, Lincoln, Nebraska, Police Department, http://www.lincoln.ne.gov/city/police/cbp.htm.; **Excerpt** on p. 36: Tom Casady, Lincoln, Nebraska, Police Department, http://www.lincoln.ne.gov/city/police/cbp.htm; **Excerpt** on p. 36: From Community Policing Dispatch, Vol. 01, Issue. 01, U.S. Department of Justice; **Figure** 2–2 on p. 37: Kenneth H Peak, Ronald W Glensor, Community and Problem-Oriented Policing: Effectively Addressing Crime and Disorder, 7e, © 2018. Pearson Education, Inc., New York, NY; **Table** 2–1 on p. 37: From Implementing Community Policing, U.S. Department of Justice; **Excerpt** on p. 39: Southern California Public Radio, "Social Cities Debate the Pros and Cons of Police Oversight Models" (July 30, 2015), http://www.scpr.org/news/2015/07/30/53450/socal-cities-debate-the-pros-and-cons-of-police-ov/; **Exhibit** 2–4 on p. 40: Based on Barbara Ludman, "How Community Policing Works," City of Johannesburg, South Africa, January 18, 2016, http://joburg.org.za/ index.php?option=com_content&task=view&id=88&Itemid=9;

Exhibit 2–5 on p. 40: From Boston Police Department: Enhancing Cultures of Integrity, U.S. Department of Justice; **Table** 2–2 on p. 41: Based on Office of Juvenile Justice and Delinquency Prevention Balanced and Restorative Justice: Prospects for Juvenile Justice in the 21st Century, 2004, pp. 467–509, https://www.ncjrs. gov/pdffiles/framwork.pdf; **Exhibit** 2–7 on p. 43: David Leitenberger, Pete Semenyna, and Jeffrey B. Spelman, "Community Corrections and Community Policing," FBI Law Enforcement Bulletin (November 2003): 20–23; **Exhibit** 2–8 on p. 44: From Active Calls For Service. Copyright © by Clearwater Florida Police Department. Used with permission of Clearwater Florida Police Department; **Excerpt** on pp. 35–36: From Community Based Policing, Lincoln Police Department.

Chapter 3

Excerpt on p. 49: Quote by Justice Thurgood Marshall; **Exhibit** 3–1 on p. 52: Anthony Strianese, "Community Policing in the Delray Beach, Florida, Haitian Community," The Police Chief 78 (March 2011), pp. 32–33, http://www.policechiefmagazine.org/magazine/ index.cfm?fuseaction=display_arch&article_id=2333&issue_ id=32011; **Exhibit** 3–2 on p. 53: Christine Mai-Duc, "Deportee accused of killing Kathryn Steinle to stand trial on murder charge," Los Angeles Times, September 4, 2015, http://www.latimes.com/ local/lanow/la-me-ln-kathryn-steinle-sf-shooting-murder-trial-20150904-story.html; **Exhibit** 3–3 on p. 55: Greg Botelho and Sonia Moghe, "North Charleston reaches $6.5 Million settlement with family of Walter Scott," CNN, October 9, 2015, http://www.cnn. com/2015/10/08/us/walter-scott-north-charleston-settlement/index. html; **Excerpt** on p. 55: From Nobody Knows My Name: More Notes of a Native Son by James Baldwin. Published by Dell Publishing Company, © 1962; **Exhibit** 3–4 on pp. 57–58: BBC News, "Papua New Guinea Profile – Overview," October 7, 2015, http://www.bbc.com/news/world-asia-15592917; **Excerpt** on p. 57: From Interim Report of The President's Task Force on 21st Century Policing, U.S. Department of Justice; **Excerpt** on p. 58: From 2013 OIS Web Summaries, Case # 311475A, Dallas Police Department; **Table** 3–1 on p. 59: Pew Research Center/USA Today, August 2014; **Excerpt** on p. 61: From "Considering Police Body Cameras" by Developments in the Law, Vol. 128, No. 06, pp. 1794–1817. Published by Harvard Law Review, © 2015; **Excerpt** on p. 62: U.S. Department of Justice, Office of Community Oriented Policing Services, Community Policing Dispatch, "Preparing for Crime in a Bad Economy," http://www.cops.usdoj.gov/html/dispatch/ January_2009/crime_economy.htm; **Excerpt** on p. 62: Reprinted from The Police Chief, Vol. 72, No. 02. Copyright held by the International Association of chiefs of Police Inc., 44 Conal Center Plaza Suite 200, Alexander, VA, 22314. Further reproduction without express permission for IACP is strictly prohibited; **Exhibit** 3–5 on p. 63: Police Executive Research Forum. 2015. Critical Response Technical Assessment Review: Police Accountability—Findings and National Implications of an Assessment of the San Diego Police Department (Washington, DC: Office of Community Oriented Policing Services, 2015), p. ix, http:// www.sandiego.gov/police/pdf/perfrpt.pdf; **Excerpt** on pp. 61–62: From Interim Report of The President's Task Force on 21st Century Policing, U.S. Department of Justice.

Chapter 4

Excerpt on p. 69: Quote by Muhammad Atta; **Excerpt** on p. 69: Quote by Justice Arlen Specter; **Excerpt** on p. 72: From Remarks by Secretary of Homeland Security Jeh Johnson at the Canadian American Business Council, Department of Homeland Security; **Exhibit** 4–1 on p. 72: Majority and Minority Staff of the Senate Committee on Homeland Security and Governmental Affairs, Zachary Chesser: A Case Study in Online Islamist Radicalization and Its Meaning for the Threat of Homegrown Terrorism (Washington, DC: United States Senate, 2012); **Exhibit** 4–2 on p. 72: Khalid Aldawsari, "Complaint Affidavit," The Washington Post (February 23, 2011), http://www.washington-post.com/wp-srv/world/documents/khalid-aldawsari-complaint-affidavit.html; **Excerpt** on p. 79: The Rockefeller Institute of Government, "The Federalism Challenge: The Challenge for State and Local Government," "The Role of 'Home' in Homeland Security: Symposium Series," Number 2, March 24, 2003.

Chapter 5

Excerpt on p. 87: Quote by Albert Einstein; **Figure** 5–1 on p. 88: From Community Policing Defined, U.S. Department of Justice; **Excerpt** on p. 89: Problem-Oriented Policing by Herman Goldstein. Published by Herman Goldstein, © 1987; **Figure** 5–2 on p. 89: From Problem Solving, Problem-Oriented Policing In Newport News by John E Eck and William Spelman, U.S. Department of Justice; **Figure** 5–3 on p. 90: From Problem Solving, Problem-Oriented Policing In Newport News by John E Eck and William Spelman, U.S. Department of Justice; **Figure** 5–4 on p. 91: From Problem-Solving Tools Series: Problem-Oriented Guides for Police, No. 13, Identifying and Defining Policing Problems, U.S. Department of Justice; **Figure** 5–5 on p. 95: From The Problem Analysis Triangle, http://www.popcenter.org/about/?p=triangle. © Center for Problem-Oriented Policing. Reprinted with permission; **Figure** 5–6 on p. 96: Adapted from The Problem Analysis Triangle, http://www.popcenter.org/about/?p=triangle. © Center for Problem-Oriented Policing. Reprinted with permission; **Excerpt** on p. 97: From Problem Solving, Problem-Oriented Policing In Newport News, National Criminal Justice Reference Service (NCJRS); **Box** 5–1 on p. 98: Adapted from Herman Goldstein, Problem-Oriented Policing (New York: McGraw-Hill, 1990), pp. 140–141. Used with permission of McGraw-Hill; **Excerpt** on p. 98: From Problem-Solving Tips: A Guide to Reducing Crime and Disorder Through Problem-Solving Partnerships, U.S. Department of Justice; **Box** 5–2 on p. 99: Adapted from Implementing a Problem-Oriented Approach: A Management Guide by John E Eck. Copyright © 1990. Used with permission of Police Executive Research Forum; **Figure** 5–7 on p. 100: From Problem-Solving Tools Series: Problem-Oriented Guides for Police, No. 01, Assessing Responses to Problems, An Introductory Guide for Police Problem-Solvers by John E Eck, U.S. Department of Justice; **Excerpt** on p. 101: W. G. Skogan, S. M. Hartnett, J. DuBois, J. T. Comey, M. Kaiser, and J. H. Lovig, Problem Solving in Practice: Implementing Community Policing in Chicago (Washington, D.C.: U.S. Department of Justice, National Institute of Justice, 2000); **Excerpt** on p. 101: W. G. Skogan, S. M. Hartnett, J. DuBois, J. T. Comey, M. Kaiser, and J. H. Lovig, Problem Solving in Practice: Implementing Community Policing in Chicago (Washington, D.C.: U.S. Department of Justice, National Institute of Justice, 2000); **Exhibit** 5–1 on p. 102: New Zealand Police, "Top POP Cops head to Christchurch for final," June 23, 2015, http://www.police.govt.nz/news/release/top-pop-cops-head-christchurch-final; **Excerpt** on p. 102: Based on Problem-Solving Tips: A Guide to Reducing Crime and Disorder Through Problem-Solving Partnerships (2d ed.)

(Washington, D.C.: Office of Community Oriented Policing Services, July 2011); **Figure** 5–8 on p. 103: From Community Policing Defined, U.S. Department of Justice; **Excerpt** on pp. 100–101: From Community Policing: Can it Work? By Wesley G Skogan. Published by Thomson Learning, © 2004.

Chapter 6

Excerpt on p. 107: Quote by Thomas Fuller; **Excerpt** on p. 107: Quote by H G Wells; **Excerpt** on p. 108: Quote by Richard Mellard; **Excerpt** on p. 108: From Crime Prevention in America: Foundations for Action. Published by The National Crime Prevention Council, © 1990; **Table** 6–1 on p. 109: From Crime Prevention Brief: Crime Prevention Through Environmental Design, U.S. Department of Housing and Urban Development; **Excerpt** on p. 111: From Crime Prevention and Community Policing: A Vital Partnership, U.S. Department of Justice; **Exhibit** 06–01 on p. 112: Association of State and Territorial Health Officials, "Crime Prevention Through Environmental Design" (Arlington, VA: Author, n.d.); **Excerpt** on p. 114: National Crime Prevention Council, Designing Safer Communities: A Crime Prevention Through Environmental Design Handbook (Washington, D.C.: Author, 1997), pp. 7–8; **Excerpt** on p. 115: Greg Saville and Gerry Cleveland, "2nd Generation CPTED: An Antidote to the Social Y2K Virus of Urban Design." Paper presented at the Third Annual International CPTED Conference, Washington, D.C., December 14–16, 1998; **Exhibit** 6–2 on p. 116: From Problem-Oriented Guides for Police Problem-Solving Tools Series No. 01, Using Crime Prevention Through Environmental Design in Problem-Solving by Diane Zahm, U.S. Department of Justice; **Excerpt** on p. 117: From Situational Crime Prevention. Copyright © by Center for Problem-Oriented Policing. Reprinted with permission; **Excerpt** on p. 118: Based On Ronald V. Clarke, "The 10 Principles Of Crime Opportunity," In U.S. Department Of Justice, Center For Problem-Oriented Policing, "Twenty-Five Techniques Of Situational Prevention," Http://Www.Popcenter.Org/25Techniques/; **Table** 6–2 on p. 119: From "Opportunities Precipitators and Criminal Decisions: A Reply to Wortley's Critique of Situational Crime Prevention" by Derek B Cornish and Ronald V Clarke in Theory for Practice in Situational Crime Prevention, Crime Prevention Studies, Vol 16, pp. 41–96 Edited by Martha J Smith, Derek B. Cornish. Copyright © Lynne Rienner Publishers ; **Excerpt** on p. 120: Used with permission of the International Association of Chiefs of Police. Further reproduction without express permission from IACP is strictly prohibited; **Table** 6–3 on p. 121: U.S. Department of Justice, Office of Community Oriented Policing Services, Center for Problem Oriented Policing, "Police Publicity Campaigns and Target Audiences," http://www.popcenter.org/responses/crime_prevention/2 (Accessed September 22, 2010); **Excerpt** on p. 124: CPTED Ontario; **Excerpt** on p. 121–122: From "Crime Placement, Displacement, and Deflection" by Robert Barr and Ken Pease in Crime and Justice, Volume 12. Published by University of Chicago Press, © 1990.

Chapter 7

Excerpt on p. 127: Western Sheriff; **Excerpt** on p. 129: From The Evolution and Development of Police Technology by Lee P Brown. Published by Seaskate Inc., Copyright © 1998; **Excerpt** on p. 130: From Introductory Guide To Crime Analysis and Mapping, U.S. Department of Justice; **Excerpt** on p. 130: From Future Trenda In Police. Copyright © 2014, U.S. Department of Justice; **Excerpt** on p. 130: From Future Trenda In Police. Published by Police Executive research Forum, © 2014; **Excerpt** on p. 130: From Future Trenda In

Police. Copyright © 2014, Target; **Figure** 7–1 on p. 131: From Introductory Guide To Crime Analysis and Mapping, U.S. Department of Justice; **Excerpt** on p. 131: International Association of Crime Analysts, "What Crime Analysts Do," http://www.iaca.net/dc_analyst_role.asp; **Excerpt** on p. 132: From What is Crime Analysis? Copyright © by International Association of Crime Analysts. Reprinted with permission; **Excerpt** on p. 133: From Police Department Investments in Information Technology Systems: Challenges Assessing Their Payoff by Brian A Jackson, Victoria A Greenfield, Andrew R Morral and John S Hollywood. Copyright © by RAND Corporation; **Exhibit** 7–3 on p. 138: Adapted from Office of Justice Programs, Bureau of Justice Assistance, "Intelligence-led Policing," http://www.ojp.usdoj.gov/BJA/topics/ilp.html; **Exhibit** 7–4 on p. 141: Based on Los Angeles Community Policing, "Community Policing in Europe: Structure and Best Practices in Sweden, France, Germany http://www.lacp.org/Articles%20-%20Expert%20-%20Our%20Opinion/060908-Community-PolicingInEurope-AJ.htm; **Excerpt** on p. 142: From Defining Civic Hacking by Jake Levitas. Published by Code of America, © 2013. Used by permission of Code of America. Reprinted with permission; **Exhibit** 7–1 on pp. 132–133: Adapted from Based on City of Mesa, Arizona, Police Department, "Crime Analyst Job Description"; **Exhibit** 7–2 on pp. 136–137: Information Builders, "Houston Police Department Creates Real-Time Crime Center," n.d., http://www.informationbuilders.com/applications/houston

Chapter 8

Excerpt on p. 149: Quote by R D Laing; **Excerpt** on p. 150: From Constitutional Policing as a Cornerstone of Community Policing: A Report by the Police Executive Research, U.S. Department of Justice; **Excerpt** on p. 154: "Judge Rejects New York's Stop-and-Frisk Policy." The New York Times, August 12, 2013. http://www.nytimes.com/2013/08/13/nyregion/stop-and-frisk-practice-violated-rights-judge-rules.html?hp&_r=1&; **Excerpt** on p. 155: From Constitutional Policing as a Cornerstone of Community Policing: A Report by the Police Executive Research, U.S. Department of Justice; **Excerpt** on p. 156: From Good To Great Policing: Application of Business Management Principles in the Public Sector, U.S. Department of Justice; **Excerpt** on p. 163: From "Six Things Police Leaders Can Do About Crime" by James Q Wilson in College of Criminal Justice, Vol. 14, Issue. 13. Published by Criminal Justice Center, © 1997; **Excerpt** on p. 164: From Problem Printed Policing by Herman Goldstein. Published by McGraw-Hill, © 1990; **Excerpt** on p. 164: From Problem-Oriented Policing by Herman Goldstein. Published by McGraw-Hill Companies, © 1990; **Excerpt** on p. 164: From "Implementing Community Policing: The Administrative Problem" by George L. Kelling and William J. Bratton in Perspective on Policing, No. 17, U.S. Department of Justice; **Exhibit** 8–6 on p. 164: From Supervising Problem-Solving. Copyright © 1990 by Police Executive Research Forum. Used with permission of Police Executive Research Forum; **Exhibit** 8–1 on pp. 151–152: From Values: Our Mission Statement and Codes of Ethics. © by St. Louis County Police Department. Reprinted with permission; **Exhibit** 8–2 on pp. 157–158: Based on Los Angeles Community Policing, "Community Policing in Europe: Structure and Best Practices in Sweden, France, Germany; **Exhibit** 8–3 on pp. 158–159: Office of Community Oriented Policing Services, "COPS Hiring Program (CHP)—How Decisions were Made to Allocate the $123 Million When More than $425 Million was Requested," http://www.cops.usdoj.gov/pdf/2014AwardDocs/CHP/2014CHP-Methodology.pdf; **Excerpt** on pp. 159–160: Wilsom, et al., Police Recruitment and Retention for the New Millennium, pp. 83–85; **Exhibit** 8–5 on pp. 161–162: Based on Joseph E. Brann

and Suzanne Whalley, "Community Policing and Problem Solving: The Transformation of Police Organizations," in California Department of Justice, Attorney General's Office, Crime Prevention Center, Community Oriented Policing and Problem Solving (Sacramento, Calif.: Author, 1992), p. 72.

Chapter 9

Exhibit 9–3 on p. 25: From Helpful Hints for the Tradition-Bound Chief by John E Eck. Copyright © 1992 by Police Executive Research Forum. Used with permission of Police Executive Research Forum; **Excerpt** on p. 168: From Chapter 6, Pig and Pepper in Alice's Adventures in Wonderland by Lewis Carroll. Copyright by Macmillan; **Figure** 9–1 on p. 169: From Community Policing Defined, U.S. Department of Justice; **Excerpt** on p. 170: From Strategic Thinking or Strategic Planning? In Long Range Planning, Vol. 31, Issue. 03, pp. 481–487. Published by Heracleous, © 1998; **Excerpt** on p. 171: "Brief History of Strategic Planning," http://www.des.calstate.edu/glossary.html, p. 2; **Excerpt** on p. 171: Brief History of Strategic Planning, http://www.des.calstate.edu/glossary.html, p. 2; **Excerpt** on p. 172: From Director's Column in The E-Newsletter of the COPS Office, Vol. 04, Issue. 06, U.S. Department of Justice; **Exhibit** 9–1 on p. 174: David Kurz, Strategic Planning: Building Strong Police-Community Partnerships in Small Towns (Alexandria, VA: International Association of Chiefs of Police, n.d.), pp. 1–5; **Figure** 9–2 on p. 175: Kenneth H Peak, Ronald W Glensor, Community and Problem-Oriented Policing: Effectively Addressing Crime and Disorder, 7e, © 2018. Pearson Education, Inc., New York, NY; **Excerpt** on p. 175: From Problem Solving, Problem-Oriented Policing In Newport News by John E Eck and William Spelman, National Institute of Justice; **Excerpt** on pp. 178–179: Based on Joel B. Plant and Michael S. Scott, Effective Policing and Crime Prevention: A Problem-Oriented Guide for Mayors, City Managers, and County Executives (Washington, D.C.: U.S. Department of Justice, Office of Community Oriented Policing Services, 2009), pp. 13–14; **Exhibit** 9–2 on p. 178: Workshop presentation, Mary Ann Wycoff, Police Executive Research Forum, "The 8th Annual International Problem Oriented Policing Conference: Problem Oriented Policing 1997," November 16, 1997, San Diego, California; **Figure** 9–3 on p. 181: Kenneth H Peak, Ronald W Glensor, Community and Problem-Oriented Policing: Effectively Addressing Crime and Disorder, 7e, © 2018. Pearson Education, Inc., New York, NY; **Figure** 9–4 on p. 183: Kenneth H Peak, Ronald W Glensor, Community and Problem-Oriented Policing: Effectively Addressing Crime and Disorder, 7e, © 2018. Pearson Education, Inc., New York, NY; **Exhibit** 9–4 on p. 185: Based on Edward Maguire and William Wells (eds.), Implementing Community Policing: Lessons from 12 Agencies (Washington, D.C.: U.S. Department of Justice, Office of Community Oriented Policing Services, July 2009); **Excerpt** on pp. 171–172: Based on Richard Myers, Joseph Schafer, and Bernard H. Levin, Police Decision-Making: A Futures Perspective, Police Futurists International, Futures Working Group White Paper Series, Vol 1. No. 2. September 2010, pp. 20–26.

Chapter 10

Excerpt on p. 189: Quote by Mark Twain; **Excerpt** on p. 190: Quote by Helen Thomas; **Exhibit** 10–1 on p. 193: Based on Community Policing Dispatch, Vol. 02, Issue. 11. Published by U.S. Department of Justice; **Excerpt** on p. 195: From Davis v. City of Dallas, 777 F.2d 205 (5th Cir. 1985), United States Court of Appeals for the Fifth Circuit; **Exhibit** 10–2 on p. 196: Based on Christopher Moraff, "Can Different Training Make Police Officers Guardians, Not Warriors?" Next City,

December 4, 2014, https://nextcity.org/daily/entry/change-police-training-task-force-empathy-policing; **Excerpt** on p. 197: From Andragogy in Action by Malcolm S Knowles. Published by John Wiley & Sons, © 1981; **Excerpt** on p. 198: From The Fifth Discipline: The Art and Practice of the Learning Organization by Peter M Senge. Published by Doubleday/Currency, © 1990; **Excerpt** on p. 198: Based on George Cartwright, "A Learning Organization," Law and Order, September 2008, pp. 71–73; **Excerpt** on p. 189: Quote by Thomas H. Huxley.

Chapter 11

Excerpt on p. 3: Used by permission from Merriam-Webster's Collegiate® Dictionary, 11th Edition ©2016 by Merriam-Webster, Inc. (www.Merriam-Webster.com); **Excerpt** on p. 207: From The American Scholar, Ralph Waldo Emerson; **Excerpt** on p. 207: Quote by Albert Einstein; **Exhibit** 11–1 on p. 209: From Process and Outcome Evaluation of the G.R.E.A.T. Program, U.S. Department of Justice; **Exhibit** 11–2 on p. 212: The Evidence-Based Policing Matrix. Journal of Experimental Criminology, 7(1), 3-26 by Cynthia Lum, Christopher Koper and Cody Telep. Published by George Mason University/Special Collections and Archives © 2011; **Exhibit** 11–2 on p. 212: "New Tool Translates Research to Practice," Bureau of Justice Assistance; **Excerpt** on p. 213: From "Problem-Solving Initiatives: Assessment and Evaluation" by Melchor L de Guzman in Encyclopedia of Community Policing and Problem Solving by Kenneth J Peak. Published by SAGE Publications Inc, © 2013; **Exhibit** 11–3 on p. 215: From RAND Benchmark: Accurate Police Officer Performance Benchmarking and Evaluation. Copyright © by RAND Corporation; **Excerpt** on p. 216: Timothy S. Bynum, Using Analysis for Problem-Solving: A Guide for Law Enforcement (U.S. Department of Justice, Office of Community Oriented Policing Services, 2002), pp. 25–26, http://www.cops.usdoj.gov/pdf/e08011230.pdf; **Exhibit** 11–4 on p. 217: Los Angeles Community Policing, "Community Policing in Europe: Structure and Best Practices in Sweden, France, Germany," http://www.lacp.org/Articles%20-%20Expert%20-%20Our%20Opinion/060908 CommunityPolicingInEurope-AJ.htm

Chapter 12

Excerpt on p. 2: Quote by Branch Rickey; **Exhibit** 12–1 on p. 225: Kenneth H Peak, Ronald W Glensor, Community and Problem-Oriented Policing: Effectively Addressing Crime and Disorder, 7e, © 2018. Pearson Education, Inc., New York, NY; **Figure** 12–1 on p. 226: Kenneth H Peak, Ronald W Glensor, Community and Problem-Oriented Policing: Effectively Addressing Crime and Disorder, 7e, © 2018. Pearson Education, Inc., New York, NY; **Exhibit** 12–2 on p. 229: Adapted from National Institute of Justice, CrimeSOLUTIONS.GOV, "Rockford Pulling Levers Drug Market Intervention," http://www.crimesolutions.gov/ProgramDetails.aspx?ID=400; **Exhibit** 12–3 on p. 230: Kenneth H Peak, Ronald W Glensor, Community and Problem-Oriented Policing: Effectively Addressing Crime and Disorder, 7e, © 2018. Pearson Education, Inc., New York, NY; **Exhibit** 12–4 on p. 230: Adapted from National Institute of Justice, CrimeSOLUTIONS.GOV, http://www.crimesolutions.gov/ProgramDetails.aspx?ID=51; **Exhibit** 12–5 on p. 235: National Institute of Justice, "Project Safe Neighborhoods: Gun Violence Programs: Project Safe Neighborhoods," http://www.nij.gov/topics/crime/gun-violence/prevention/pages/project-safe-neighborhoods.aspx; **Exhibit** 12–6 on p. 235: Based on the Antigraffiti Ordinance of Lakewood, Colorado, 0–91–29, Title 9, Article 85, Chapter 9.85. Taken from city website, at: http://www.lakewood.org/City_Clerk/Codes_and_Laws/Municipal_Code/Title_9_-_Public_Peace_and_Safety/VIII__Nuisances/Chapter_9_85_-_Defaced_Property/2147490059/; **Exhibit** 12–7 on p. 238: Based on Zoe Mentel, "Shutting the Door on Foreclosure and Drug-Related Problem Properties: Two Communities Respond to Neighborhood Disorder," Community Policing Dispatch 2(7) (July 2009), http://cops.usdoj.gov/html/dispatch/July_2009/communities_respond.htm; **Exhibit** 12–8 on p. 239: Based on Green Bay Police Department, "Neighborhood Policing," http://www.gbpolice.org/?page_id=93

Chapter 13

Excerpt on p. 244: Quote by Winston Churchill; **Exhibit** 13–1 on p. 247: Adapted from Christian Mason, Tod W. Burke, and Stephen S. Owen, "Responding to Persons with Mental Illness: Can Screening Checklists Aid Law Enforcement?" FBI Law Enforcement Bulletin (February 2014), https://leb.fbi.gov/2014/february/responding-to-persons-with-mental-illness-can-screening-checklists-aid-law-enforcement; **Exhibit** 13–2 on p. 248: Adapted from Gary Cordner, "People with Mental Illness," p. 2; **Exhibit** 13–3 on p. 249: Kenneth H Peak, Ronald W Glensor, Community and Problem-Oriented Policing: Effectively Addressing Crime and Disorder, 7e, © 2018. Pearson Education, Inc., New York, NY; **Exhibit** 13–4 on p. 250: Adapted from San Diego Family Justice Center (FJC). Copyright © by The California Evidence-Based Clearinghouse for Child Welfare; **Exhibit** 13–5 on p. 251: Adapted from Federal Bureau of Investigation, "Cyber Stalker: A Cautionary Tale About Online Romance and Revenge," December 23, 2013, https://www.fbi.gov/news/stories/2013/december/cautionary-tale-of-online-romance-and-revenge/cautionary-tale-of-online-romance-and-revenge; **Exhibit** 13–6 on p. 254: Based on A Financial Crimes Task Force in Pennsylvania Taken from: https://www.justice.gov/usao-wdpa/task-forces#financial; **Excerpt** on p. 255: Based on Provisions of New Fair and Accurate Credit Transactions Act Will Help Reduce Identity Theft and Help Victims Recover: FTC, Federal Trade Commission, © 2004; **Exhibit** 13–7 on p. 257: Used with permission of the International Association of Chiefs of Police. Further reproduction without express permission from IACP is strictly prohibited; **Excerpt** on pp. 247–248: Based on Gary Cordner, "People with Mental Illness," p. 2.

Chapter 14

Excerpt on p. 264: From Predictive Policing: What Can We Learn from Wal-Mart and Amazon about Fighting Crime in a Recession? by Charlie Beck in The Police Chief, Vol. LXXVI, No. 11. Published by International Association of Chiefs of Police, © 2009; **Excerpt** on p. 264: From Predictive Policing Symposiums, U.S. Department of Justice; **Exhibit** 14–1 on p. 270: United Nations Interregional Crime and Justice Research Institute (UNICRI), Improving Urban Security through Green Environmental Design: New Energy for Urban Security, p. 22, http://www.unicri.it/news/2011/1104-2_urban_security/110414_CRA_Urban_Security_sm.pdf; **Excerpt** on pp. 269–270: Paul Rosenzweig, "Future of Policing: 4 Factors to Consider When Deploying New Technologies, Government Technology, December 4, 2015.

INDEX